For Buck, Carlotta, and Mark Stahl

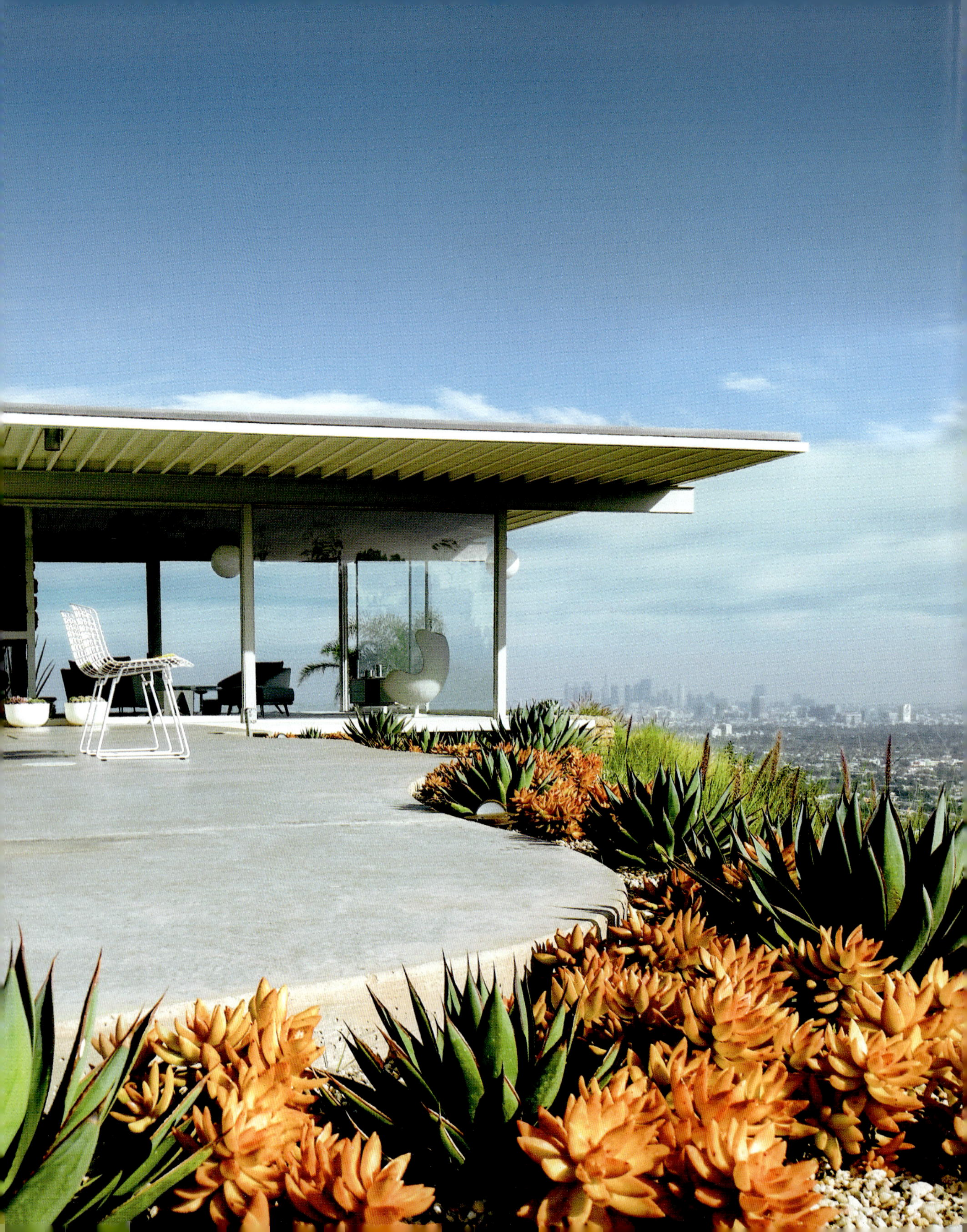

THE STAHL HOUSE

CASE STUDY HOUSE #22

The Making of a Modernist Icon

By Shari Stahl Gronwald, Bruce Stahl,
and Kim Cross

CHRONICLE CHROMA

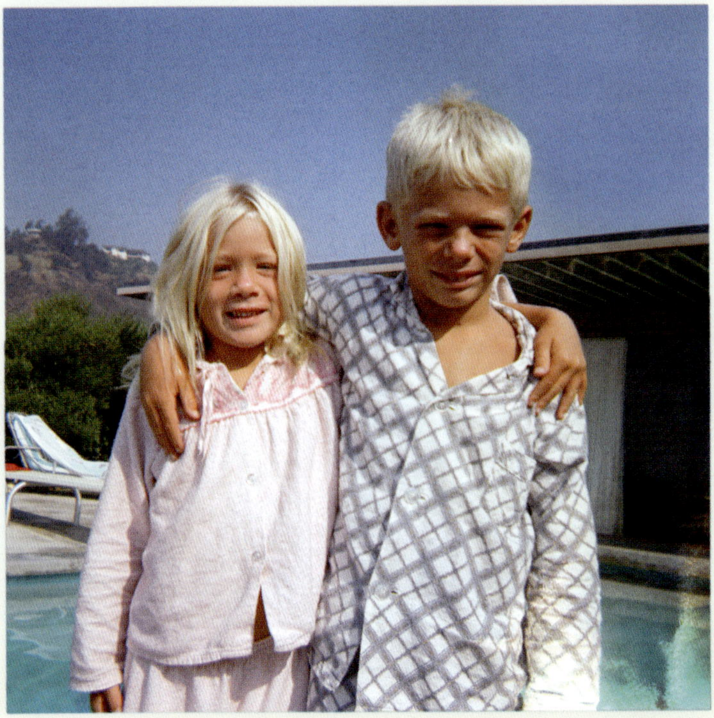

FOREWORD

When visitors step into the Stahl House they often ask: *What about the family who lives here?*

We wrote this book to answer that question. Despite all that's been published about our house—in thousands of books, magazines, and newspaper stories—very little is known about our family.

We weren't famous. Or wealthy. Or powerful. Our parents, Buck and Carlotta Stahl, were middle-class Americans with "champagne tastes and a beer budget," as Pierre Koenig once said. They never set out to build a house that would one day be a celebrity in its own right. They simply built their dream home.

It wasn't easy. Nothing about this house has ever been easy. But our parents had a vision of the life they wanted, and they were willing to put in the work to realize a dream that many considered impossible. They had to beat the long odds of economics, building codes, and experts who called their plan unbuildable.

With the help of key people, Mom and Dad proved everyone (including their family) wrong. They raised three kids in a two-bedroom, glass-walled house surrounded on three sides by cliffs (we all survived). Through an unlucky turn of circumstance, they were forced to move out—and fought for years to get back home.

In August 2019, *Newsweek* declared the Stahl House one of the great architectural wonders of Los Angeles, and *the* greatest example of mid-century modern architecture in Southern California.

"If I had to choose one snapshot, one architectural moment, of which I would like to have been the author," wrote the British architect Norman Foster, "this is surely it."

But Case Study House #22 had no one single author. It was the product of vision, hard work, and perseverance—of a constellation of players. Pierre Koenig. Julius Shulman. John Entenza. Buck and Carlotta Stahl. If any one of them had been missing, this house, this icon, might not exist. We want you to know the story—the whole story—of how those stars aligned.

People often told our father how lucky he was to have such a magnificent house.

"Luck," he'd growl with a knowing grin, "didn't have a goddamn thing to do with it!"

As kids, we didn't know our house was special. It was simply "home." We want to show you what our life was like there. We want you to meet our parents and our younger brother, who made this house what it is—not only a cultural icon, but a warm and welcoming place to celebrate Christmas, birthdays, and summer afternoons.

Time magazine named Julius Shulman's "Two Girls" photograph—the image on the cover of this book—one of the 100 Most Influential Photographs of All Time. Of all the images of the Stahl House, this one "burns more brightly and stays on the retina just that bit longer," wrote Foster, who said it captured "the whole spirit of late twentieth-century architecture." A vintage Shulman print of our house may sell at high-end galleries for as much as fifty thousand dollars.

This photo plays an important role in the story of our house. But it's not the entire story.

You may know about the Case Study House Program. You might be familiar with the architectural history of #22. You may even have taken a tour of the house and stood inside its walls. But we want to open the doors of our home—as our mother did for nearly half a century—and welcome you in as a guest.

When you look at this monument of steel and glass and stone, we want you to appreciate something more than architecture. We want you to look at our house, then look again, and see something more than a house. See the blueprints of your own improbable dream and believe you can build it, too.

This book is not a historical tome, an architectural textbook, or an academic publication. It's a biography of a house. It's a story about people. We hope the story will live on with the house even after we, too, are gone. This story defines the threshold between the structure of a house and the geometry of home.

—*Shari Stahl Gronwald and Bruce Stahl*

What good is a dream house if you haven’t got a dream?

—Julius Shulman

CHAPTER 1
THE DREAM

March 1954—Hollywood, California

Drenched in sunshine, swimming in sky, the ridge swept out from the mountain like a buttress on a cathedral. The newlyweds could see it from the one-bedroom flat they rented in the Hollywood Hills. Northwest of downtown Los Angeles, the Santa Monica mountains paraded along the Pacific, a curtain of ridges and canyons fading into the coastal mist. To Buck and Carlotta Stahl, one ridge stood out from the rest. Surrounded on three sides by cliffs, it seemed to float above Sunset Boulevard. On its tip was a lot that stood alone, an island in a sea of blue sky.

Every day in the spring of 1954, Buck and Carlotta would gaze up at the lot. They could see it through the sliding glass doors of their living room, between the eucalyptus trees rustling on their patio, and from the patch of dirt on Hillside Avenue where they parked their convertible.

"This lot was in pure view—every morning, every night," Carlotta told historian Philip Ethington. Their apartment faced downtown Los Angeles, which was still a grove of midrise buildings rising up from the gridded flats. But the ridge in the foreground dominated their view, and the lot on its precipice became their obsession.

It was nothing then but an empty lot, a flat spot roughly graded for development, the runt of a handful of terraces sculpted into the hillside. "Even though it was the smallest one," Carlotta said, "this is the one that caught our eye." It was a cocktail napkin of real estate, and on it Buck and Carlotta sketched the blueprints of their future. Parties with homemade cakes and spirited toasts. Barefoot children running around in pajamas. Quiet nights under a rising moon, city lights twinkling below. They imagined how their lives might unfold on that modest patch of dirt, that little notch carved in a Hollywood hill.

The newlyweds started calling it "our lot."

They were a blue-collar couple with white-collar dreams.

Clarence Henry Stahl, forty-two, was a barrel-chested 6 foot 3, 230 pounds of muscle. Everyone called him Buck. Hazel-eyed with olive skin and dark brown hair slicked back, he was ruggedly handsome, a man's man who conquered a room with his booming voice and moved with a stride and confidence that called to mind John Wayne. He was brought up on wrestling, boxing, and football, with a lineman's shoulders and hands that made a basketball look like a softball. People who knew him described him as "larger than life."

Born in St. Louis in 1912 to a milkman and a homemaker, Buck was not only a natural athlete but also a gifted artist. His talent for drawing and painting emerged early, when he was a student at Cleveland High School in St. Louis. At fifteen, he was hired to paint the names on planes at Lambert Field Airport. In 1928, at sixteen, Buck graduated from Cleveland High with a two-year Manual Training Certificate in Mechanical Drawing. He then entered the David Ranken, Jr. School of Mechanical Trades, where he spent two years studying painting. He graduated in 1930, in the midst of the Great Depression.

In 1935, a pilot friend invited Buck to join him on a brief flight to Los Angeles. He fell in love with the mountains, sun, and sea, and promptly decided to leave the muggy heat of St. Louis behind. In LA he found work as a commercial

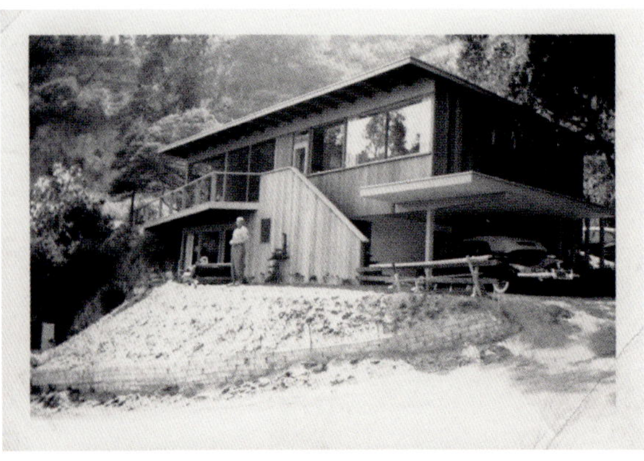

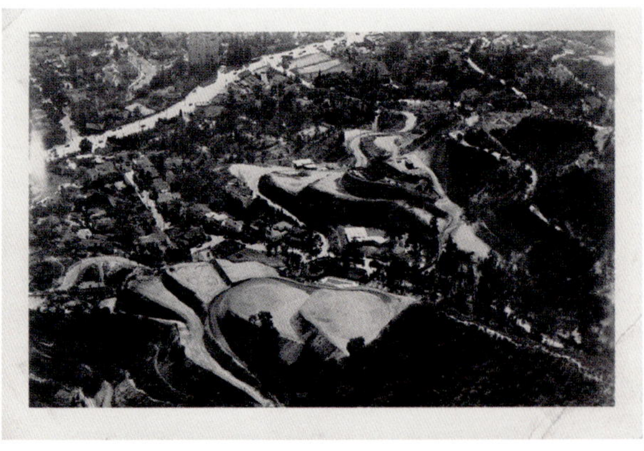

artist, designing logos and ads for various companies, and then was hired by Farmers Automobile Insurance Exchange, where he was promoted to ad manager. In 1942, months after the attack on Pearl Harbor, Buck decided to join the US Navy. Seeking a job as a physical fitness instructor, he wrote a letter to a naval officer he knew through boxing.

Gene Tunney was the Irish American boxer who defeated slugger Jack Dempsey twice—first to win the title himself, and then to defend it in the bout known as The Long Count, one of the sport's most famous and controversial moments. Tunney, an ex-marine, was now a lieutenant commander of the naval reserve, in charge of a physical fitness program for training student pilots. When a position opened up, Tunney hired Buck as one of the instructors at Naval Station Great Lakes, the navy's bootcamp near Chicago. Buck would regale his future children with stories of playing semi-professional football in Chicago in an era when players wore leather helmets. In his downtime, he read the Bible and the dictionary from cover to cover.

After the war, Buck returned to his commercial art career, creating hand-drawn advertisements for a variety of products. He drew the latest fashions of Rough Rider slacks, an announcement for the opening of the Flamingo Casino in Las Vegas, and ads for Sparkeeta UP: "a wonderful mixer—not too sweet!" His alluring depictions of Carmen Miranda in the film *Something for the Boys* (1944) and Gene Tierney in *Laura* (1944) were splashed on billboards around LA.

One of his favorite clients was Howard Hughes, the producer of such notable films as *Hell's Angels* (1930), *Scarface* (1932), and other big-budget movies. In 1932, Hughes formed the Hughes Aircraft Company, a major aerospace and defense company that built the Hughes H-4 Hercules, a heavy-transport flying boat better known as the Spruce Goose. Buck designed movie posters for Hughes, who would invite him into his office and spread the drawings over a conference table. Once, they even met on the Spruce Goose. Buck told his family that Hughes had an uncanny ability to remember, without pulling out paper records, exactly which invoices were paid and unpaid.

In 1950, Buck went to work for Hughes Aircraft as a purchasing agent, earning a salary of ten thousand dollars a year—a solid, middle-class income. It was not only a stable job but also a path that would lead him to Carlotta.

Carlotta May Gates was 5 feet 10, a natural blonde with kind blue eyes, a generous smile, and a pin-up figure. She was the living embodiment of California sunshine, a natural talker who radiated warmth and charmed everyone in her orbit. The distinct ring of her laugh is still remembered fondly. "It was very unique and infectious," said Michael Hicks, a longtime family friend. "You could pick it out of a crowd."

Carlotta had grown up riding horses and playing in the lima-bean fields that surrounded her home in the rural flats of Culver City. Her father, an avid hunter and fisherman from Missoula, Montana, worked as a rare-coin dealer, and her mother ran the house. They made a living through Carlton's Coin Shop and decorated their home with arrowheads, antique guns, and Native American artifacts.

Carlotta never liked being told what to do. She was headstrong and spirited, with a dash of her father's temper. She dreaded practicing the marimba and the piano, both of which she played beautifully (if not willingly) at her mother's insistence.

"She was the most stubborn bugger I think I ever met," recalled her brother, Bud, two years younger. "And boy could she punch! I tried not to get into too many fights with her, 'cause I always lost." She occasionally went rabbit hunting with her father and once, by accident, shot herself in the foot while carrying a loaded .22.

"She had the muzzle resting on her foot," said her daughter, Shari. "Something spooked her in the bushes, and she reflexively pulled the trigger." Carlotta loved showing off that scar, a tiny dot on her pretty right foot.

At Venice High School "she was the most popular gal in the school," according to her brother, who didn't mind when her girlfriends came out to the house and danced with him in the living room. She had a lot of boyfriends, "but she got tired of the guys pretty fast."

After graduating high school in 1948, Carlotta got a job as a receptionist at North American Aviation, an aerospace manufacturer that supplied B-25 Mitchell bombers and P-51 Mustang fighter planes for the war. When Buck stopped by on a sales call, he could not help but notice the stunning blonde with the brilliant smile behind the front desk.

Hollywood was experiencing a postwar boom as a new generation of Americans, freed from the years of world conflict, moved to California in search of the American dream, seeking to live the life of opportunity they saw in movie theaters (and increasingly in their living rooms every night on television). It was a time to dream big. California's population would grow from ten million in 1950 to more than fifteen million in 1960.

During this decade, no place was more glamorous or alluring than Hollywood. Stars like Marlon Brando, Paul Newman, Ava Gardner, and Audrey Hepburn ruled the silver screen. Marilyn Monroe would marry Joe DiMaggio, and Grace Kelly would become the princess of Monaco. The Academy Awards began to be broadcast on television, and black-and-white films exploded into full color. The voices of Frank Sinatra, Tony Bennett, Dean Martin, and Nat King Cole crooned over the radio.

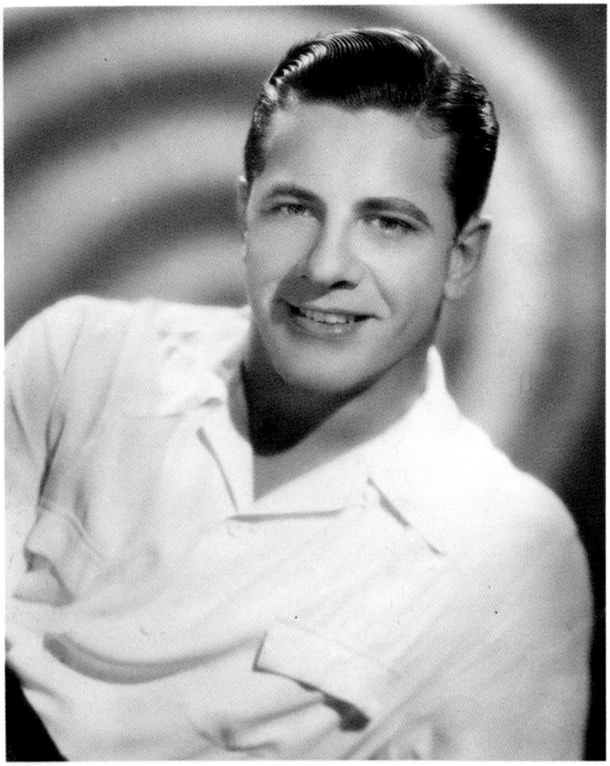

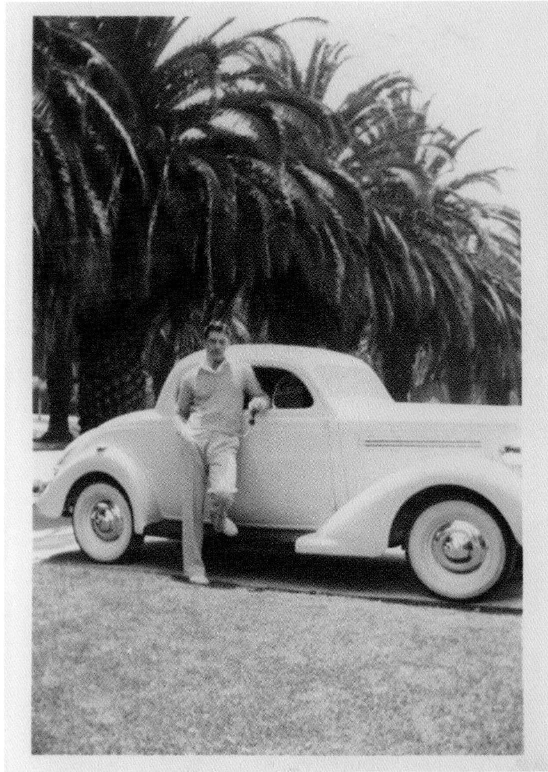

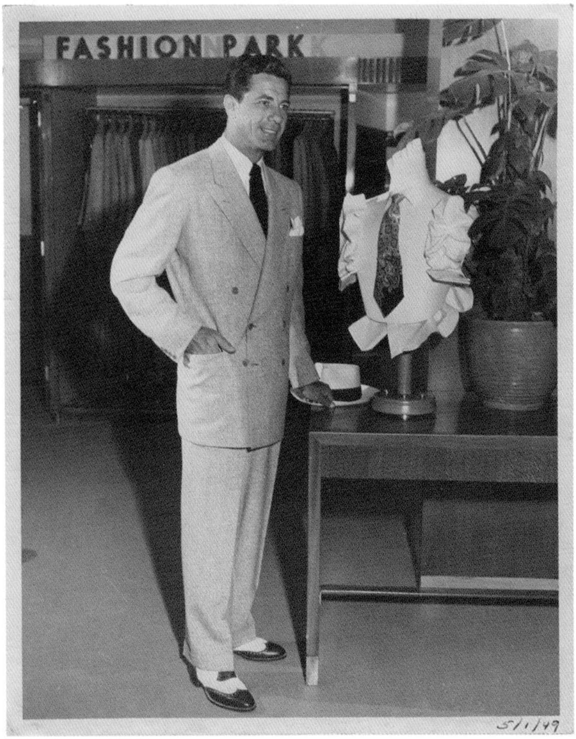
FASHION PARK
5/1/49

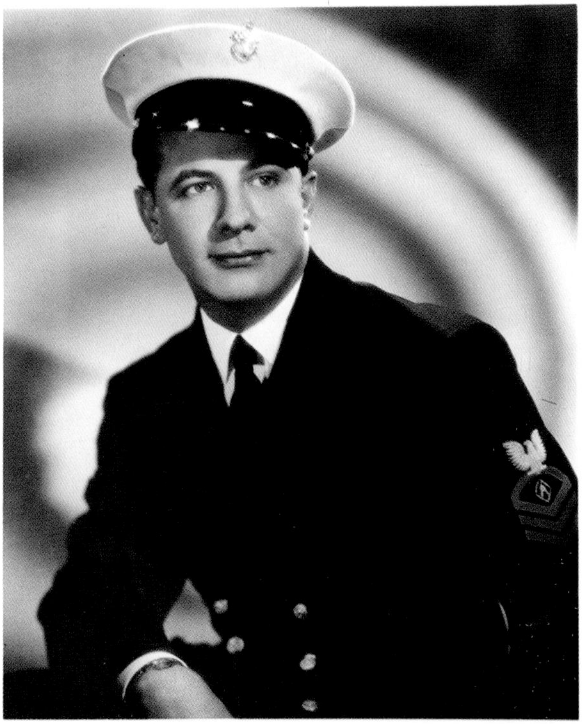

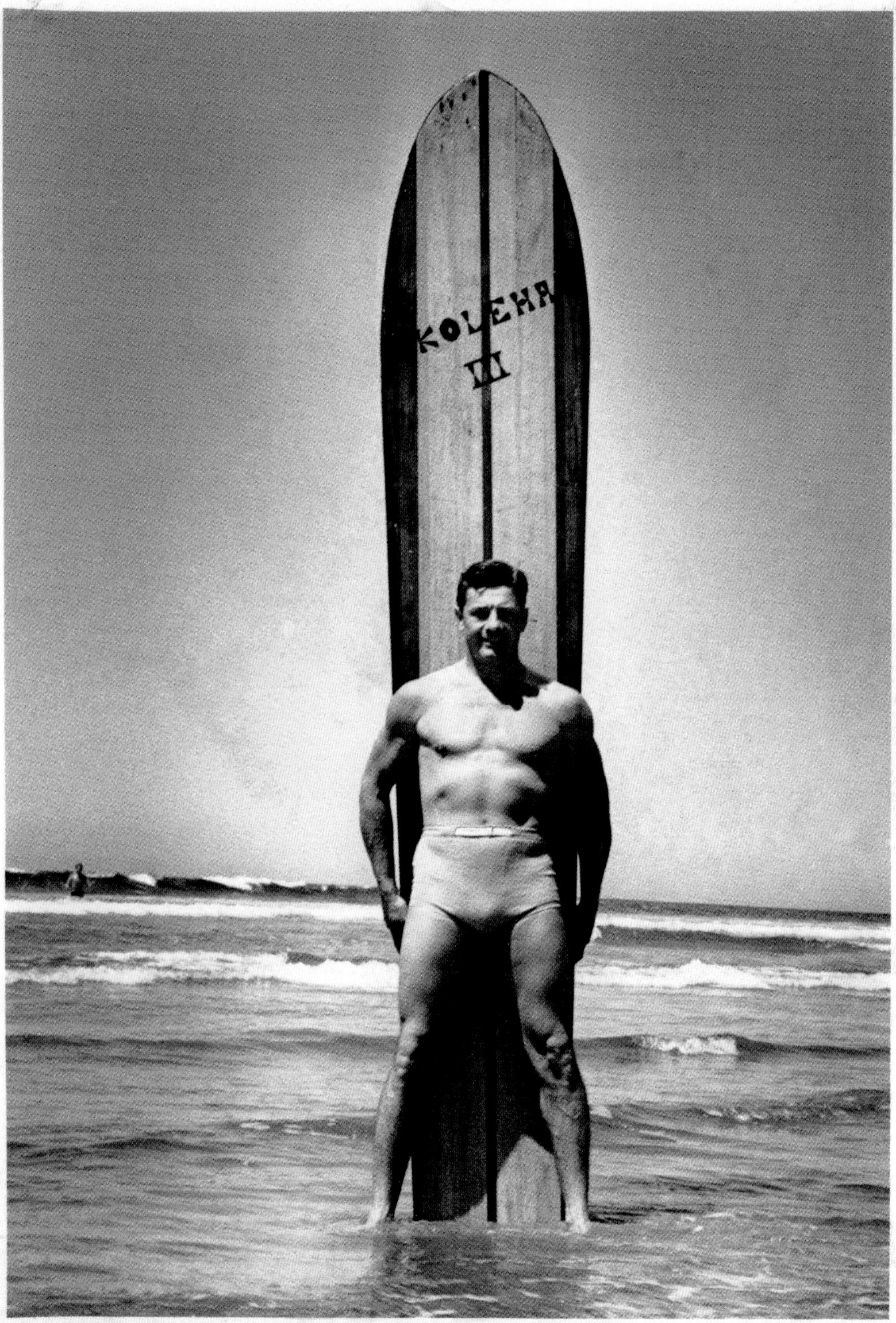
KOLEHA
III

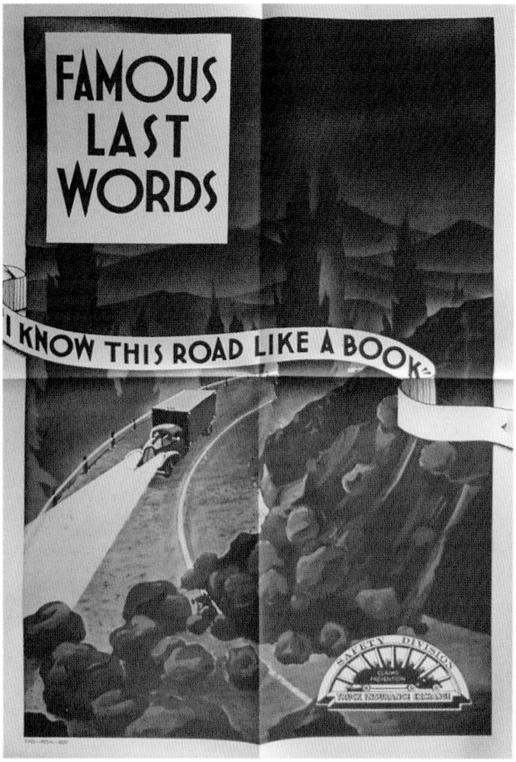
FAMOUS LAST WORDS
"I KNOW THIS ROAD LIKE A BOOK"
SAFETY DIVISION
CLAIMS PREVENTION
TRUCK INSURANCE EXCHANGE

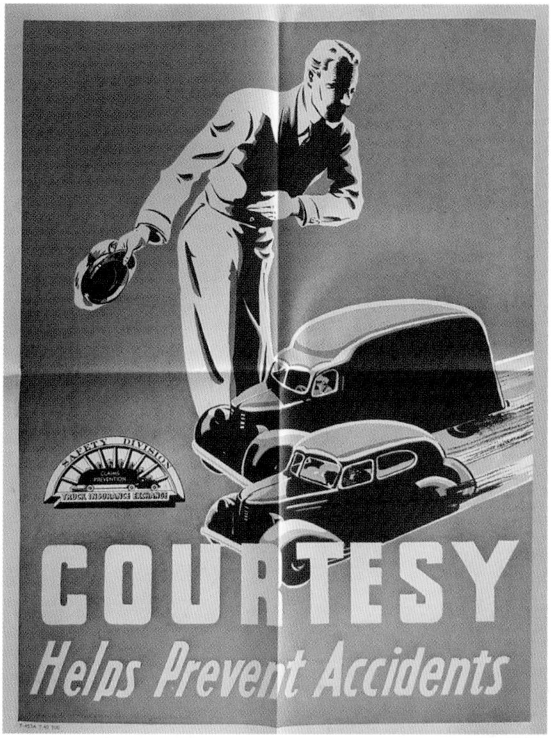
SAFETY DIVISION
CLAIMS PREVENTION
TRUCK INSURANCE EXCHANGE
COURTESY
Helps Prevent Accidents

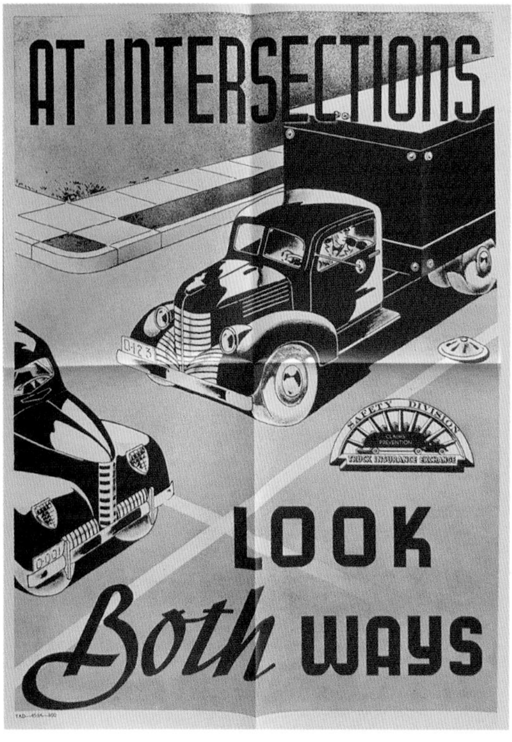
AT INTERSECTIONS
SAFETY DIVISION
CLAIMS PREVENTION
TRUCK INSURANCE EXCHANGE
LOOK
Both WAYS

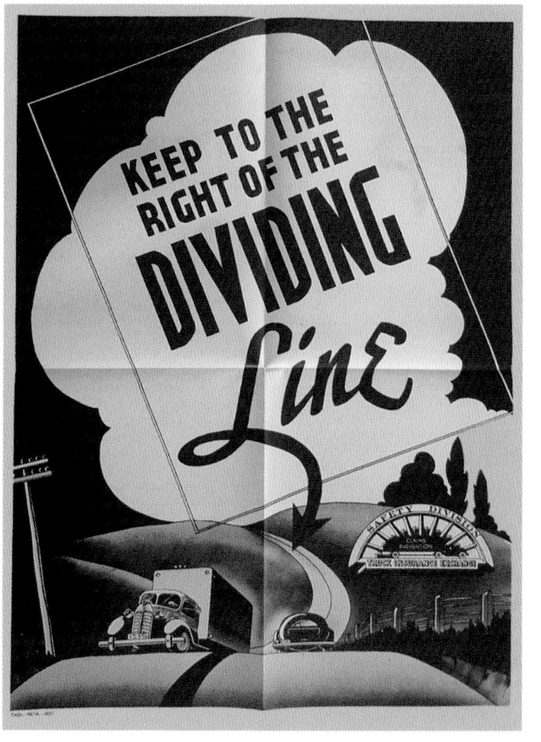
KEEP TO THE RIGHT OF THE
DIVIDING
Line
SAFETY DIVISION
CLAIMS PREVENTION
TRUCK INSURANCE EXCHANGE

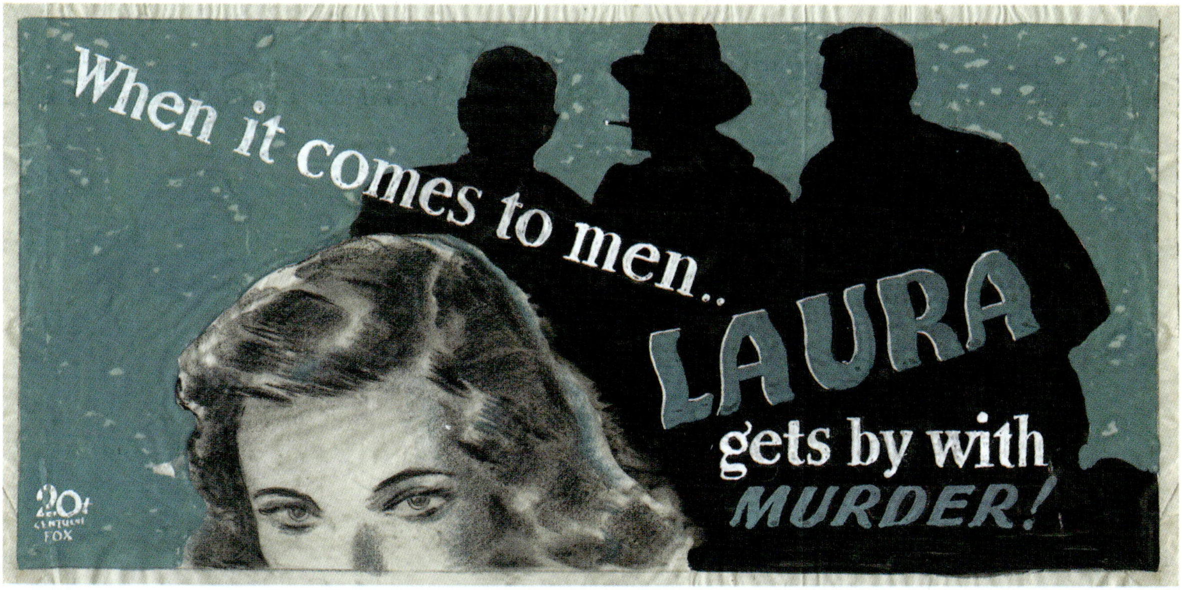

When it comes to men...
LAURA
gets by with
MURDER!
20th CENTURY FOX

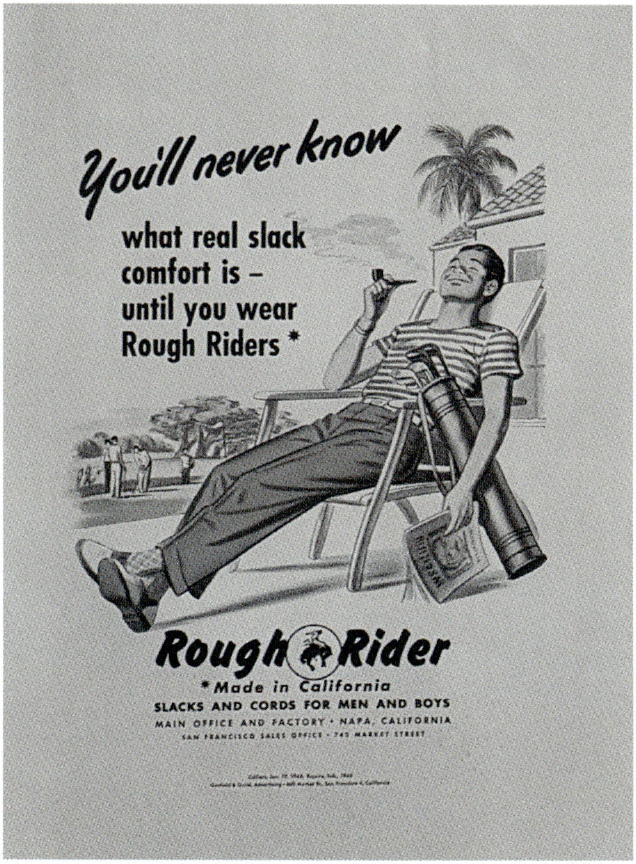

You'll never know
what real slack comfort is – until you wear Rough Riders *
Rough Rider
* Made in California
SLACKS AND CORDS FOR MEN AND BOYS
MAIN OFFICE AND FACTORY • NAPA, CALIFORNIA
SAN FRANCISCO SALES OFFICE • 745 MARKET STREET

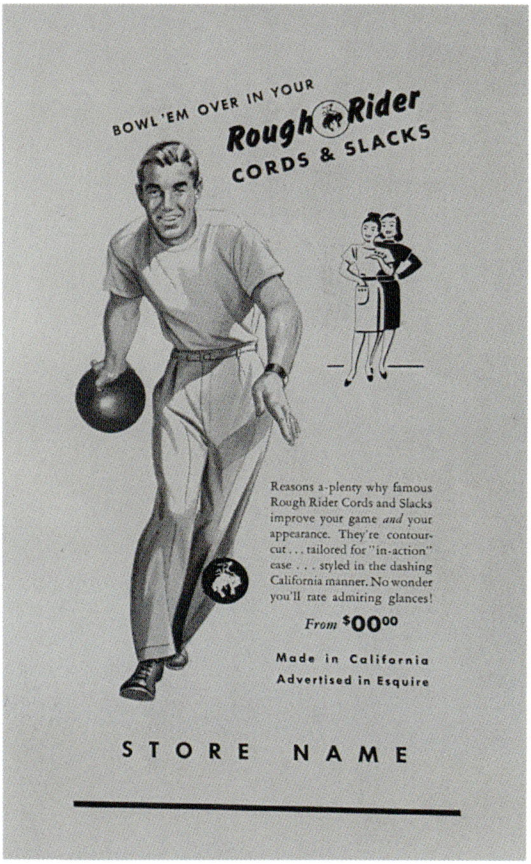

BOWL 'EM OVER IN YOUR
Rough Rider
CORDS & SLACKS
Reasons a-plenty why famous Rough Rider Cords and Slacks improve your game *and* your appearance. They're contour-cut . . . tailored for "in-action" ease . . . styled in the dashing California manner. No wonder you'll rate admiring glances!
From $00.00
Made in California
Advertised in Esquire
STORE NAME

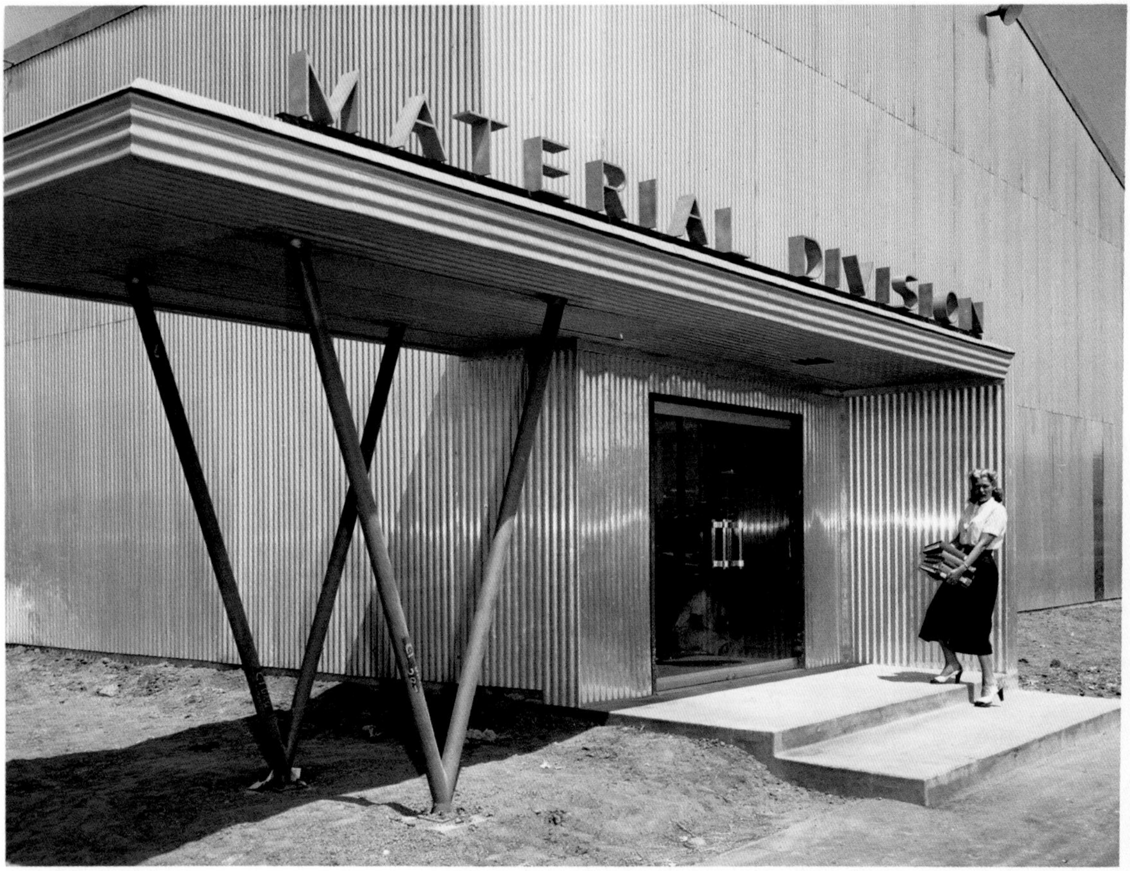
MATERIAL DIVISION

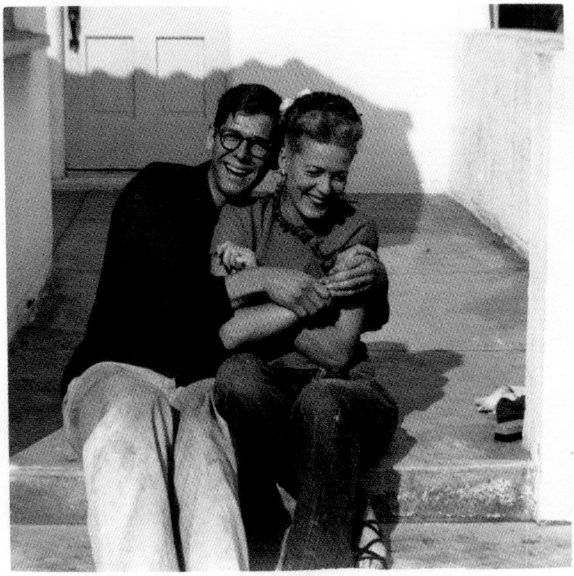

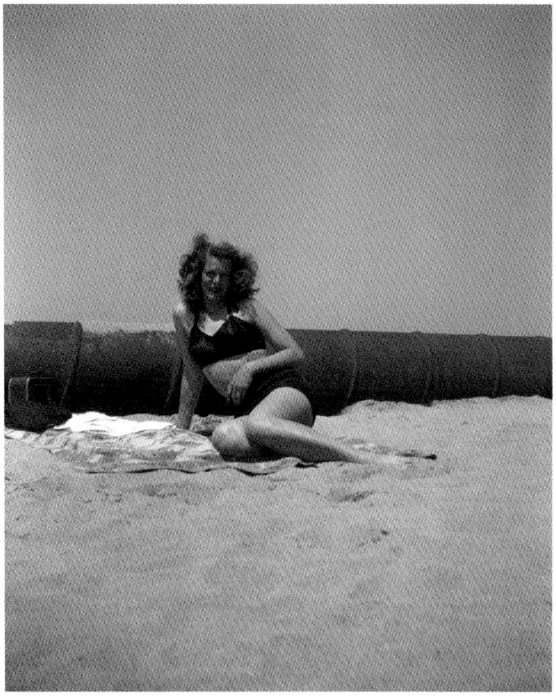

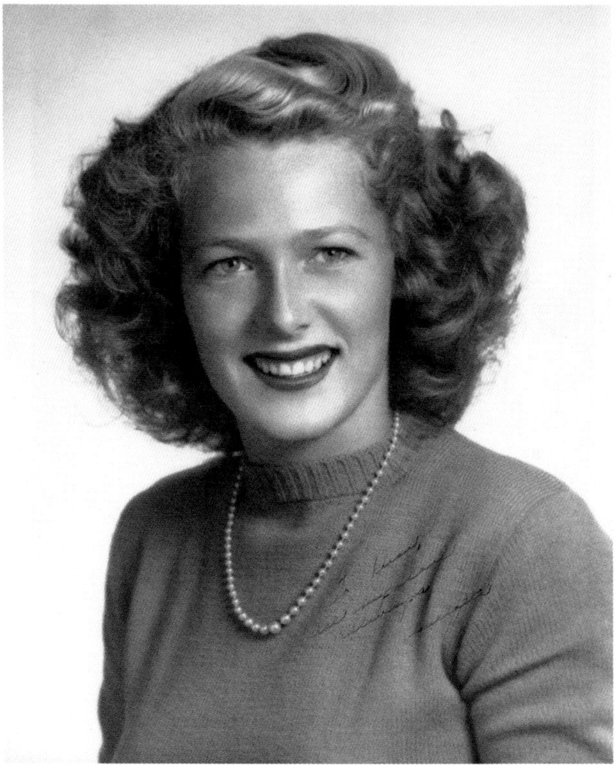

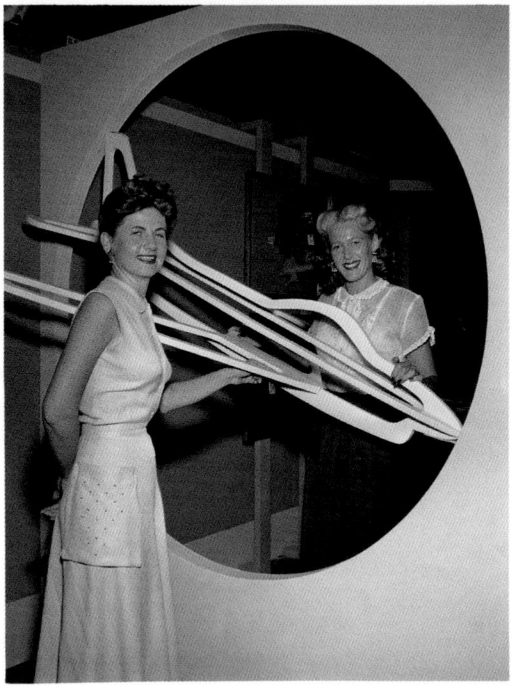

Looking every bit like a Hollywood couple themselves, Buck and Carlotta courted on La Cienega Boulevard's Restaurant Row, where Carlotta turned heads in sequined gowns and cocktail dresses, many of which Buck had custom-made for her. They loved dancing to big-band music and often dined at The Flight Deck, a restaurant with a view of jet planes soaring off the runways at LAX. Carlotta's parents initially frowned upon the seventeen-year age difference—Buck was forty-one years old, Carlotta twenty-four—but warmed up when they saw how much they loved each other. Within a year, the couple decided to marry.

It was not the first marriage for either of them. In the summer of 1936, after his move to LA, Buck had married, but the relationship ended in April 1948, about a year before Carlotta married her high-school sweetheart. That marriage, too, ended in divorce almost four years later.

In the spring of 1954, Buck and Carlotta drove to Las Vegas and got married in a small chapel. Carlotta had chosen a white, tea-length, lace dress. To Buck, it seemed too demure for his bride, so, with an artist's eye for detail, he trimmed the fabric covering her décolletage and dyed the lace in black coffee. They exchanged vows in a simple ceremony attended by a couple of friends. They emerged from the chapel hand in hand, beaming radiant smiles, on March 20. Five days later, the classic dramatic war romance, *From Here to Eternity*, swept the Oscars.

Carlotta moved into the one-bedroom apartment Buck had been renting on the bottom floor of a two-story house on Hillside Avenue, a two-lane road that switch-backed up into the Hollywood Hills. The gridded streets of Los Angeles already smothered the flats, but the hills were still blanketed with trees and coastal scrub. The lot they coveted was not yet a scarce commodity, just one of many tempting spaces waiting for new construction. It was known to some locals as "Pecker Point," a scenic overlook that happened to be a popular spot for necking. Despite the intensity of their longing, the Stahls assumed they would never be able to afford this kind of real estate, not even with two incomes and no kids.

One gorgeous day in May 1954, not quite two months after the wedding, Buck and Carlotta felt the urge to explore it in person. Although they had spent long hours staring up at their place in the sky, they had never dared to set foot there. "We decided, let's go and see our lot!" Carlotta said. "We had already claimed it, even though we'd never been there." They climbed into Buck's convertible, wove through the maze of narrow hillside roads, and pulled up to the nose of the ridgeline they had gazed upon for months. They stepped out of the car and took their first sweeping, unobstructed view of Los Angeles, rolling out toward a seam of blue sea on the edge of the horizon. How could they not fall even deeper in love with this place?

What would it be like to live with this view? The daydream was interrupted by the crunch of tires on dirt. "All of a sudden, a car comes in," Carlotta recalled. "It turns out to be the owner of the lot, who lived in La Jolla, down by San Diego." Purely by chance, he too had taken a drive that day. The man introduced himself as George Beha and said the lot was, in fact, for sale. The smallest of the lots carved out on the ridge, it was a 5,500-square-foot blip of real estate, barely one-eighth of an acre, shaped like a slice of pie. Its value lay not in its size but in a view that could never be impeded. Beha was actually hoping to sell *two* parcels—"their" lot, plus an adjacent one to the east, larger and slightly lower. He offered them both for twenty-five thousand dollars.

That sum was well out of reach for the Stahls, who could not even afford the median $19,300 price tag of a new home and a lot at the time. Perhaps they could afford *one* lot—but only with a mortgage. Buck Stahl and George Beha negotiated the terms of the sale on the spot.

"At the end of two hours, we bought a lot," Carlotta said. The deal: $13,500 for the smaller lot, with Beha carrying the mortgage. Only when it was paid off in full could the building begin. Buck offered one hundred dollars in earnest money, and the men sealed the deal with a handshake. "I feel like this whole thing has been planned by someone," Carlotta said. "We just happened to walk out there on a given day, and he was on his way in his car. And it all came together."

"You are crazy!" Carlotta later recalled her friends and family saying. Why would anyone buy a "chunk of dirt" when the couple could own a three-bedroom home—plus the land on which it stood—for thirteen thousand dollars?

"Nobody understood what we were doing," Carlotta told interviewer Fumi Yamanaka in 2004. "We decided, we are not going to argue. We are just going our way."

Buck knew exactly what he wanted—to hell with what anyone thought. He wanted a view from every room (including the shower). He wanted walls of glass and a roof that swept up and out, angled like the wings of a butterfly. "I want to stand in one place and see the whole view just by turning my head," he said. His island in the sky provided a 270-degree panorama, and he didn't want to waste any bit of it.

"We loved this lot so much," Carlotta said. "We'd drive up to sit and dream."

But building a house there seemed as far out of reach as Catalina Island. The lot sat empty for four long years, as Buck and Carlotta paid it off with monthly installments of two hundred dollars plus interest, each payment handwritten in ballpoint pen in a pocket-sized ledger. Buck spent "two

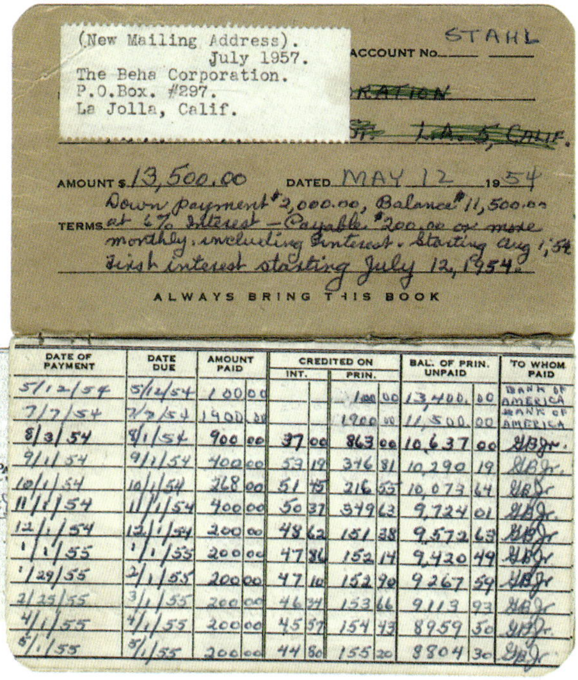

(New Mailing Address).
July 1957.
The Beha Corporation.
P.O.Box. #297.
La Jolla, Calif.

ACCOUNT No. STAHL

~~RATION~~

~~L.A. 5, CALIF.~~

AMOUNT $ 13,500.00 DATED MAY 12 1954

TERMS Down payment $2,000.00, Balance $11,500.00 at 6% Interest – Payable $200.00 or more monthly, including Interest. Starting Aug 1, 54 First interest starting July 12, 1954.

ALWAYS BRING THIS BOOK

DATE OF PAYMENT	DATE DUE	AMOUNT PAID	CREDITED ON INT.	CREDITED ON PRIN.	BAL. OF PRIN. UNPAID	TO WHOM PAID
5/12/54	5/12/54	100 00		100 00	13,400.00	BANK OF AMERICA
7/7/54	7/7/54	1900 00		1900 00	11,500.00	BANK OF AMERICA
8/3/54	8/1/54	900 00	37 00	863 00	10,637 00	GBJr.
9/1/54	9/1/54	400 00	53 19	346 81	10,290 19	GBJr.
10/1/54	10/1/54	268 00	51 45	216 55	10,073 64	GBJr
11/1/54	11/1/54	400 00	50 37	349 63	9,724 01	GBJr.
12/1/54	12/1/54	200 00	48 62	151 38	9,572 63	GBJr
1/1/55	1/1/55	200 00	47 86	152 14	9,420 49	GBJr
1/29/55	2/1/55	200 00	47 10	152 90	9267 59	GBJr
2/25/55	3/1/55	200 00	46 34	153 66	9113 93	GBJr
4/1/55	4/1/55	200 00	45 57	154 43	8959 50	GBJr.
5/1/55	5/1/55	200 00	44 80	155 20	8804 30	GBJr

years of weekends" improving the lot so they could one day build a home there. He and Carlotta would drive around Los Angeles, eyeing the refuse piles at building sites. "She and I used to see a building going up and see a pile of broken concrete out there waiting to be hauled away," Buck said.

Carlotta added, "We'd ask them, can we have your broken concrete?" They would load it in the trunk of Buck's Cadillac, which rode lower under the weight as it struggled up the hill to Woods Drive. "Group by group," Carlotta said, "we finally got enough."

Buck could not afford to lease grading equipment or heavy machinery, so he squared off edges and leveled the lot "by hand—the hard way." He used what he had—two arms and a forty-two-year-old back made strong by sports and the navy. Sweating under the California sun, shirtless and tanned, he lifted concrete chunks that weighed between twenty and fifty pounds. One by one, he arranged the chunks into retaining walls, filling the cracks and smaller gaps with decomposed granite shoveled from the hillside. By building a perimeter around nearly the entire lot, he enlarged the lot's buildable surface by around six feet. He shaped one corner of the sloping lot into six terraces, reducing hillside erosion.

Buck had no formal training for this, but he had been given a few tips by someone who did. Initial developer Richard Larkin, who was the first to see the potential of the properties on the ridge, "was a very astute, smart man," Buck said. "He taught me how to lay 'em." Larkin had "cruised these hills and appraised these lots, [and] picked out the ones he wanted. And then he went down and made an offer to the City. He ended up with some nice lots. And this mountain was one of them. I don't know what he paid … but he got them for taxes."

Larkin saw another opportunity in the postwar period, when freeways were beginning to sprawl across the landscape, requiring millions of tons of decomposed granite for the roadbeds. "To tell you how smart this guy was … it didn't cost him anything to haul the dirt away," Buck said. "The City came in and cut the roads, cut the lots, and hauled it all away. And they did it for free because they wanted the decomposed granite for the LAX runway." A notch in the Stahls' lot, by the swimming pool, shows the gully where tons and tons of excess grit was funneled down the hill and trucked off to pave Los Angeles International Airport.

In August 1956, two years after buying the lot, and shortly after completing the terraces, Buck turned his imaginary blueprint for a house into a three-dimensional model. He ripped the legs off of a 4-by-5-foot card table and on it built a replica of the lot, sculpting its curves and terraces out of empty soda and beer cans.

"He put clay over it," Carlotta said. "He molded the whole thing." He had memorized every contour of this tiny lot. Its size and dimensions limited—but also inspired—the possibilities of what might be built there. The house he had already raised in his mind soon emerged in miniature form. Nearly half a century later, when asked what inspired his design, he would say with exasperation: "This lot!"

Buck's model was an L-shaped house with glass walls and a butterfly roof. The street-facing rear wall of the house had a concave curve that followed the bend in the road. A carport was located in the middle of the one wing, between the master suite and second bedroom. Part of the living room cantilevered over the cliff.

Buck approached several architects and showed them the model. None of them saw the possibilities that Buck and Carlotta envisioned, and none would take on the project. Their reasons varied: Such large walls of glass would be too heavy for a wood-framed house. Cantilevering part of the house over a cliff would violate building codes. The lot was too small. Some called it unbuildable. All of them turned him down.

Buck took "no" to mean "not just yet."

Then, as they were flipping through the *Los Angeles Examiner*, a photo of a house caught their attention. "Pierre Koenig's picture appeared in the Sunday magazine section," Buck said. "It was his ideas of glass and steel in the use of a home." Buck did not know it yet, but this man also refused to take "no" for an answer. The Stahls could not have found a better architect to realize their improbable dream.

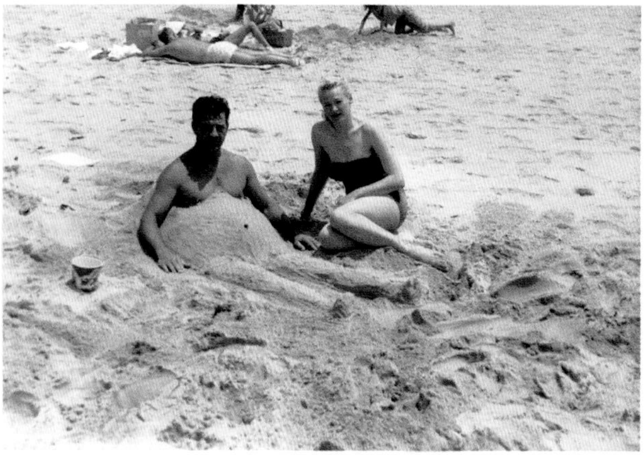

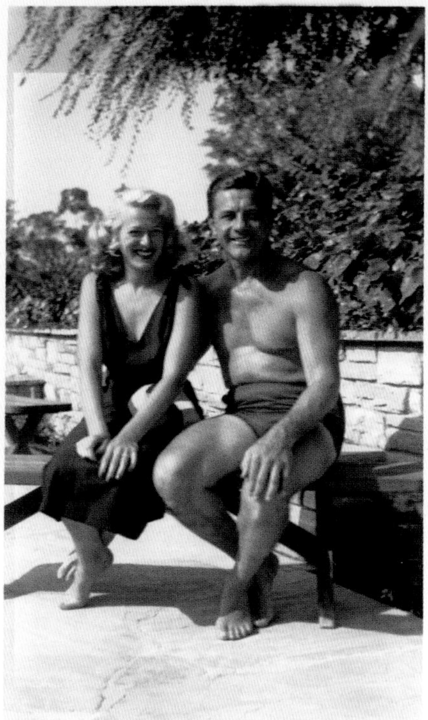

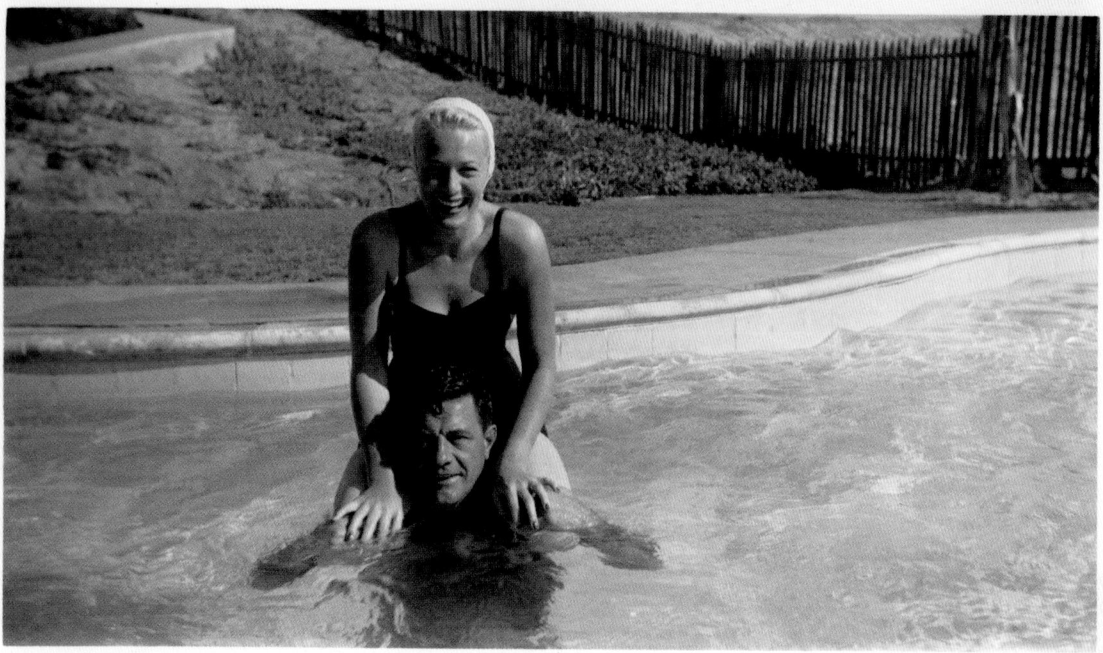

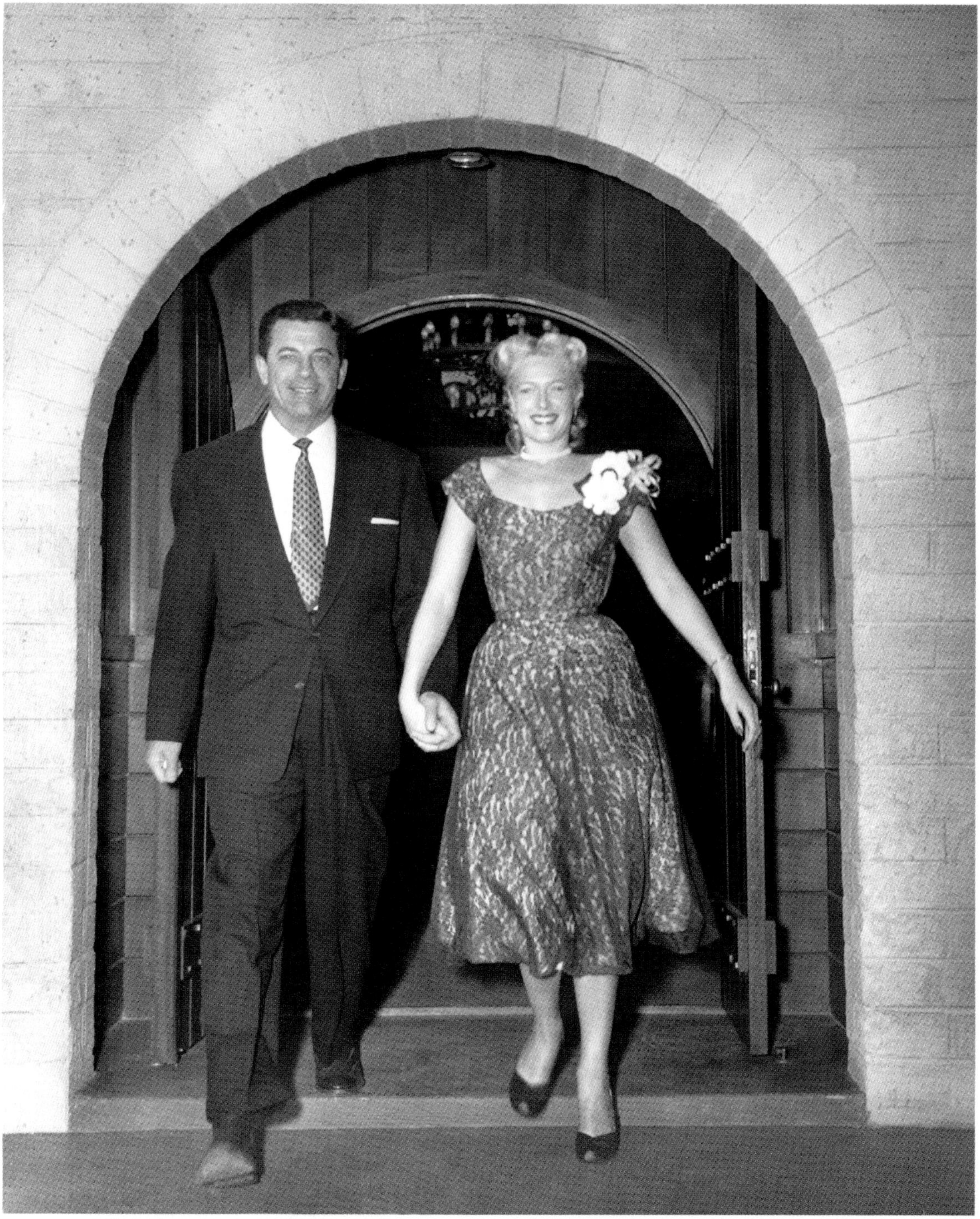

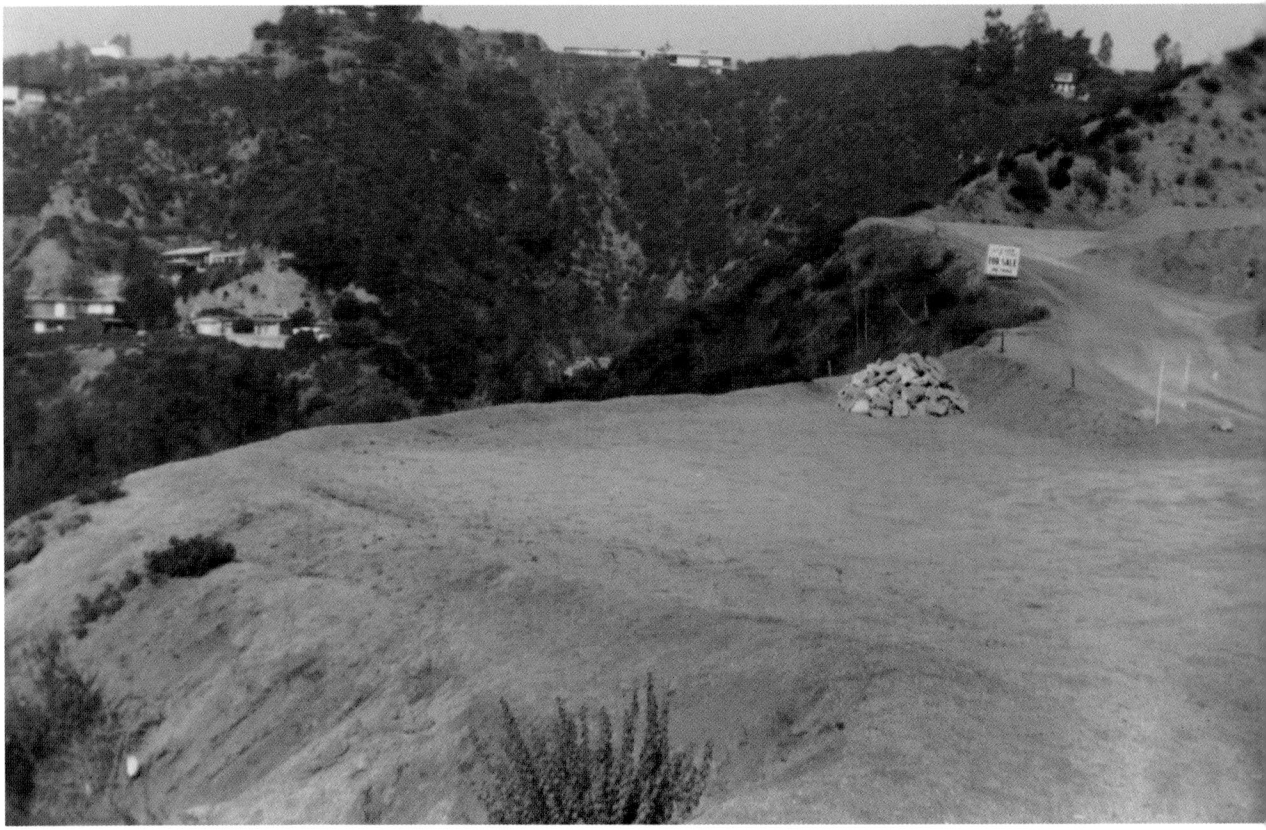

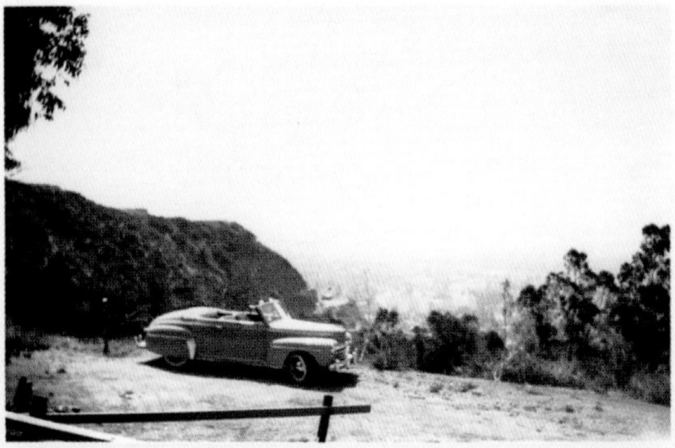

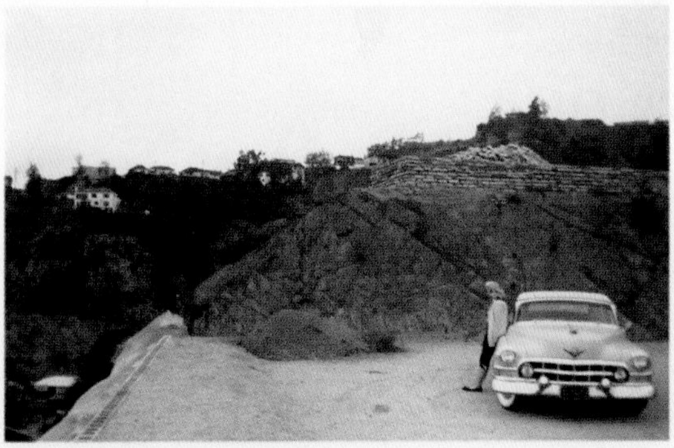

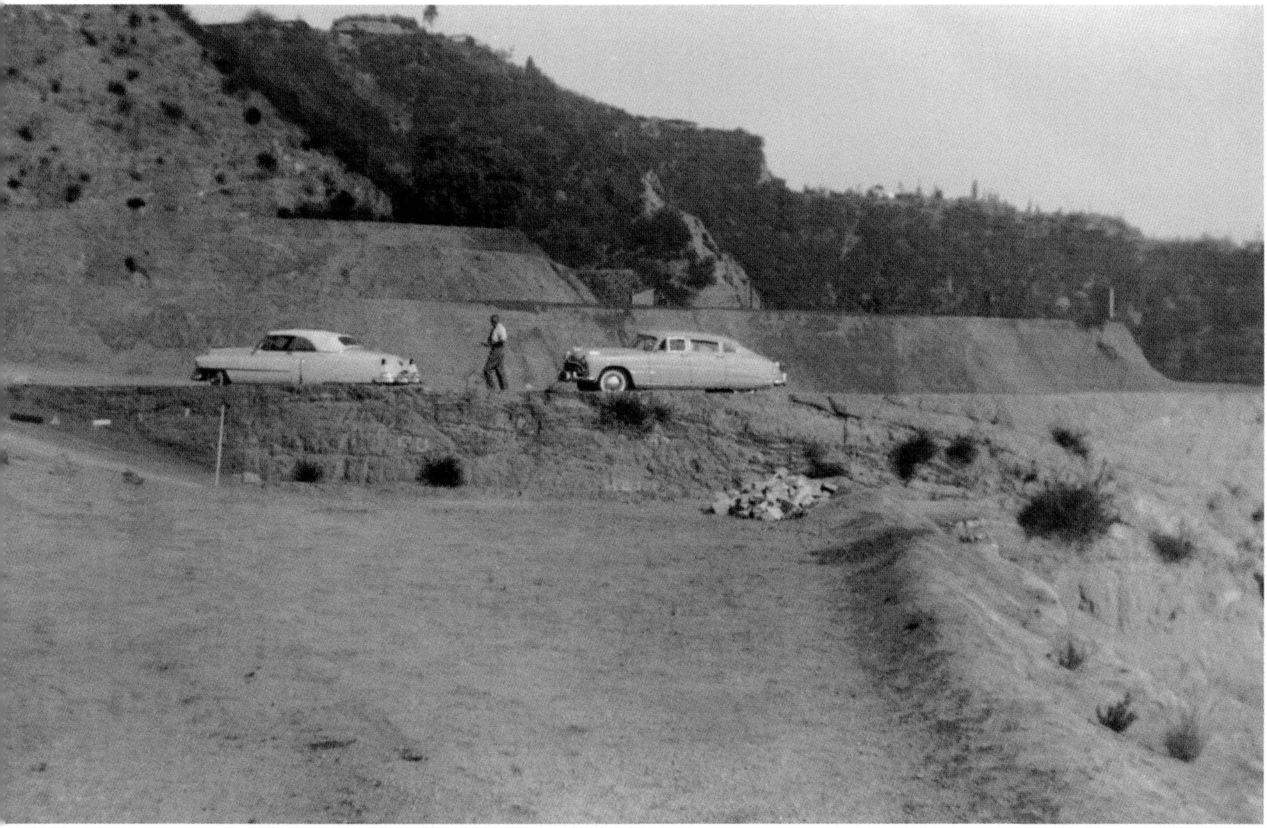

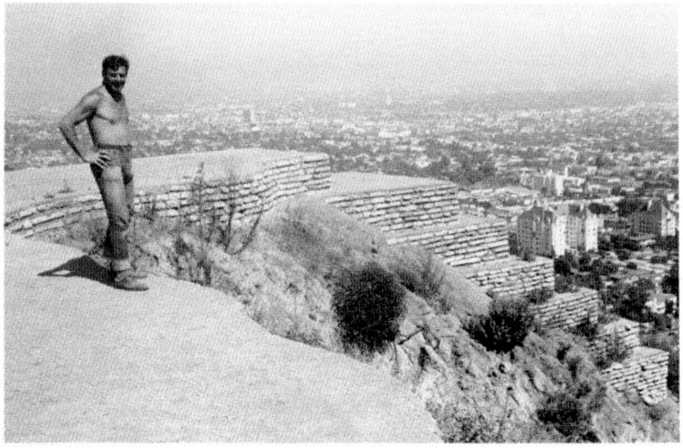

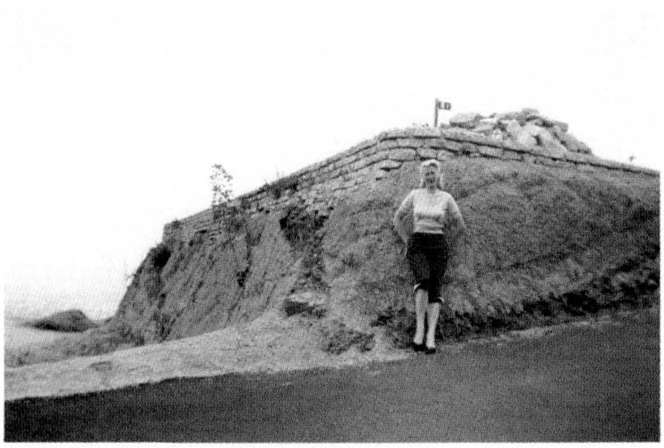

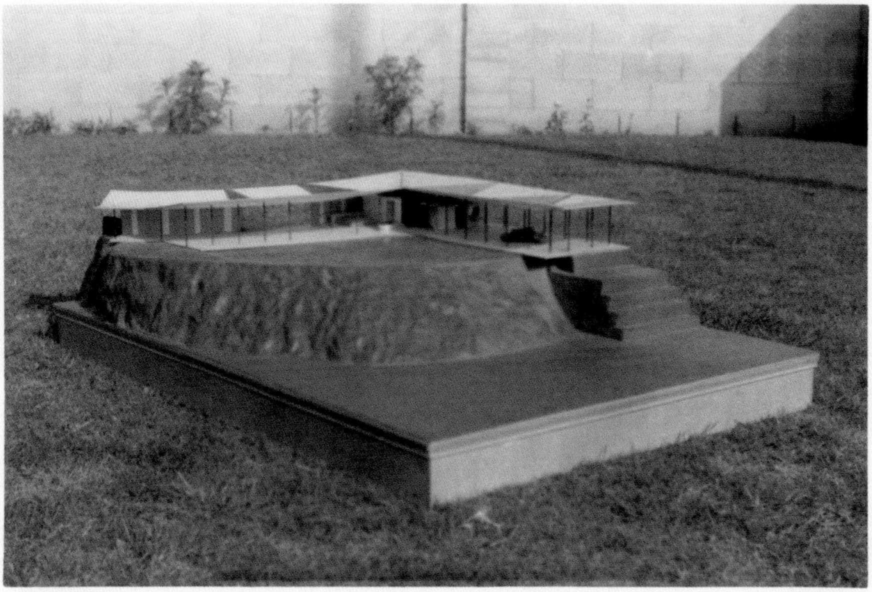

AUG • 56

AUG • 56

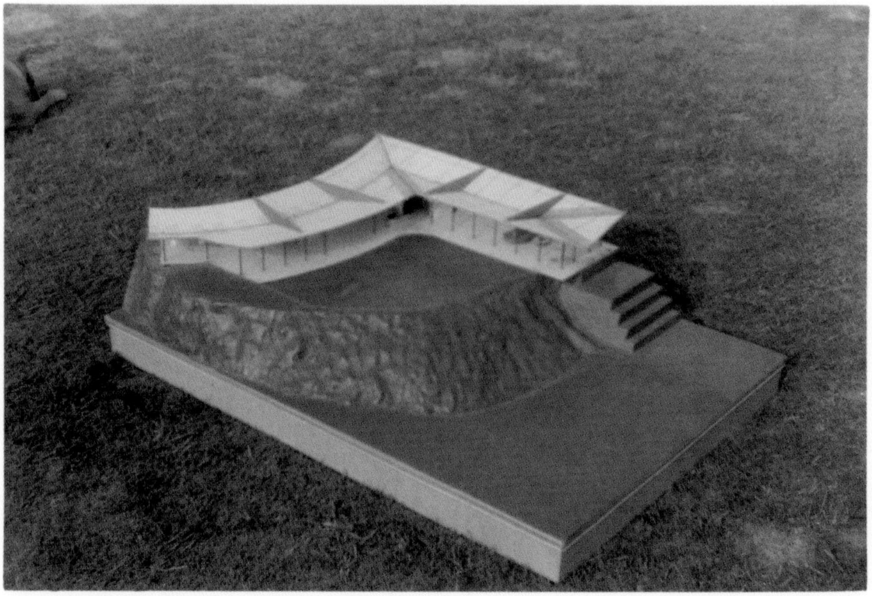

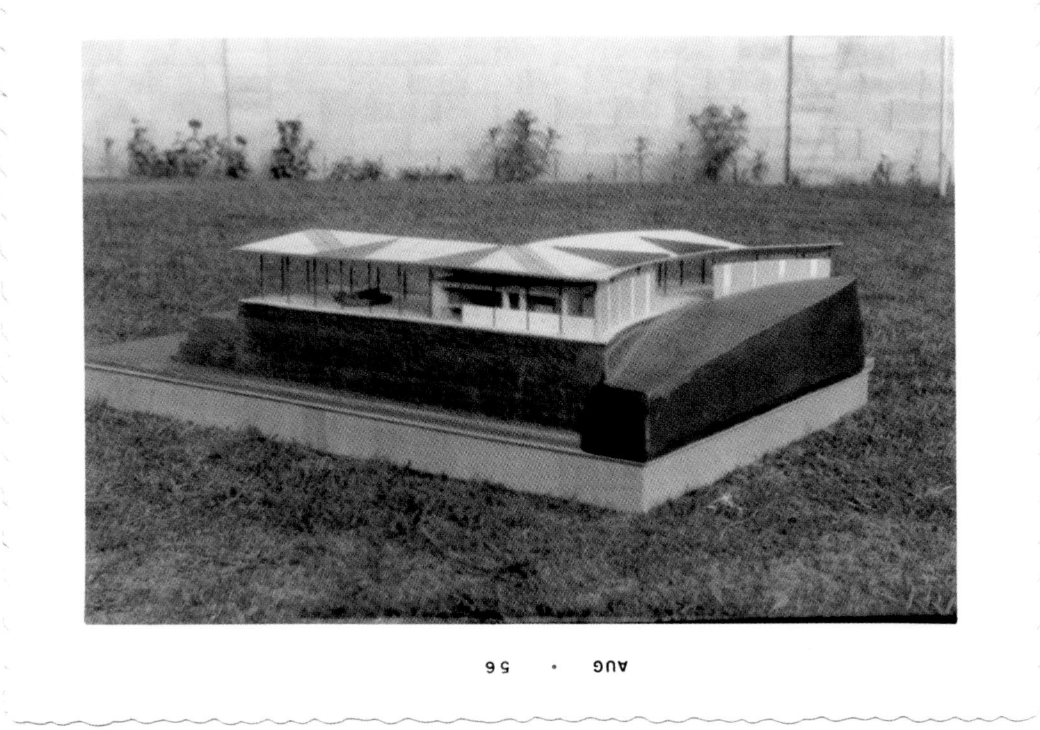
AUG • 56

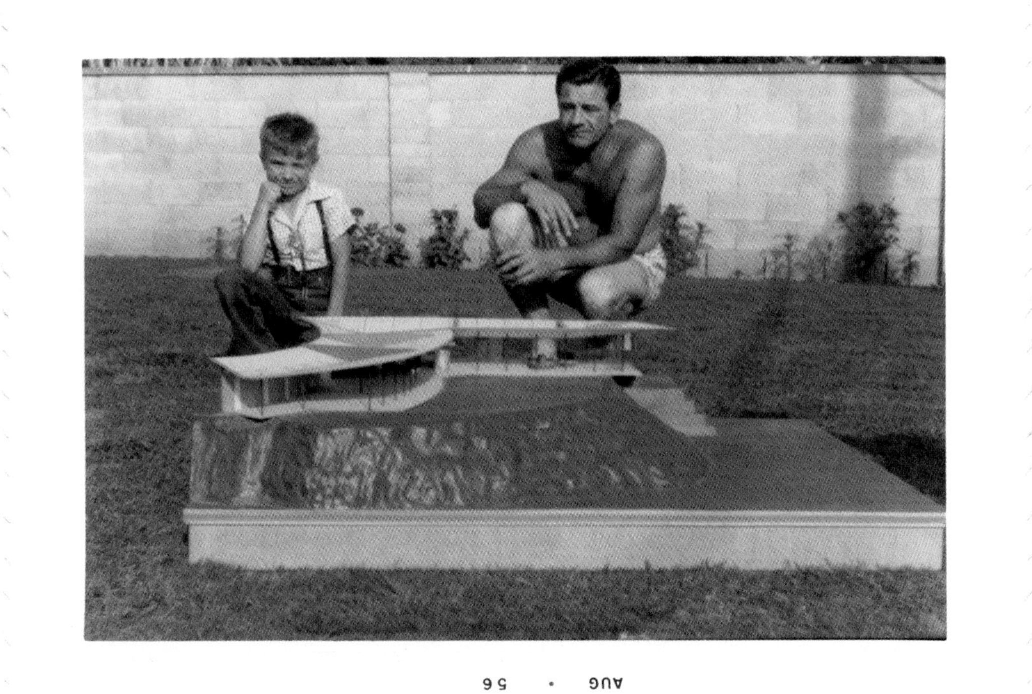
AUG • 56

CHAPTER 2
THE CONFLUENCE

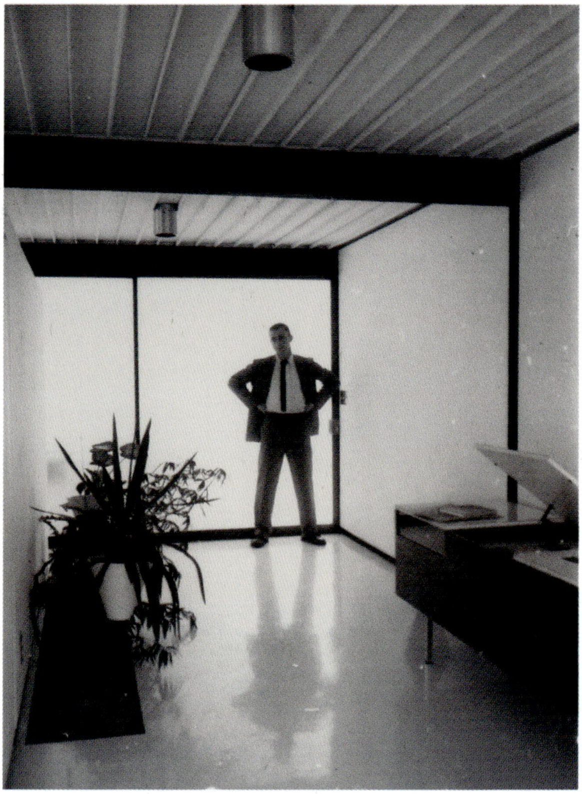

In 1956, Pierre Koenig was a thirty-year-old rising star of modernism. Though not yet a licensed architect—he wrote a letter to correct an editor who prematurely printed this title—he had already worked on several steel houses and had learned from the pioneers. As an architecture student at the University of Southern California, he had interned with Raphael Soriano, a prominent, second-generation modernist who in turn had worked for Richard Neutra, a first-generation master. Now, four years into his professional practice, Koenig had the confidence and experience to solve the particular riddles of building with steel, but he was still young and ambitious enough to be hungry for a challenge.

Like Buck, Koenig came from modest means. The son of a salesman and a homemaker, he was born in San Francisco in 1925. As a child, he had ginger hair and freckles. "I made sure I didn't get picked on by being tough, angry, and a hard worker," he told *The Guardian* in 1998. Growing up near Golden Gate Park and the marina, he loved wandering along the industrial waterfront. Koenig's affinity for drawing, like Buck's, emerged early, and the loading docks became a favorite sketching spot. "The structures I'd loved as a child in San Francisco hadn't even been buildings," Koenig said. "I used to head off from school and watch the great steel cranes loading and unloading ships in the docks. Or stop by the railroad yards to study the great steam locomotives, some of which had stormed all the way across the plains from Chicago at one hundred miles per hour."

Sometimes he and his father would climb into a DeSoto coupe and chase the Coast Daylight, an orange-and-silver passenger train that streaked down the coast to LA. "I wasn't brought up with very much art and history," Koenig admitted, "but I was passionate about this modern world of steel and rivets and energy working all around me."

In 1939, when Koenig was fourteen, his family moved to Southern California, settling east of Los Angeles in San Gabriel. After graduating from Alhambra City High, where a friend dedicated his yearbook inscription "to a super draftsman," Koenig enrolled in the University of Utah's College of Engineering. It was the fall of 1943, when Italy declared war on Germany. By year's end, as a member of the Enlisted Reserve Corps, Koenig was called to report for service. While Buck was training cadets in the navy, Koenig was going through basic training and becoming an expert rifleman as a private in the army.

Koenig toured England, France, and Germany as part of the 292nd Field Artillery Observation Battalion, whose objective was to identify the source and location of enemy fire. Within this unit he endured shelling and a truck accident that sent him to the hospital. Throughout his time at war, Koenig kept a combat diary in which he drew military ships and fighter planes in dive-bombing flight, further developing the skills he had learned in aeronautical drafting classes. He recorded the position of enemy troops in hand-drawn maps and sketched cartoonish scenes from London and Paris, where he celebrated VE Day. After two years and four-and-a-half months, he came home aboard the Queen Mary, arriving in New York harbor on August 2, 1945, "amid wild celebration." He came out of the war "feeling different about things" and shaped by what he had endured.

"If the experience of the war had given Koenig anything," wrote architect and historian Neil Jackson, "it was an inner strength and the courage to take risks."

Koenig was one of the many GIs who returned with college ambitions. He applied to the University of Southern California, but because of the sudden deluge of applicants, his admission was delayed by two years. During that time, he enrolled in Pasadena City College, where he took as many architecture courses as he could. Two years later, when he returned to apply at USC, he found himself put off once again. In response, Koenig and his friend George Foy parked themselves in the lobby of the dean's office from 8:00 a.m. to 5:00 p.m. every day for a week, wishing him good morning when he arrived and good afternoon when he left. After a week, the dean relented and granted them admission. In the fall of 1948, Koenig entered the USC School of Architecture program, the premiere architectural program on the West Coast.

The USC faculty was brimming with modernist visionaries, including Gregory Ain, Harwell Hamilton Harris, and Richard Neutra. Under their influence, Koenig contemplated the nation's housing shortage. He came to believe the single-family dwelling was "the only type of unit that offers all the advantages of maximum living needs." He also saw a unique opportunity to apply the processes and efficiencies of industrial mass production to the nation's growing appetite for affordable single-family homes. To this end, he envisioned houses designed with "a modular system of parts" that would decrease or eliminate "expensive cutting on the job that costs time and wastes material." As a student, he wrote that "the fabrication of parts at the factory is less expensive than the high-priced, rather awkward, mode of fabricating on-site."

His revolutionary approach came at just the right time. As the war had shaped Koenig's perspective, it had also dramatically influenced the world of architecture. During World War II, home construction had virtually ground to a halt, as nearly all the nation's materials and resources were diverted to the war effort. Now, many of the new materials and processes that had been developed for the war—including innovative welding methods, new polymers and adhesives, and novel uses of construction resources—were freed up for domestic use. Manufacturers of those materials were eagerly seeking new markets and applications. It was the perfect confluence of supply and demand, necessity and invention.

"When I came out of the war, there was a great impetus to change," Koenig recalled in a 1990 talk at the San Francisco Museum of Modern Art. "Industrialization and mass production had reached their zenith during the war, and there was a great need to provide homes and all types of buildings. Many architects started experimenting with new methods and different materials of building to replace the old methods. There was a certain excitement in the air—a feeling any problem could be solved."

At USC, Koenig questioned the status quo. In a third-year class called Housing, Wood, and the Community, he proposed using steel instead of wood. At the time, steel was used almost exclusively for commercial building, considered too cold and industrial for a home. But Koenig was determined to test his hypothesis. His instructor, Calvin Straub, was skeptical. "I don't agree with what you are doing," Straub told him, "but I'll let you do it." The more he was told he couldn't do something, the more Koenig wanted to do it. He completed the design for his class, but not without errors that would cost him academically.

"Probably due to his ignorance of steel construction, his grades plummeted, and he failed the year," wrote Neil Jackson.

Koenig learned from his mistakes and continued to experiment. The following summer, before graduating from USC, Koenig tested his theories with a real-world project. Since "no one had approached the problem of the steel house," Koenig said, "I thought the best way to learn this lesson was to build one."

This first big experiment—a house for himself—was a 1,000-square-foot modular structure with steel bones in place of wood framing. He designed the L-shaped plan on a 10-foot grid, with a 20-foot sliding glass door that swept open, connecting the backyard patio with the living room. (These details would echo in his future projects, including the Stahl House.) His professors were again skeptical, but he proceeded, nonetheless. "I was too innocent then to know that it was different," Koenig told historian Esther McCoy. "But that has an advantage. When you're too young to distinguish between the possible and the impossible, you often accomplish more."

Before he could build this experiment, he needed a place to put it—a lot that would suit his design needs as well as his modest budget. He had heard about "tax sales," in which the local government auctioned off real estate with unpaid property tax. After World War II, there was an abundance. Koenig paid a visit to the tax assessor's office and obtained a list of delinquent properties. He drove around Los Angeles, sizing up the potential at each address, and made a short list of his favorite lots. But when he went to the auction to bid on them, the best lots were missing. He wondered: *What's going on here?* A little digging revealed that savvy buyers were scoping out lots ahead of time and approaching property owners directly to purchase them prior to auction. Koenig employed the same strategy to purchase his lot in Glendale, as he explained to interviewer Mohamed Sharif in 2003. At eleven o'clock one night before auction, an elderly man offered him the Glendale lot—plus a second property on Sunset Plaza Drive—for a grand total of five hundred dollars. He had that much from his army discharge, so he purchased both. Shortly after the purchase, he got a phone call from a designer who'd heard, through word of mouth, that Koenig had an extra lot on his hands. Koenig sold it to him for five hundred dollars.

Koenig's budget for the house was a five-thousand-dollar bank loan, countersigned by his parents. He sent his design out to bid with various sub-contractors, and he was taken aback when their quotes added up to twelve thousand dollars. "Undaunted, I set out to find what was wrong with my plans," he said in a 1998 interview with his wife, Gloria Koenig. "I was convinced that I could build my steel house for five dollars per square foot." Seeking answers to his many questions, he reached out to a local steel company that invited him to spend a week at the plant, learning. "They taught me how to weld," Koenig told Sharif, "and showed me how to design for steel."

Koenig's hands-on exploration revealed to him the flaws in his original design that made it so expensive to build. "What I had done was design a wooden house ... but substituted steel," he told Sharif. "So I went back and designed it for steel." As he explained to Gloria Koenig, he adapted his design based on what he'd learned from his time at the steel plant:

I learned how to turn the beams on the long direction of the plan—instead of a traverse like a wood house. I learned how to minimize the number of parts by increasing spans. I learned how to cut down on waste. Then I went to a sliding glass door company, and I learned much the same thing—bigger and fewer doors were more economical. Armed with my new knowledge, I redesigned my house, and sure enough, the new bids added up to five thousand dollars, including retaining walls for the hillside. These simple lessons have served me for my entire career and have given me the basis for expanding my knowledge to bigger and more elaborate solutions.

Serving as general contractor and performing some of the labor himself, he began building this new, economical plan on the Glendale lot he had purchased for next to nothing: a north-facing plot on Los Encinos Avenue. Koenig House #1, as it came to be known, "went up in a day," Koenig later said. The cost savings on materials and the speed of construction (which also saved money) was extremely encouraging. Koenig knew he was really on to something.

As he built this house in 1950, Koenig was still technically a designer—he called himself an "architectural draftsman"—not yet licensed as an architect but able to practice the craft. In need of a summer job, he was hired by USC grad Raphael Soriano, a pioneer in the use of prefabricated steel in modern architecture. At the time, Soriano was working on four steel-framed houses, including the Olds House, which would come to be known as "Case Study House 1950." Koenig prepared the perspective drawings of the house that ran in the August 1950 issue of *Arts & Architecture* magazine.

Another of Soriano's big projects that summer was a steel-and-glass home commissioned by architectural photographer Julius Shulman, whose ability to capture the essence of modern design would play a key role in the Stahl House.

In 1950, Shulman was entering the most productive period of a prolific seventy-two-year career. This was the year he opened his studio, part of the 4,000-square-foot home Soriano created for him at a cost of thirty-eight thousand dollars. Supporting his wife, Emma, and their six-year-old daughter, Judy, Shulman worked an average of four photo assignments a week—an incredible volume he sustained throughout the 1950s. While modern architecture was his calling card and his passion, he rarely turned down a job; and his clients ranged from magazines to manufacturers, his subjects including elevators, fixtures, and housewares. He meticulously recorded each job in a logbook and took pride in his efficiency, always looking for opportunities to maximize the return on his efforts.

"When photographing a home or a corporate headquarters, he would get in a few shots of the toilets, say, or the boiler rooms, hoping to resell those pictures to the manufacturers," wrote Mary Melton in *Los Angeles* magazine. "He produced an average of ten negatives per project, which saved time as well as film stock." While most photographers burned through dozens of rolls of film, bracketing each shot with an array of f-stops and shutter speeds, Shulman was precise and minimal in his exposures. After painstakingly composing an image, he took only one negative in black and white, and a single color transparency, earning the nickname "One-shot Shulman."

Born in Brooklyn in 1910 to parents who had emigrated from Russia, Julius Shulman was the third of seven children in a family of even more modest means than that of Buck Stahl or Pierre Koenig. When Julius was only a few months old, the Shulman family moved to Connecticut, where his father farmed, tilling the soil with a horse-drawn plow. His mother pumped water by hand and cooked on a wood-and-coal stove in a house lit by kerosene lamps.

"The toilets were outside—Sears, Roebuck catalogs for paper," Shulman told Taina Rikala De Noriega in a 1990 oral history interview for the Archives of American Art. He recalled seeing the first neighbor to own a Ford Model T.

In 1920, the family of nine moved by train to California. "In those days, California was magic," Shulman said. "It was the land of gold, and you heard stories from people. It was a land of opportunity. It was a land of endless possibilities, physically, climate, and economically." They settled in Los

Angeles, where Julius and his siblings went to school at Alpine Street School, near Sunset Boulevard and Figueroa Street. His father ran a dry goods store a few blocks away, on Temple Street.

Shulman's first exposure to photography was in the 11th grade, when he was given a choice between an art-appreciation class and one of the nation's first high-school photography classes. He chose the latter. Using his family's Eastman box camera—in those days, no one called them Kodak—he would wander around Hollenbeck Park, a few blocks from Roosevelt High School, taking pictures of the lake and an old wooden bridge. He learned how to develop film and make prints in a darkroom.

He didn't get his first professional camera—a Vest Pocket Kodak camera—until five or six years later, when he was a college student at the University of California, Los Angeles. "And that was just by accident," he said. "Somebody gave me the camera, for a birthday or something." In the fall of 1929, he was studying electrical engineering at UCLA, but dropped out of the program after a couple of weeks. "Then the ensuing years I wandered around UCLA, auditing courses," he said. "I wasn't enrolled for a major because I didn't know what I wanted to be." He moved with a friend to Berkeley, where he started taking pictures of buildings on the campus of the University of California, Berkeley, photographing the Campanile Building framed by the arch of the Hearst Memorial Mining Building. But by February 1936, he had had enough of life as "an academic drifter" and decided to return to LA.

That was the year he met his first architectural client, Richard Neutra, one of the first-generation Southern California Modernist masters. In March 1936, a friend working for Neutra as a draftsman invited Shulman to accompany him to the construction site of a project nearing completion. It was the Kun House, a residence overlooking the LA basin from the Hollywood Hills near Laurel Canyon. As Neutra inspected the construction, Shulman took "about five or six" pictures of the house with his Vest Pocket camera. He printed 8-by-10 black-and-white photographs and gave them to his friend, who passed them along to the architect. "On Sunday, March 5, I got a call from him," Shulman recalled in 1990. "He said, 'Mr. Neutra has seen the pictures. He liked them. He'd like to purchase them from you.'"

Neutra told Shulman he should meet an up-and-coming architect who had worked for him before starting his own practice. "Why don't you drive up there and meet Soriano?" Neutra asked Shulman, pointing at the hill above Silver Lake, where Raphael Soriano was finishing his first residential commission, the Lipetz House. Shulman drove up the hill that day and met the architect who would become renowned as a second-generation Southern California Modernist, and who would, in turn, mentor Pierre Koenig, a third-generation master.

> **In a sense, it's one of those moments in the cosmos where you feel like stars have aligned, with Buck, Carlotta, Pierre, and Julius. There were a variety of players that came together to create an icon. —Mark Stahl**

"We became good friends," Shulman said. "We started our respective careers that same year." And when the Lipetz house was completed, Julius Shulman photographed it. Fourteen years later, Shulman would hire Soriano to design the home and studio where he would spend the rest of his life.

That serendipitous meeting with Neutra launched Shulman's meteoric career. Neutra hired Shulman for additional jobs and introduced him to Gregory Ain, Rudolph Schindler, J.R. Davidson, and Harwell Hamilton Harris. "The early pioneers were all beginning," Shulman said. "And here I was with my Vest Pocket Kodak."

One of the skills that set Shulman apart was his technical prowess for balancing ambient light with flash. This was particularly necessary (and especially challenging) when photographing houses with copious glass—a hallmark of modernist style. While the human eye and brain can merge the bright outdoors with a dimly lit interior, film lacks the capability to capture such wide dynamic range. It is up to the photographer to augment natural outdoor light with precisely placed pops of flash to bring out the detail in shadows. There was also the challenge of working with reflections in glass. Few of Shulman's contemporaries possessed his talent for managing these technicalities, and Shulman was not shy about pointing out that "they would draw the draperies or photograph at nighttime, and still leave the draperies closed." At a time when there was no way to preview an image before the darkroom, no Photoshop for post-production correction of suboptimal exposures, it was even more impressive that he had the skill and confidence to nail an image in one shot—without even using a light meter.

Yet Shulman considered the camera "the least important element" of his job. "Photography is dependent on the eye, the mind, the heart, and the soul of the photographer," he said. He studied the way the sun moved through a building, minute by minute, sculpting new patterns of shadow and light. His awareness extended to the natural world that surrounded a building, and his images expressed the relationship between a building and its site. He often preached to his students: "A photograph is a design in which you assemble thoughts in your mind." Technical proficiency was of little use without an artist's eye and an innate instinct for composition and light.

When Shulman started photographing architecture for magazines, he realized that "very few photographers used people." He became one of the first photographers to add occupants—occasionally models, but typically everyday folks—to bring warmth and domesticity to spaces that might otherwise appear lifeless and cold. People provided a sense of human scale, a breath of air, and "a feeling of natural activity." Architects did not always agree with this, because they didn't want people—or in some cases, even furniture—to distract from their work. Richard Neutra insisted on removing the owner's living-room furniture from one of his projects before Shulman photographed the house.

"He didn't want anybody interfering with his architecture," Shulman said. Editors, Shulman argued, "want to show a house *lived-in* . . . occupied by a human being." Neutra stood his ground, and Shulman complied. But after photographing Neutra's "naked" room, Shulman pulled the homeowner aside. "I would like to photograph your house the way you live in it," he told her. "May I come back?"

Shulman also inserted greenery, staging potted plants in living rooms and asking assistants (or even architects) to stand or lie just out of the shot, holding out branches to frame the image. On this, he and Neutra agreed. "He was always bringing loads of branches," Shulman said. "It's a joke among many of the architects who used to apprentice for Neutra. I'd see them at conventions, or meetings, or seminars, and they'd say, 'Hey, Julius! I remember we used to hold branches for you!'"

By the mid-1930s, Julius Shulman's editorial clients included the *Los Angeles Times* and other newspapers as well as magazines ranging from *House & Garden* and *Good Housekeeping* to architectural publications. He was already working for *Arts & Architecture* when the magazine was taken over in 1938 by a new and brilliant editor, John Entenza. The convergence of Shulman, Koenig, and Entenza would play a key role in delivering Buck Stahl's vision to the world.

The '50s were glorious years. . . . The population was booming—people were coming to Los Angeles from all over the world. And architects were given free rein. They were allowed to experiment, not in the way that is being done today—these horrible monstrosities being made in the name of post-modernism—but with integrity. The architects of the period—people like Richard Neutra, Pierre Koenig, Gregory Ain—they respected the client. Every line they drew was drawn with the client in mind. —Julius Shulman

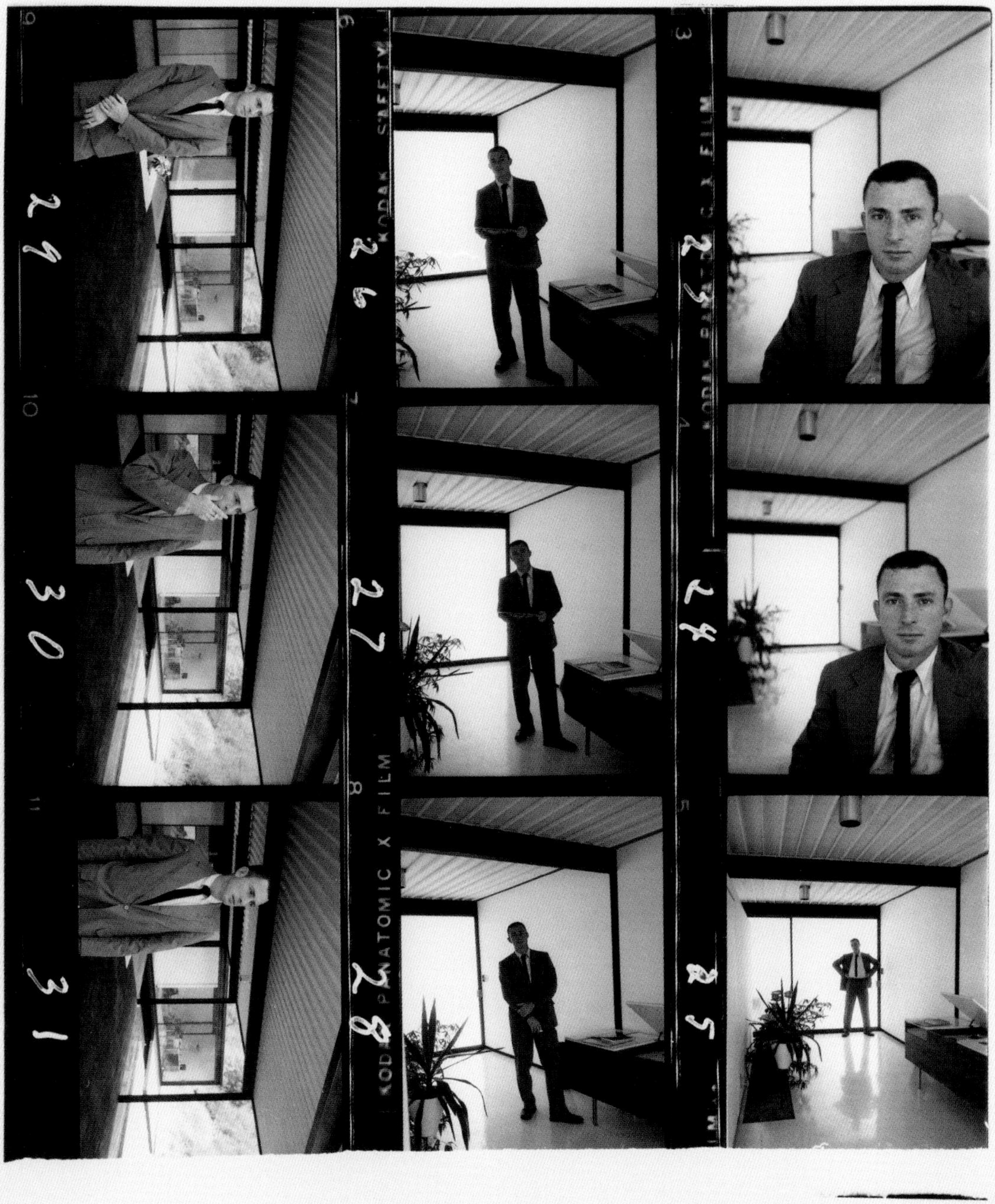
29
30
31
26
27
28
23
24
25
PANATOMIC X FILM

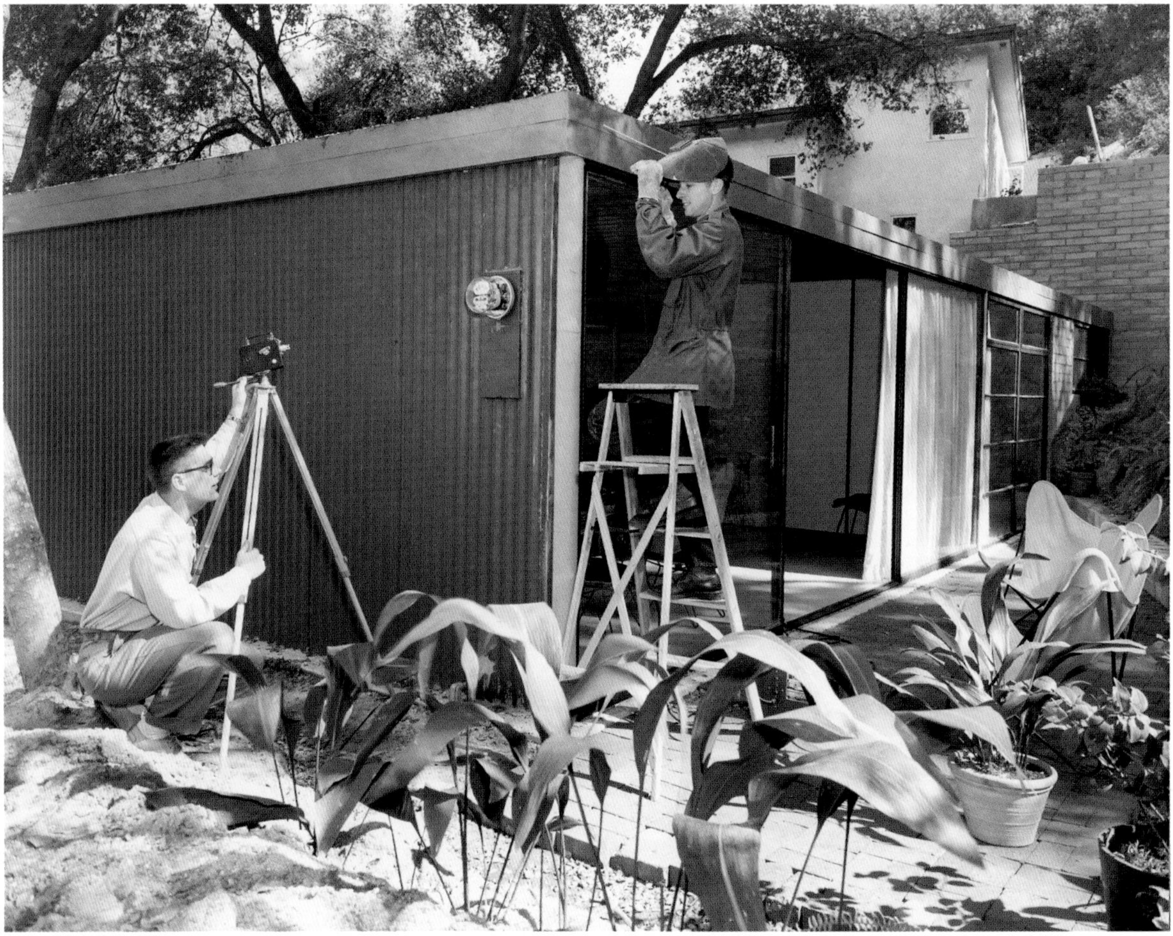

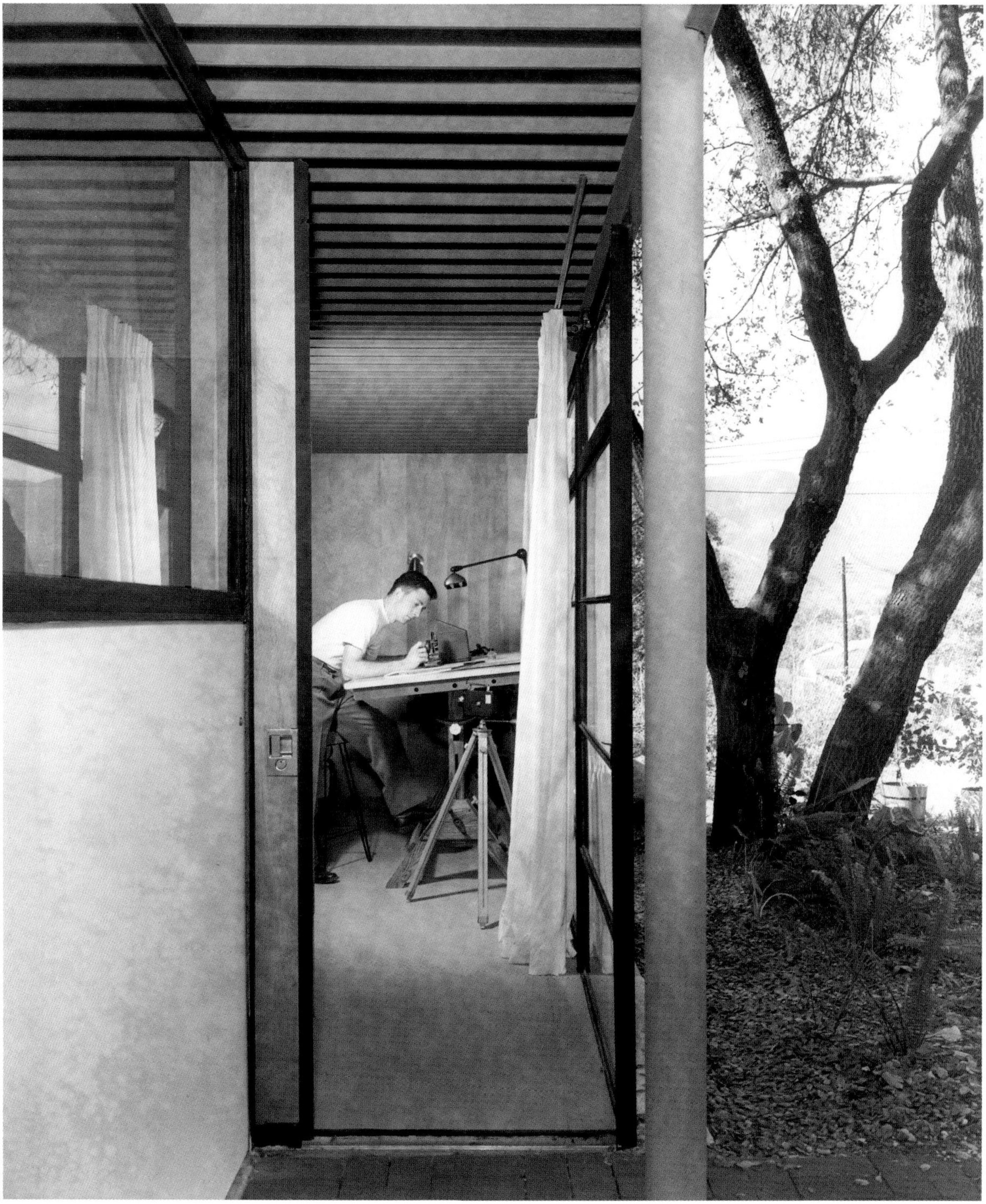

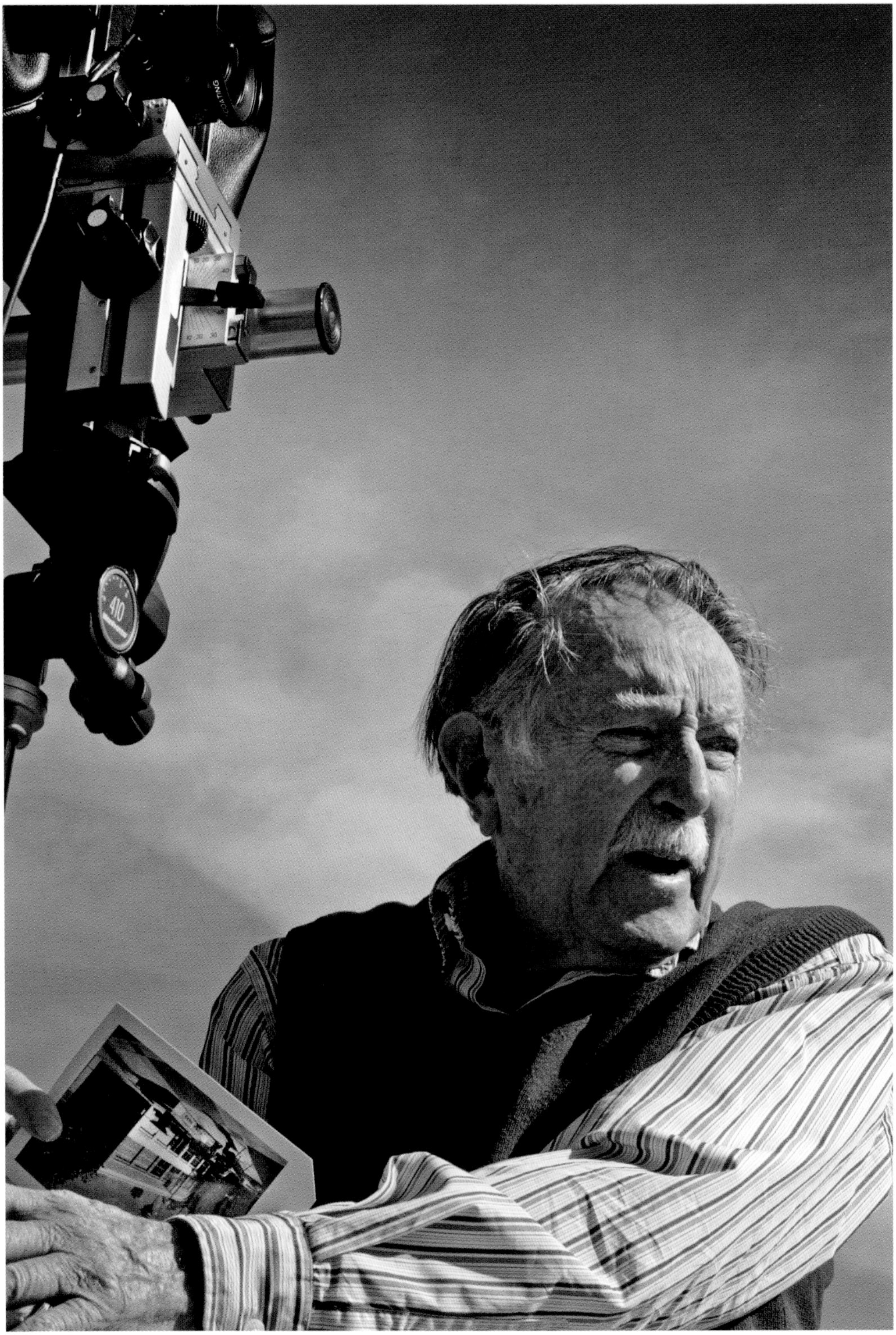
410

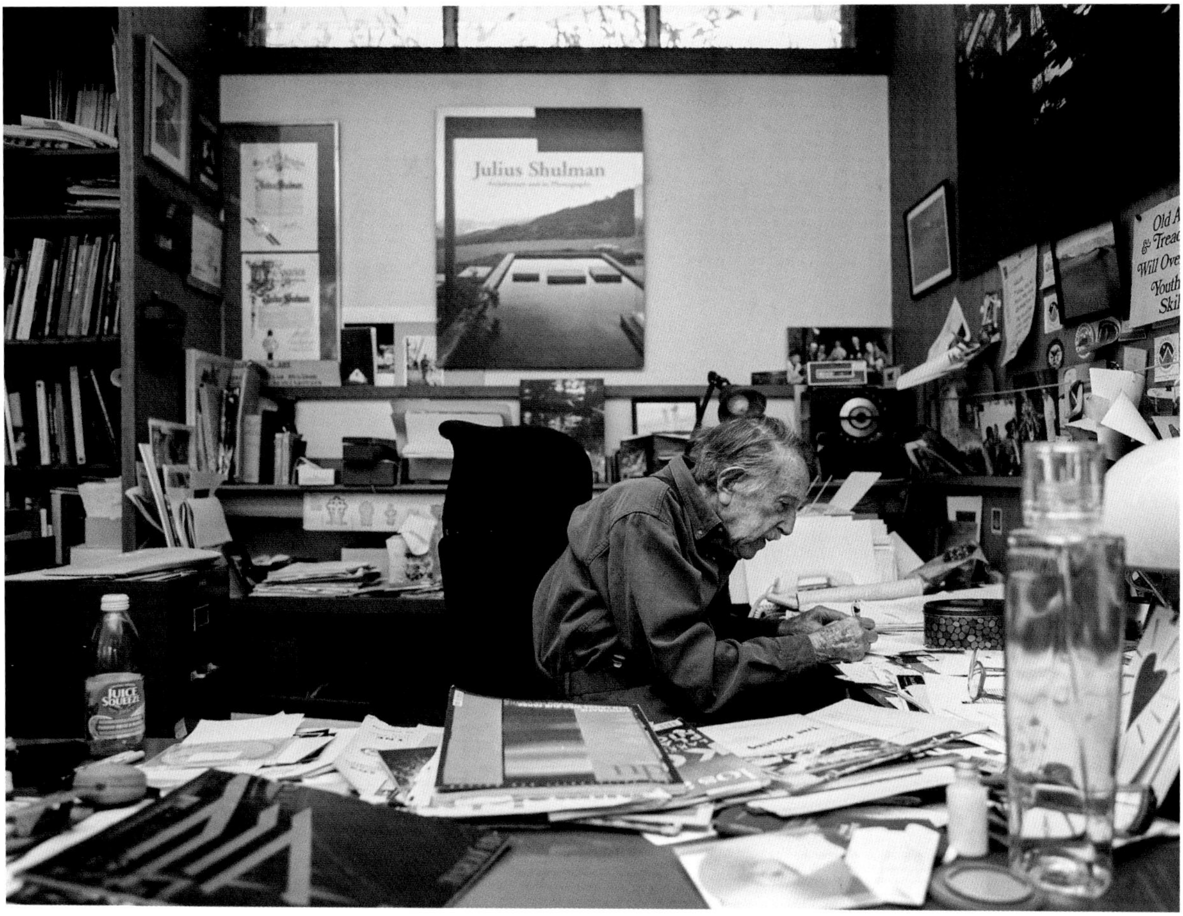
Julius Shulman
JUICE SQUEEZE

CHAPTER 3
THE CATALYST

As World War II drew to a close, John Entenza was contemplating the future of American homes. The thirty-nine-year-old editor of LA-based *Arts & Architecture* magazine perceived an imminent problem and a tremendous opportunity. The US Armed Forces would soon send home 7.6 million men and women stationed abroad. Where would they all live?

Residential construction had been on hold for years, as building materials and resources were redirected to the war effort. In order to stave off a looming housing crisis, America would need thousands of affordable homes, built quickly and efficiently, to shelter them in the coming boom years. Like Pierre Koenig, Entenza believed that the materials and technologies developed for war could be put to new use in residential building. Forward-thinking architecture could finally bring well-designed homes within reach of the average family, and his magazine could help.

Arts & Architecture would commission the nation's best contemporary architects to reinvent the middle-class home and reimagine the entire American lifestyle. They would be encouraged to incorporate new materials, efficient floor plans, and a sleek, modern aesthetic. The end goal: affordable, well-designed prototypes that could be mass-produced nationwide. Each house "must be capable of duplication" Entenza wrote, "and in no sense be an individual 'performance.'"

Seven months before the official end of the war, the editor unveiled his concept—The Case Study House Program—in the magazine's January 1945 issue.

The conditions and timing for such an experiment could not have been more auspicious. It was the end of a long, lean era for American architects, whose work had largely been put on hold for decades, first by the Great Depression and then the war. Now, nourished by an atmosphere of unbridled optimism, American architecture would once again start to flourish. There was "something electric in the air," noted historian Esther McCoy, "a particular sort of excitement that comes from the sound of hammers and saws after they have been silent for too long." Suddenly the nation was flush not only with building resources but the hopeful, forward-looking will to create what architect Edward Killingsworth called "a new way of life, better living."

The war, of course, had altered the trajectory of everyone's life. While Buck Stahl was training cadets in the navy, and Pierre Koenig was tracking enemy fire for the army in England and France, Julius Shulman was working in an army hospital as a medical and surgical photographer. American architects were designing barracks and airplane factories. In the postwar era, they would all have new tools and a burgeoning market. The materials, resources, and labor now freed up for domestic use would help ignite the peacetime economic boom.

Los Angeles was primed for postwar prosperity. The federal government had invested billions of dollars in the city, which was coming into its own as a powerhouse of industry and culture. As historian Richard Lillard noted: Los Angeles "handled more seaport tonnage than San Francisco, landed more fish than Boston and Gloucester, and together with satellite cities, it made more planes than any other metropolis on Earth. Los Angeles also assembled more cars than any city but Detroit, baked more tires than any city but Akron, made more furniture than Grand Rapids, and stitched together more clothes than any city except New York. . . ."

War veterans were relocating to the golden land they had glimpsed while passing through on their way to the Pacific theater. Around one million moved to Los Angeles in the immediate postwar years. Two million more came in the 1950s. By 1960, the LA population had swelled to six million people, many of whom were just starting families and came in search of a casual lifestyle that called for a new kind of shelter. "The Case Study House Program was the answer to the need for well-designed, two-bedroom houses that were easy to maintain without servants," penned McCoy, who wrote about the program for *Arts & Architecture* and other publications.

Young architects had been starving for opportunity, and the Case Study Program would provide an outlet for their creative energy. It also created an economic model that encouraged experimentation with new materials, buffering the cost through a mutually beneficial relationship between architects, homeowners, and home-building suppliers. Suppliers supported the program by donating products or offering dramatically reduced rates, which allowed architects to experiment with state-of-the-art materials while staying within homeowners' budgets. In turn, the suppliers benefited from the publicity of being featured in these high-profile houses, which were each highlighted (with a list of products and materials) in the magazine. Photographs of the construction process were accompanied by comments from the architect. After completion, each house was opened for public tours.

What man has learned about himself in the past five years will, we are sure, express itself in the way in which he will want to be housed in the future. Only one thing will stop the realization of that wish, and that is the tenacity with which man clings to old forms because he does not yet understand the new.

—John Entenza

Everyone involved in the Case Study House Program had great faith in the power of architecture to effect social change. "They were true believers," said historian Thomas S. Hines. "Modern architecture was going to not just improve the world but might save the world. Much of the modern movement was made up of heroic romantics, or romantic heroes, who were out to slay the dragons, and who did believe that they had the solutions."

These heroes, whom we now call the modernists, had the courage to abandon classical forms, such as single-point perspective in painting (Pablo Picasso) or plot structure in literature (James Joyce). In the visual and literary arts, they sought new aesthetics that matched the "machine age" of industry, motion pictures, airplanes, and automobiles. Modern architects were more than ready to break with the neoclassical tradition, which "had reigned supreme from the Renaissance to the Victorian age," according to historian Philip Ethington. "Reflecting bygone social worlds, the wedding-cake ornamentation and Greek temple facades lost their relevance in a world of speedy trains, steel construction, and the telephone."

Architectural modernism emerged in Chicago at the turn of the nineteenth century, when American architect Louis Sullivan coined the phrase, "Form ever follows function." His disciples included Frank Lloyd Wright, who harmonized nature with machine-age utility, and Austrian architect Adolf Loos, who denounced ornamentation as "a crime." Loos mentored Austrians Richard Neutra and Rudolph Schindler, encouraging them to move to Chicago to work with Frank Lloyd Wright.

Meanwhile, architects on both sides of the Atlantic were influenced by the Vienna Secession, an art movement that aimed to unify fine art, decorative arts, and architecture with a streamlined aesthetic that embodied the taut minimalism of the machine age. "Less is more" declared Ludwig Mies van der Rohe, who directed the Bauhaus, a German art and design school founded in 1919 that merged the principles of mass production with the individual elegance of fine arts and the functionality of crafts.

The Bauhaus approach to architecture—which came to be known as the International Style—went beyond the aesthetic. "Modernism in architecture became central to movements for social reform," said Ethington, "because buildings are the footprints of social forms." In order to build a more equitable society, the thinking went, we must change the way people live. Such teachings were denounced by the Nazis as communist. Under pressure, Mies van der Rohe closed the school in 1933 and took refuge in Chicago.

In the 1920s, after working with Frank Lloyd Wright, Neutra and Schindler moved from Chicago to Southern California to work for Wright's offices in Los Angeles. There, in the temperate climate and stunning topography, they evolved International Style into Southern California Modernism, which envisioned an indoor-outdoor lifestyle not possible in Chicago winters.

The Case Study House Program's focus on modernism was anything but coincidence; it went deeper than John Entenza's personal taste. It was rooted in an ideology that manifested in design. He believed that the materials and manufacturing practices of the machine age could be harnessed to place good architecture within reach of middle-class American families like the Stahls—if you put them in the hands of the right designers. Could modern architecture truly save the world? The Case Study House Program would put that question to a real-world test.

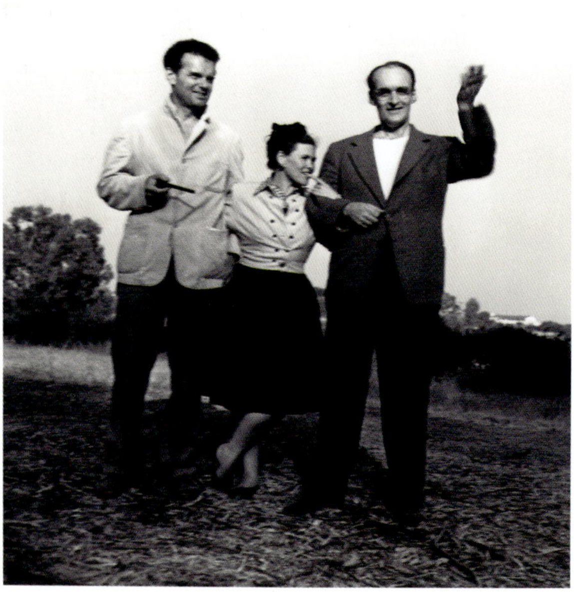

John Entenza (right) with Charles and Ray Eames.

It would be one of the most famous experiments in American architecture.

John Dymock Entenza was not an architect, but he was a champion of modernism in all forms. A discriminating editor with sophisticated taste, Entenza curated a culturally diverse, intellectually ambitious magazine that featured varied topics, from Orson Welles discussing theater to articles on wine tasting. Esther McCoy, who knew Entenza personally, described *Arts & Architecture* as being "as thin as a tortilla and as sleek as a Bugatti." Despite its slim profile, the magazine had a fantastic reach, distributed in forty-one countries.

Everybody was very idealistic. Everybody wanted to produce answers to the housing problems. —Pierre Koenig

John Entenza was a hardworking, deep-thinking man with a moral compass and a passion for new ideas. He carried himself with dignity and dressed in immaculate dark suits. "His shoes and his mind were always nicely polished," wrote McCoy, who met him in Los Angeles in 1932, when "LA, even Santa Monica, was déclassé." Despite his Protestant work ethic, he rarely got to the office before noon. "He loved gossip, but never reached for it," McCoy observed. "It was given."

Born in Michigan in 1903 to a Spanish attorney and a Scottish mining heiress, Entenza was well-educated and culturally literate. He studied liberal arts at Tulane University and the University of Virginia before training for a job with the Department of Labor in Washington, DC. He changed careers and moved to California, where he worked as a writer on experimental films for MGM from 1932 to 1936, when his unit folded in the Great Depression.

Entenza's interest in modern architecture began when his father's law partner, a female attorney, commissioned a house by Harwell Hamilton Harris, an architect who had apprenticed with Richard Neutra. That house was never built, but in 1937 Entenza hired Harris to design one for himself. Soon thereafter, Entenza began working as an editor for what some considered "a rather staid provincial publication" called *California Arts & Architecture,* founded in 1929. In 1938, he bought the magazine, and two years later assumed the role of editor, steering it into a new era.

A believer that good design has no borders, he dropped California from the title and set out to reinvent the magazine from within. He replaced "cozy eclecticism" with "carefully selected modern buildings, innovative art and design, and progressive politics," wrote architectural writer Michael Webb. *Arts & Architecture* was "a shoestring operation," as McCoy put it, with one paid assistant, a small circulation, and editorial pages sparsely populated with ads. "I would go further," wrote David Travers, who succeeded Entenza as editor and publisher in 1962. "It was a shoeless operation."

While *Arts & Architecture* lacked the budget to compete with East Coast architectural journals, it nurtured West Coast architectural talent, which "grew and flourished under its rays," according to Travers. Entenza wanted to champion young architects, to whom he was generous, kind, and supportive. Calvin Straub, featured in the magazine as one of those relative newcomers, recalled that Entenza didn't exhibit a trace of intellectual snobbery. "He was a warm guy. He encouraged us."

Entenza surrounded himself with smart people who had innovative ideas. His office on Wilshire Boulevard became "a rallying point" for progressive thinking about design, whether design applied to houses, landscapes, furniture, textiles, or other industrial arts. As Esther McCoy noted:

Those were exciting and electric times. We thought we were part of a brave new world. New things were happening, new directions that would take part in the lives of the ordinary people.

—Ralph Rapson

"It created a climate which not only encouraged but bred talent." He always opened his door to architects in need of encouragement or art students with an idea for a cover. Young architects considered it a mark of prestige to be published in *Arts & Architecture*.

Underlying the content of the magazine's pages was a political awareness and progressive ideology that transcended arts and architecture. In his editorials, he weighed in on international diplomacy, expressing support for America's Soviet ally and the new United Nations, while also decrying incidents of prejudice back home, such as the infamous Zoot Suit Riots of 1943, in which lawmen and service members attacked minority youths in Los Angeles. The editor's "moral seriousness—leavened by his wry humor—infused the magazine," wrote Travers.

The experiment began as Entenza commissioned eight architectural firms to design eight Case Study houses. He knew the architects personally, and most of them were young—in their twenties and thirties—though a few were older. Among them was Richard Neutra, who would mentor Raphael Soriano, who would mentor Pierre Koenig.

Julius Shulman, who began working for *Arts & Architecture* long before Entenza's arrival, was intimately involved with the Case Study House Program from the start, and not only as a photographer. "I worked closely with the advertising manager of the magazine because A) there was no money for the magazine to perform the production of the Case Study Program without sponsors, and B) there was no money for photographs." Not all products met the editor's discerning standards. "Entenza would be the judge of whether it was accepted," Shulman said. It wasn't a particularly profitable arrangement for *Arts & Architecture*, on which Entenza lost money. Of the twenty-six Case Study houses that would ultimately be built, Shulman would photograph eighteen of them.

The twenty-one-year Case Study House Program would evolve into three phases, each distinct in retrospect. The first phase (1945 to 1949) reflected limited material shortages after the war. With one notable exception (No. 8, the Eames House), these homes reflected a transition between the familiar plans of prewar homes and the dramatically different designs of the 1950s. The second phase (1950 to 1960) was defined largely by experimentation with steel. The third phase (1960 to 1966) broadened its focus beyond the single-family home to community planning.

The beginning of the second phase in the summer of 1950 would be fortuitous in the story of the Stahl House. Though Buck and Carlotta's paths had not yet crossed, instrumental people, ideas, and events were clicking into place in ways that would shape their future. Buck was transitioning to his new job at Hughes Aircraft, the role in which he would meet Carlotta. The Case Study House Program was pivoting to the use of steel, and Raphael Soriano was completing Case Study House 1950, a steel-framed house composed of 10-feet-by-20-feet modules. Working for Soriano, Pierre Koenig, still a third-year architecture student at USC, was preparing drawings of CSH 1950 for publication in *Arts & Architecture*. Koenig was also building his own house, that first L-shaped foray into steel, on his five-thousand-dollar budget.

When John Entenza heard of this house, he told Koenig: "Call Julius Shulman to come out, and if he likes it, he'll photograph it. And if he likes it, I'll publish it." In 1952, Shulman went out to investigate. He liked what he saw and took a few photos of the house, as well as a portrait of the twenty-seven-year-old architect bent over his drafting table, framed by a doorway. Five black-and-white photographs and the floorplan of the Koenig House #1, as it would come to be known, were published in the February 1953 issue of *Living for Young Homemakers*, in an article titled "The Pioneering Urge in Action." Seven months later, the house was featured in the October 1953 issue of *Arts & Architecture*, which praised it as a "simple, light, and spacious structure" that "takes full advantage of a heavily wooded site by opening to the front and rear with large expanses of glass and sliding doors."

Entenza, with his eye for talent, had found his next recruit. "John asked me to come in one day and . . . said, 'If you ever have a good house with some good clients, tell me and we'll make it a Case Study House,'" Koenig later recalled. "That was Case Study House 21."

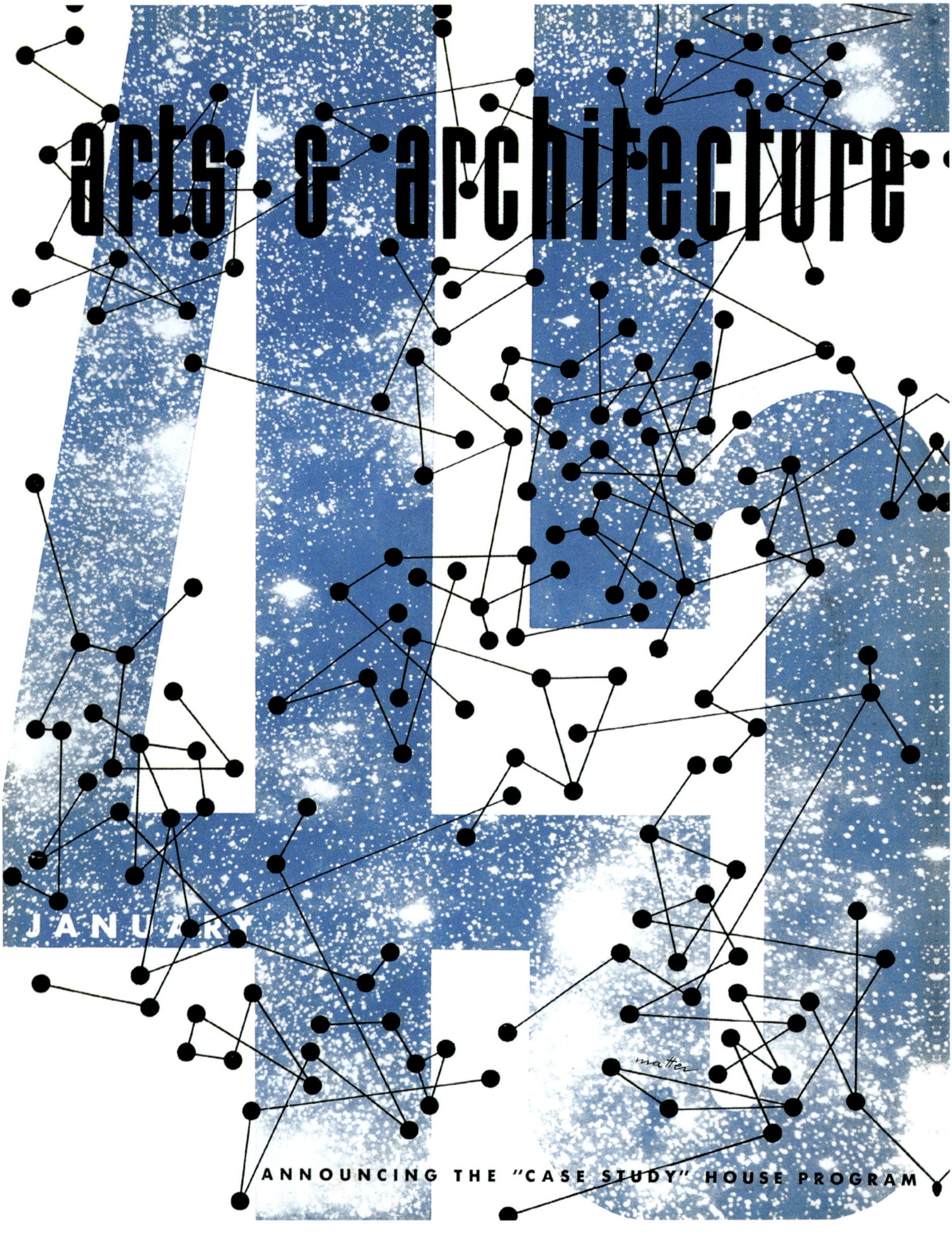
arts & architecture
JANUARY
matter
ANNOUNCING THE "CASE STUDY" HOUSE PROGRAM

ANNOUNCEMENT

the case study house program

Because most opinion, both profound and light-headed, in terms of post war housing is nothing but speculation in the form of talk and reams of paper, it occurs to us that it might be a good idea to get down to cases and at least make a beginning in the gathering of that mass of material that must eventually result in what we know as "house—post war".

Agreeing that the whole matter is surrounded by conditions over which few of us have any control, certainly we can develop a point of view and do some organized thinking which might come to a practical end. It is with that in mind that we now announce the project we have called **THE "CASE STUDY" HOUSE PROGRAM.**

The magazine has undertaken to supply an answer insofar as it is possible to correlate the facts and point them in the direction of an end result. We are, within the limits of uncontrollable factors, proposing to begin immediately the study, planning, actual design and construction of eight houses, each to fulfil the specifications of a special living problem in the Southern California area. Eight nationally known architects, chosen not only for their obvious talents, but for their ability to evaluate realistically housing in terms of need, have been commissioned to take a plot of God's green earth and create "good" living conditions for eight American families. They will be free to choose or reject, on a merit basis, the products of national manufacturers offering either old or new materials considered best for the purpose by each architect in his attempt to create contemporary dwelling units. We are quite aware that the meaning of "contemporary" changes by the minute and it is conceivable that each architect might wish to change his idea or a part of his idea when time for actual building arrives. In that case he will, within reason, be permitted to do so. (Incidentally, the eight men have been chosen for, among other things, reasonableness, which they have consistently maintained at a very high level.)

We will try and arrange the over-all plan so that it will make fairly good sense, despite the fact that building even one house has been known to throw a client off balance for years. Briefly, then, we will begin on the problem as posed to the architect, with the analysis of land in relation to work, schools, neighborhood conditions and individual family need. Each house will be designed within a specified budget, subject, of course, to the dictates of price fluctuation. It will be a natural part of the problem however to work as closely as possible within this budget or give very good reasons for not being able to do so.

Beginning with the February issue of the magazine and for eight months or longer thereafter, each house will make its appearance with the comments of the architect—his reasons for his solution and his choice of specific materials to be used. All this predicated on the basis of a house that he knows can be built when restrictions are lifted or as soon as practicable thereafter.

Architects will be responsible to no one but the magazine, which having put on a long white beard, will pose as "client". It is to be clearly understood that every consideration will be given to new materials and new techniques in house construction. And we must repeat again that these materials will be selected on a purely merit basis by the architects themselves. We have been promised fullest cooperation by manufacturers of products and appliances who have agreed to place in the hands of the architects the full results of research on the products they intend to offer the public. No attempt will be made to use a material merely because it is new or tricky. On the other hand, neither will there be any hesitation in discarding old materials and techniques if their only value is that they have been generally regarded as "safe".

Each architect takes upon himself the responsibility of designing a house which would, under all ordinary conditions be subject to the usual (and sometimes regrettable) building restrictions. The house must be capable of duplication and in no sense be an individual "performance".

All eight houses will be opened to the public for a period of from six to eight weeks and thereafter an attempt will be made to secure and report upon tenancy studies to see how successfully the job has been done. Each house will be completely furnished under a working arrangement between the architect, the designer and the furniture manufacturer, either to the architect's specifications or under his supervision.

This, then, is an attempt to find out on the most practical basis known to us, the facts (and we hope the figures) which will be available to the general public when it is once more possible to build houses.

It is important that the best materials available be used in the best possible way in order to arrive at a "good" solution of each problem, which in the over-all program will be general enough to be of practical assistance to the average American in search of a home in which he can afford to live.

We can only promise our best efforts in the midst of the confusions and contradictions that confront every man who is now thinking about his post war home. We expect to report as honestly and directly as we know how the conclusions which must inevitably be drawn from the mass of material that these very words will loose about our heads. Therefore, while the objective is very firm, the means and the methods must of necessity remain fluid in order that the general plan can be accommodated to changing conditions and conceptions.

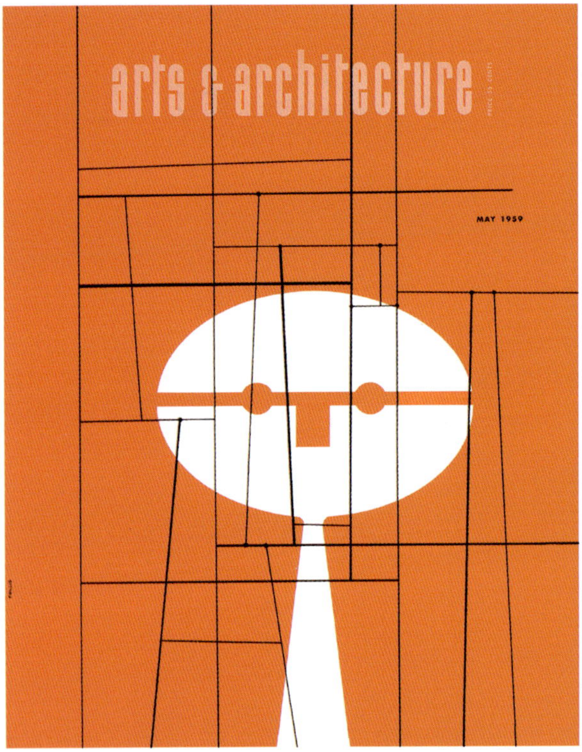
arts & architecture
MAY 1959

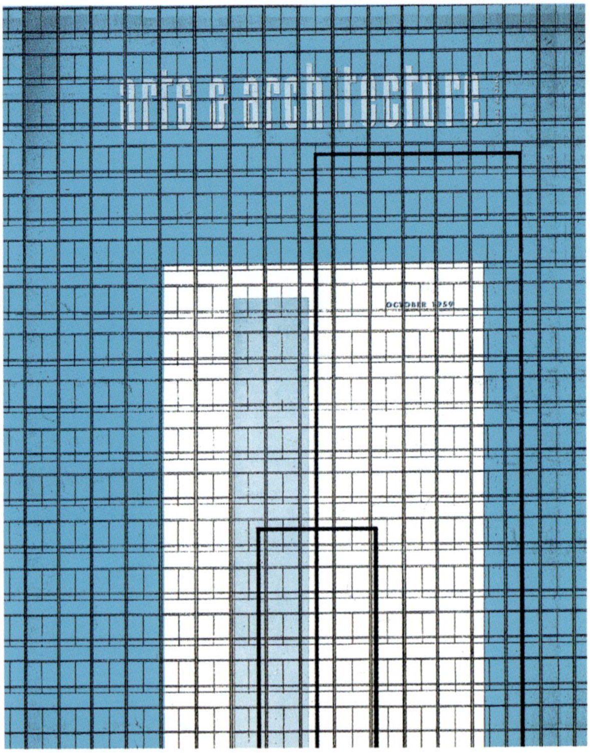
OCTOBER 1959

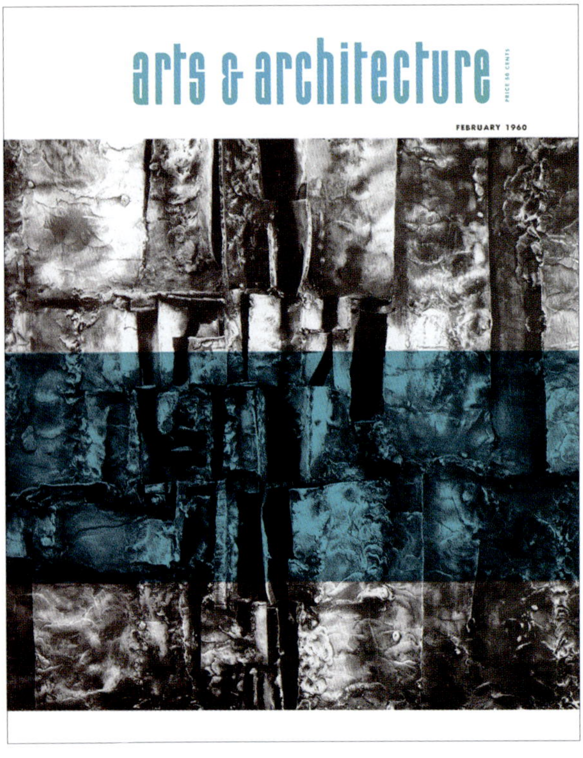
arts & architecture
FEBRUARY 1960

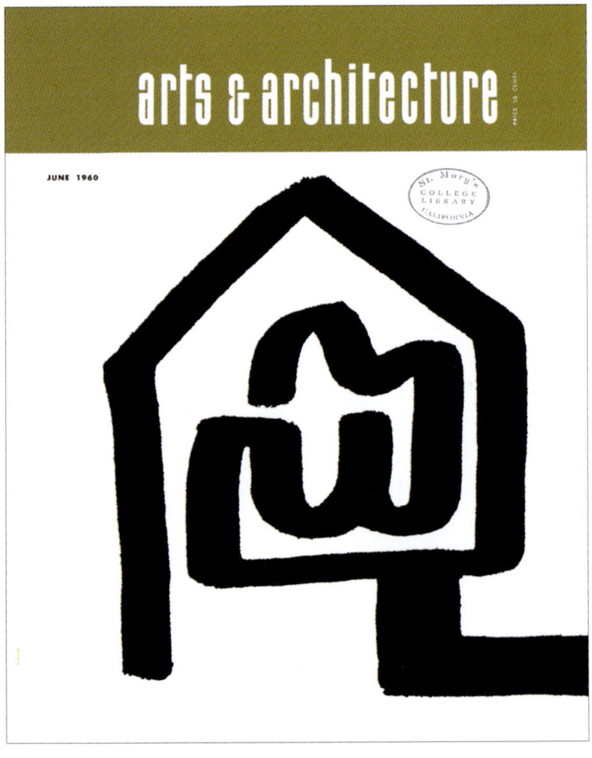
arts & architecture
JUNE 1960
St. Mary's
COLLEGE
LIBRARY
CALIFORNIA

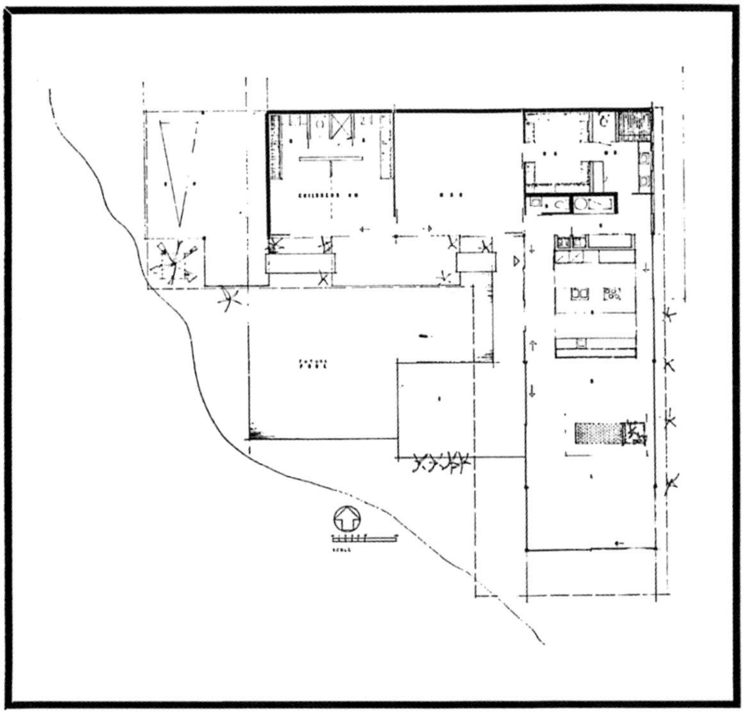

The construction photographs shown here were taken at the early stages of construction with the structural steel frame and the Bellevue steel sliding doors in place. The house at this stage is ready for steel roof deck and concrete grade beams. The foundation photographs show the reinforcing steel in what will be the system of cantilevered grade beams. The piers are not under the columns in this case but are set back from five to seven feet. In this way any possibility of damaging erosive action is eliminated. The columns are bearing at the ends of the concrete beams and are encased with twelve inches of concrete for resistance to seismic forces. With glass on all exterior walls except the street side, all horizontal forces can be resisted in this manner.

A working platform is constructed at one corner of the house and lot and is 125 feet above the first street directly below. Although the house is situated on a precipice the ground conditions are excellent with no extraneous water problems and without fill.

The sequence of construction calls for the setting of the base first, erection of steel frame and roof deck, installation of sliding door frames and wall decking, pouring of piers and grade beams, rough mechanical and electrical ducts and pipes, pouring of finish slab and finish, in that order. The usual sequence of fabrication on these houses was complicated by the fact that the piers are not directly under the columns. Special arrangements had to be made to support the columns before pouring structural concrete. The finish slab will be poured up to about the sill of the sliding door frames. The finish floor can thus be determined at this time by noting the location of the door sills.

(Continued on page 35)

PROGRESS REPORT — CASE STUDY HOUSE NO. 22 BY PIERRE KOENIG, ARCHITECT

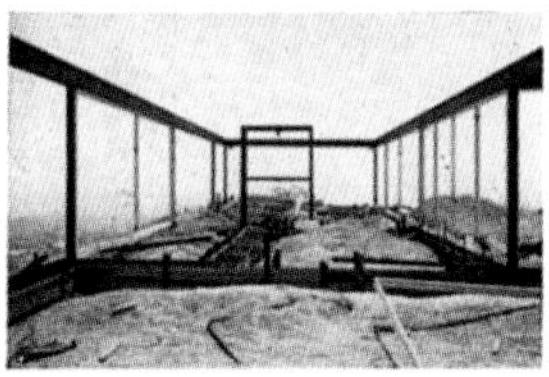

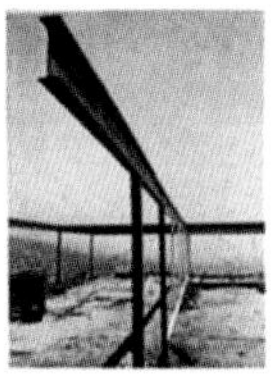

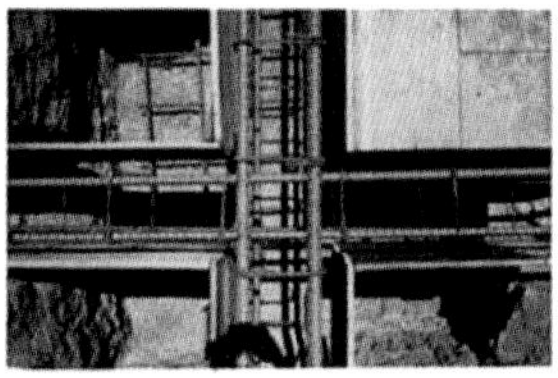

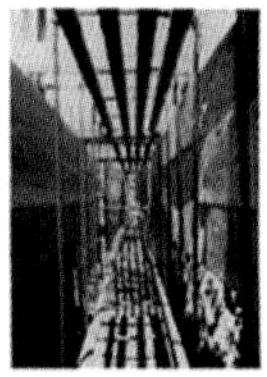

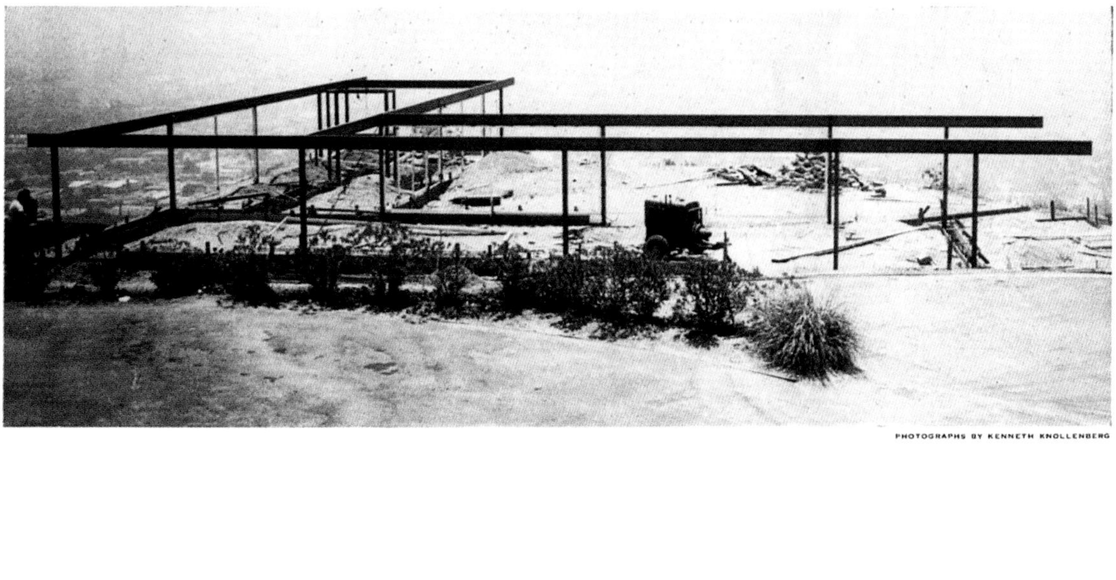

PHOTOGRAPHS BY KENNETH KNOLLENBERG

CHAPTER 4
THE PLAN

As Buck and Carlotta Stahl were beginning to search for an architect in 1956, Pierre Koenig was beginning Case Study House #21, a glass-and-steel masterpiece that would turn out to be one of his two most famous creations. This house would come to be considered as the truest embodiment of the Case Study ideology: an efficient, affordable prototype that could be replicated and mass produced. John Entenza would call it "some of the cleanest and most immaculate thinking in the development of the small, contemporary house."

It was not yet part of the Case Study House Program, however. Los Angeles psychologist Walter Bailey and his wife, Mary, a social worker, had commissioned Koenig to design a small house—1,200 to 1,300 square feet—suited to their lifestyle. They had no children and wanted an informal, open floor plan with two or three bedrooms. Koenig hoped to create "an efficient, social, and exciting plan that people could afford."

As John Entenza put it: "Minimal house, maximum space."

While Koenig commenced work on the Bailey House, Buck Stahl was heaving the last few hundred chunks of concrete into place on his empty lot. Buck and Carlotta had purchased the first home of their own, a one-story dwelling on Slauson Avenue in Culver City. Working in the garage, he began crafting a three-dimensional mock-up of the house that stood so clearly in his mind. "The garage was never more for cars," Carlotta joked. This miniature house was more important to Buck than even his treasured Cadillac. In August 1956, Buck set the completed model in the grass and knelt beside it for a few photographs (see photos on pages 22–23). His seven-year-old nephew, Bobby, who was visiting with his parents from St. Louis, jumped into one of the photos.

This was the year that Elvis Presley appeared on the music charts with "Heartbreak Hotel," and Norma Jean Mortensen changed her name to Marilyn Monroe. The Dow Jones Industrial Average closed above 500 for the first time in history, and "In God We Trust" replaced *E pluribus unum* on the US dollar. The Capitol Records Building became the newest Hollywood landmark, with its thirteen-story profile, shaped like a stack of records, rising 150 feet—the maximum height that zoning restrictions would allow. The Eames Lounge Chair and Ottoman were released by Charles and Ray Eames, whose Case Study House #8 marked the end of the program's first phase in 1949. As Reyner Banham wrote, #8 "was the bridge to the fully developed steel-and-glass style of the younger generation of [Craig] Ellwood and Koenig."

Steel had not yet entered Buck and Carlotta's vocabulary when they spoke about their dream home. But Buck's model emphasized the glass walls, open floor plan, and minimalist lines that were becoming hallmarks of modernism.

After Buck finished his model that summer, he and Carlotta began searching for an architect, flipping through the phone book and cold calling six candidates, several of whom agreed to meet at the lot on Woods Drive. One of them was Craig Ellwood, a second-generation modernist who was not (and never would become) a licensed architect, but who would design three Case Study Houses. In 1956, Ellwood was completing the second of these, Case Study House #17, a U-shaped steel house with floor-to-ceiling windows that framed a swimming pool.

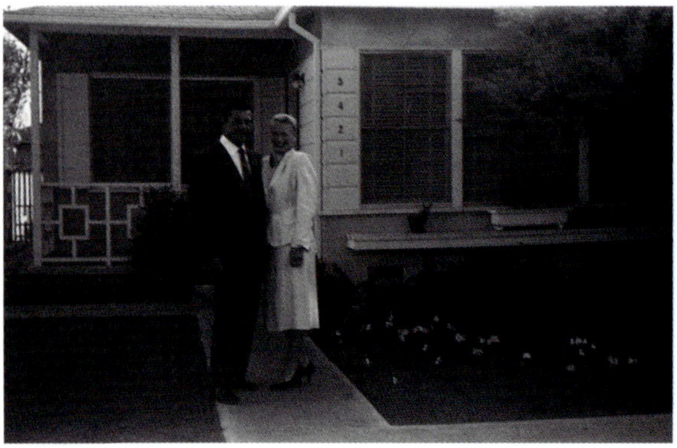

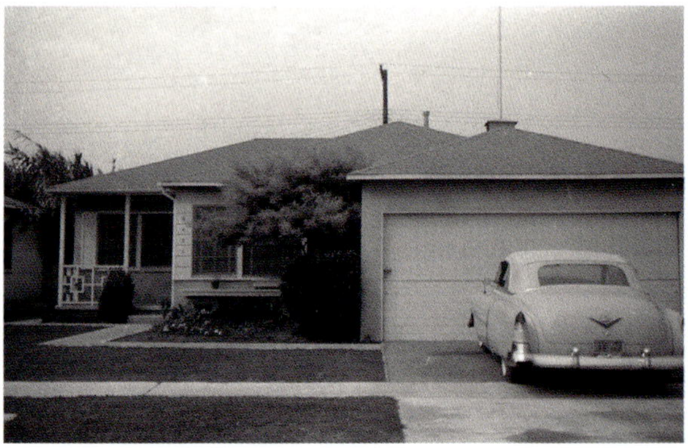

Everybody said, "No way!" because we had it hanging over space. And the house was all glass. —Carlotta Stahl

One by one, the architects visited the Stahls' lot on Woods Drive, assessed the difficulties of the building site, and studied Buck's model. Their response was unanimous. "No way do I want any part of this," Carlotta recalls one candidate saying, echoing the thoughts of the others. "They wouldn't risk it."

As Buck told historian Philip Ethington: "They didn't think it was a possibility."

Then, while flipping through *Pictorial Living*, a tabloid-size lifestyle section of the *Los Angeles Examiner*, Buck and Carlotta saw a story that caught their eye. "Steel Around the Pacific," by Esther McCoy, featured photographs of Pierre Koenig's Lamel House, a 1,000-square-foot steel-frame house with sliding glass doors, designed for a couple on a tight budget.

That same month, the same house appeared in *Arts & Architecture* magazine, featured in a U.S. Steel advertorial. "How to stretch a twelve-thousand-dollar budget . . . using steel" the copy read. "It's a familiar story: young couple . . . house hunting . . . small budget . . . big plans. Usually, couples like this must either lower their sights or wait until their savings grow. Usually—but not always." The copy seemed written with Buck and Carlotta in mind.

Buck Stahl called Koenig, who visited the site and walked across the empty lot and its newly finished terraces. Drinking in the expansive views of the city and the sea, Koenig saw the possibilities. Standing on that modest patch of dirt, engulfed by open sky, felt like looking out from "an eagle's nest." He immediately understood what Buck and Carlotta wanted. No wall, no matter how exquisitely designed, was worthy of obstructing any part of this view.

It would be a challenge. But Koenig loved a challenge, and he knew he had the vocabulary to make it happen. "We didn't think in terms of steel," Carlotta said. "But it was Pierre Koenig who said, 'We'll have to do all cement and steel in order to hold everything together up there.' So it took two men to really get this thing going."

Buck Stahl and Pierre Koenig hit it off immediately. Both men exuded confidence, determination, and an unwavering faith, not only in their ideas but in their ability to transmute those ideas into practical realities. Both were resourceful, able to stretch a budget through logic and creative problem-solving. And they were stubborn as hell.

"Pierre and my dad were renegades," as Bruce Stahl put it. "They didn't take no for an answer." What sealed the deal was Koenig's desire to tackle the challenge that other architects had considered impossible.

"Pierre was the one with the enthusiasm," Carlotta added. "It was like, 'I want this house! I want to do this house!'"

To Koenig, the question was not whether this house could be built, but rather which features would give way to the limited budget, and how well the clients would collaborate on those necessary changes. Koenig was still learning the intimate dance of an architect and a client, but he understood that his role involved much more than drawing blueprints. "An architect has to be a diplomat, psychiatrist, and financier, as well as engineer and draughtsman," he told *Echoes* magazine in 1999. "You have to know how to talk to couples, for whom house building is a very stressful time. A lot of couples get divorced over it."

Like the majority of first-time home builders, the Stahls had big ideas, but little knowledge of their costs. "I envisioned a glass house with a butterfly roof and a waterfall cascading down the cliff," Buck recalled.

"That would have cost a million dollars!" Koenig replied—expensive to build, shape, and weld. "So I slowly began chipping away at their original demands. First, the butterfly roof went, then the waterfall. Buck wanted stone somewhere in the plan, so I compromised and put it in the base of the fireplace." Fortunately, Buck and Carlotta were also willing to compromise—enough to make the house buildable, but not so much as to erode their dream. "We had visions of what we wanted," Carlotta said. "But now things had to be changed a little bit."

Koenig replaced Buck's butterfly roof with a more economical flat roof. As for the waterfall, Koenig had worked with water features before—Case Study House #21 was surrounded by shallow reflecting pools fed by a stream of water flowing off the roof—but he eliminated Buck's water feature, primarily because of the cost. Buck envisioned the carport in the middle of the sleeping wing, separating the children's room from the master suite. Koenig moved it to the western end, providing parking space for one car and an entryway to the courtyard.

The five years Koenig had invested in studying the most economical ways to design with steel now informed his every decision. "In those five years I developed schemes, and I priced out everything, and I went through testing it, in my mind or on paper, or sending it out to bid," Koenig told interviewer Mohamed Sharif in 2016. Applying what he had learned about building with steel through the trials and errors of past projects, he straightened the curve in Buck's street-facing wall, which eliminated the need for additional custom welding and shaping. "Pierre said, 'Let's go with straight lines,'" Carlotta said. Straight lines not only created a streamlined elegance but also allowed Koenig to use off-the-shelf materials, such as steel I beams.

"I was trying to solve a problem," Koenig told *Los Angeles* magazine. "The client had champagne tastes and a beer budget."

Buck and Carlotta accepted these changes, relieved that their most important priority—an unobstructed view—was still intact. "We knew that he was the architect, not us," Carlotta said. "And he had a good reason for everything that he said."

On November 20, 1957, a month after receiving his architectural license from the state of California, Pierre Koenig sent Buck Stahl a formal agreement. The contract specified an architect's fee of 10 percent of the actual construction costs, noting "the owner intends to provide materials and products at a reduced cost." It granted Koenig "or his agent" the exclusive right to photograph or film the house and allowed "the architect and party admission to the house at least once a week during daylight hours at the owners [sic] convenience for one year after completion."

On December 4, Buck signed the contract. The Stahl House was a go.

The following month, in January 1958, Koenig had completed the plot plan, which mapped out the orientation of the building on the site. That same month, Buck and Carlotta celebrated this milestone along with even bigger news: Carlotta was pregnant. The baby was due that summer.

Meanwhile, they were scrambling to move into a temporary rental house. Buck and Carlotta were among the quarter of a million people displaced by the construction of the interstates—527 miles of arteries built to accommodate the expanding population. Their home on Slauson Avenue stood in the path of Interstate 405, the San Diego Freeway, which would run through Culver City. The City had bought their house in December to make way for "the 405," which eventually would become the nation's busiest and most congested interstate. With the money they received from the City, Buck and Carlotta found a rental house and simultaneously made their final $11.46 payment on the lot. It was an eventful beginning to the new year.

Pierre Koenig had big news of his own. The Bailey House had officially become part of the Case Study House Program, announced in the May 1958 issue of *Arts & Architecture* as "Case Study House XXI." Koenig described it as "a comprehensive integration of steel structure and plan" that maximized every dollar and every square foot. In the Case Study spirit, Koenig had designed #21 with an elegant simplicity that would lend itself to duplication.

Case Study House #22 required another approach. Respecting the bones of Buck's model, Koenig elevated the Stahl House design into a masterpiece very different from Case Study House #21. While the Bailey House was not site-specific, the Stahl House was a unique union of site and structure. The small lot and commanding view presented a "contextual problem" that Koenig solved by creating "an interior space that was an extension of the exterior." This structure was designed to merge with its surroundings. The roof's large overhangs enhanced this connection, and its transparency dissolved the traditional boundary between interior and exterior. "The house is supposed to fit in with the environment and relate to it," Koenig said. "You don't see the house when you're in it; you see the view, and you're living with the environment, the outside."

In the short time between the Bailey House and the Stahl House, new construction products had come out. One of them, economical long-span decking, was a game-changer. Where the Bailey House was designed with 10-foot modules, the Stahl House had 20-foot modules. Increasing the space between support beams minimized any obstruction to the view, and the bigger rooms seemed a more proportionate fit for a taller-than-average couple. Considered together, Case Study House #21 and #22 proved Koenig's theory that the same materials and design philosophy could be successfully applied to a site-specific house as well as a prototypical house that could fit on almost any given site.

One of Koenig's most brilliant site-specific decisions was to orient the Stahl House to the grid pattern of Los Angeles. He extended the beams beyond the house, aligning them precisely with streets that converged toward the horizon like a perspective drawing. The city and the house would be linked in perfect harmony, each an extension of the other.

Another key instinct was restraint. He saw how one could go too far in designing a house that would overshadow the site, the view. "I could see how easy it is to destroy something that you have," Koenig told Sharif. "You must know when to stop and not overdo anything. … By having everything very simple, straightforward, I was able to magnify the magnificent view and not destroy it."

Koenig had designed a structure that, viewed from within or without, did not compete with its environment. "I had to suppress the idea of building something egotistical that says, 'Look at me, here I am sitting on top of this hill as a great house,'" Koenig said. "All my statements are not

I had only a year to do Case Study House #22, which I saw essentially as a contextual problem because of the unusual and challenging site. At the time I couldn't see anything other than to create an interior space that was an extension of the exterior. In order to do that I had to minimize what I was doing myself. I had to suppress the idea of building something egotistical that says, "Look at me, here I am sitting on top of this hill as a great house." Like all design processes, after you conceptualize it, you have to constantly hold yourself in range and ask yourself why you're doing something—and sometimes fight to keep yourself to your original notion. It's easy to get lost in the process. You constantly have to go back and remember the important things. I think that is what I did successfully in this case so that Los Angeles becomes an extension of the house, and vice versa. The house is just a part of the city.

—Pierre Koenig

inward—look at the house, look at the form of it, look at the shape. I don't do that. I look outward, and the people inside are projected outward to whatever is around them."

For an architect whose last notable assignment was earning wide acclaim, it was an act of humility to design a house that would, in a way, vanish. "Pierre Koenig was not a romanticist in any sense of the word," Julius Shulman said. "He was a bread-and-butter steel man. He understood engineering. Not many architects could do this."

Six months after completing the initial design, Koenig began submitting blueprints to the City of Los Angeles. That's when the unique design elements of the house began to work against its construction. The lot's unusual shape and tight dimensions were atypical and didn't fit existing building codes. Its precipitous perch on a cliff-bound ridge amplified concerns expressed by the LA Department of Building and Safety.

"Board Action required to build on this site," the department noted, "because of the extremely high, steep slopes on the east and south sides."

As Carlotta recalled, "Inspectors would come up and say, 'Oh, I don't even know what I'm looking at. How can I inspect this?'" It wasn't simply a matter of a house not being up to code. This was a design that pushed boundaries that had not been defined and broke rules that hadn't been written. "There was nothing on the books that said we couldn't do a lot of the things that we wanted," Carlotta said.

After Koenig had spent months meeting with city planners, explaining the design through technical drawings, and defending his use of steel, he was infuriated when the City still wasn't ready to approve the building permit. So, he took a bold new tactic: *Show me a rule that says I can't do this.* Otherwise, he was doing it. During the months he spent struggling to get the permit approved by city hall, Koenig worked doggedly to push it through the red tape.

"He fought the battle with city hall for us," Buck would always say with pride.

One of the central sticking points concerned the living room, which cantilevered 18 feet over the cliff. Koenig eventually compromised and shortened the overhang by 10 feet, which decreased the footprint of the house, compressing the living room. He also eliminated a catwalk originally designed around the exterior of the cantilevered living room. The changes are evident in apparent revisions to a plan (see page 131) preserved in Pierre Koenig's archive at the Getty Research Institute. Koenig resubmitted the plans he believed the City would finally approve.

The next challenge was to find a bank willing to finance the construction loan for a house that defied precedents. Building in the hills was a proposition that made risk-averse bankers run for the flats. The forward-thinking design was an impediment to securing a loan from bankers accustomed to traditional homes with wooden frames and pitched roofs, cookie-cutter lots and predictable floor plans. They didn't quite know what to make of this glass-and-steel anomaly. When Buck approached prospective lenders in 1958, bank after bank turned him down. "They were dead set against cliff dwellers," he said.

Meanwhile, financial and family pressures were mounting. As Koenig was butting heads with city hall in July 1958, Carlotta was ready to give birth. To stay home with the baby, she would leave her receptionist job at North American Aviation, which paid $4,326 a year. Buck was now working for Garrett Corp. AiResearch Manufacturing for an annual salary of $10,000. The Stahls would soon be a single-income family.

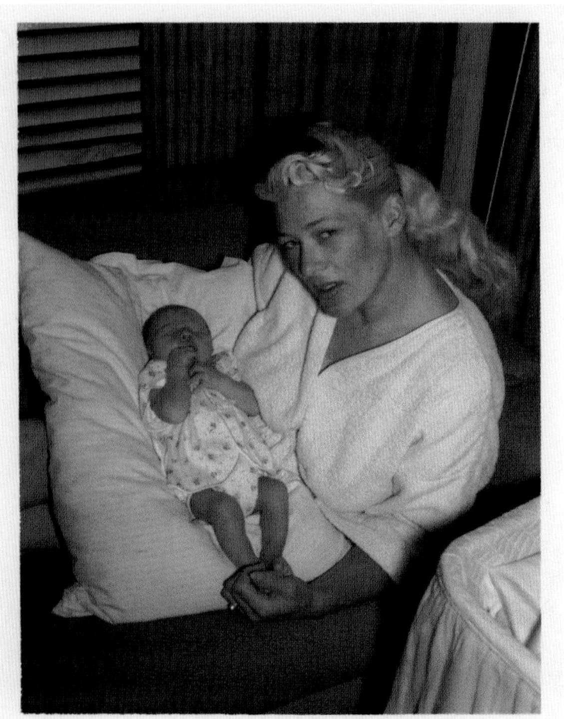

On August 6, 1958, Carlotta gave birth to Bruce Allen Stahl at St. John's Hospital in Santa Monica, the same hospital where Carlotta was born twenty-eight years before. Buck and Carlotta took the infant home to the rental house in Culver City, where they'd moved eight months earlier.

Meanwhile, exceeding the duties of an architect, Pierre Koenig stepped in and aggressively searched for a lender. "No one would loan on flat-roof housing or hillside sites," Koenig said. Working his way through his personal and industry contacts, he found a bank willing to take the risk. "Finally, in desperation, I found the Broadway Savings and Loan."

Like the Stahl House and its creators, the bank was a precedent-breaker and a pioneer of its time. Broadway Federal Savings and Loan Association was an African American-owned bank founded in 1946 to provide financial services to minority consumers and businesses being ignored or exploited by traditional financial institutions, or essentially barred from lending.

"The board of directors included Black architect Paul Williams, whose modern houses I knew were flat-roofed," Koenig said. One of the first certified African American architects in the West, Paul Revere Williams would go on to become an award-winning legend in his profession, designing thousands of private homes in Los Angeles. This architectural connection may have played some part in the bank's decision.

When Pierre told Buck that he could get a loan from the minority-owned bank, Buck replied with characteristic bluntness: "I don't care what color their skin is, as long as their money is green." Buck submitted the loan application in October 1958. On November 5, it was approved.

Broadway Federal's role in the creation of the Stahl House is extraordinary. "The incredible irony is that a Black family could not have gotten a loan in that neighborhood at that time," said historian Philip Ethington, a professor at USC. "Because the banks had redlined it. They wouldn't loan to a person of color because of this orthodoxy that mixed-race neighborhoods brought property values down. Ironically, a Black bank was willing to do something adventurous in terms of modern architecture."

What's more, the Black-owned bank underwrote a white family's dream home in a development where "Covenants, Conditions, and Restrictions" discriminated against non-whites. Still in place were covenants from 1948 that declared no part of the property could "be occupied at any time by any person not of the Caucasian race." There was one notable exception: "servants of other than the Caucasian race may be employed and kept thereon." Today, Broadway Federal remains LA's last surviving Black-owned bank.

Broadway Federal not only underwrote the $34,000 loan to build the Stahl House, it influenced the design in a significant way. The loan agreement spelled out two requirements: "carport space for two cars" and a "swimming pool" with "filter, heater, and diving board." The swimming pool was a particularly curious—and pivotal—condition for the loan. Municipal pools, popular in American cities during the 1920s through 1940s, were giving way to private backyard pools in the 1950s, so this new luxury amenity would increase the overall value of their investment. But there was one other unusual condition to this loan: "They wouldn't finance the pool," Carlotta said. The pool would add $3,454.71 to the building costs, but that wasn't included in the mortgage.

Buck's model left the elbow of the L-shaped plan undefined. "They just thought they would have a regular yard," Shari said. "They didn't think they could afford anything else." Here Koenig placed the pool, 20 feet wide and 26 feet long, ranging in depth from 2 to 9 feet. Turquoise water lapped the glass walls of the bedrooms in several spots, and concrete footbridges provided an entry path from the carport to the kitchen.

The pool enhanced the interplay of the house with its environment. Every room except the bathrooms and laundry room looked out upon the water, which would mirror the sky and the house in a way that magnified both. On windless days, the pool would echo Koenig's elegant lines. Weather would stir the water into mesmerizing textures. West Coast sunsets would multiply in the reflections off glass and water. By day, light ripples would send shadows of light dancing over the walls and ceilings. At night, the pool would become a lightbox that illuminated the entire property.

The pool not only completed the house, it created the quintessential California lifestyle.

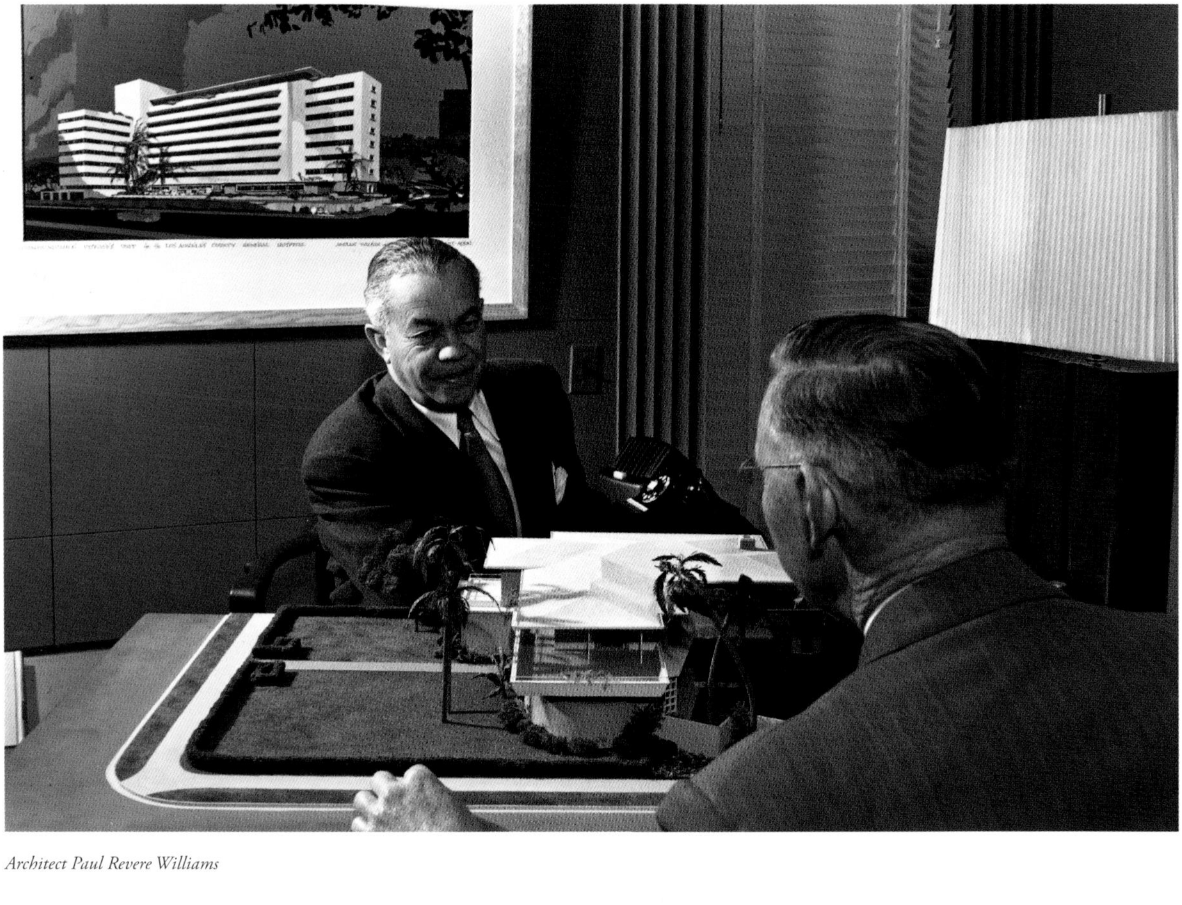

Architect Paul Revere Williams

GR 37L34

A. I. A. Form B102
(Rev. 6-1-53)

THE STANDARD FORM OF AGREEMENT BETWEEN OWNER AND ARCHITECT

ISSUED BY THE AMERICAN INSTITUTE OF ARCHITECTS FOR USE WHEN A PERCENTAGE OF THE COST OF THE WORK FORMS THE BASIS OF PAYMENT, AND ENGINEERS' FEES ARE INCLUDED IN THE ARCHITECT'S FEE.

THIS AGREEMENT made the 20th.

day of NOVEMBER in the year Nineteen Hundred and 57

by and between MR. & MRS. CLARENCE H. STAHL

5421 SLAUSON AVE., ~~LOS ANGELES,~~ CULVER CITY CALIF.

hereinafter called the Owner, and

PIERRE KOENIG

hereinafter called the Architect,

11681 SAN VICENTE BLVD., LOS ANGELES 49, CALIF.

WITNESSETH, that whereas the Owner intends to erect A RESIDENCE

AT LOT 3, TRACT 13044 MB 309-11 LOS ANGELES, CALIF.

, hereinafter called the Work,

NOW, THEREFORE, the Owner and the Architect, for the considerations hereinafter named, agree as follows:

The Architect agrees to perform, for the above-named Work, professional services as hereinafter set forth.

The Owner agrees to pay the Architect for such services a fee of TEN per cent of the cost of the Work, with other payments and reimbursements as hereinafter provided, the said percentage being hereinafter called the Basic Rate.

A. I. A. Form B102
(Rev. 6-1-53)

ESTIMATE SHEET

Catalina POOL CO.

6719 RESEDA BOULEVARD • RESEDA, CALIFORNIA • DIckens 5-5110
8821 LAKEWOOD BOULEVARD • DOWNEY, CALIFORNIA • TOpaz 1-5410
6116 BLACKSTONE AVENUE • FRESNO, CALIFORNIA • BAldwin 2-5712

Customer's Name MR. C.H. STAHL
Address 1635 WOODS DR City HLWD HILLS
Phone EX 12783 Salesman John West Date 1-16-60
Private X Public ______ Semi Public ______
FOLLOWING SPECIFICATIONS FOR 20' x 36' POOL. DEPTH 2'-6" to 9'-0" POOL DESIGN CUSTOM RECTANGLE

BASE PRICE OF POOL	2895.00
PLANS, BUILDING PERMITS, LAYOUT & FORMS	INC.
EXCAVATION: DIRT REMOVED X DIRT REMAINS	INC.
NORMAL SOIL GRANIT EXPANSIVE SOIL	INC.
DEEP END DIG X SUR-CHARGE CONSTRUCTION	50.00
HAND DIG	—
STEPS IN SHALLOW END	INC.
OFFSET STEPS (size) x OVER SIZE	55.00
RECESSED SKIMMER	INC.
6 x 6 WATERLINE TILE X (color)	INC.
COPING: (color AS PER OWNERS PLANS (coping no.)	INC.
FLAGSTONE FLAGSTONE & ROCK	—
FILTER: (make) SPIN TYPE (model) 8-DISC (type) DIAT EARTH	INC.
PUMP: BRONZE HORSE POWER MOTOR 3/4 H.P.	INC.
DRY WELL	—
MARINE LIGHT 500 WATT	INC.
AUTOMATIC FILTER TIME CLOCK	INC.
ELECTRICAL HOOKUP TO 85' TO EXISTING SERVICE X	INC.
CHROME VACUUM OUTLET	INC.
FILL SPOUT	INC.
DIVING BOARD 10' GLASS COVERED STANDARDS X	INC.
LADDER X GRAB RAILS	INC.
CHLORINATOR	—
CERAMICS	—
ROPE RINGS	INC.
GUNITE INSPECTION	—
HEATER: (make) (btu) INSTALLATION	—
COMPLETION BOND 1% OF TOTAL CONT. IF DESIRED	—
MISCELLANEOUS 2ND OFFSET PART OF POOL -	96.00
C-B WALL & SLAB FOR FILTER SYSTEM	56.00
TOTAL PRICE OF POOL & ACCESSORIES	$ 3152.00

FINANCING AVAILABLE 5 YRS DOWN $ 25.00 INTEREST FOR 60 MONTHS
PAYMENTS WILL BE $ 67.17 PER MONTH WITH $ 52.00 DOWN
Estimate will remain in effect for ______ days and is based on normal access to property.

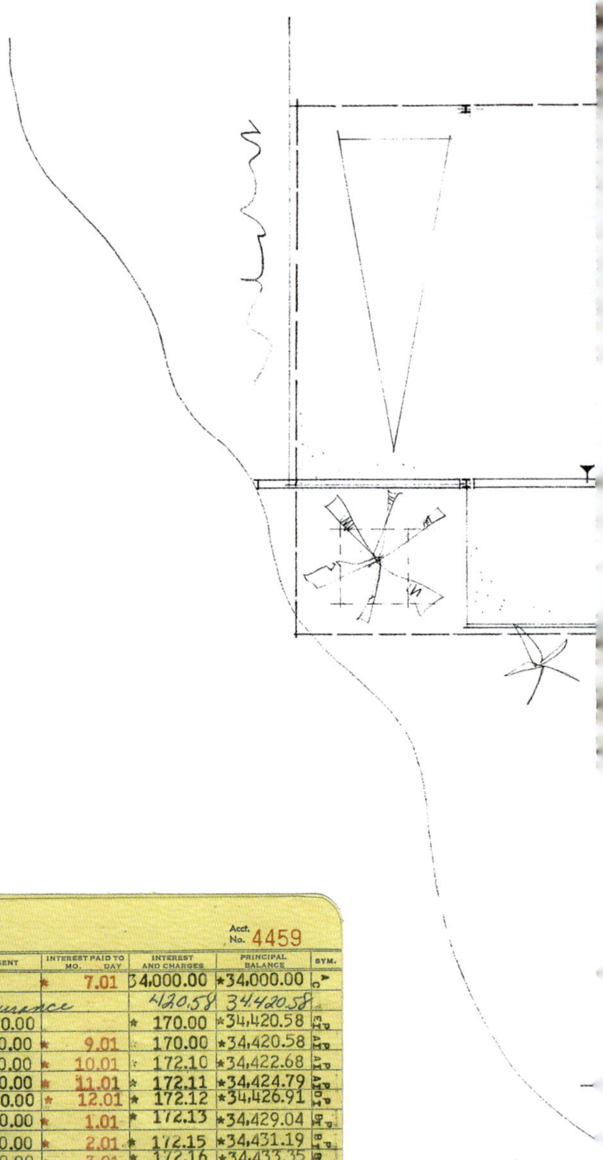

LOAN ACCOUNT

FEDERAL HOME LOAN BANK SYSTEM · MEMBER

SAFETY OF YOUR SAVINGS INSURED UP TO $10,000

FEDERAL SAVINGS AND LOAN INSURANCE CORPORATION · INSURED UP TO $10,000

ACCOUNT NO. 4459 (P.L.)

BROADWAY FEDERAL SAVINGS AND LOAN ASSOCIATION

4501 SOUTH BROADWAY

LOS ANGELES 37, CALIFORNIA

ALWAYS BRING THIS BOOK WITH YOU OR MAIL WITH PAYMENT

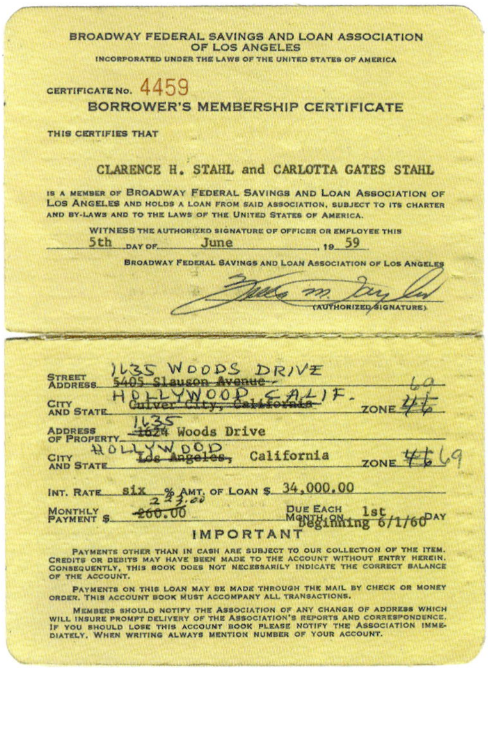
BROADWAY FEDERAL SAVINGS AND LOAN ASSOCIATION OF LOS ANGELES

INCORPORATED UNDER THE LAWS OF THE UNITED STATES OF AMERICA

CERTIFICATE No. 4459

BORROWER'S MEMBERSHIP CERTIFICATE

THIS CERTIFIES THAT

CLARENCE H. STAHL and CARLOTTA GATES STAHL

IS A MEMBER OF BROADWAY FEDERAL SAVINGS AND LOAN ASSOCIATION OF LOS ANGELES AND HOLDS A LOAN FROM SAID ASSOCIATION, SUBJECT TO ITS CHARTER AND BY-LAWS AND TO THE LAWS OF THE UNITED STATES OF AMERICA.

WITNESS THE AUTHORIZED SIGNATURE OF OFFICER OR EMPLOYEE THIS 5th DAY OF June, 19 59

BROADWAY FEDERAL SAVINGS AND LOAN ASSOCIATION OF LOS ANGELES

(AUTHORIZED SIGNATURE)

STREET ADDRESS 1635 WOODS DRIVE ~~5405 Slauson Avenue~~

CITY AND STATE HOLLYWOOD, CALIF. ~~Culver City, California~~ ZONE ~~46~~ 69

ADDRESS OF PROPERTY 1635 ~~1624~~ Woods Drive

CITY AND STATE HOLLYWOOD ~~Los Angeles,~~ California ZONE ~~46~~ 69

INT. RATE six % AMT. OF LOAN $ 34,000.00

MONTHLY PAYMENT $ 2?3.00 ~~260.00~~ DUE EACH MONTH ON 1st DAY Beginning 6/1/60

IMPORTANT

PAYMENTS OTHER THAN IN CASH ARE SUBJECT TO OUR COLLECTION OF THE ITEM. CREDITS OR DEBITS MAY HAVE BEEN MADE TO THE ACCOUNT WITHOUT ENTRY HEREIN. CONSEQUENTLY, THIS BOOK DOES NOT NECESSARILY INDICATE THE CORRECT BALANCE OF THE ACCOUNT.

PAYMENTS ON THIS LOAN MAY BE MADE THROUGH THE MAIL BY CHECK OR MONEY ORDER. THIS ACCOUNT BOOK MUST ACCOMPANY ALL TRANSACTIONS.

MEMBERS SHOULD NOTIFY THE ASSOCIATION OF ANY CHANGE OF ADDRESS WHICH WILL INSURE PROMPT DELIVERY OF THE ASSOCIATION'S REPORTS AND CORRESPONDENCE. IF YOU SHOULD LOSE THIS ACCOUNT BOOK PLEASE NOTIFY THE ASSOCIATION IMMEDIATELY. WHEN WRITING ALWAYS MENTION NUMBER OF YOUR ACCOUNT.

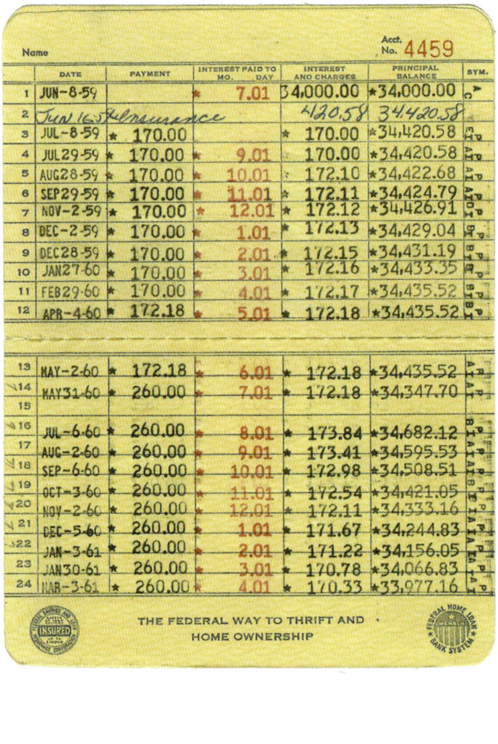
Name

Acct. No. 4459

	DATE	PAYMENT	INTEREST PAID TO MO. DAY	INTEREST AND CHARGES	PRINCIPAL BALANCE	SYM.
1	JUN-8-59		★ 7.01	34,000.00	★34,000.00	[illegible]
2	Jun 16 59 Insurance			420.58	34420.58	
3	JUL-8-59	★ 170.00		★ 170.00	★34,420.58	[illegible]
4	JUL29-59	★ 170.00	★ 9.01	170.00	★34,420.58	[illegible]
5	AUG28-59	★ 170.00	★ 10.01	172.10	★34,422.68	[illegible]
6	SEP29-59	★ 170.00	★ 11.01	★ 172.11	★34,424.79	[illegible]
7	NOV-2-59	★ 170.00	★ 12.01	★ 172.12	★34,426.91	[illegible]
8	DEC-2-59	★ 170.00	★ 1.01	★ 172.13	★34,429.04	[illegible]
9	DEC28-59	★ 170.00	★ 2.01	★ 172.15	★34,431.19	[illegible]
10	JAN27-60	★ 170.00	★ 3.01	★ 172.16	★34,433.35	[illegible]
11	FEB29-60	★ 170.00	★ 4.01	★ 172.17	★34,435.52	[illegible]
12	APR-4-60	★ 172.18	★ 5.01	★ 172.18	★34,435.52	[illegible]
13	MAY-2-60	★ 172.18	★ 6.01	★ 172.18	★34,435.52	[illegible]
14	MAY31-60	★ 260.00	★ 7.01	★ 172.18	★34,347.70	[illegible]
15						
16	JUL-6-60	★ 260.00	★ 8.01	★ 173.84	★34,682.12	[illegible]
17	AUG-2-60	★ 260.00	★ 9.01	★ 173.41	★34,595.53	[illegible]
18	SEP-6-60	★ 260.00	★ 10.01	★ 172.98	★34,508.51	[illegible]
19	OCT-3-60	★ 260.00	★ 11.01	★ 172.54	★34,421.05	[illegible]
20	NOV-2-60	★ 260.00	★ 12.01	★ 172.11	★34,333.16	[illegible]
21	DEC-5-60	★ 260.00	★ 1.01	★ 171.67	★34,244.83	[illegible]
22	JAN-3-61	★ 260.00	★ 2.01	★ 171.22	★34,156.05	[illegible]
23	JAN30-61	★ 260.00	★ 3.01	★ 170.78	★34,066.83	[illegible]
24	MAR-3-61	★ 260.00	★ 4.01	★ 170.33	★33,977.16	[illegible]

THE FEDERAL WAY TO THRIFT AND HOME OWNERSHIP

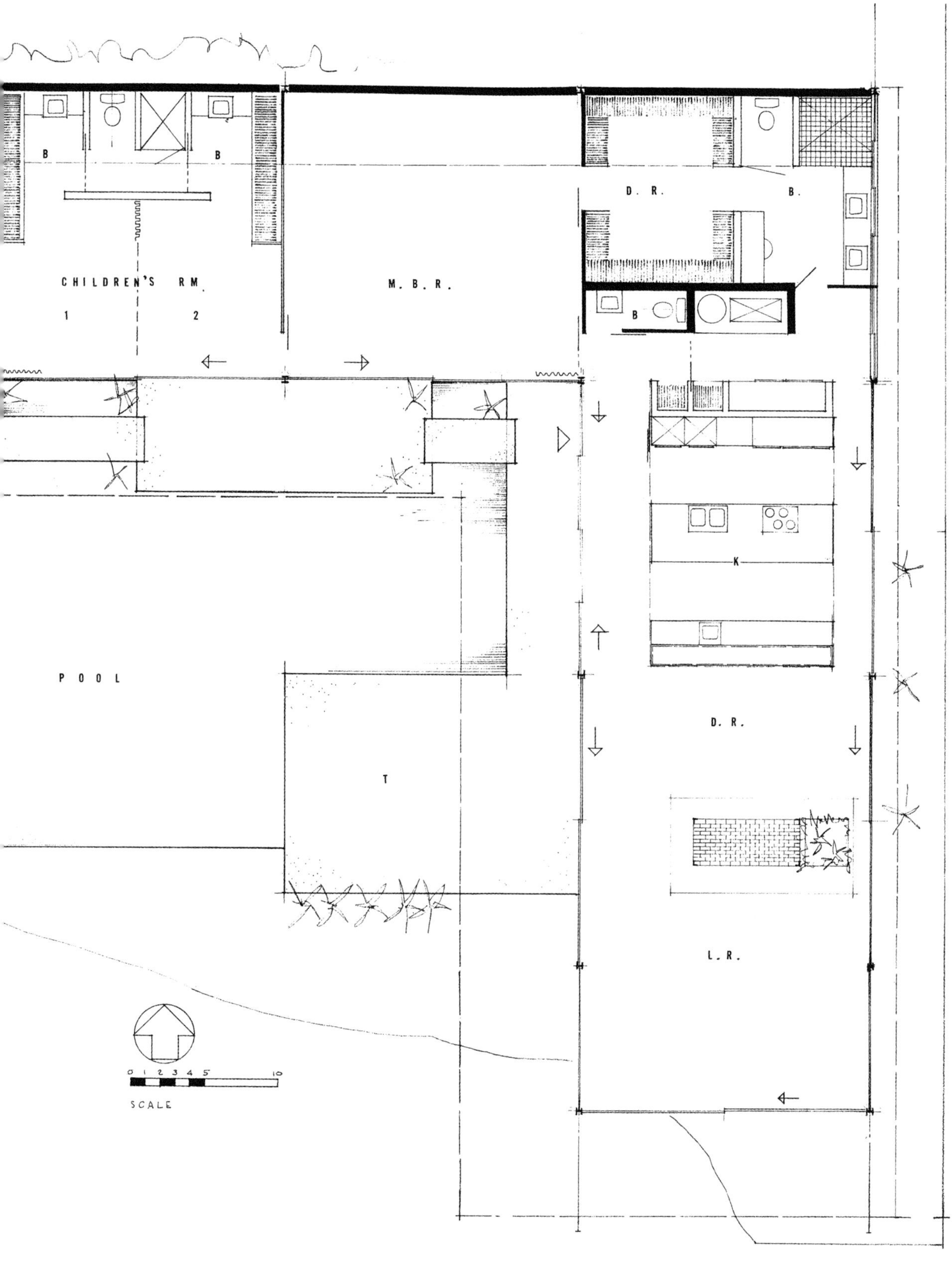
B
B
D. R.
B.
CHILDREN'S RM.
M. B. R.
1
2
B
K
POOL
D. R.
T
L. R.
0 1 2 3 4 5 10
SCALE

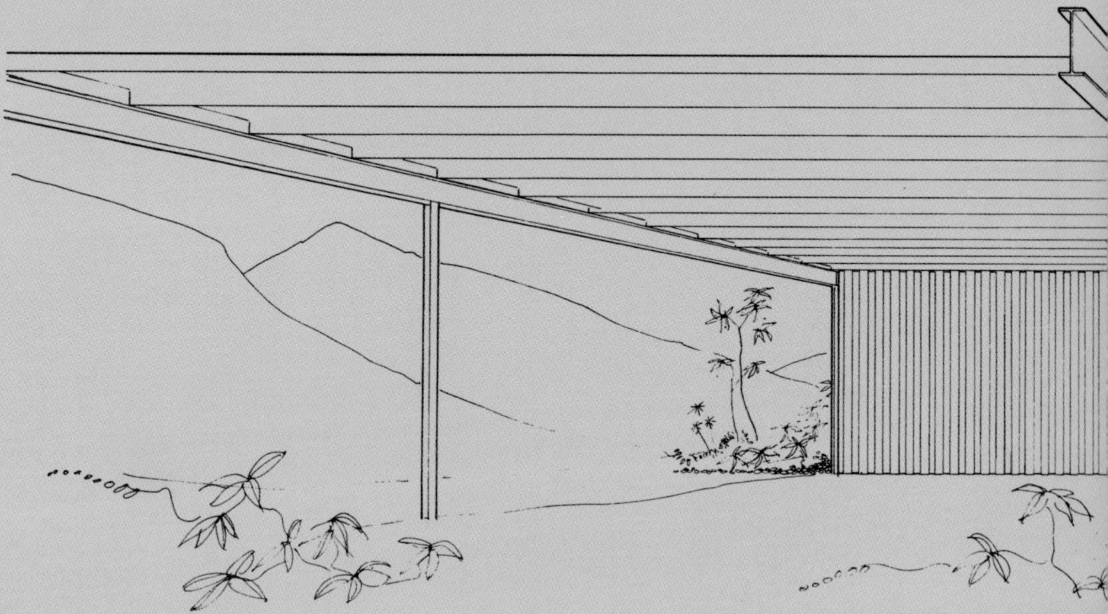

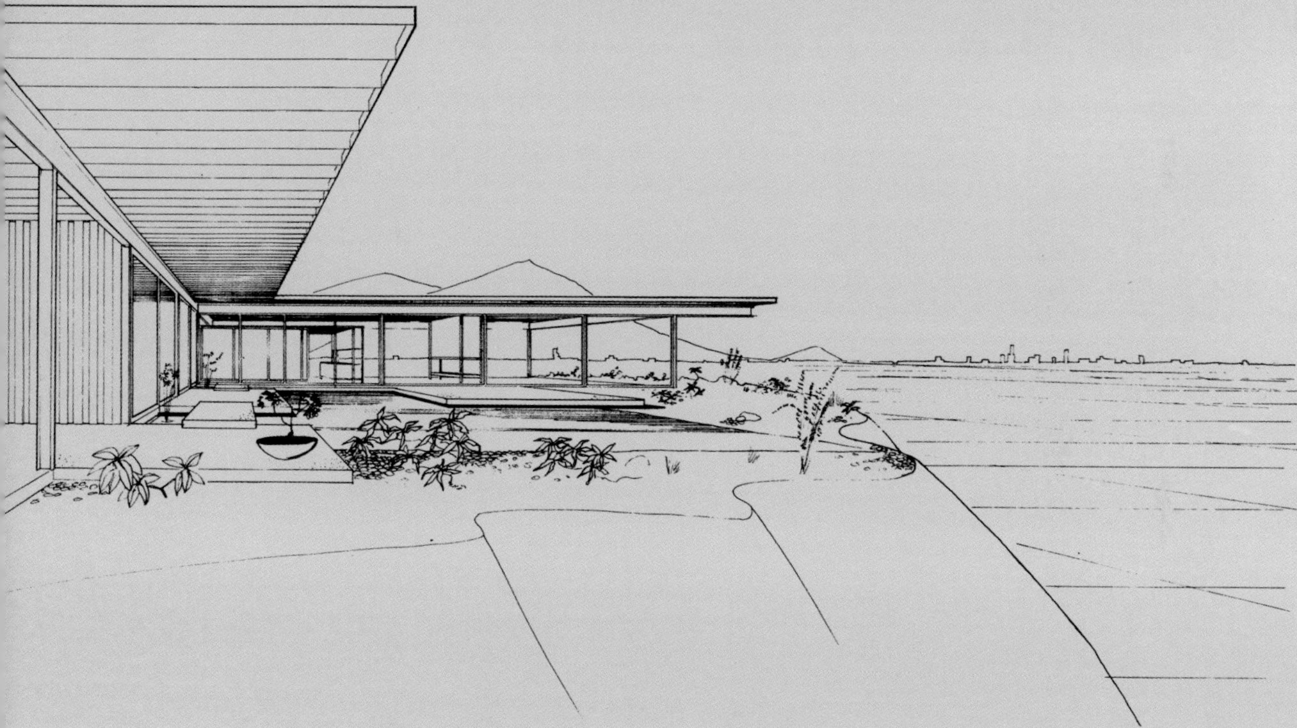

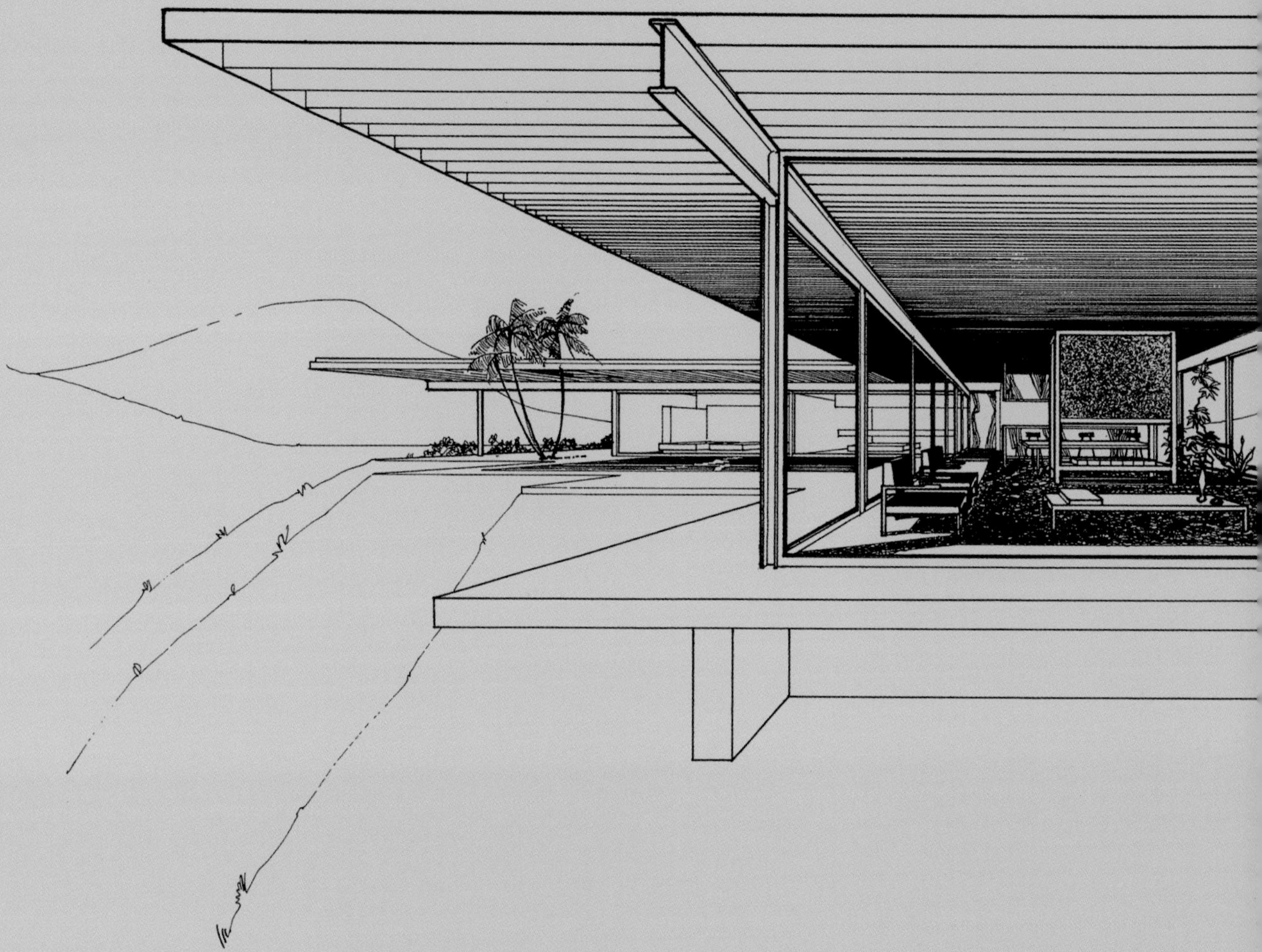

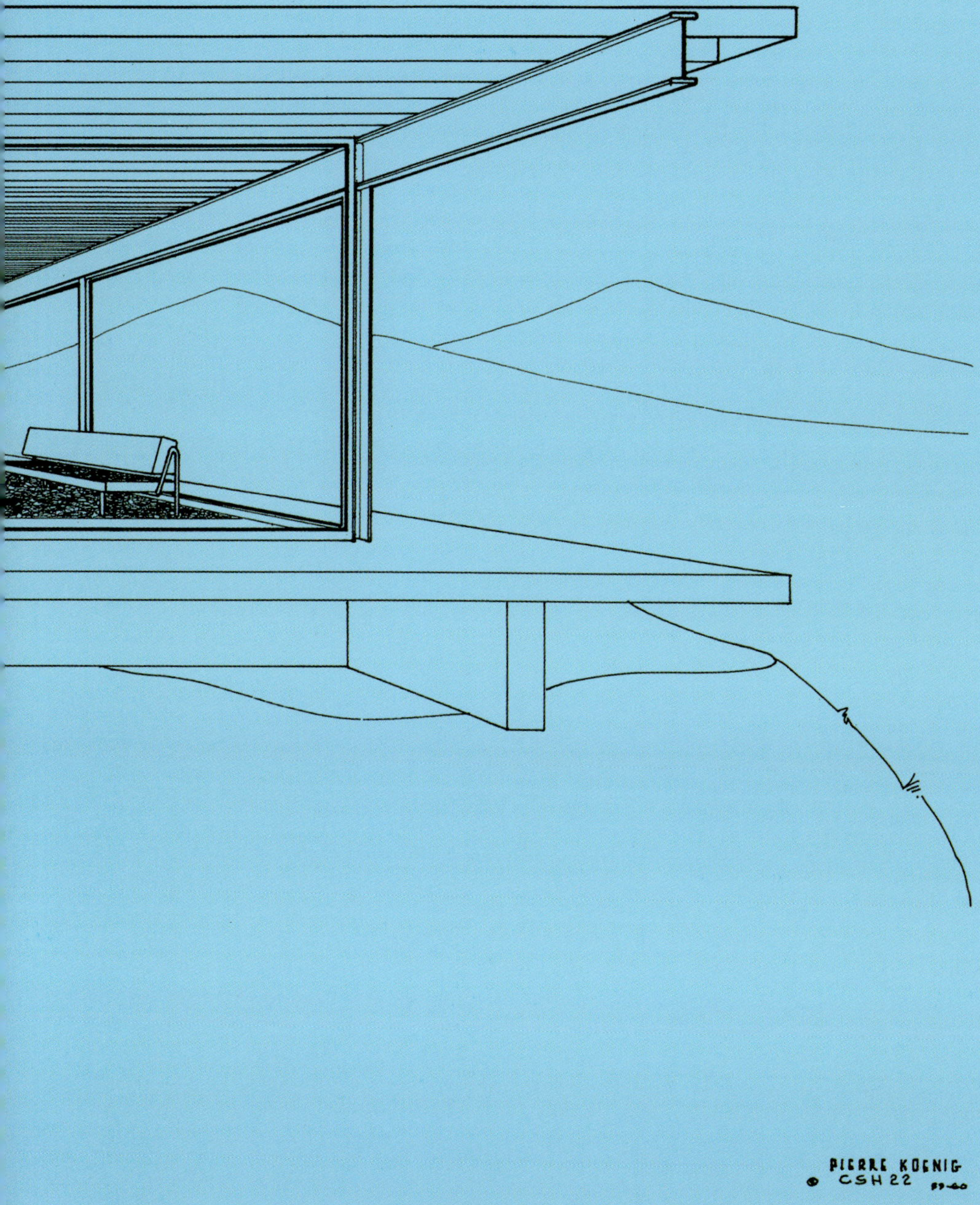
PIERRE KOENIG
© CSH 22
59-60

CHAPTER 5
GROUND BREAKING

In January 1959, less than two miles northeast of Buck and Carlotta's empty lot, Pierre Koenig's Case Study House #21 was unveiled ahead of schedule "through a number of small miracles." *Arts & Architecture* called it "one of the most interesting of our undertakings in this field" and announced that on January 3, it would open for public tours on Saturday and Sunday afternoons from 1:00 p.m. to 5:00 p.m. Over seven weekends, more than six hundred people poured through its doors to admire the two-bedroom prototype of logical thinking and clean design. These admirers included families, homemakers, architects, professors, and fifty-six students from the architectural engineering department at California Polytechnic State University, San Luis Obispo. In February, Carlotta Stahl walked through the house, took in the elegant lines of glass and steel, and had no doubt she had found the right architect.

Also in January, after Koenig shortened the cantilevered living room, the City of Los Angeles reviewed his revised plan and finally granted a building permit, albeit grudgingly.

On April 1, John Entenza dictated a brief, typewritten letter to Buck and Carlotta confirming his offer to make the Stahl House a Case Study House. "The magazine will attempt, wherever possible, to secure discounts on materials specified for the project," Entenza wrote. "These savings, whenever obtainable, will be passed on to you." This opportunity—and the benefits it would convey—was not something they were aware of when they decided to hire Pierre Koenig. But it would ultimately help them to afford their dream home.

Construction would begin as soon as possible. After completion, for the *Arts & Architecture* photo shoot, the house would be staged with furnishings approved by the editor and the architect, and the Stahls would have the right to buy the furniture at whatever discount might be offered. Finally, before they moved in, the doors would be opened for public tours. "The house," Entenza wrote, "will be known tentatively as Case Study House No. 22."

The timing could not have been better. Koenig had approached Bethlehem Steel in 1957 about developing a program for residential architects. The company didn't see a big enough need at the time to justify a formal program. However, in 1959, Bethlehem Steel introduced a new division to work with architects, and the company wanted Koenig's insights. Though his second Glendale house had been featured in a U.S. Steel advertorial in *Arts & Architecture*, Bethlehem Steel became the official steel sponsor of the Stahl House. "They let dad have the steel at cost," Bruce said.

Koenig had already begun to assemble his building team. He called upon William Porush, a structural engineer with whom he had worked on several steel houses, including his first home in Glendale. A native of Russia who came to the United States in 1922, Porush would go on to engineer more than half of Koenig's projects. The builder was Robert. J. Brady, a thirty-two-year-old former schoolteacher who "did building on the side," according to a 1959 Dun & Bradstreet report that said he gave up teaching to start a limited partnership that did "speculative building." Raymond Equipment and Welding Company was hired to do the steelwork.

Compared to the glacial pace of the permitting process, construction moved fairly quickly. In May, the septic system was installed. In June, workers poured a concrete foundation.

One of the officials said ... [there'll] never be another house built like this. They didn't like the big windows. That was one of the things that bothered them more than anything, and the fact that we're cantilevered.

—Carlotta Stahl

In July, the steel bones of the house were assembled on-site by a team of five men, who used a 180-degree stinger crane to frame the entire structure in a single, nine-hour day. This speed reflected Koenig's use of off-the-shelf industrial components combined with the efficiencies of mass production. "There are too many advantages to mass production to ignore it," Koenig said. As the efficiency of the assembly line had made automobiles ubiquitous, Koenig was convinced that mass production would make homes "available to anyone."

"Our civilization is a machine civilization," he said, so houses should be made by machines. "If you use industrial techniques for residential designs, the savings are tremendous." The challenge was getting the rest of the world—clients, lenders, and the market—to share his enthusiasm for industrial materials and the economy and beauty they could provide.

Koenig's research on steel construction—for his own house and others—had given him an intimate understanding of the economic opportunities of building with steel. To keep costs down, he never had steel custom-fabricated to his designs. In fact, he did the reverse. He was now testing the concept he had described as a student: houses designed with "a modular system" of prefabricated parts that would minimize on-site cutting and waste.

With the steel structure and foundation in place, attention turned toward the answer to a question posed by building a house with glass walls: Where do you hide the guts of a house—the electrical wiring, plumbing, and ductwork—that typically are concealed by drywall?

Fortunately, this house had no ductwork or HVAC, which solved one part of the question. Despite the 1950s boom in residential air conditioning, the Stahl House would forego such a system, cooled instead by 20-foot sliding glass doors that rolled open, inviting a sea-cooled cross breeze. Once again, the lot made this possible. "Where you sit on the globe dictates the kind of weather you have," Bruce Stahl said, "so the latitude and longitude really came into play."

With no traditional walls to hide the electrical and plumbing system (nor a basement or a crawl space) the basic electrical system and galvanized steel water pipes of the plumbing system were embedded within the concrete floor slab, which also contained the radiant heating system: a snaking network of copper pipes through which hot water flowed, warming the house from underfoot. Photos taken during this phase of construction clearly show these systems in place in advance of the concrete slab being poured. Since the glass walls could have no insulation—and were made of single-pane plate glass—the radiant heating was a primary source of heat, supplemented by passive solar heating on sunny days. A fireplace in the living room provided another source of warmth.

Having flattened the roof and straightened the walls of Buck's model, Koenig designed the revised house using only stock parts. "That is the challenge—to take these common, everyday parts and work them into an esthetically pleasing concept," he said. "The more members you repeat in a design, the more economical the job becomes." In the Stahl House, Koenig used less than sixty different building components, ranging from 12-inch, standard-length beams, to 4-inch H columns, to interlocking steel panels. His artistry lay in using this limited palette of parts to create unique and visually stunning spaces—and to do so on a budget. "You can make anything beautiful given an unlimited amount of money," Koenig said. "But to do it within the limits of economy is different."

In August and September, the steel roof deck was installed with a seamless ease that validated Koenig's instincts. The tongue-and-groove steel roof decking snapped together neatly.

"Each was laid in place, then spot-welded to the top of a twelve-inch I beam," Bruce said. As summer gave way to fall, the fireplace—which appeared to support the roof but was in fact freestanding—was installed, along with the steel frames for the sliding glass walls.

Because the steel ceiling was left exposed—for aesthetics as well as economy—there was no space overhead for ductwork. Three Prescolite pendant lights—glowing orbs the size of beach balls—were suspended in the dining room, living room, and just outside the south glass wall, wired invisibly through the roof decking. Everything else ran through the slab. However, embedding the nervous and circulatory systems of the house in concrete would make busted pipes or shorted connections inaccessible without a jackhammer.

On January 1, 1960, the sun rose upon a new decade, and the house now taking shape on the ridge would echo the vast changes the '60s would bring.

Buck and Carlotta were pleased with progress on the house, but also feeling the financial pressure of a growing family and mounting expenses. Carlotta was seven months pregnant with their second child and chasing a toddler, enjoying the work of a homemaker but missing the second income. Funds were running low. To reduce construction costs, Buck convinced contractor Robert J. Brady to let him do some of the manual labor. Buck would clean up and remove construction debris, wax the floors, clean the sash, and finish the grade—all to save . . . $450. The nearer their dream appeared, the more the Stahls struggled to afford it.

On March 17, 1960, Carlotta gave birth to Shari Lyn Stahl, an 11-pound baby girl with bright blue eyes and dark hair that would lighten to blonde. Bruce, now eighteen

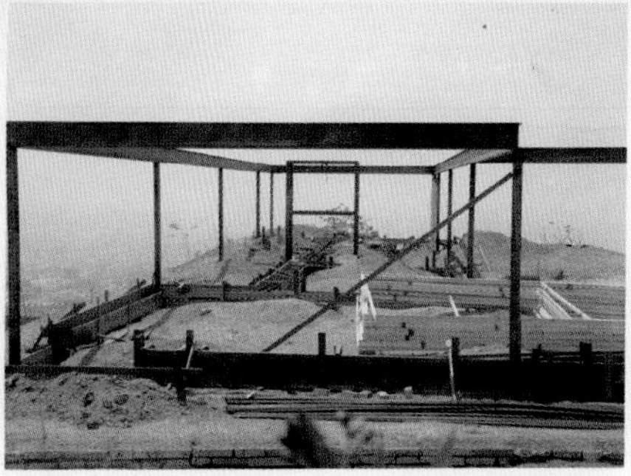
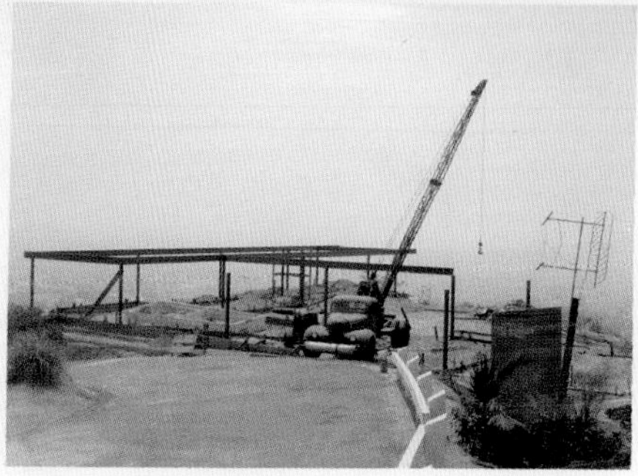
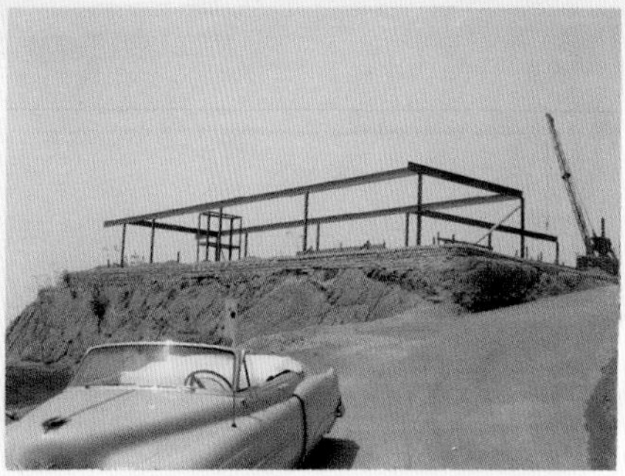
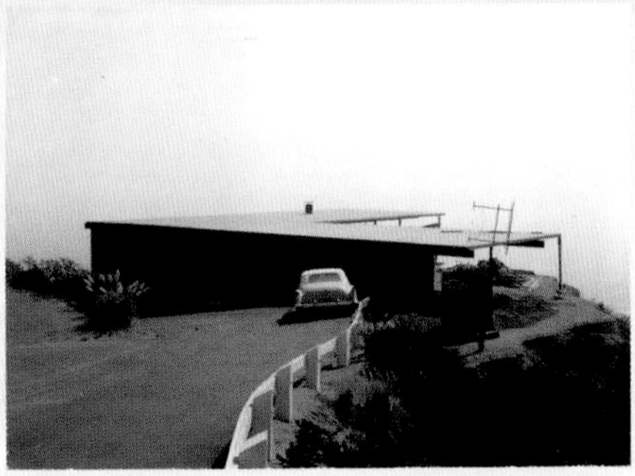
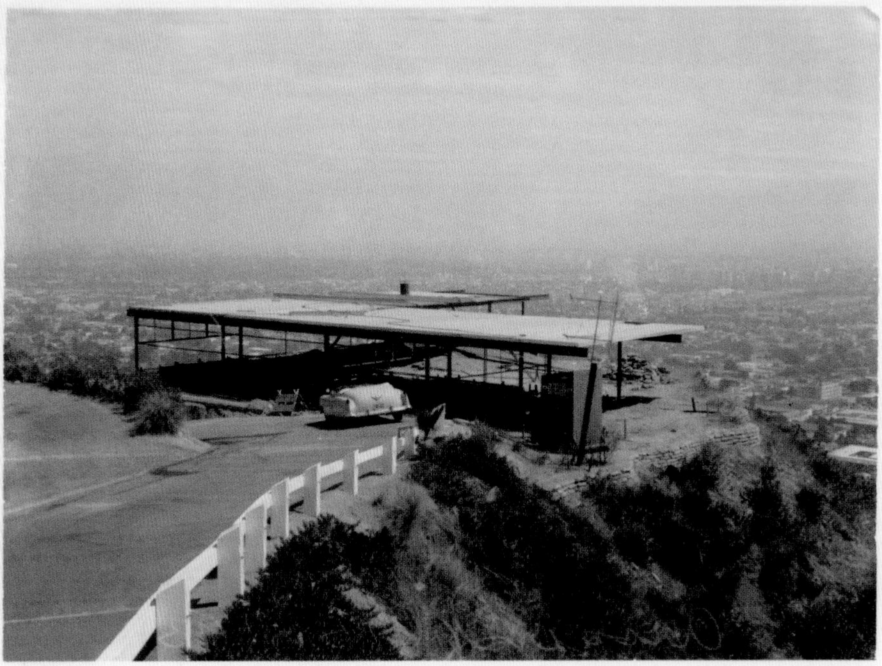

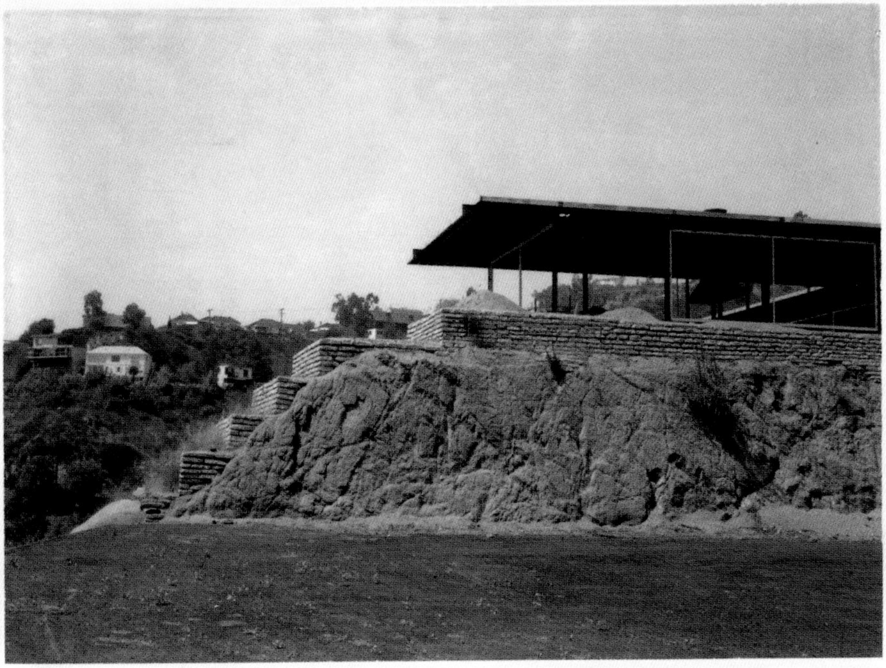

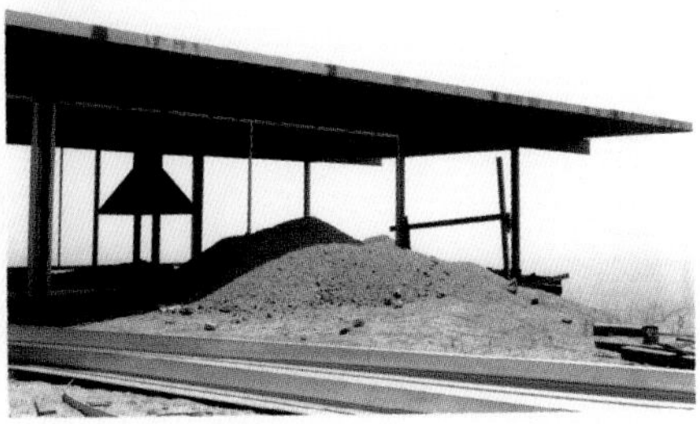

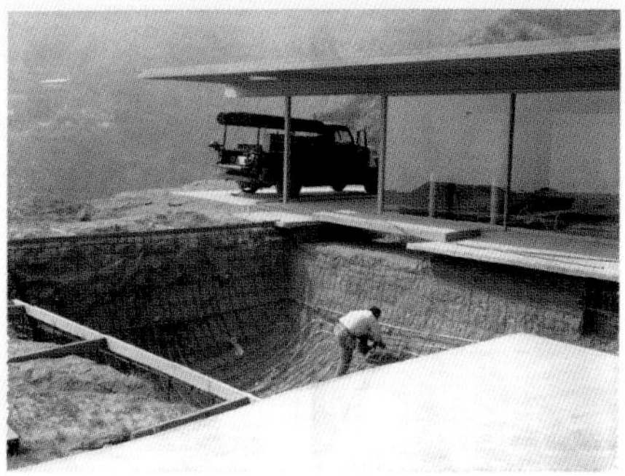

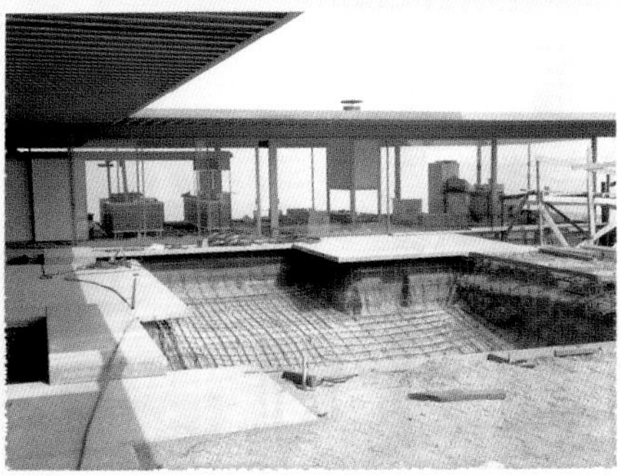

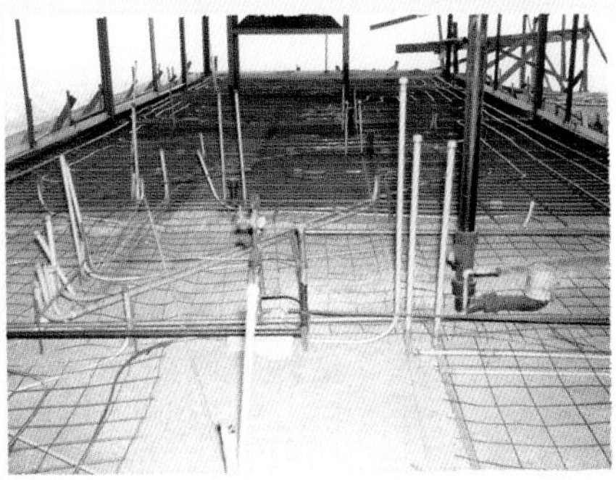

CHANGE ORDER

PIERRE KOENIG A. I. A.
11681 SAN VICENTE BLVD.
LOS ANGELES 49, CALIF.

GRanite 3-7634

ARCHITECT JOB # RS-80

CHANGE ORDER # 4

DATE 1-15-60

TO THE OWNER:

If this order is satisfactory please sign and return two 9 (2) copies to the architect. retain original.

AUTHORIZATION IS HEREBY GIVEN ROBERT BRADY (contractor)

TO MAKE CHANGES IN THE WORK FOR RESIDENCE (job)

LOCATED AT 1635 WOODS DRIVE (address)

FOR C.H. STAHL (owner)

YOUR PROPOSAL FOR MAKING THE FOLLOWING CHANGES HAS BEEN ACCEPTED.

OWNER SHALL PERFORM THE FOLLOWING TASKS AT THE JOB SITE:

1. CLEAN UP AND REMOVE ALL DEBRIS	$200.00
2. WAX FLOORS	50.00
3. CLEAN ALL SASH ETC.	150.00
4. FINISH GRADE	50.00
	450.00

THE AMOUNT OF THE CONTRACT WILL BE (~~INCREASED~~) (DECREASED) IN THE SUM OF $450.00 (DOLLARS) ($450.00)
WITH (~~INCREASE~~) (~~DECREASE~~) (NO CHANGE) IN CONTRACT TIME OF _ DAYS.

APPROVAL: OWNER C.H. Stahl DATE: 1/27/60
ARCHITECT Pierre Koenig DATE: JAN 22 1960
CONTRACTOR Robert Brady DATE: 1-15-60

The Magazine Arts & Architecture
3305 Wilshire Blvd.
Los Angeles 5, Calif.
Dunkirk 31161
Mr. John Entenza
Editor & Publisher

Mr. and Mrs. C. H. Stahl
5405 Slauson Avenue
Culver City, California

Dear Mr. and Mrs. Stahl:

This is to confirm the arrangements whereby the house designed by Pierre Koenig will be interpreted as a Case Study House in the program of the magazine, ARTS & ARCHITECTURE.

It is understood that construction will begin on this project as soon as it is reasonably possible, and that, once begun, it will be carried to completion without delay.

It is agreed that the magazine will attempt wherever possible to secure discounts on materials specified for this project, and that these savings whenever obtainable, will be passed on to you. It is understood that the magazine does not assume any responsibilities, financial or otherwise, to you or for you in the building of this house.

The house will be known tentatively as Case Study House No. 22 and is to be made available to us for public showing immediately on completion for a period of not less than eight consecutive weekends, the exact dates to be governed by the completion schedule.

It is understood that all photographic and editorial material relating to this project will be exclusively available to the magazine and to cooperating manufacturers for publication and promotion.

The furnishings of the house for exhibition and photographic purposes will be subject to the approval of the magazine and the architect. The client, however, retaining the right to buy any or all of such furnishings at whatever savings might be effected.

Now that the final arrangements have been made, I hope that construction will begin very soon, and we will proceed with the necessary announcements in an early issue of the magazine. Will you, and Mrs. Stahl, be good enough to sign this letter which is, I think, all that will be necessary between us. My best wishes.

Sincerely,

John Entenza

John Entenza
Editor and Publisher

JE:sj

Approved: C H Stahl   Carlotta Stahl

Los Angeles, 4/8/9, 1959

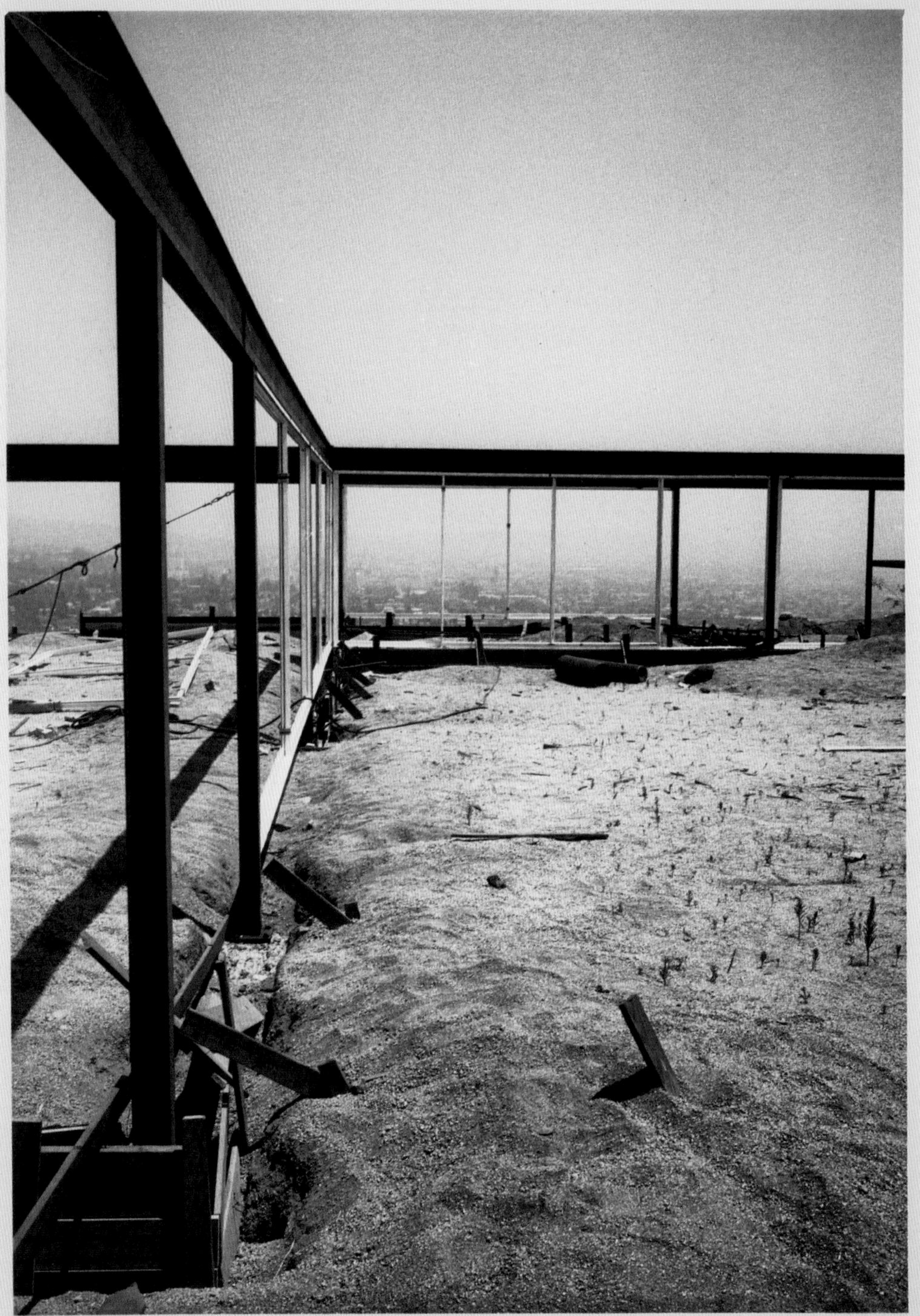

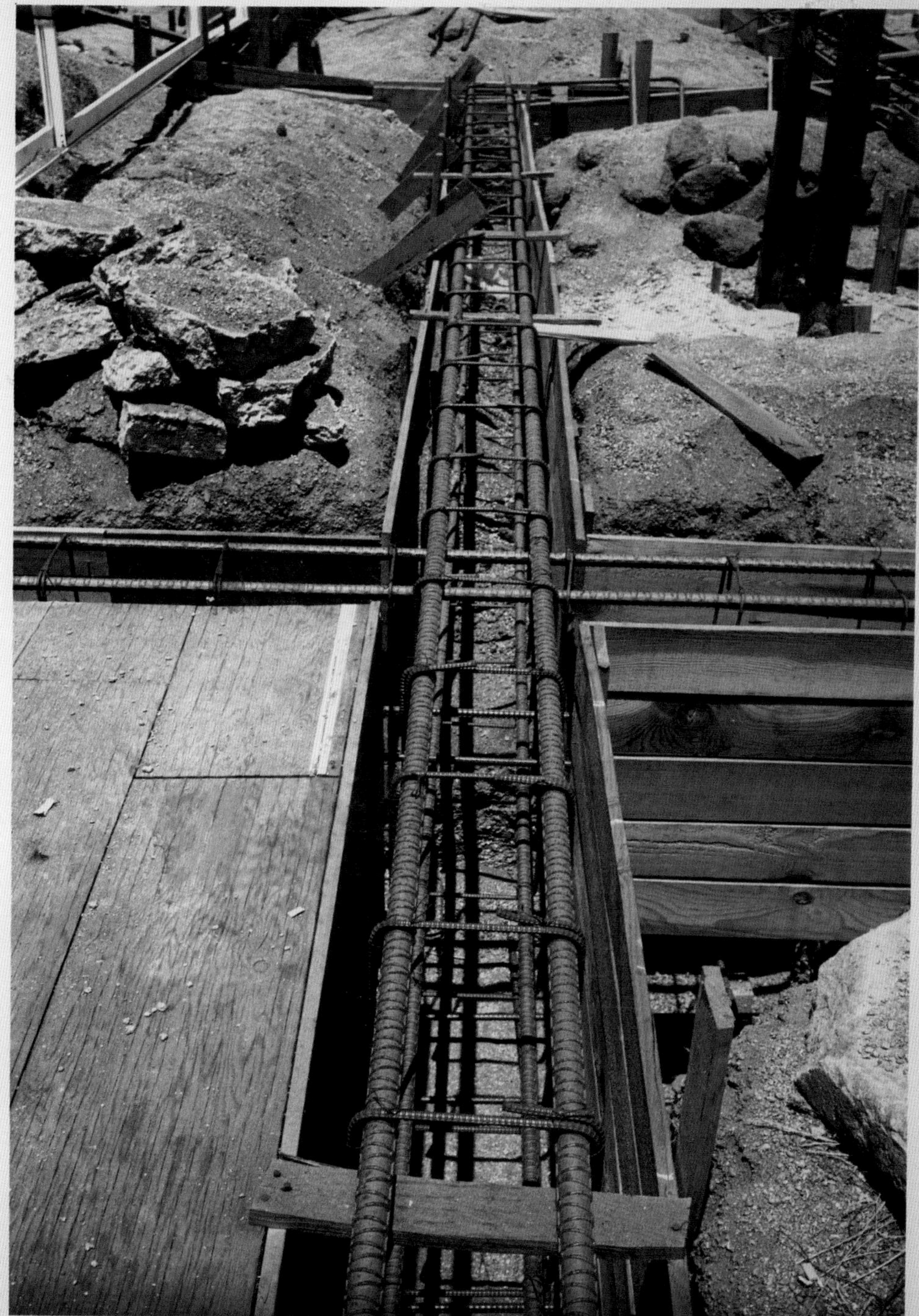

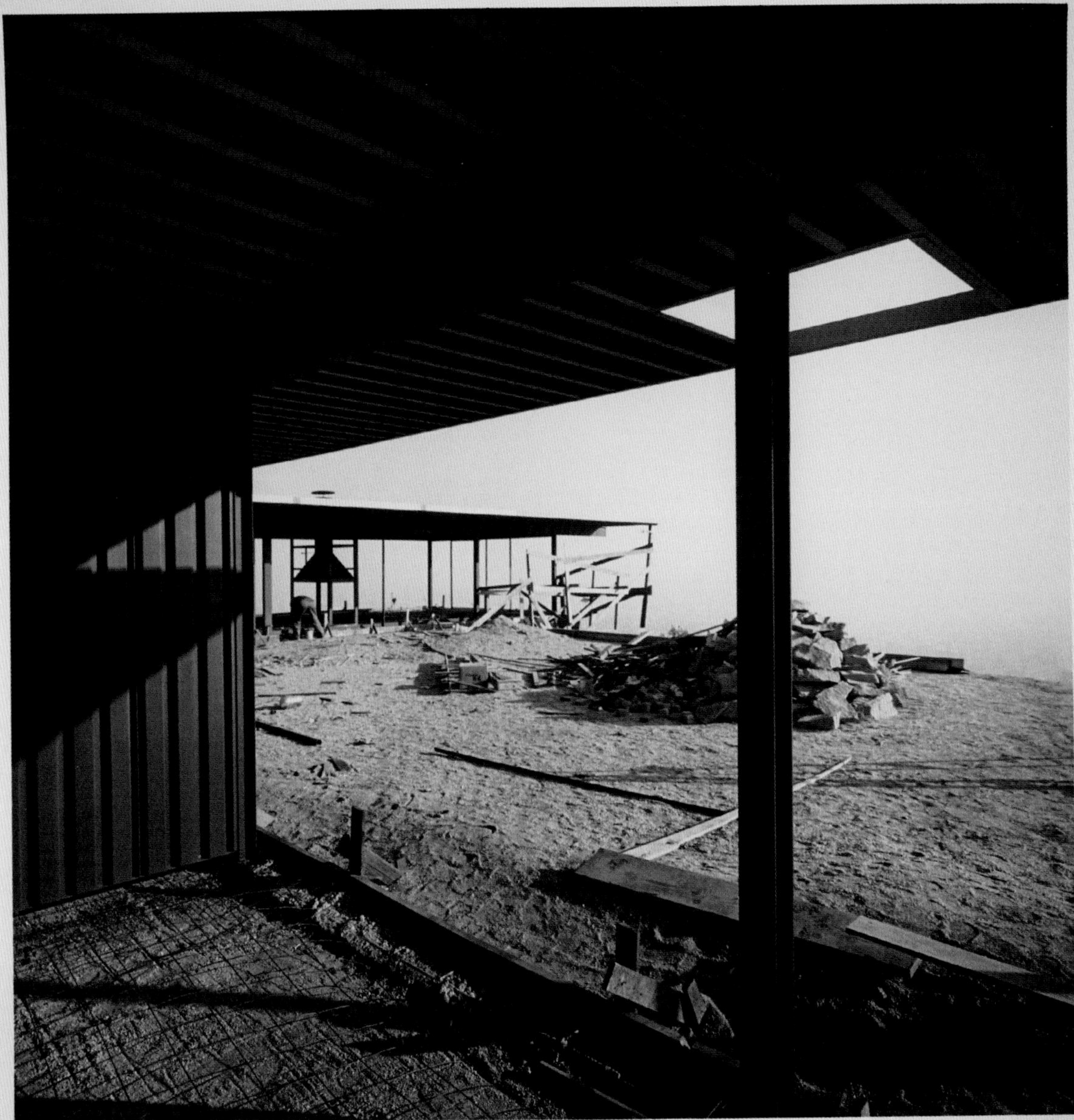

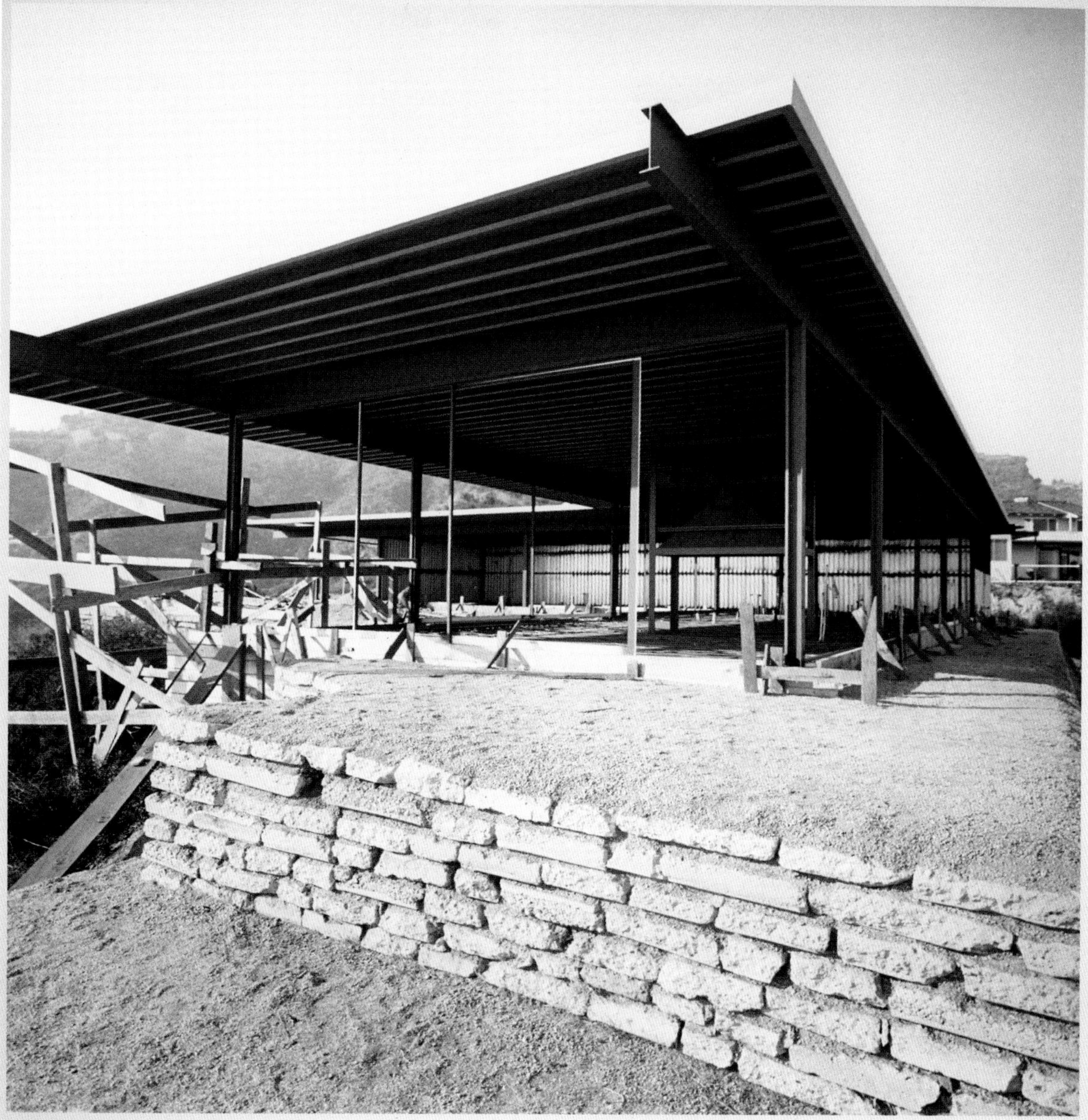

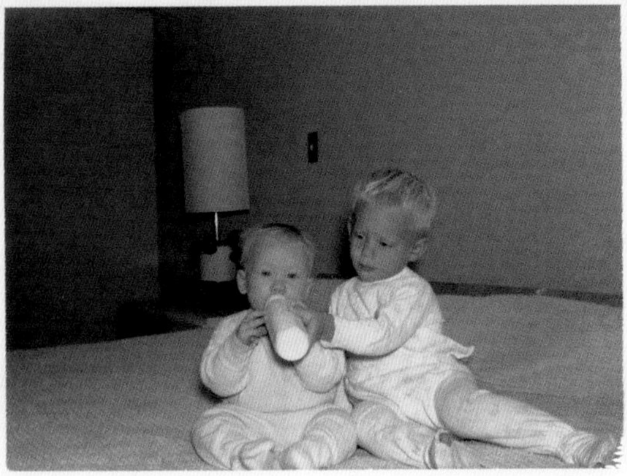

months, refused to speak to his mother for days, not realizing that this intruder she had brought into his world would grow into his favorite playmate. The next month, workers added the pool that would become the center of their childhoods.

As the house neared completion, construction was running behind schedule. Koenig faced a hard deadline: the photo shoot for *Arts & Architecture* magazine, scheduled for Monday, April 18. When that day arrived, Koenig found the house several weeks from completion and the job site mysteriously empty. On Tuesday, April 19, typing in all caps, he wrote a desperate letter to Robert Brady, the general contractor:

"As you know, we were supposed to shoot Monday," he wrote bitterly. "The deadline has been changed, but it will be impossible to change it again. The dye [sic] is set. Mr. Van Keppel is waiting to move furniture in. Shulman comes by the job every day to see when he can shoot. Mr. Entenza is shouting for photos so he can print the next issue. The president of Bethlehem [Steel] is supposed to visit the finished house this Friday. There is to be a press conference this weekend. Not to mention Mr. Stahl. This will give you an idea of the pressure being put on. I hope you will act accordingly."

With a toddler clinging to his knees and an infant in his arms, Buck was ready to move in and get settled. But that could not happen until after the photo shoot and a month-long interim when the house would be open to the public for tours.

At dawn on the day of the Shulman shoot, the Stahl house was still incomplete. Koenig's specs called for terrazzo floors and carpet, but Buck and Carlotta couldn't afford it, so the concrete floors were left bare. Plain gypsum board covered the space intended for a rock façade above the fireplace. One of Koenig's blueprints indicated Palo Verde stone on the fireplace, but that would have to be added later. And the furniture—where the hell was the furniture? Van Keppel-Green, a maker of custom modern furniture, was supposed to be staging the house. But on the Friday before the Monday shoot, the house was still unfurnished. Koenig dialed Van Keppel-Green.

"Where's the truck?"

They weren't sure. The driver was missing in action.

"We're working on it; we're tracing it now," he was told. "But we have to stop at five o'clock because that's the end of the day."

"Give me the number," Koenig said. He would call the driver himself. "I have got to have that furniture."

Koenig managed to track down the driver, who was in Kansas City, visiting his mother.

"You haul your ass out here," Koenig told him, even if that meant driving all night.

(It did.)

On the morning of Monday, May 9, 1960, Hendrik Van Keppel carried in the furniture as Julius Shulman set up his equipment. It was a smoldering, 83-degree day in LA, and the skies were heavy with smog. Koenig had every reason to be sweating. The kitchen was unfinished, plaster dust was everywhere, and the yard was trampled from all the coming and going. Assistants were running around with branches, positioning them in bare spots. Koenig ran home to gather additional props—outdoor chairs and architectural pottery—to fill the white space. His five-year-old son, Randy, who often came with him to job sites, was instructed to wait in the car.

"He positioned it in the street so [I] could see in the house," Randy Koenig recalled in 2020. "It was raw. It was barely done! It was cold, and it was four hours. I finally fell asleep." Outside of Shulman's camera frame, the scene was pure chaos. "In the background, all hell is breaking loose," Koenig recalled. "People are running around, and junk and trash is piled up. If I had a proclivity for an ulcer, I'd certainly have had one."

Julius Shulman set up a number of shots that day, directing a male and female model in various domestic scenes. He sat on the 4-foot carport wall and aimed across the bright pool, positioning a man with binoculars on Buck's top terrace. As the sun sank over the neighboring ridgeline, California's honey-glazed afternoon light faded from gold to pink to electric blue twilight. An orange glow defined the seam where the Pacific Ocean met a dome of flickering stars, as if dying embers were scattered just beyond the offing.

That's the precise moment: the instant that Shulman saw the unique interplay of the structure and the setting, what he later called "the essence" of the house. He began to assemble a composition that would distill the mastery of Pierre Koenig's design and the brilliance of Buck Stahl's vision into a single, curated image.

It was the shot to be seen 'round the world.

This photograph he captured that evening would be invoked, again and again, as one of the most essential images ever taken of Los Angeles. As *New York Times* critic Paul Goldberger would describe it, it was "one of those singular images that sum up an entire city at a moment in time." The photograph would appear in lifestyle magazines, on the walls of museums, in the pages of architecture textbooks, and on the covers of oversized fine art books. It would be published, by some estimates, more than any photograph of any house in the world. In Julius Shulman's meticulous logbooks, it was noted simply as job No. 2980.

As simple and effortless as Shulman's most famous image would appear, it demonstrated the prowess of a master fully in control. Lights had to be positioned with great care to avoid reflections in all that glass. Balancing the bright interior lights with the atmospheric glitter of the city below required a tricky double exposure. The house lights would have to be turned off when Shulman opened his shutter. During a seven-minute exposure, any people he positioned in the photo would have to sit perfectly still as the subtle glow of the city gradually burned itself into the film. Then the lights of the house would have to be turned on—with normal bulbs replaced by flashbulbs—to expose the bright interior for a brief and fleeting instant, capturing the interior. The artistry of Shulman's composition could only succeed if the exposure was executed with absolute technical precision.

None of this was what Shulman originally planned.

He had been working inside, searching for an angle that would capture the essence of the house in a single frame. His assistant, Leland Lee, was rigging lights, preparing for an interior shot. The night was warm, so Shulman stepped outside to get some air and take in the view. That's when he noticed "the girls."

They weren't models—not exactly. Ann Lightbody and Cynthia Tindle were the fiancée and friend of Jim Jennings and Don Murphy, respectively, two architecture students assisting with the shoot. They had all been invited, sort of, by Shulman. "Tell the students to bring their girlfriends," Shulman had said to Koenig in advance.

Standing beside the pool on that warm May night, Shulman saw his shot. The two young women were chatting quietly in the cantilevered corner, their white dresses aglow in the globe lights, suspended in time, as well as space, above the glittering city. He burst back into the house.

"We're changing the composition."

His Sinar 4 x 5 camera was brought outside and set up on a tripod. The lights were rearranged, and the bulbs in the globe lights were replaced with flashbulbs that would explode with light for a fraction of a second, and then go dark.

He told the women, "Just pretend you're having a conversation."

He turned off the lights and opened the shutter. Lightbody and Tindle sat in the dark for seven minutes as the city lights burned into film. Shulman closed the shutter and prepared for the next step of the exposure.

"Hold still!" Shulman said. The flashbulbs popped, the room lit up, and the shutter opened.

Click!

It would become arguably the most famous residential photograph of all time.

But Shulman himself didn't see it as that. To him, it was not a picture of a house.

"It was a picture of a mood."

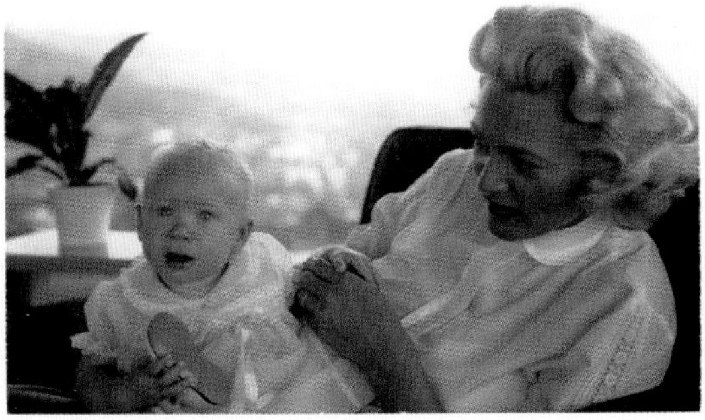

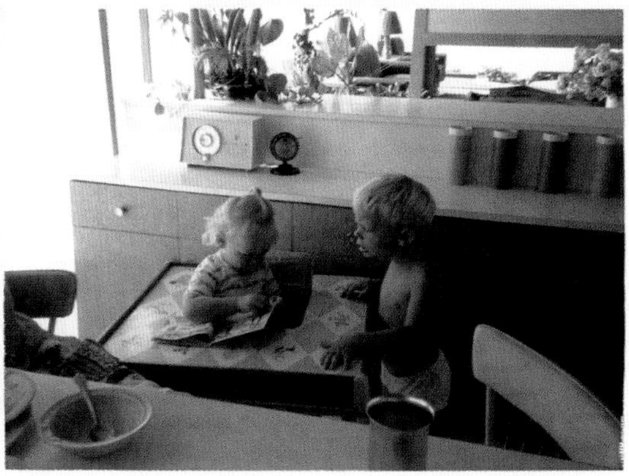

APRIL 19, 1960

DEAR BOB,

I'M LEAVING FOR SAN FRANCISCO WED. A.M. AND BECAUSE I HAVE BEEN UNABLE TO REACH YOU I MUST LEAVE THIS NOTE.

WHEN I WENT TO THE JOB MON. I WAS SHOCKED TO SEE NO ONE THERE AND MANY THINGS TO BE DONE YET. AS YOU KNOW WE WHERE SUPPOSED TO SHOOT MONDAY. THEDEADLINE HAS BEEN CHANGED ONCE BUT IT IS IMPOSSIBLE TO CHANGE IT AGAIN. THE DIE IS SET. MR. VAN KEPPEL IS WAITING TO MOVE FURNITURE IN. SHULMAN COMES BY THE JOB EVERY DAY TO SEE WHEN HE CAN SHOOT. MR. ENTENZA IS SHOUTING FOR PHOTOS SO HE CAN PRINT THE NEXT ISSUE. THE PRESIDENT OF BETHLEHEM IS SUPPOSED TO VISIT THE FINISHED HOUSE THIS FRIDAY. THERE IS TO BE A PRESS CONFERENCE THIS WEEK-END. NOT TO MENTION MR. STAHL. THIS WILL GIVE YOU SOME IDEA OF THE PRESSURE BEING PUT ON. I HOPE YOU CAN ACT IN ACCORDANCE.

ALSO, WE HAVE TO TREAT THE FLOORS BEFORE ANYTHING CAN BE PLACED ON THEM. AS I WILL BE GONE I WOULD APPRECIATE IT IF YOU CAN MAKE THE ARRAINGEMENTS WITH MR FORSTER AT WATCO-DENNIS GR. 92969 TO GET THIS DONE RIGHT AWAY!

ALSO, CALL MR. VAN KEPPELL AT EX. 31839 AND TELL HIM WHEN HE MAY FURNISH.

MANY THANKS,

Pierre Koenig

PIERRE KOENIG

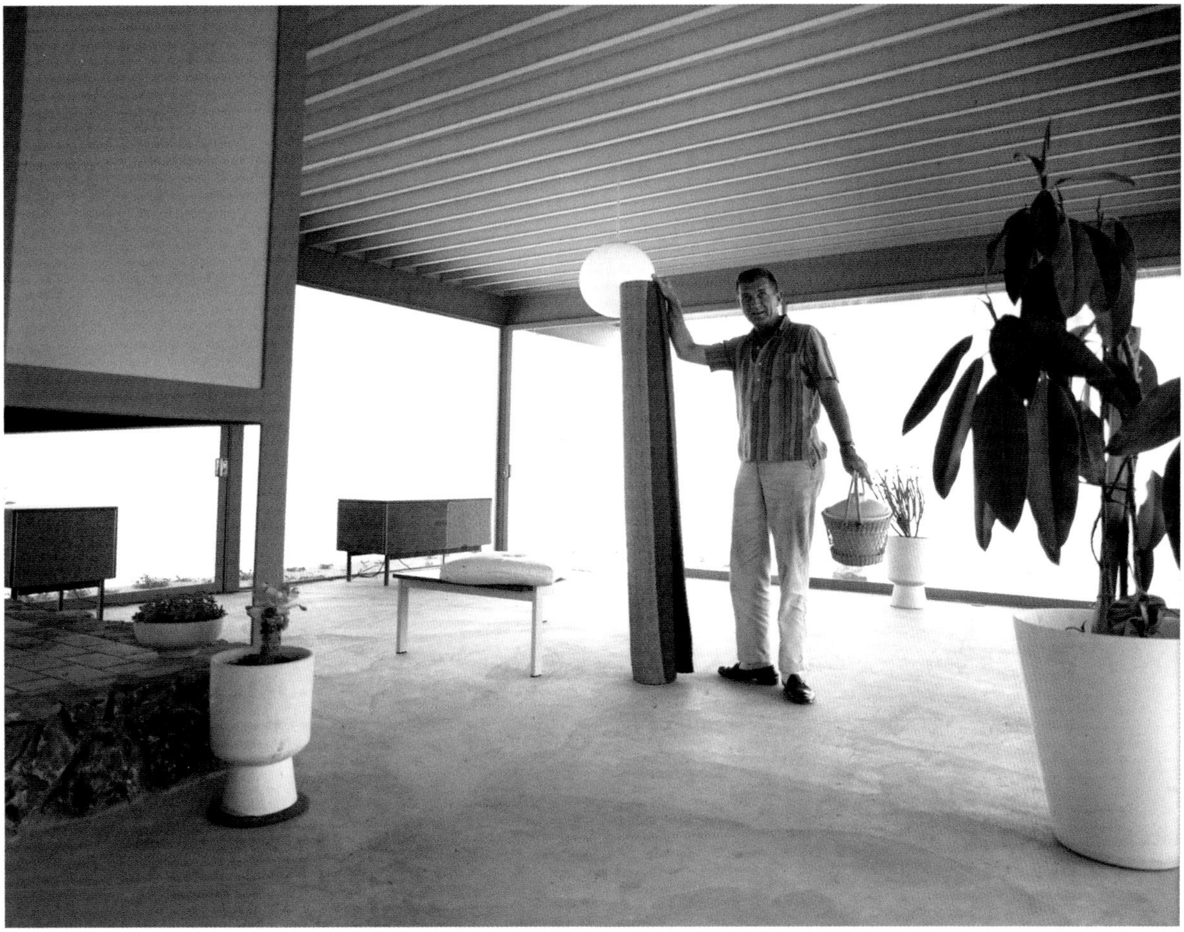

Hendrik Van Keppel, staging the house for Julius Shulman's photo shoot.

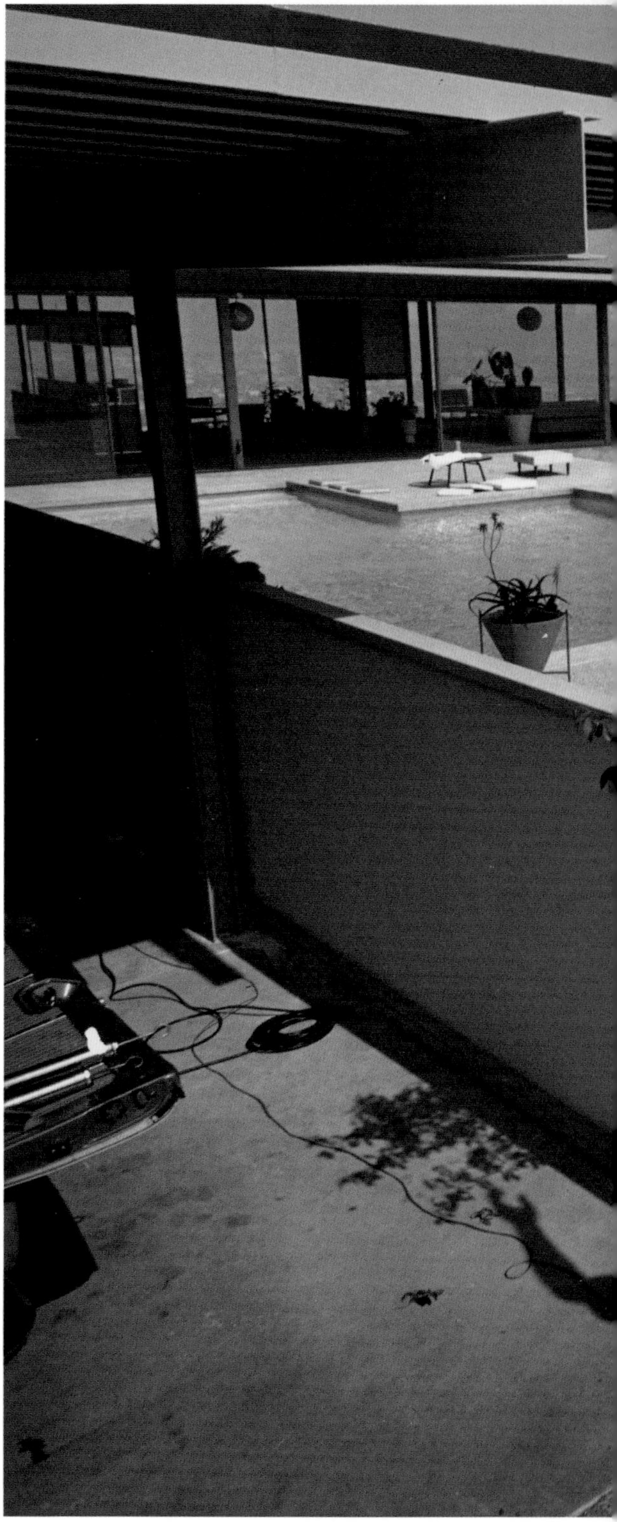

May 1960: Julius Shulman sits on the pony wall in the carport to frame a shot.

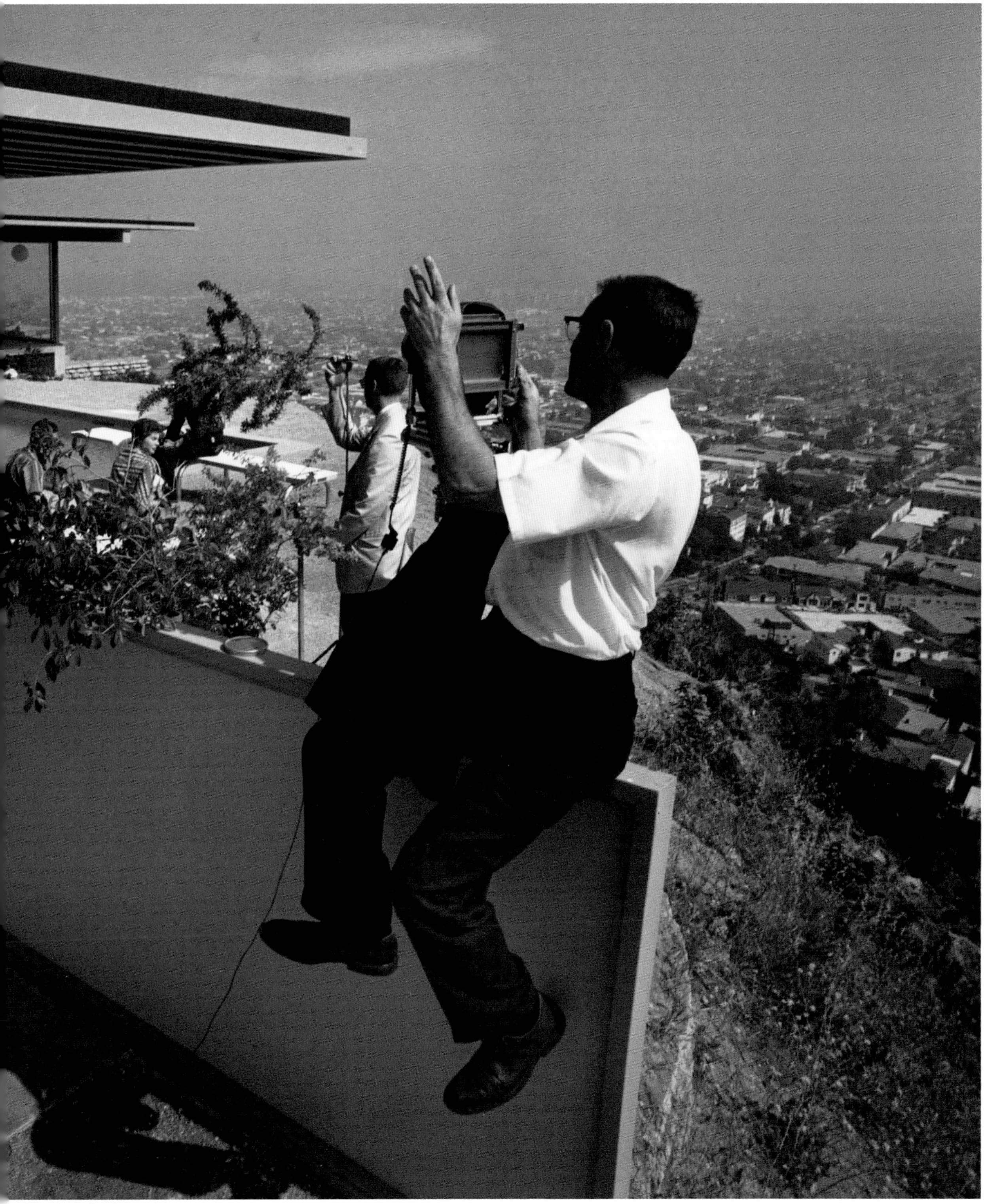

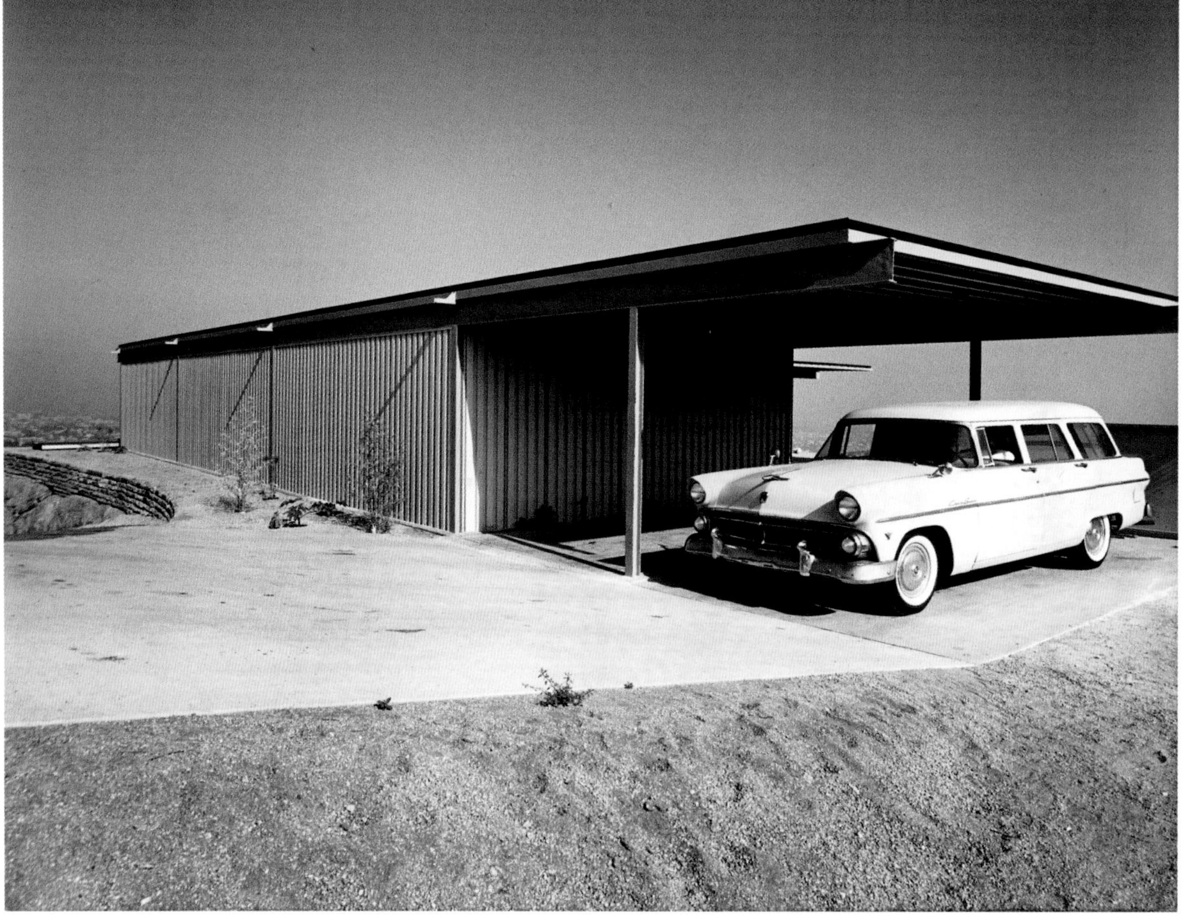

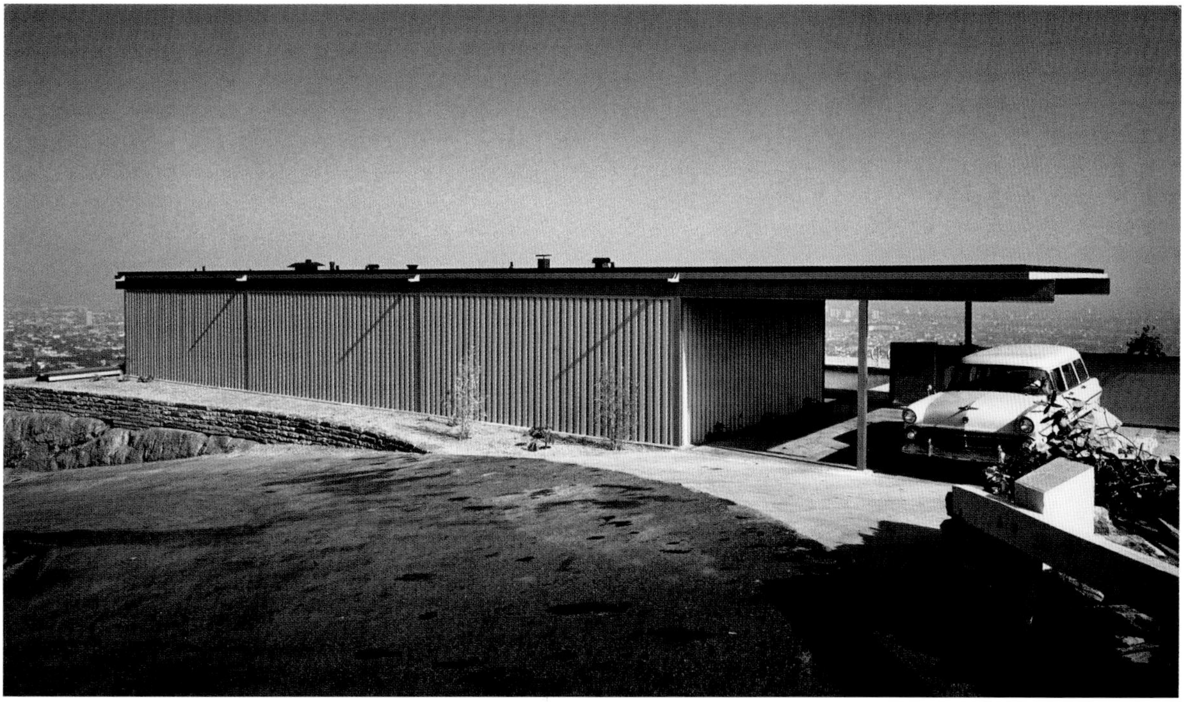

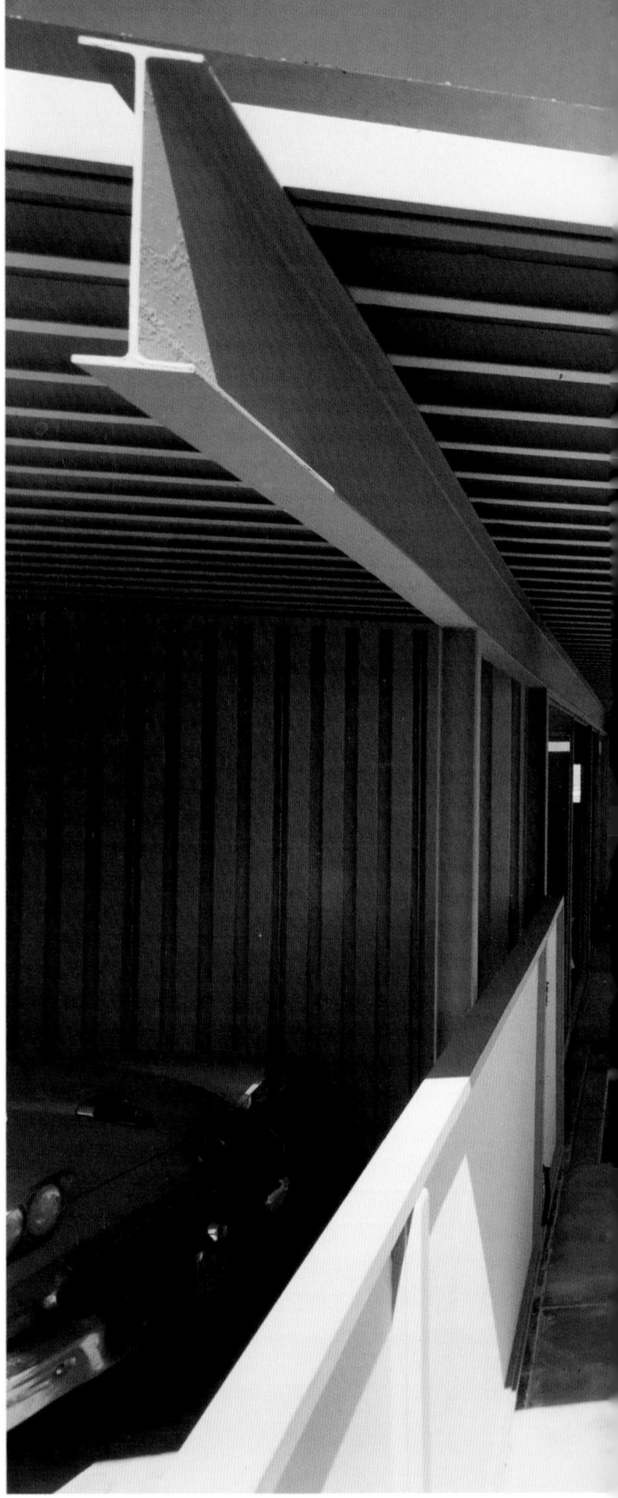

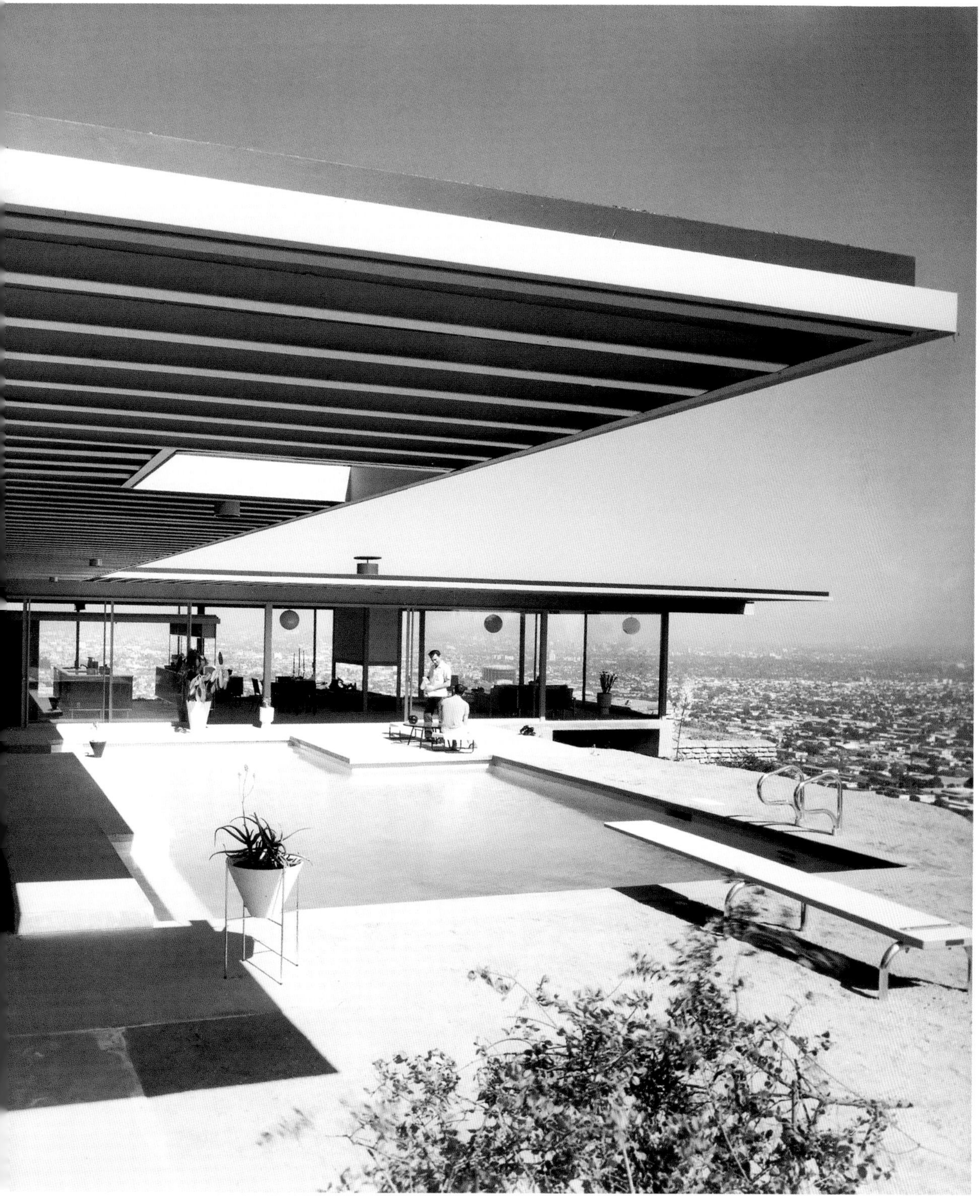

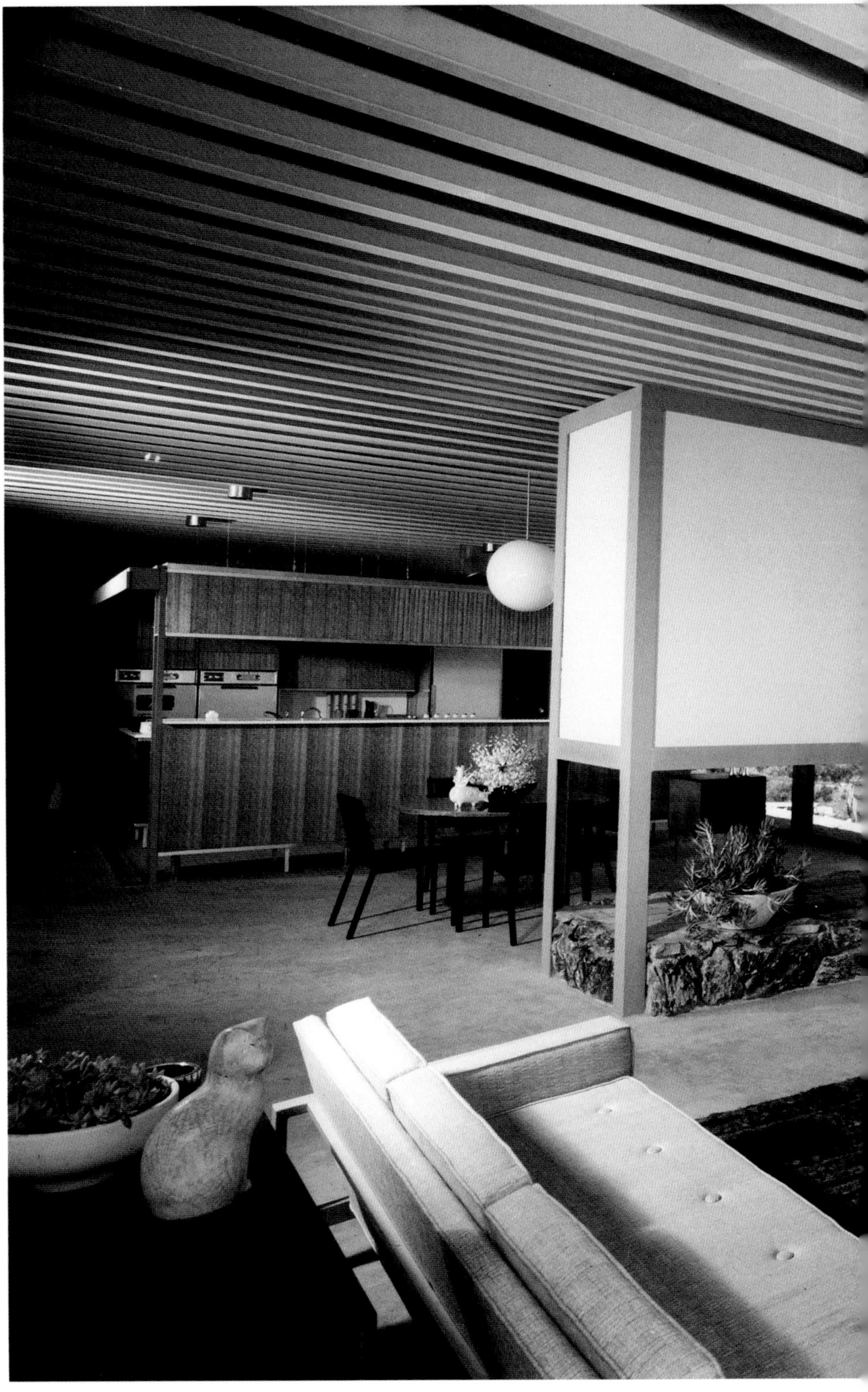

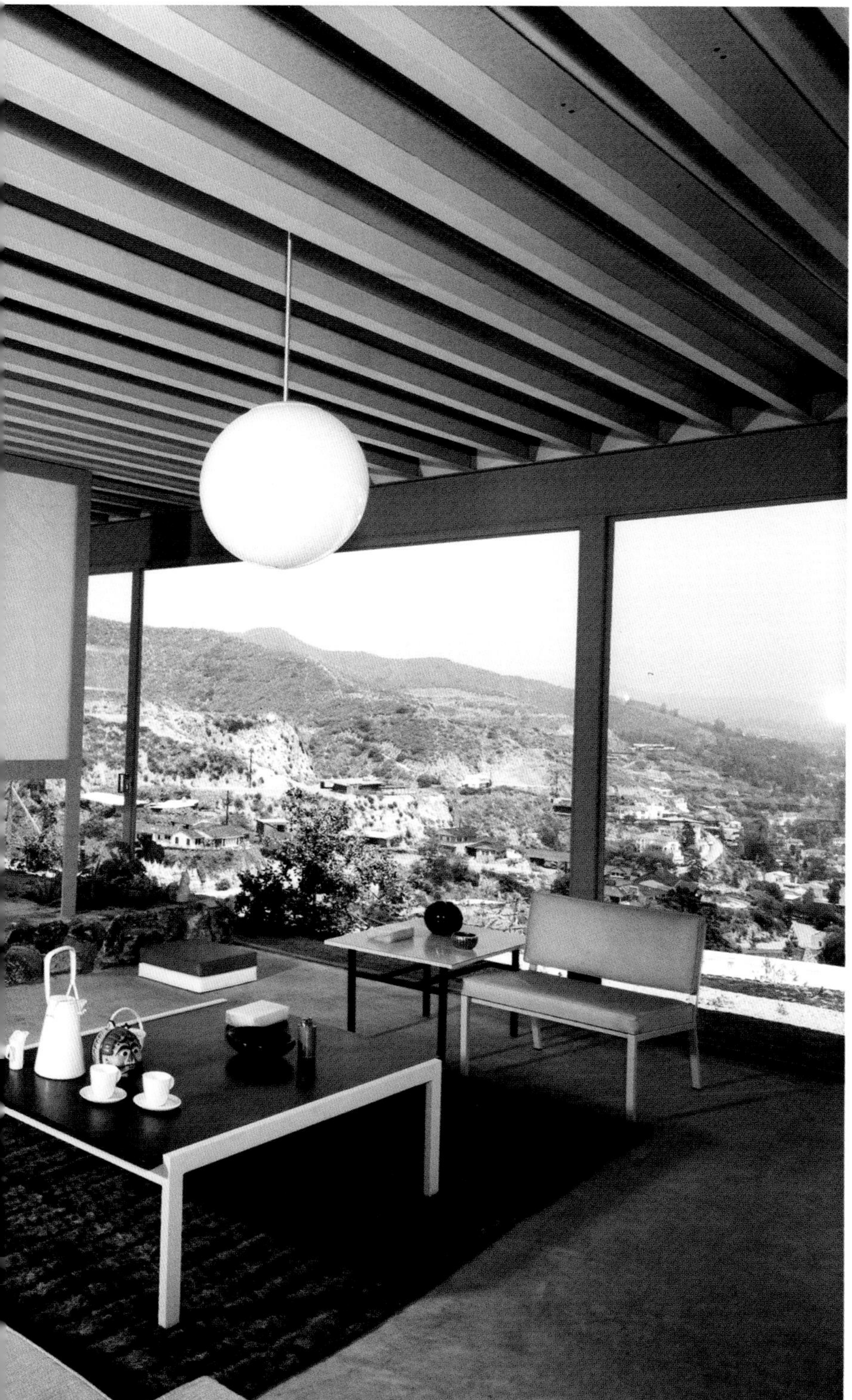

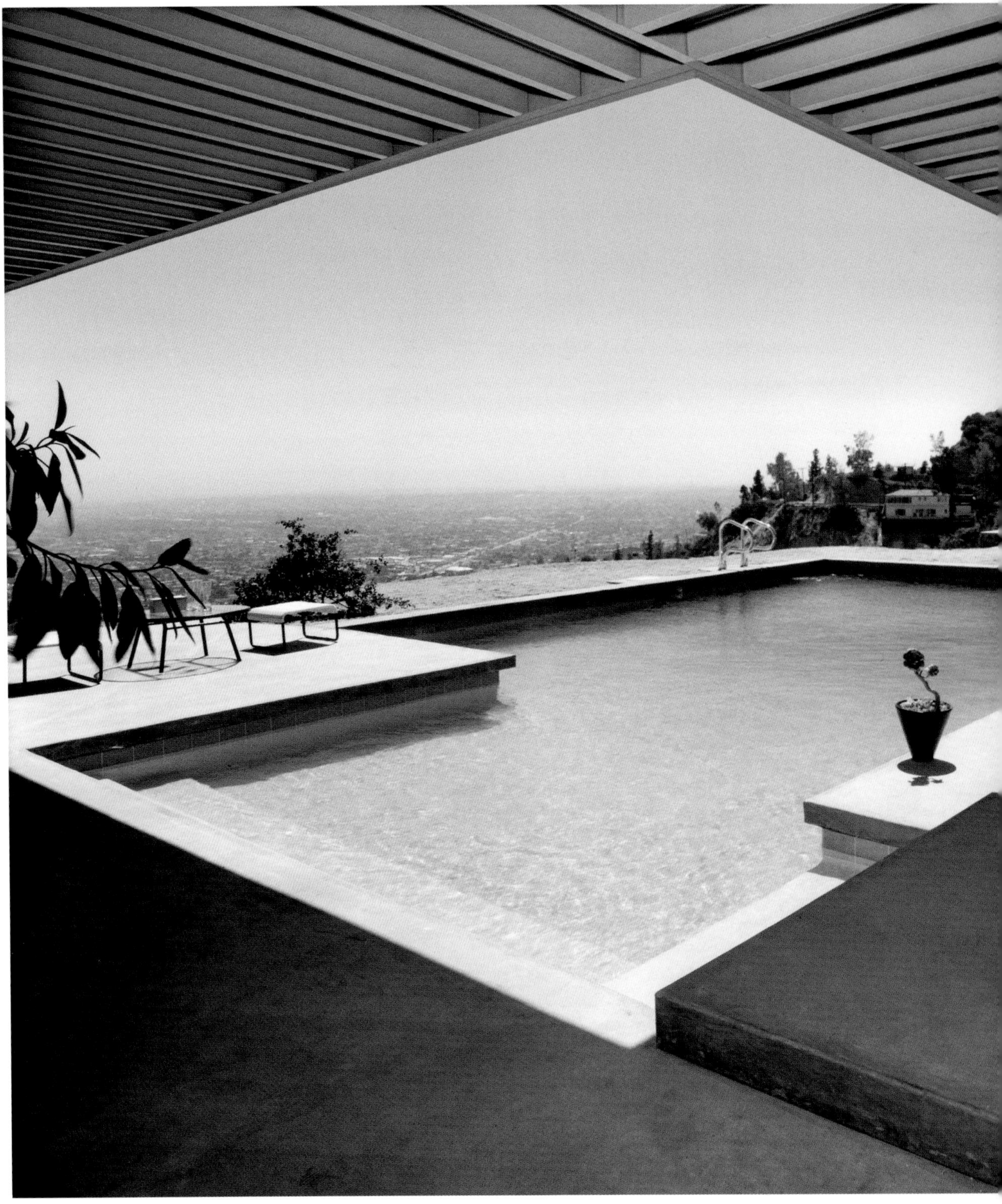

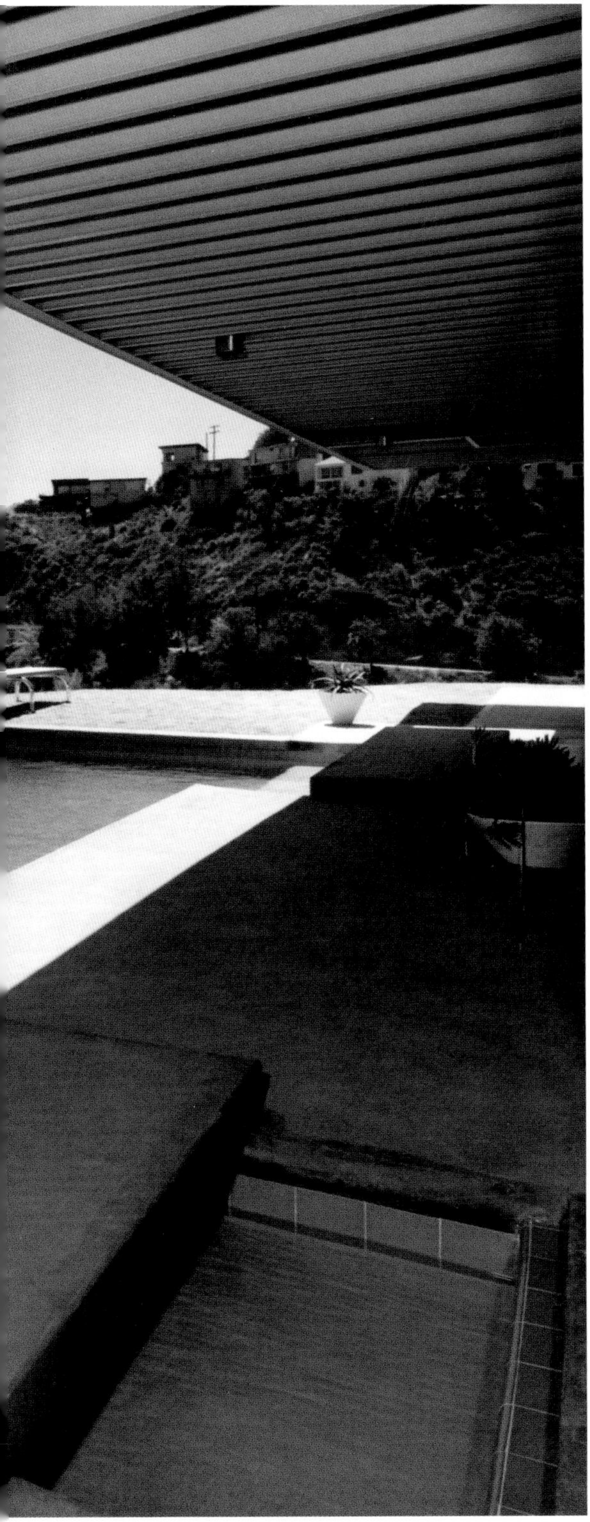

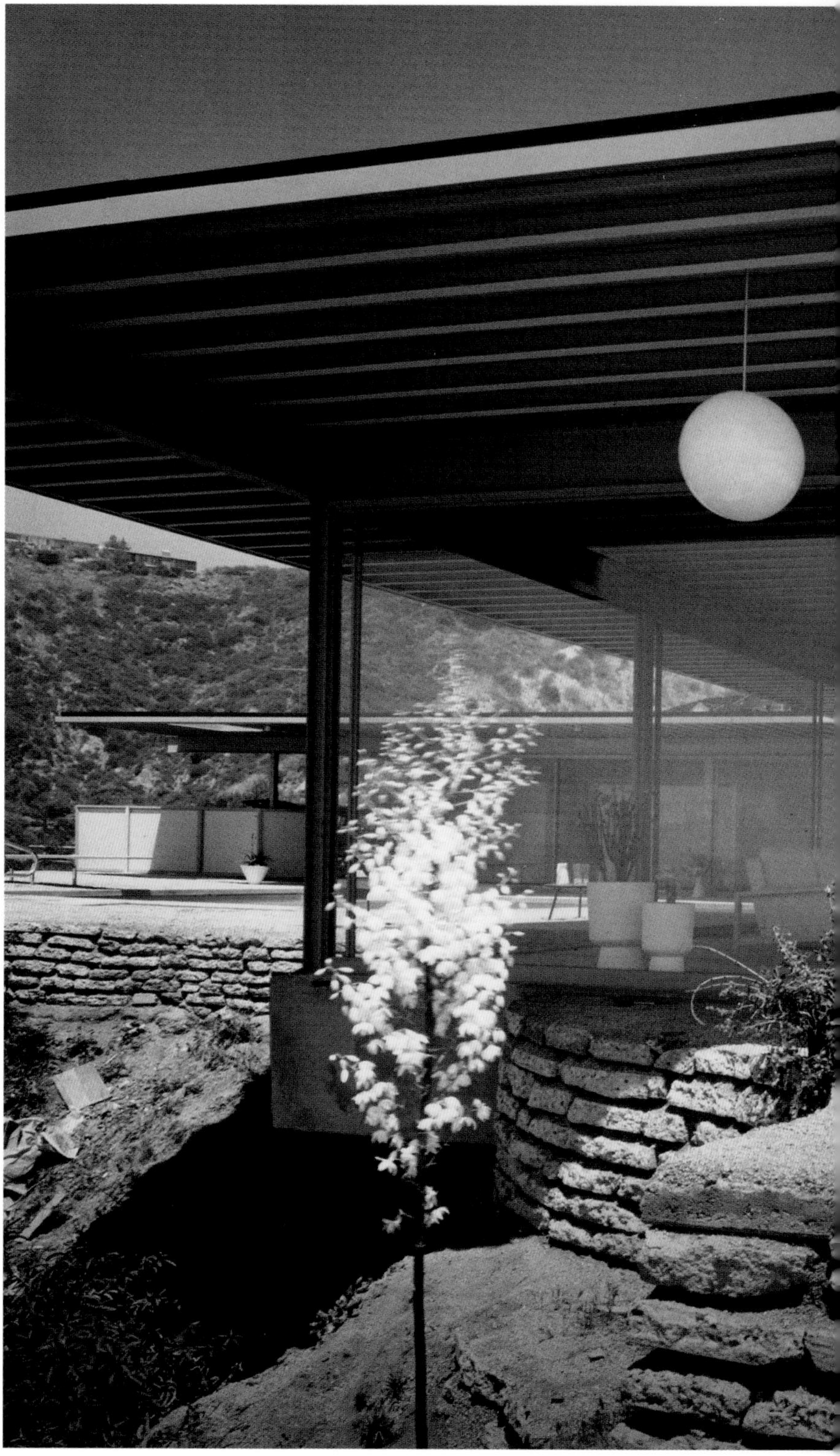

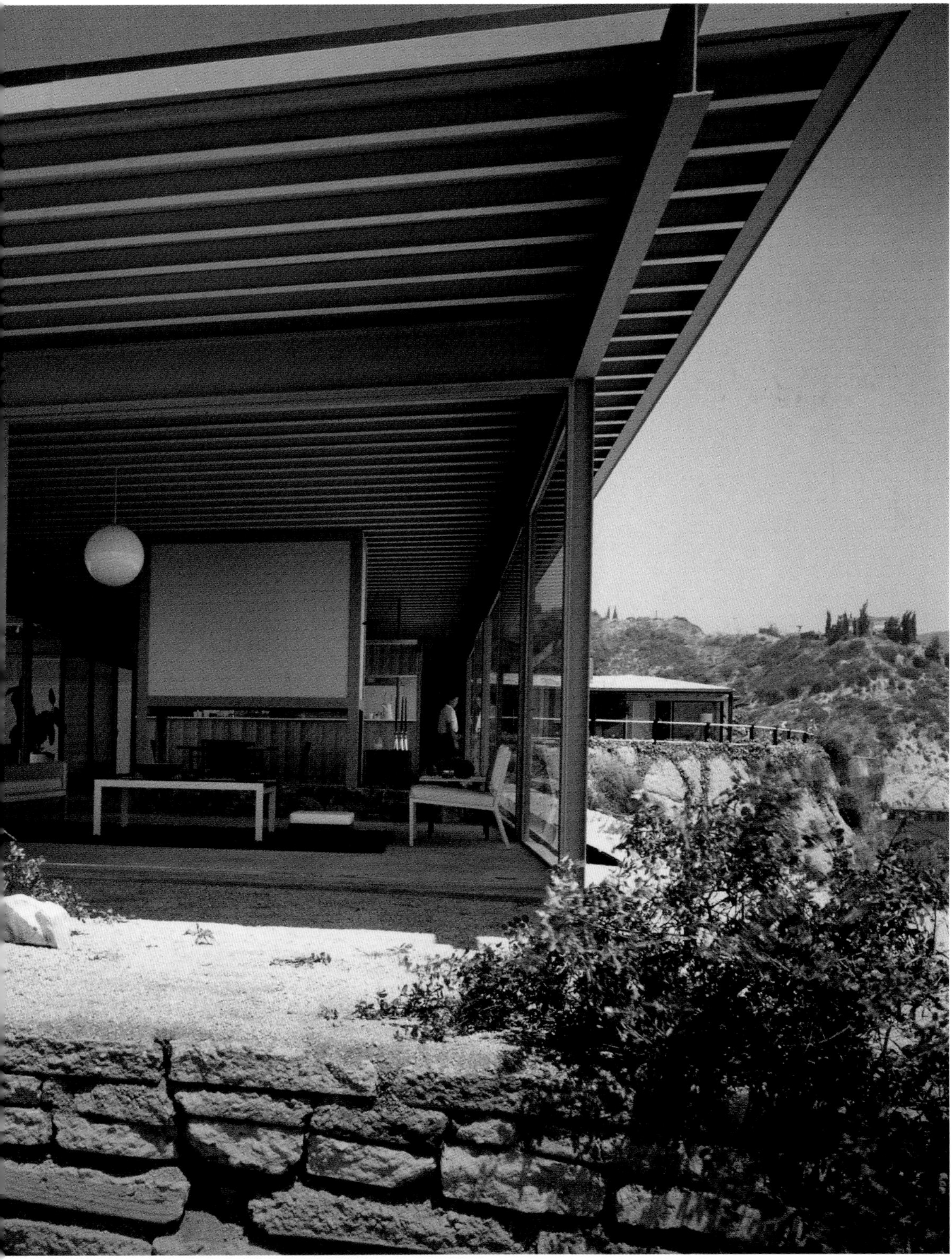

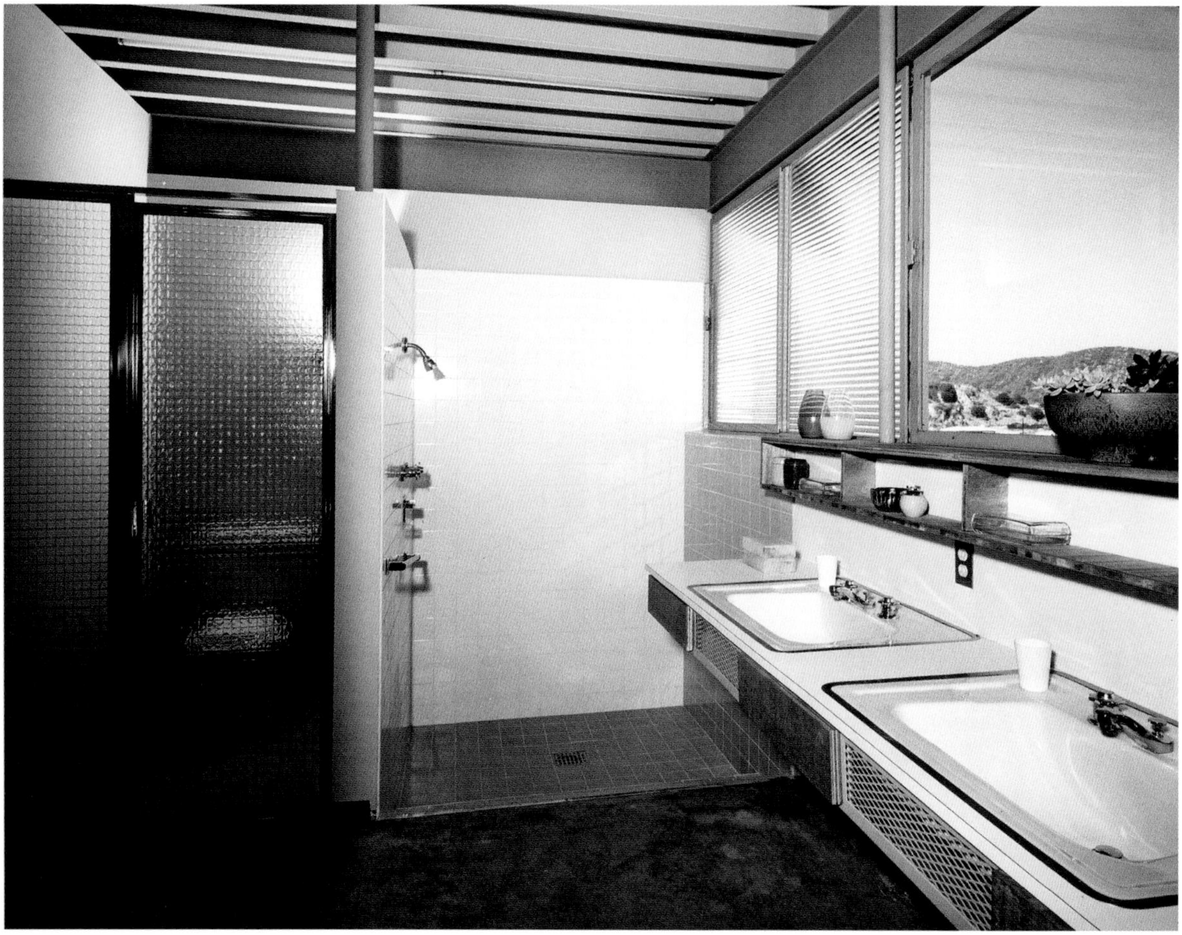

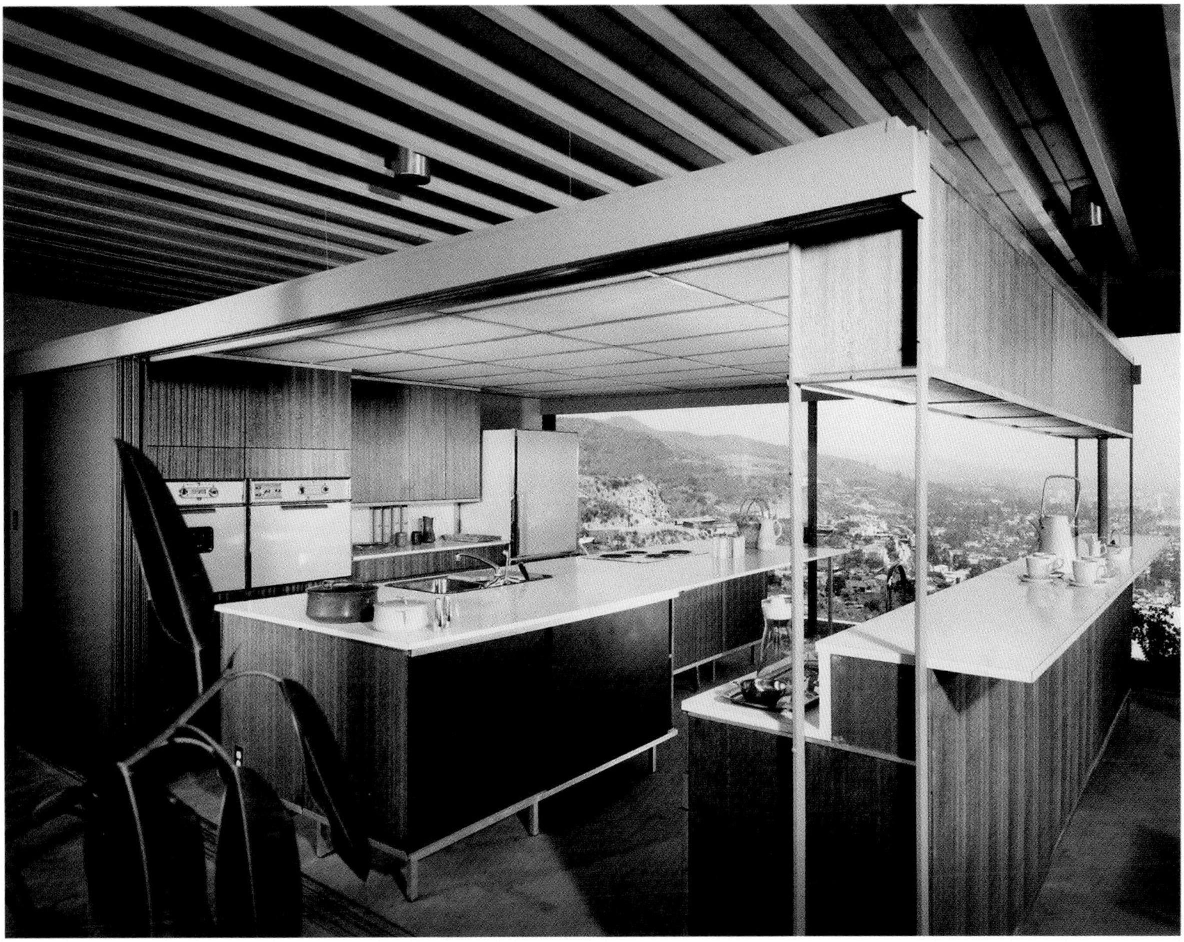

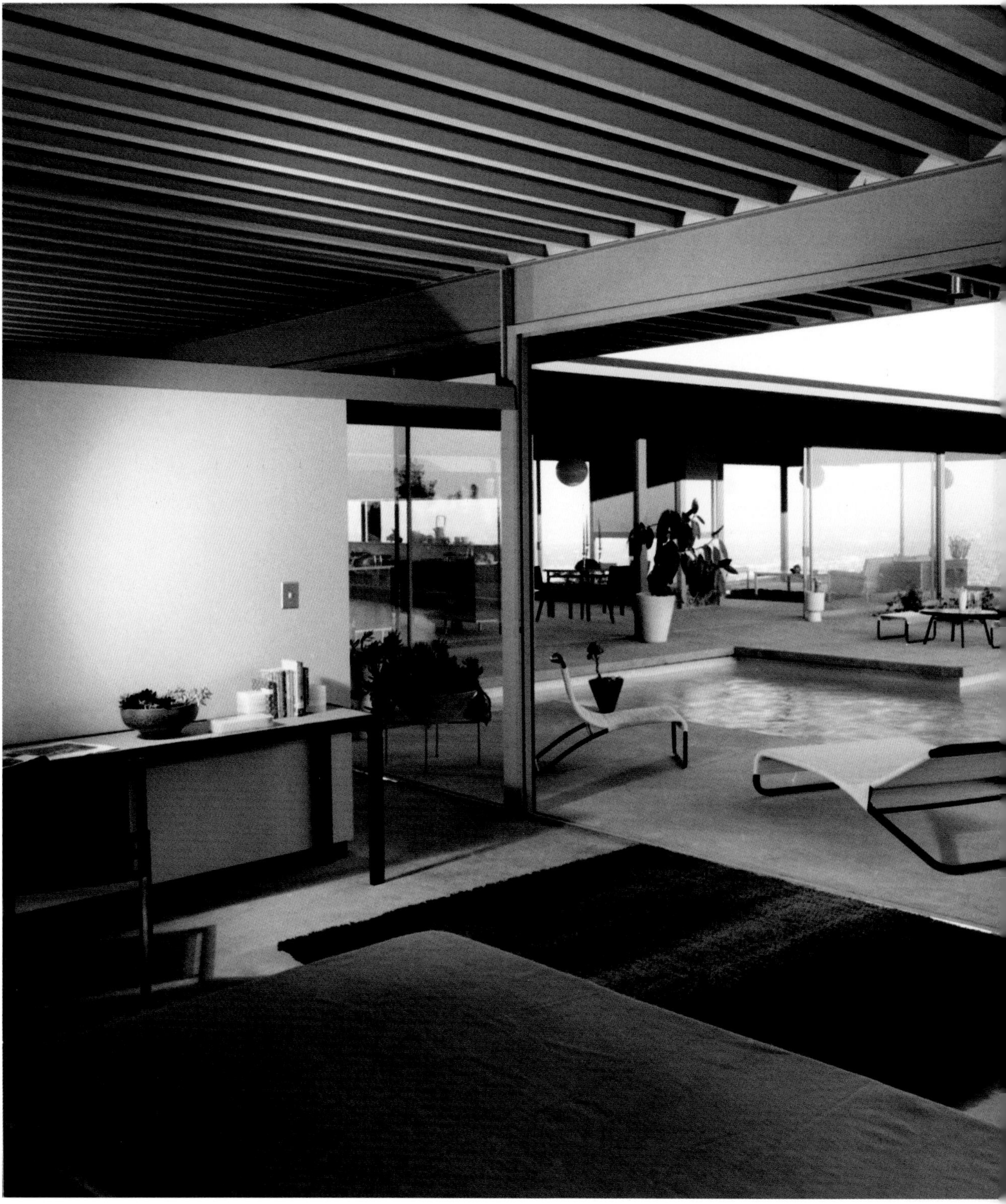

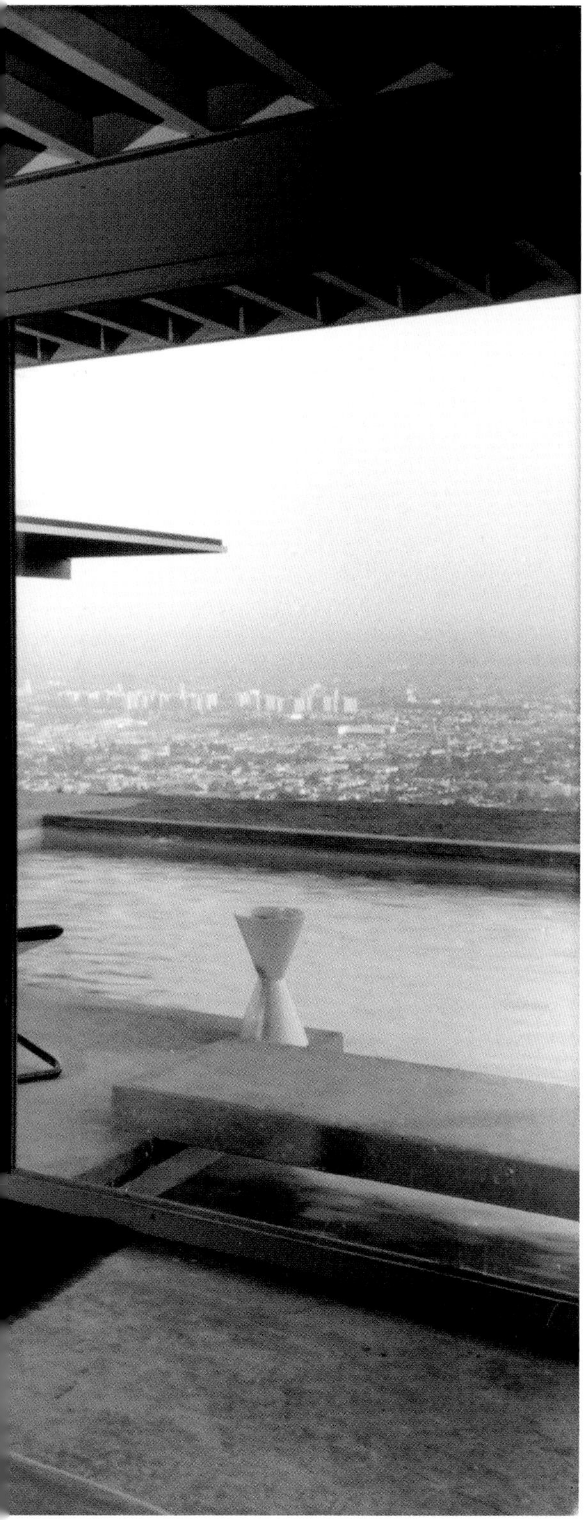

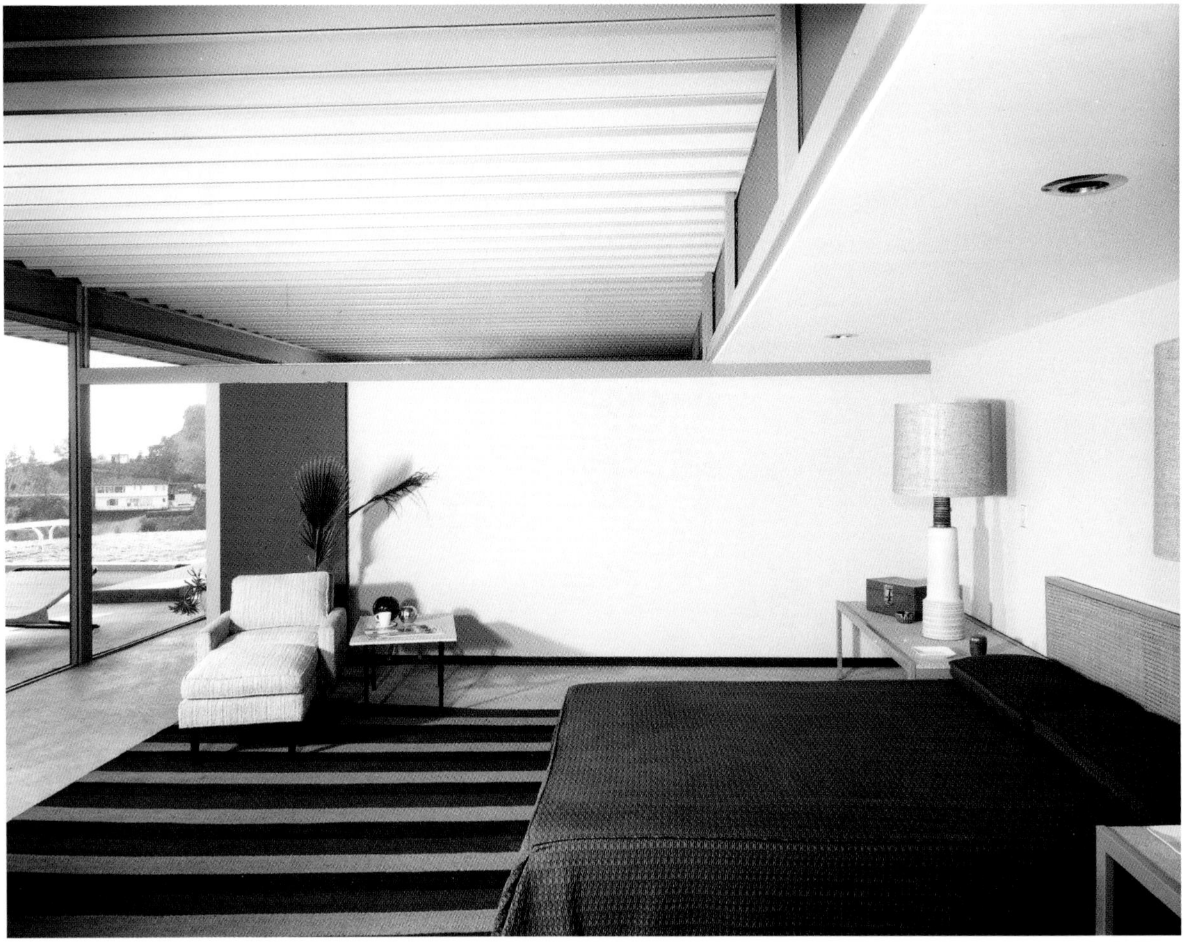

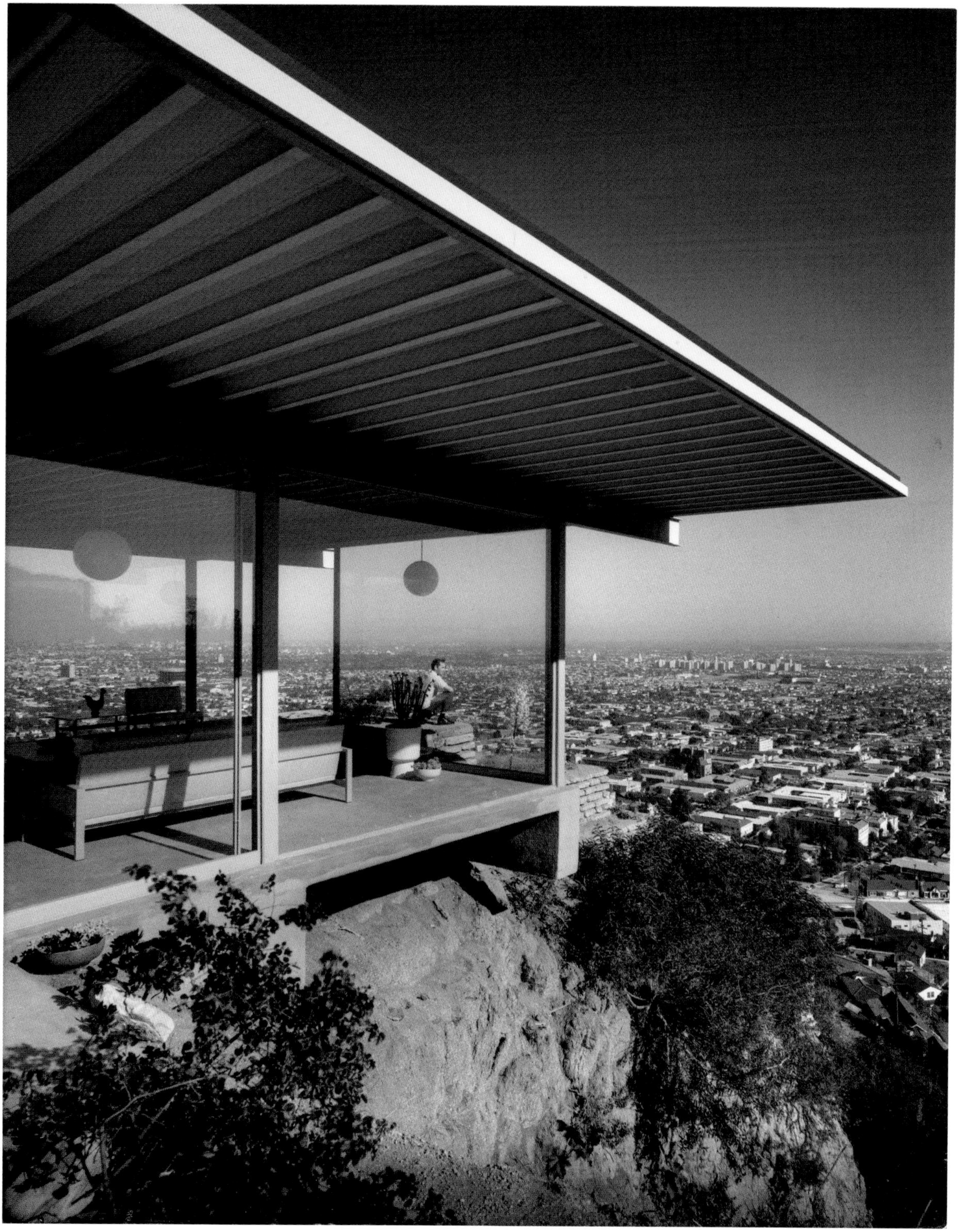

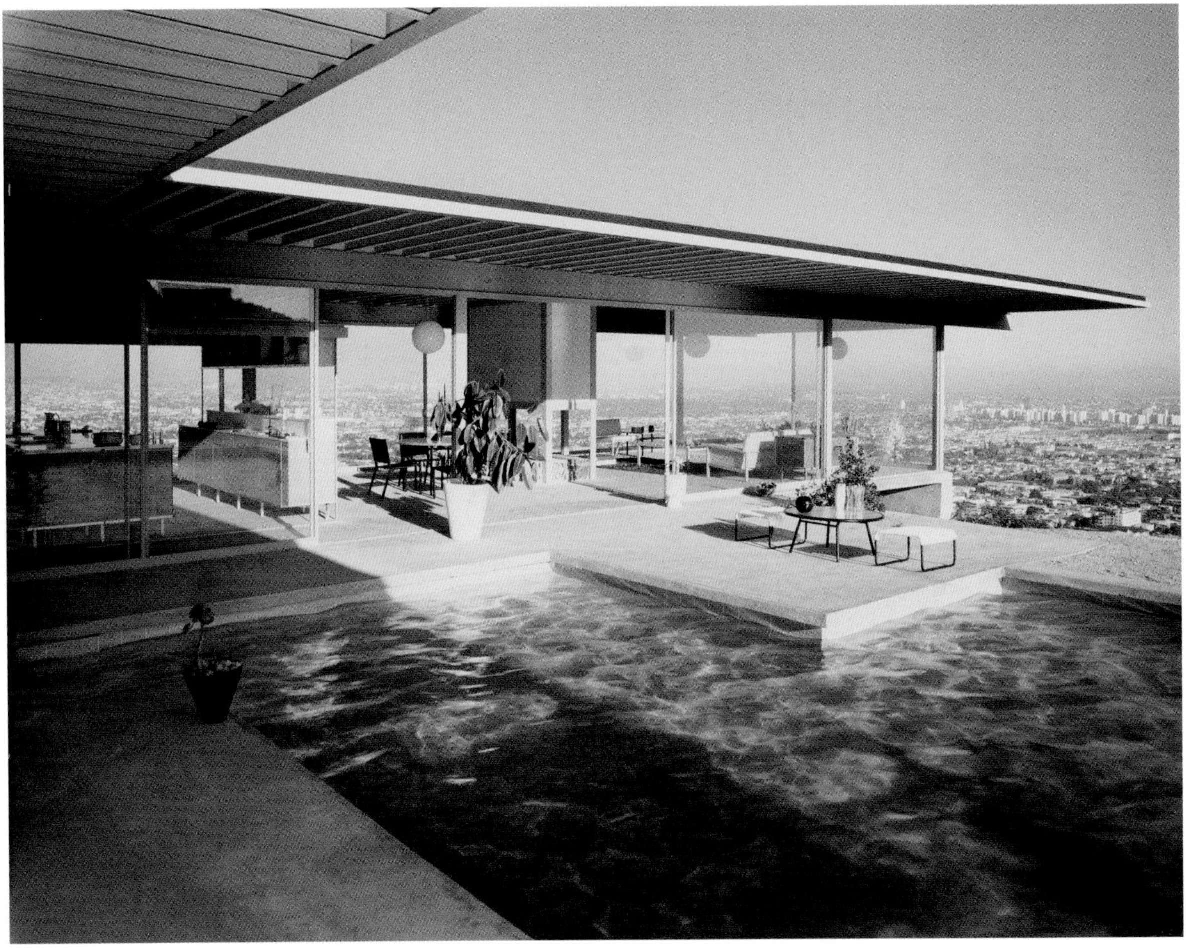

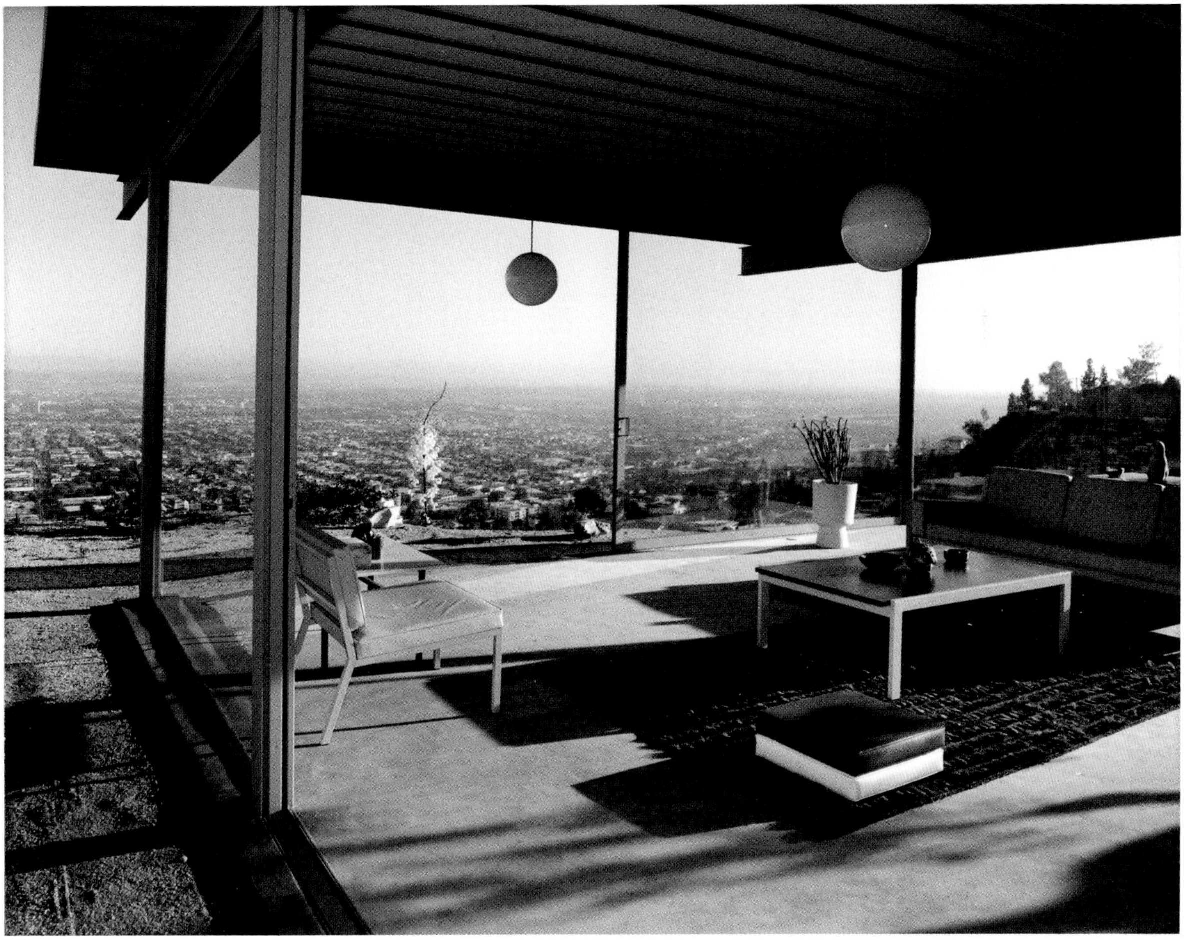

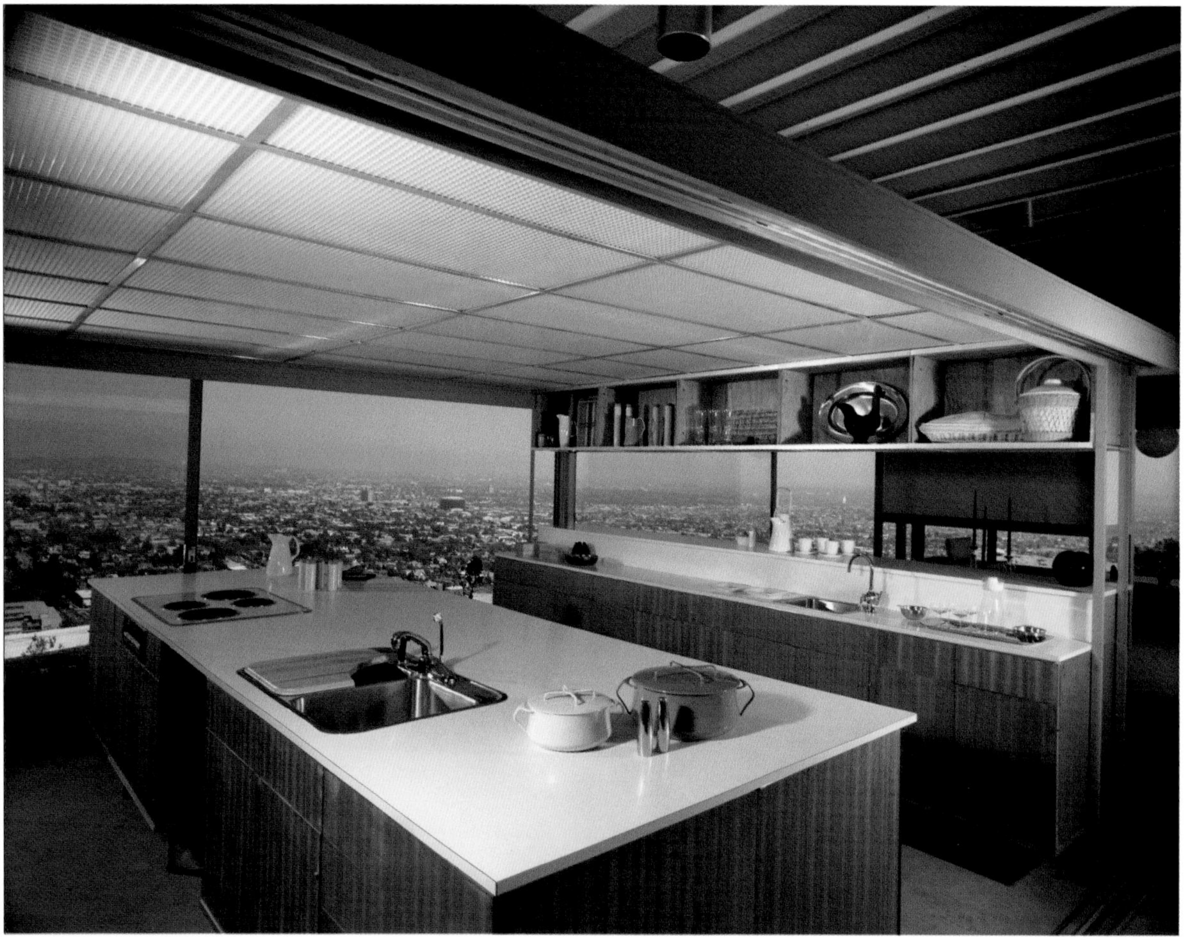

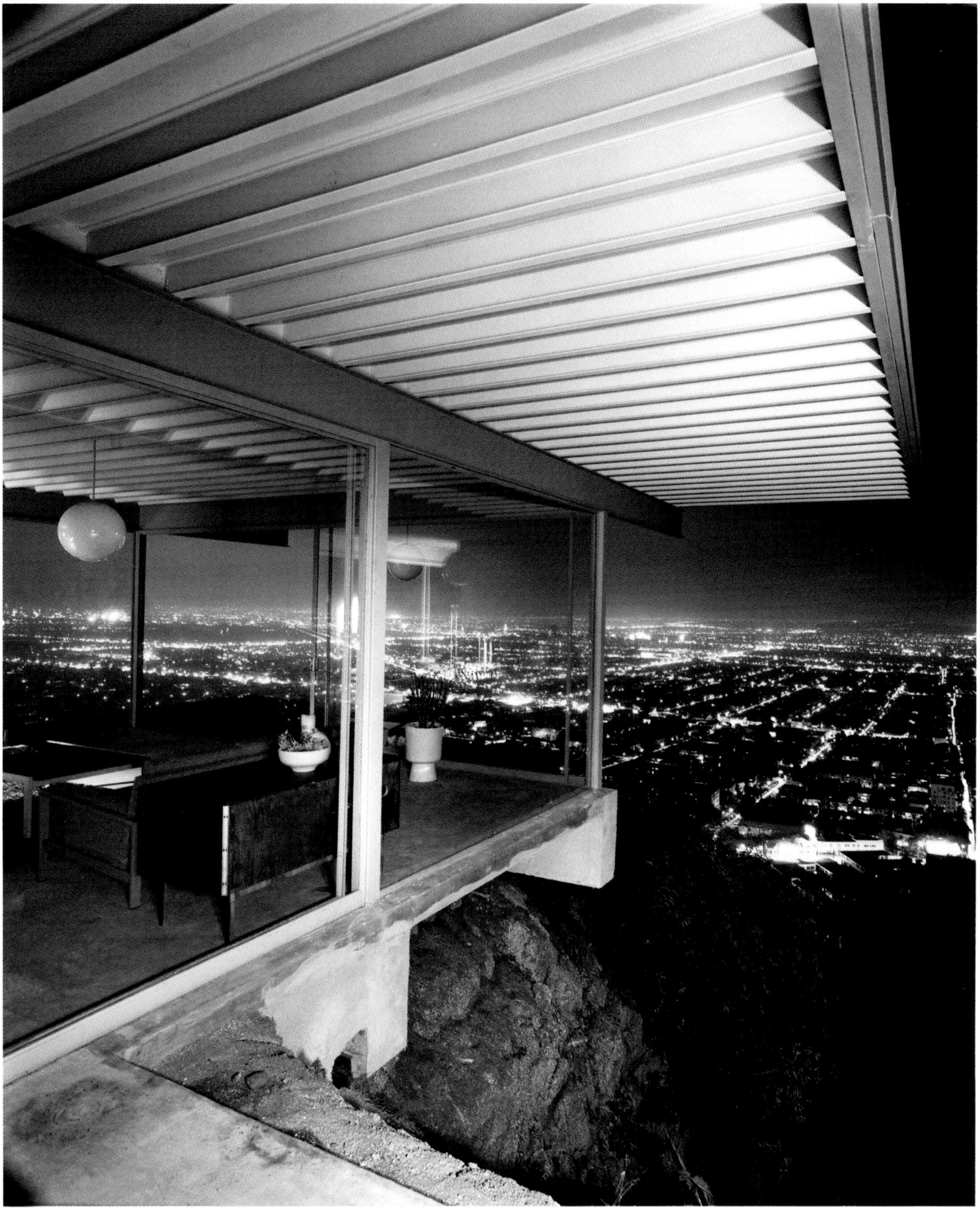

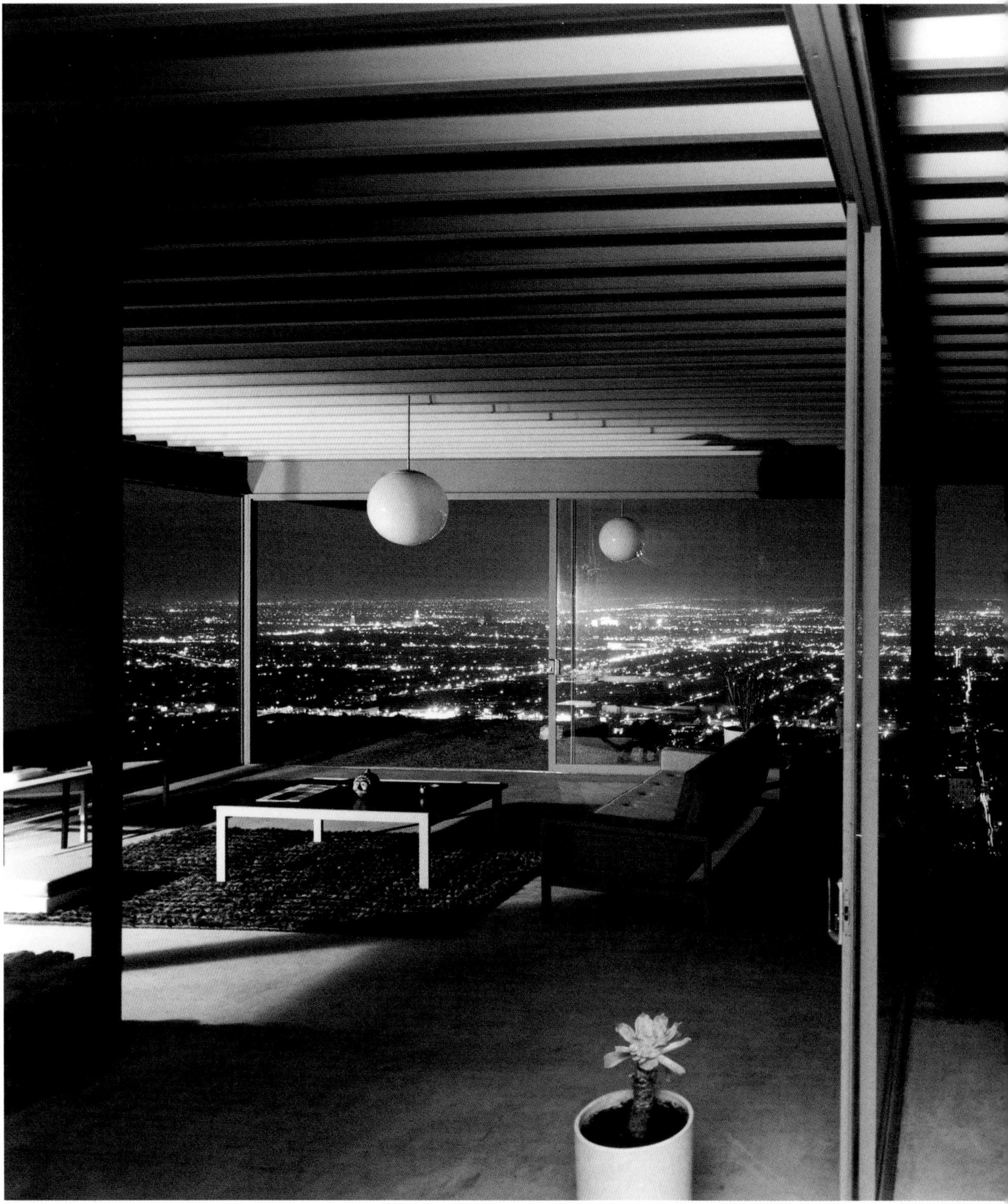

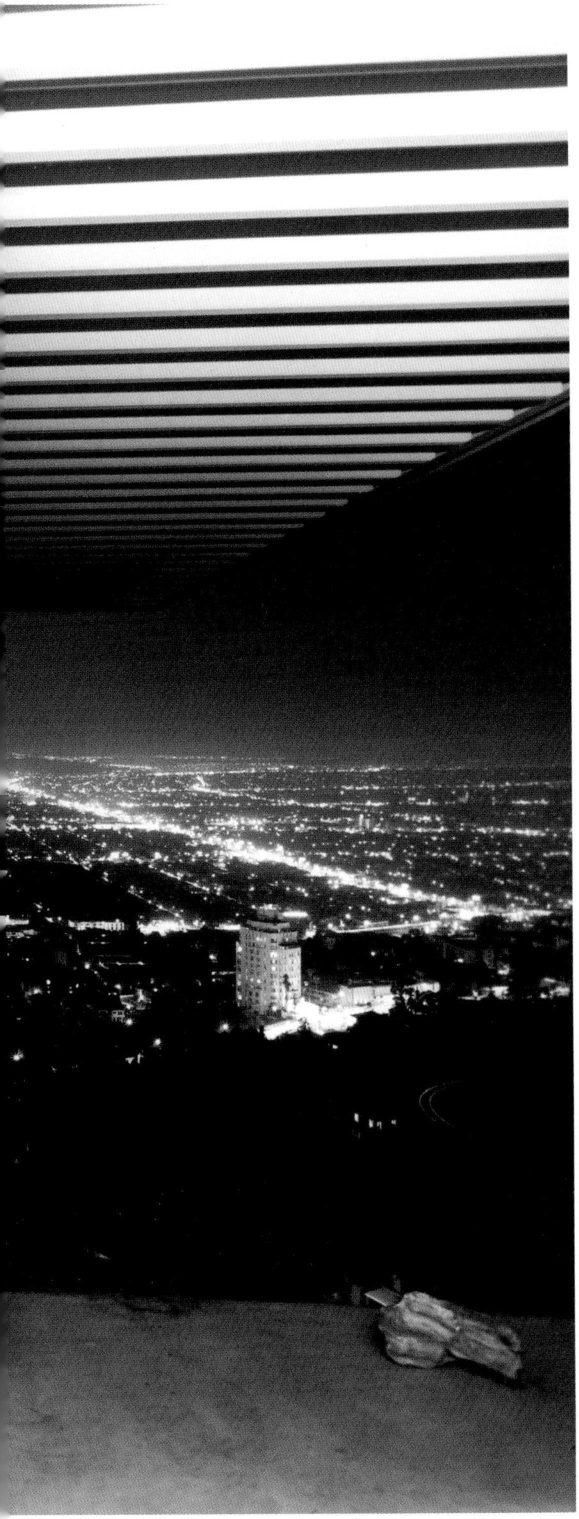

So we worked, and it got dark, and the lights came on, and I think somebody had brought sandwiches. We ate in the kitchen, coffee, and we had a nice, pleasant time. My assistant and I were setting up lights and taking pictures all along. I was outside looking at the view. And suddenly I perceived a composition. Here are the elements. I set up the furniture, and I called the girls. I said, "Girls. Come over, sit down on those chairs, the sofa in the background there." And I planted them there, and I said, "You sit down and talk. I'm going outside and look at the view." And I called my assistant, and I said, "Hey, let's set some lights." Because we used flash in those days. We didn't use floodlights. We set up lights, and I set up my camera and created this composition in which I assembled a statement. It was not an architectural, quote, unquote "photograph." It was a picture of a mood.

—Julius Shulman

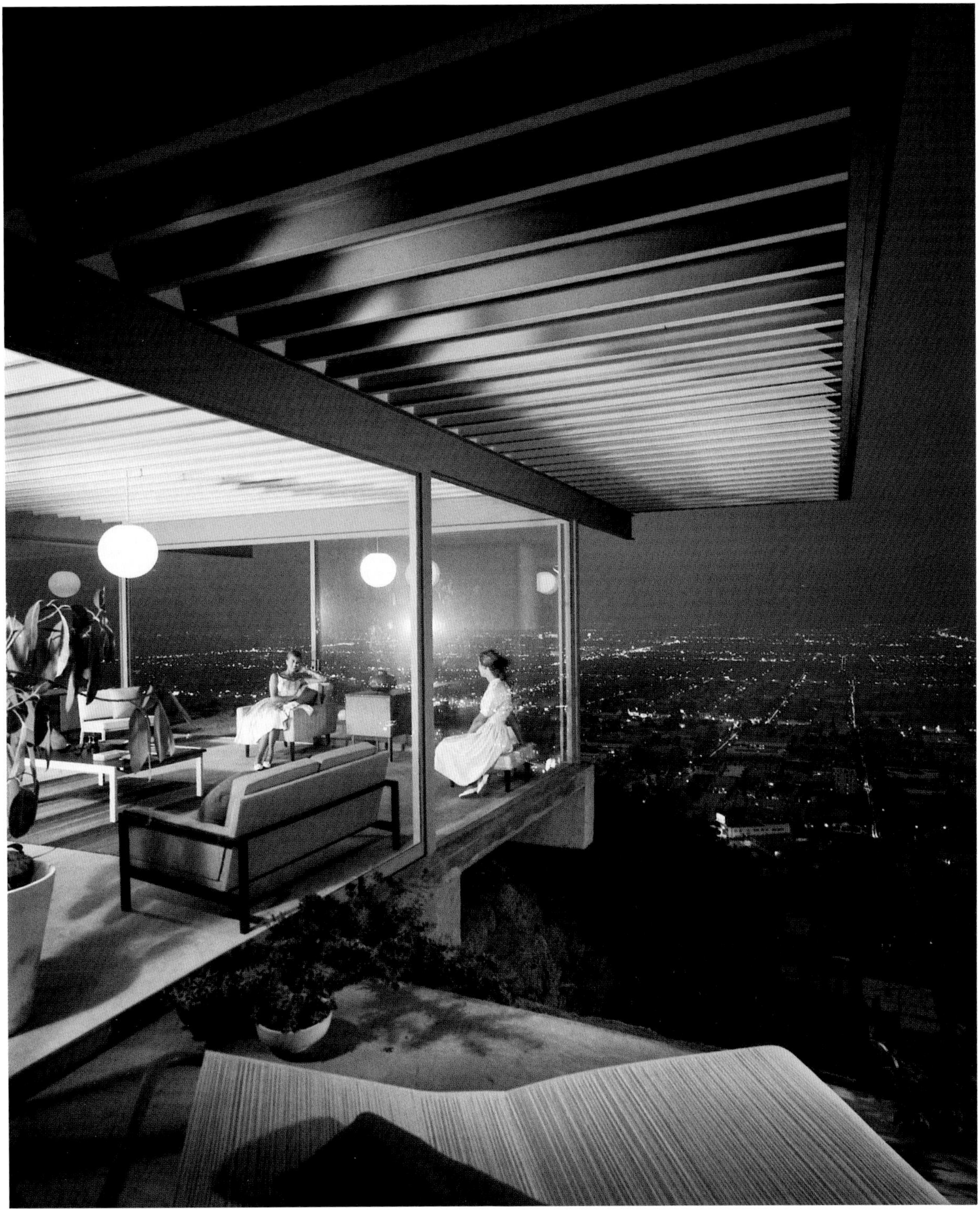

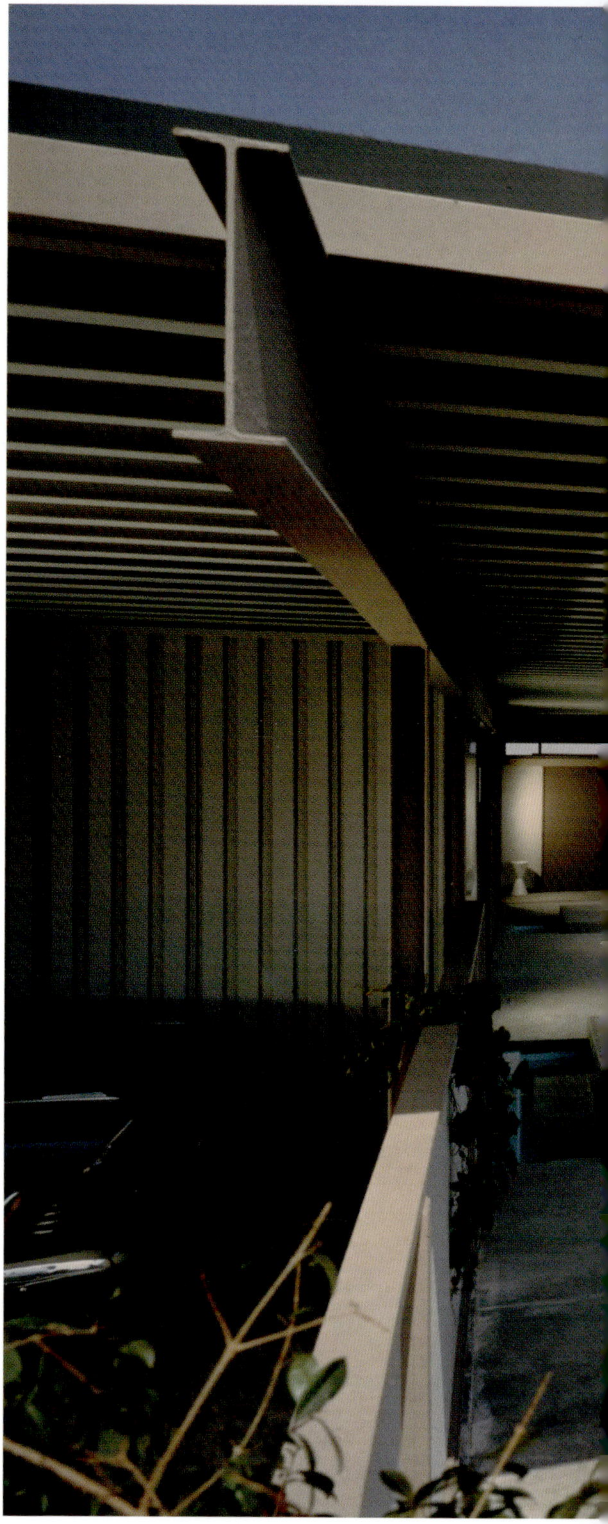

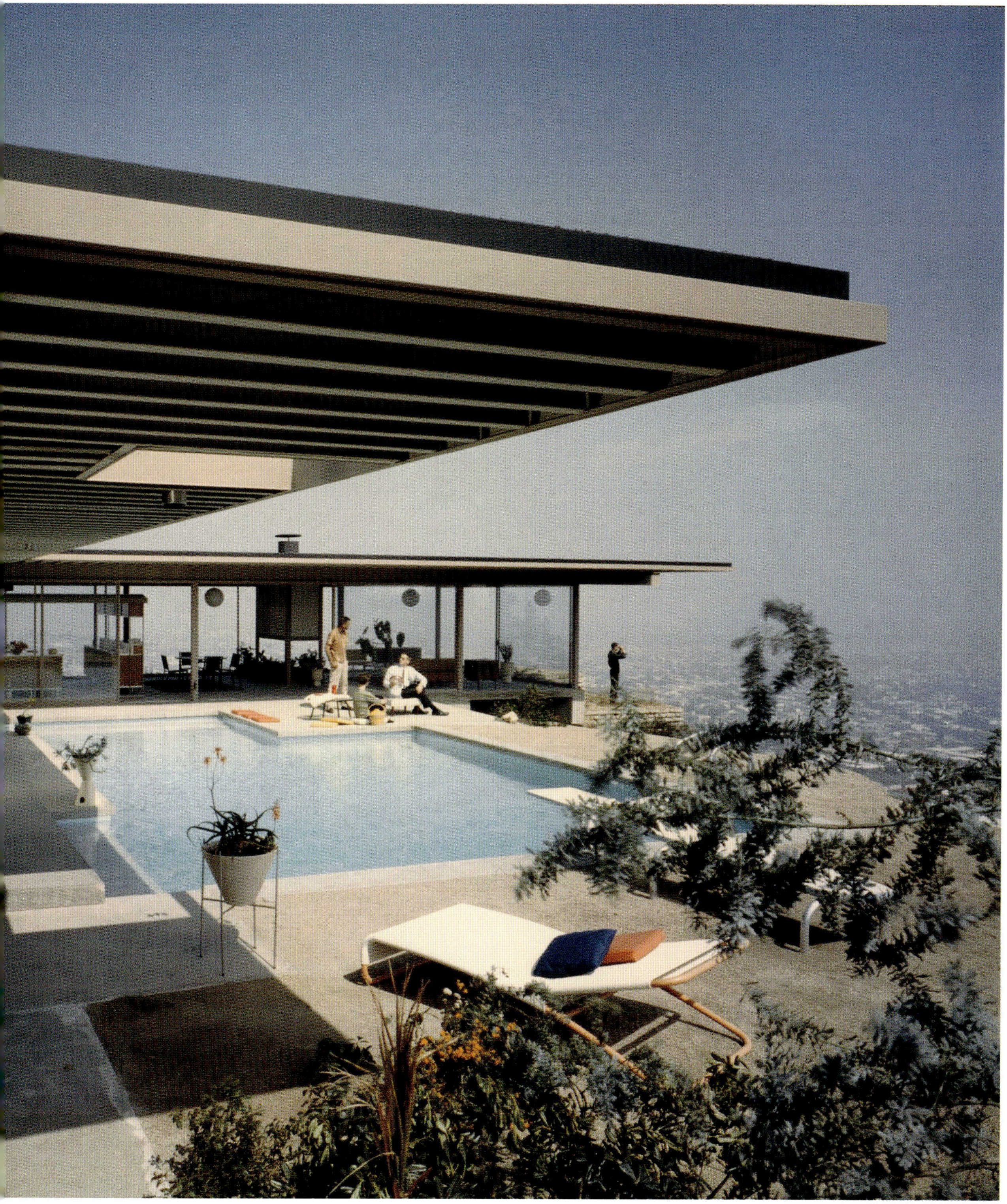

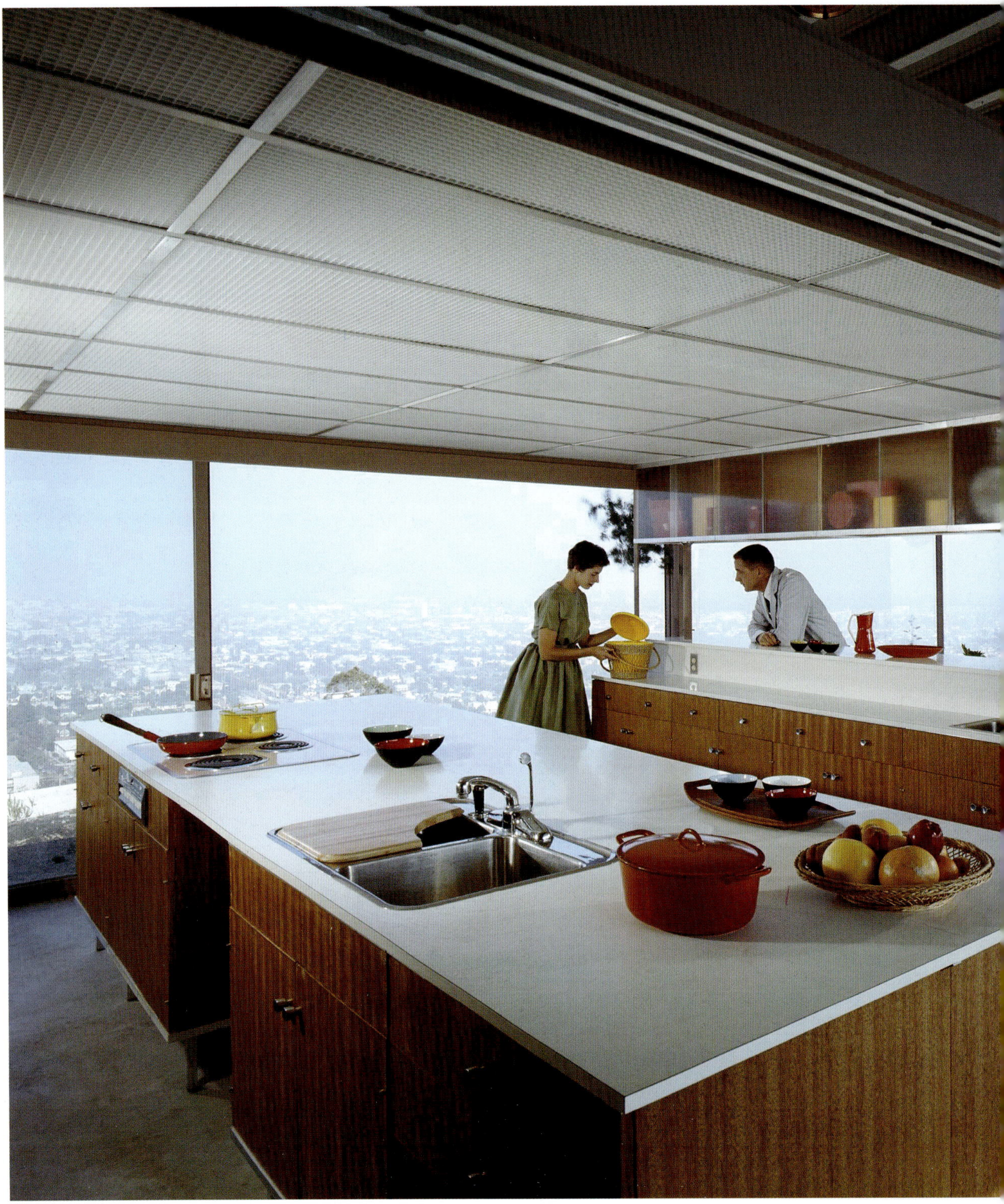

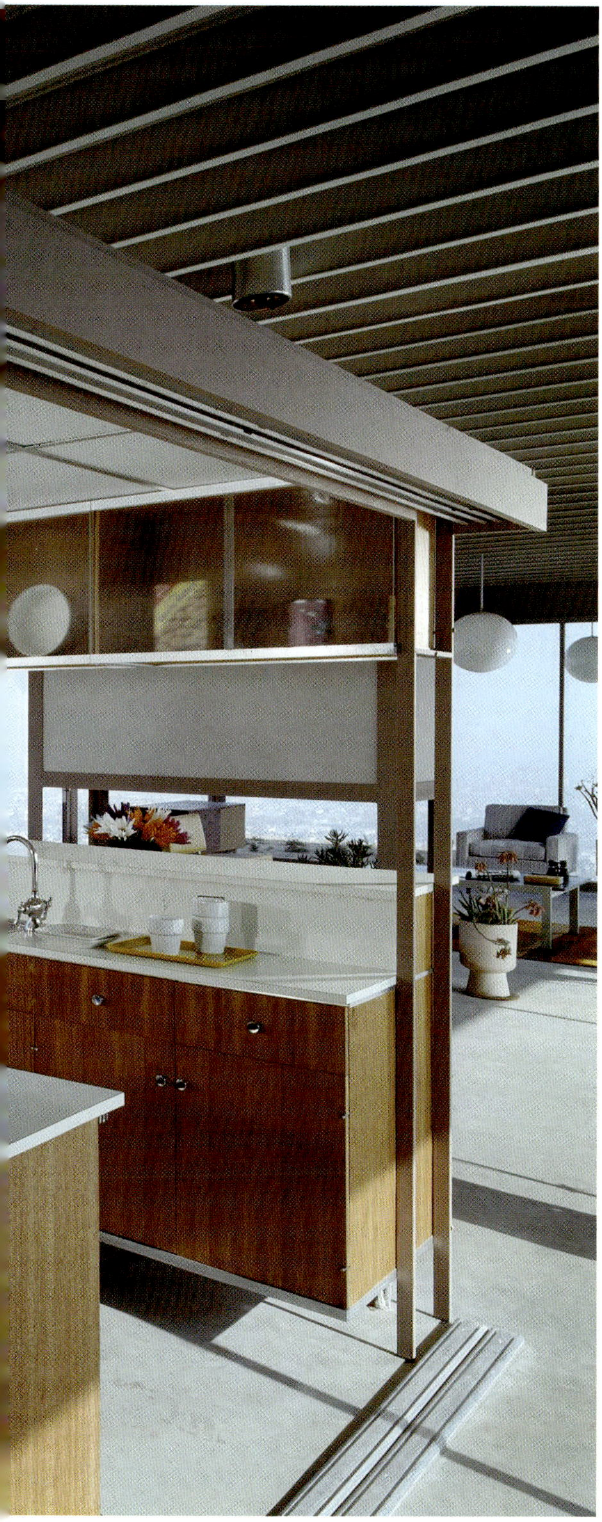

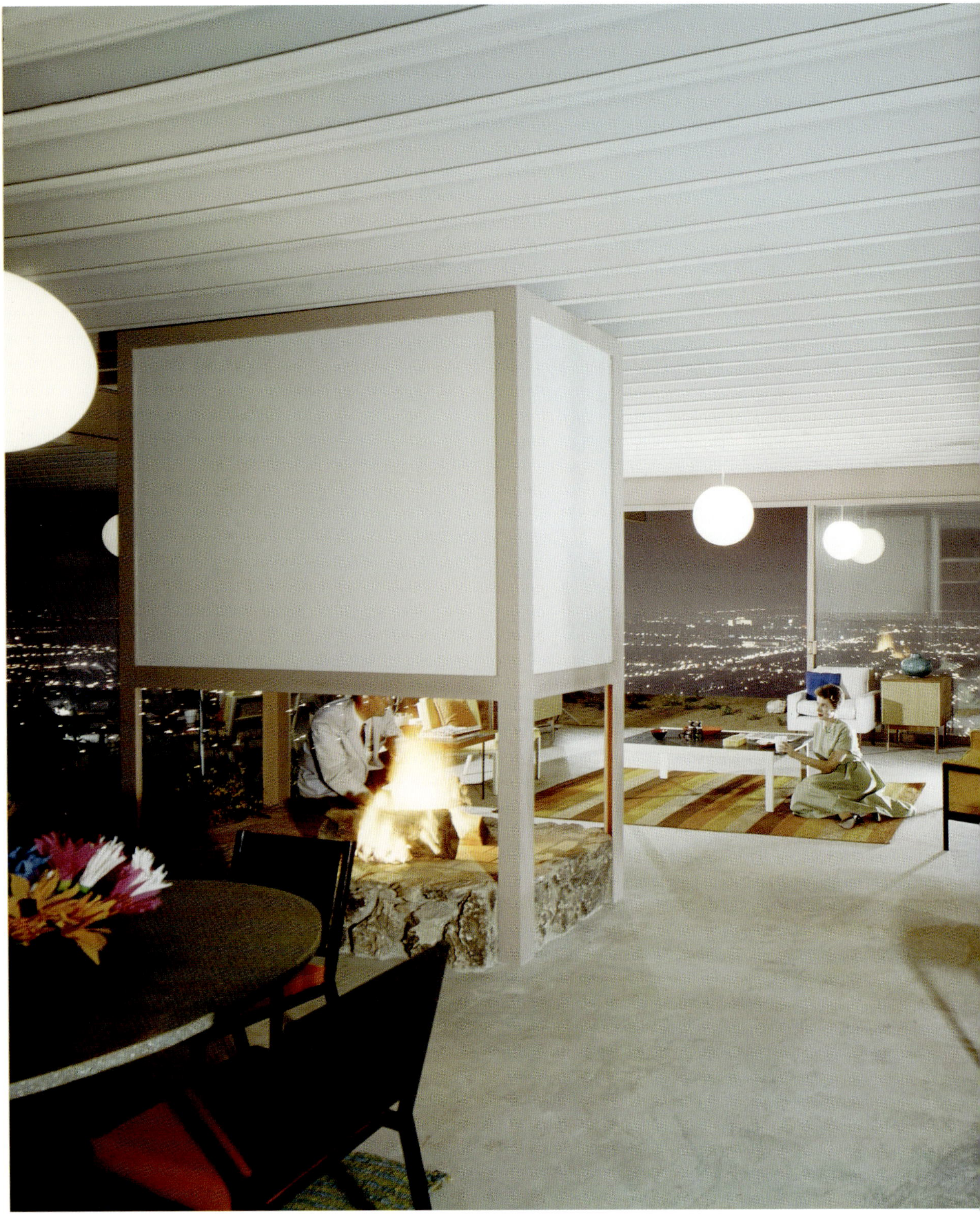

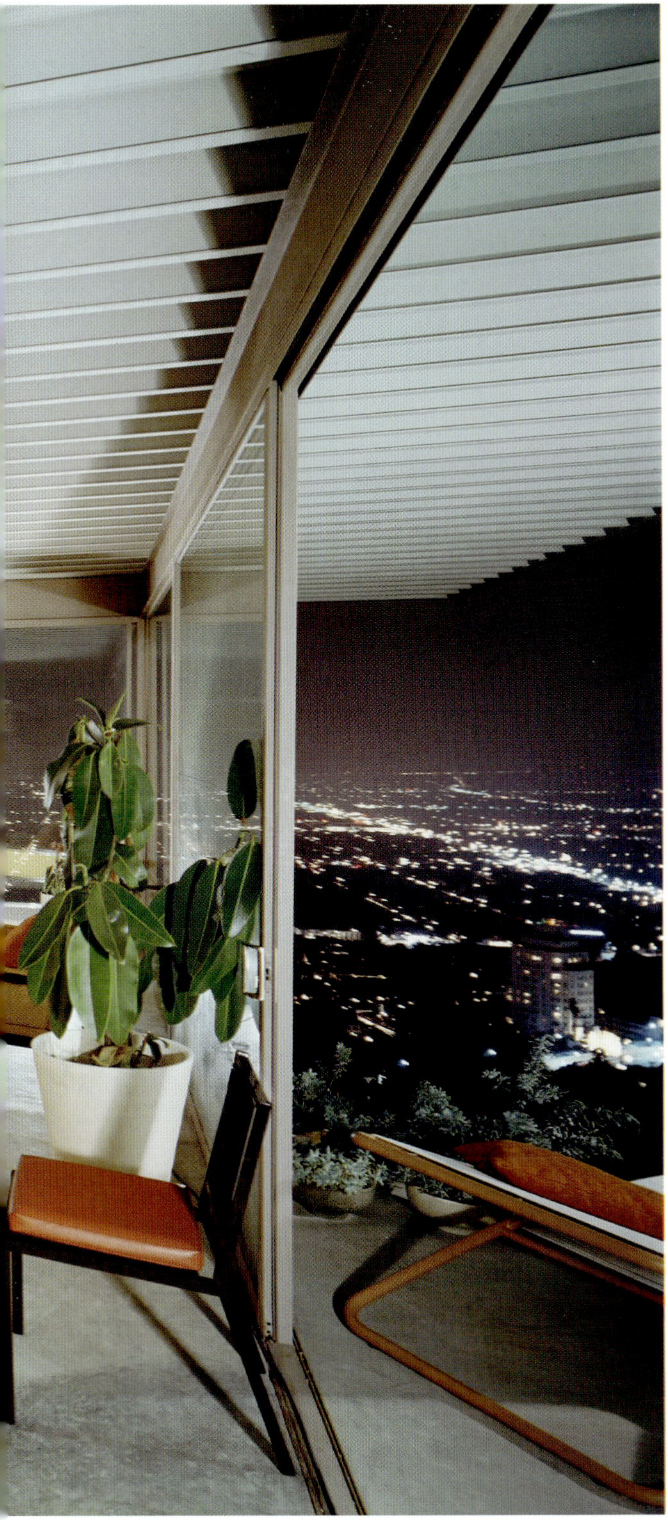

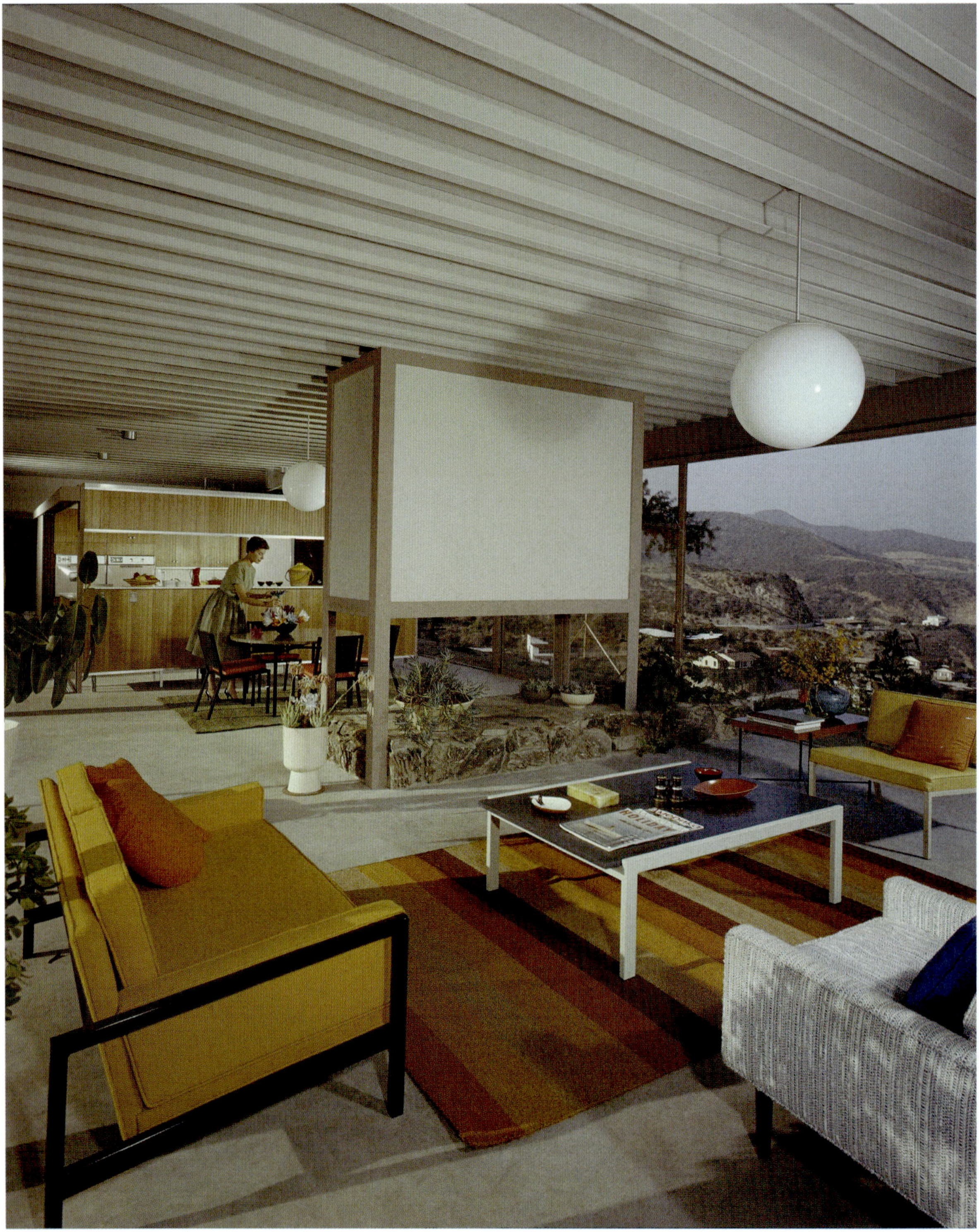

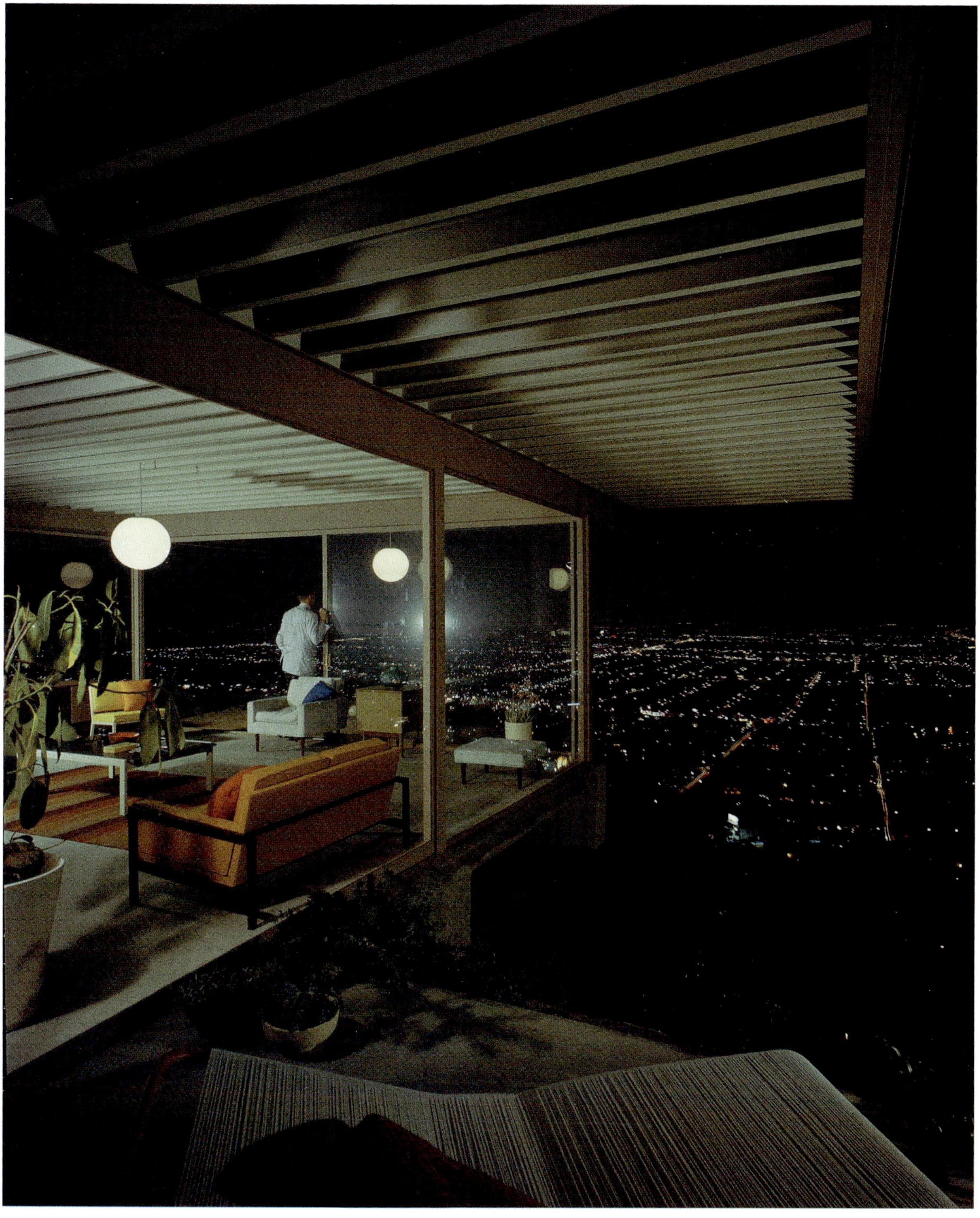

CHAPTER 6
THE GEOMETRY OF HOME

Monday, June 6, 1960, was a misty summer day in Los Angeles, the coastal skies smog-free and veiled with light drizzle. Buck and Carlotta pulled their Cadillac into the carport, walked across the concrete bridges suspended over the pool, slid open the glass door, and stepped onto the cool, concrete floor. They stood inside the walls of glass and slowly spun around, immersed in the panorama. This moment marked the crossing of another threshold: For a husband and wife, their toddler boy and baby girl, Case Study House #22 became home.

The Van Keppel-Green furniture had been hauled away. After the photo shoot, after hundreds of strangers had walked through the house and imagined sitting on those streamlined couches and modern chairs, Carlotta had wistfully watched it all go. "We had the opportunity to buy it, but after building the house, and everything we did, we had to let it go." Even with the Case Study discount, the Stahls could not afford it. Every cent they could save or borrow had gone toward construction, and even then, they'd had to cut corners. But here they were, at last, beginning the life they had imagined while staring up at that empty lot.

On clear mornings, the sun would emerge through the LA city skyline, the horizon a dynamic blend of electric blue, white, and orange. Buck would rise early, pour a cup of black coffee, and roll open the glass walls that opened onto the pool. Carlotta would find him in his favorite spot, the corner stool at the kitchen island, eating a Danish. He worked shirtless in the yard on the weekends and ended the day in the pool, one elbow draped over the south-facing edge with a cocktail in his hand.

Carlotta could often be found in the kitchen, which was outfitted with GE appliances—all pink, including the fridge. Designed as a room-within-a-room, the kitchen had a dropped ceiling that concealed the exhaust fan for the stove as well as a few wires for the kitchen can lights, and also made the space feel more intimate. The island and lower cabinets were slightly raised and seemed to float above the floor. The kitchen was divided from the dining room by a bar-height counter and upper cabinets, with enough space in between them to offer an unbroken sight line to the horizon. On a clear day, Carlotta could stand at her sink and see all the way to Catalina Island.

The movement of the sun through the house shaped the family's daily rhythms. The morning sun warmed their home with honey-colored light. When the house grew stuffy, Carlotta would slide open more walls, inviting a cross breeze that cooled the room instantly. Most days, the door between kitchen and pool remained open, functioning as the main domestic thoroughfare and also the home's front door. When the sun rose high, the roof's large overhangs shaded the rooms from the day's hottest hours. A brilliant choice by Koenig, the 2,300-square-foot house had a roof nearly twice as big, shading it from the midday sun while allowing the morning and evening light to work its magic and reveal the best aspects of their new home. The slanting rays of late-afternoon sunshine glinted off the pool and sent prismatic ribbons of light dancing across the walls and ceiling. Sunsets were magnified by the kaleidoscope of water and glass.

> **It's like standing on a furnished mountaintop—wide open, breeze blowing. All around it's like the whole world is at your feet.**
>
> **—Michael Hicks, family friend**

Bruce and Shari, still toddlers, shared the room beside the carport, which was furnished with a twin bed and a double, populated with dolls and fire trucks. This room was designed to be split in half, with separate dressing areas joined by a Jack-and-Jill bath. The children began each day with a singular ritual—strapping life vests over their pajamas—before they were allowed to leave their room. A wooden sliding door connected their bedroom with the master suite (Buck considered hallways wasted space), but the kids usually ran outside, across the concrete bridges over the pool, to reach the kitchen and living room. There were a few close calls. Shari once rode her tricycle straight into the deep end, where Carlotta spotted her big blue eyes looking up in confusion before diving in to save her. On another occasion, she caught

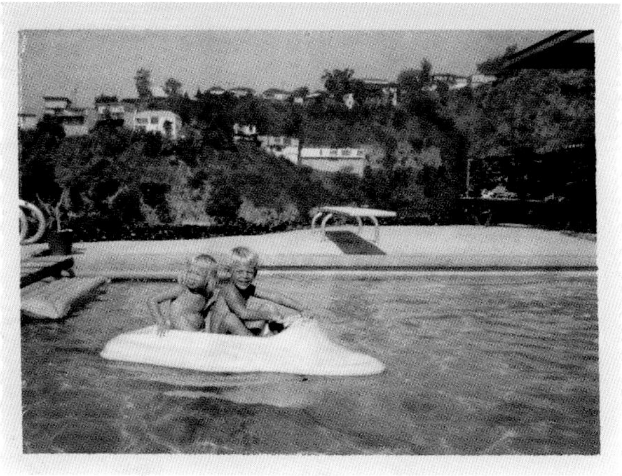

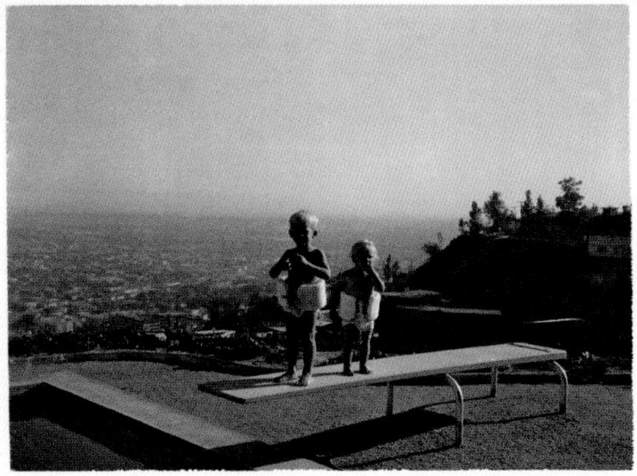

Bruce holding the vacuum cleaner over the pool, stopping him just before he managed to suck out any water.

Buck taught water safety the old-fashioned way—"Sink or swim!"—and soon the kids were amphibious. They loved diving to the bottom of the 9-foot deep end and trying to run across floats without falling in. Some days they didn't even get out of the water for lunch. Carlotta would deliver sandwiches to the edge of the pool, where it was perfect manners to eat with their elbows propped on the concrete. The pool shaped their days, bodies, and souls. Bruce's hair turned to platinum, and Shari's the color of corn silk.

One summer day, Buck propped a metal ladder against the house and climbed onto the flat, steel roof, carefully assisting Bruce and Shari. As the children stood there in their bathing suits with the whole world at their feet, the vast city unfurling from their toes to the sea, the roof seemed like some kind of magic carpet. From here, they could see everything. They could look down upon the backs of hawks soaring over the canyons below. Like the day he and Carlotta first set foot on their lot, Buck felt as if he were standing on an island in a sea of sky. Now he was king of this island.

Buck was the first to jump, landing in the deep end with an epic splash. With nervous excitement, Bruce and Shari inched toward the edge of the roof, which slightly overlapped the edge of the pool below. "Aim for the drain!" Buck called from the water. It was a moment the children would remember forever, this first leap of faith.

"We were really young, like five or six," Shari said. "It was so scary and exciting." That moment in the air, suspended between steel and splash, was something like flying, or falling off the edge of the world.

The house, meanwhile, began its own arc toward fame. In June it appeared in an eight-page story in *Arts & Architecture*, which featured one drawing of Pierre Koenig's plan and sixteen photos by Julius Shulman (plus another in the back of the magazine, featured in an ad for Catalina Pool Co.). Those photos did not include the now-famous image of the "Two Girls" photo, as Shulman and others referred to it. The *Arts & Architecture* photos were devoid of people, except for one wide-angle image in which two figures appear in the background, on the patio by the pool—so small that on first glance it's easy to miss them or mistake them for furniture.

The image Shulman would consider "one of my masterpieces" would not appear in print until August 1960, when it ran—in vibrant color—on the cover of *Pictorial Living*. The magazine feature included eleven photos of the house, five of them in color, tied together by pops of orange in the Van Keppel-Green couches, area rug, and dining-room chairs, and a fire glowing in the hearth. In several shots, a male and female model stood in for the mister and missus of the household. The presence of people and the warmth of color added a "picture yourself here" element that made the Stahl House feel more inviting, more like a home.

Amid pages with ads for Parliament cigarettes and Betty Crocker cake mix, the article, titled "A Milestone in Steel," made no mention of the Case Study House Program. But it echoed John Entenza's ideas, praising "revolutionaries" like Koenig for their vision in creating "machine-built houses which would be better and cheaper than today's product." Koenig predicted in the story that steel would be fabricated in an increasing array of components, enabling "an almost infinite variety of house designs available in steel."

The writer (unnamed) described Koenig's design as "a vast steel umbrella" that provided "an unbroken view of more than 200 square miles." It was one of the few publications that acknowledged Buck's sweat equity, mentioning the "dozens of weekends terracing the steep south and west slopes with sections of discarded paving." The story contained a few errors, including a mention of the "two young Stahl boys" sharing a room that "can be divided in two with a sliding panel." But it showcased the house beautifully and declared this "milestone on a hilltop" as a harbinger of the future of American homebuilding. "This house," the story declared, "shows how steel can have a future in housing."

After appearing on the cover of *Pictorial Living*, Julius Shulman's photograph began to collect awards. In 1960, the American Institute of Architects announced its first-ever award for a color photograph, and first prize went to a full-color version of Shulman's "Two Girls" photo. The Smithsonian Institution included it in a traveling show exhibited at nearly a dozen museums and art galleries around the country from 1962 to 1964. The photograph then faded into relative obscurity for nearly a decade.

As their home was being shown in museums and art galleries, Bruce and Shari were busy being kids. They raced across the concrete floors on roller skates with metal wheels and smudged the windows with fingerprints. When they weren't swimming or picking tarantulas and scorpions out of the pool, they were poking around in the dirt that sloped away beneath their floating living room. Once they were old enough to roam, Buck built a chain-link fence to keep them from falling off the cliff, where they loved to go "on safari." The surrounding hills had no trails and very few houses, and they often hiked to a favorite tree. With the discovery of matches came the joy of setting fire to twigs. "I'm surprised we didn't set the hill ablaze," Shari said. Once, Bruce tied Shari's Barbie to a skateboard, struck a match, and sent her streaking downhill like a comet. Shari was incensed. But there weren't a lot of kids on Woods Drive, so she eventually forgave him.

With a large portion of their income going to the house, Buck and Carlotta had little money left for furnishings, so what they couldn't afford, Buck either built or reconditioned. He enjoyed bargain shopping for damaged furnishings at Levitz Furniture and fixing it up in the carport. He constructed the kids' nightstands from scratch and, as a gift for Carlotta, transformed a pile of scrap wood into a frame for a painting of wild horses. A child of the Depression, he scavenged scrap wood and saved used nails, hammering bent ones straight and storing them in coffee cans and peanut butter jars. When someone gave them an odd-sized mattress, even bigger than a California King, he built a bed frame to fit it. "Mom had to buy fabric and sew sheets for the bed, since you couldn't buy any that size," Shari said. Carlotta also stitched most of the children's clothes on her sewing machine in the master bedroom.

While some might call the Stahl family "house-poor," they considered themselves cash-poor and house-rich. They rarely went out to eat, and the only family vacation they could afford was a road trip to San Diego (they stayed with Carlotta's parents in Mission Bay, where they had retired and purchased a modest trailer close to the water). But they lived in a house that made every day feel like a holiday. Over the carport entrance, Buck hung a sign he built out of white Romex cable twisted into free-form cursive letters that spelled out *Isle of Sky*.

By understating the structure, a balanced relationship has been established between house, pool, sky, and view. In this project, a happy combination of site, soil, height, and location combined to suggest a solution in which it was possible to take advantage of all elements without the necessity of compromising the design.

—*Arts & Architecture*, June 1960

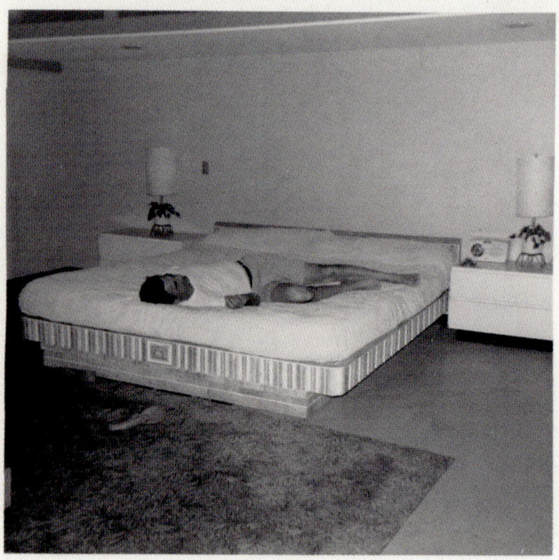

The 1960s marked the end of one era and the birth of another in Los Angeles, where the conformity of the 1950s began to intersect with more freewheeling and creative attitudes. Over the course of the decade, Pacific Electric trolleys and passenger trains gave way to the rise of the freeways. LAX unveiled the Los Angeles Theme Building, a space-age spider of a structure that embodied the Googie architectural style. Downtown buildings stretched skyward, and from their living room, Buck and Carlotta witnessed the rise of a skyline in Century City. The Dodgers built a vast stadium in Elysian Park.

Even as some men began to be shipped to Vietnam, other young people started growing out their hair as the Summer of Love approached. The Beach Boys began crooning earnestly about surfing, cars, and girls. Whisky a Go Go, a hot new nightclub on the Sunset Strip, began booking a new band called the Doors. Laurel Canyon, not far from the Stahl House, was becoming the epicenter of a new wave of music, home to Joni Mitchell, Neil Young, the Eagles, and many more artists who would create the soundtrack of the 1960s and '70s. Two members of the Mamas and the Papas, a folk-rock vocal group famous for the counterculture anthem "California Dreamin'," briefly lived in the house across the street from the Stahl House, where they were welcomed as neighbors. "My father told us they loved hanging out by the pool and walking around naked," Shari said.

Once again, Los Angeles was being reinvented to suit a new age. Historic buildings were torn down to make room for new construction, and architectural preservationists formed the Los Angeles City Cultural Heritage Board. New houses popped up in the Hollywood Hills like mushrooms after a rain. Once empty lots now buzzed with construction, and Buck loved walking through newly framed houses with the kids, pointing out pipes and floor plans and asking, "What room do you think this is?" Conservative lenders were letting go of their qualms about underwriting "cliff dwellers," and property values rose as houses "in the hills" became as fashionable as candy-colored muscle cars.

The Stahl House suddenly seemed emblematic of this new era. In February 1962, *Life* magazine published a photograph of Buck dangling over the city, tending to his terraces with a rope tied around his waist, for a story called "California's Dizzy Hillside Homes." The rope was a prop for dramatic effect, not something he actually used. His kids would later tease him about the loafers and Bermuda shorts he put on for the shoot—they were used to seeing him shirtless, in jeans, while working in the yard.

In 1962, the Stahl House made its film debut in *Smog*, a black-and-white Italian drama by director Franco Rossi. The movie depicted an Italian attorney who spends a day in Los Angeles while waiting for a visa. Attending a party with Italians living in LA, he meets a beautiful Italian woman who lives in a house that seems to float above the city. Their brief affair plays out at the house and in the pool. The Stahl House proved to be the perfect location, but the city of LA and its famous smog didn't quite cooperate. "When they came up, it was a clear day," Carlotta said. "So they had to spray gunk on the windows to make it look like you were looking out at smog."

In the film, the Stahl House transcended the role of an average location. It became a character in and of itself, capable of projecting a spectrum of nuanced moods and personalities. In morning light, with Girl Scouts knocking on the glass to sell cookies for fifty cents a box, it was wholesome and earnest. With late-afternoon sun dancing on the pool, its waters trembling around the embracing couple, it was sensual. At night, the glowing pool enveloped the female star with a pulsing light that hinted at things not shown on screen. *Smog* was far from a blockbuster, but it was an effective screen test that demonstrated the role the Stahl House could play in a film.

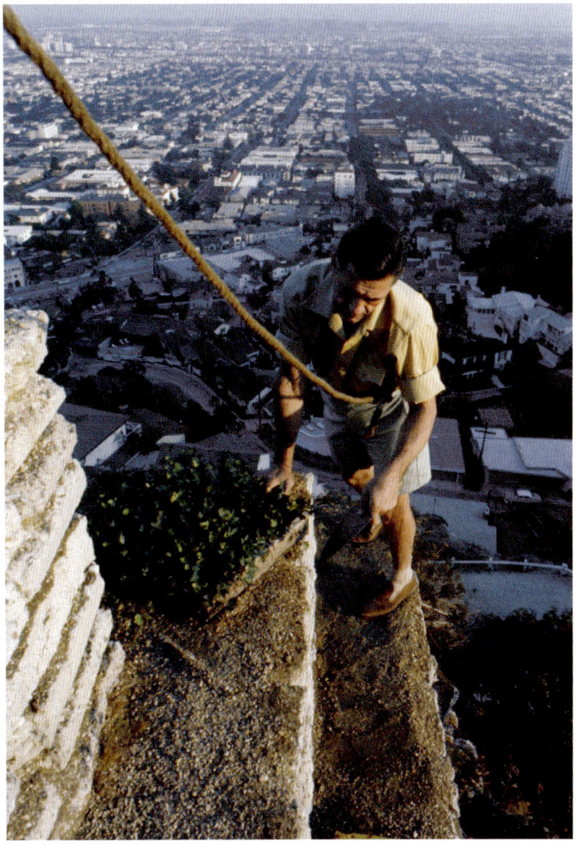

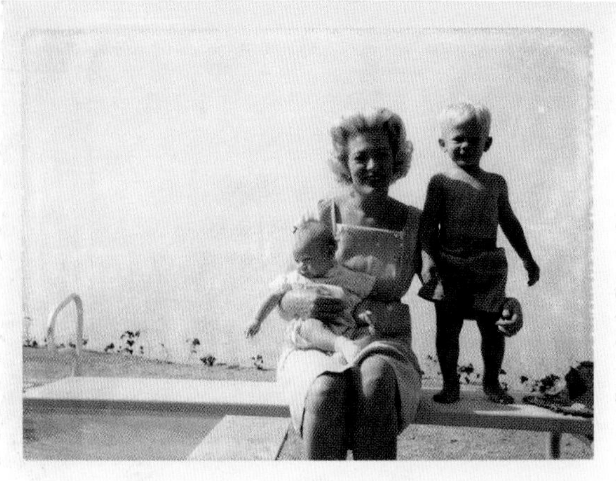

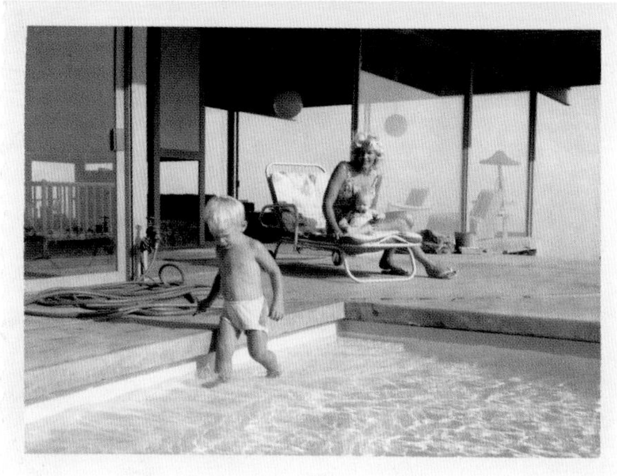

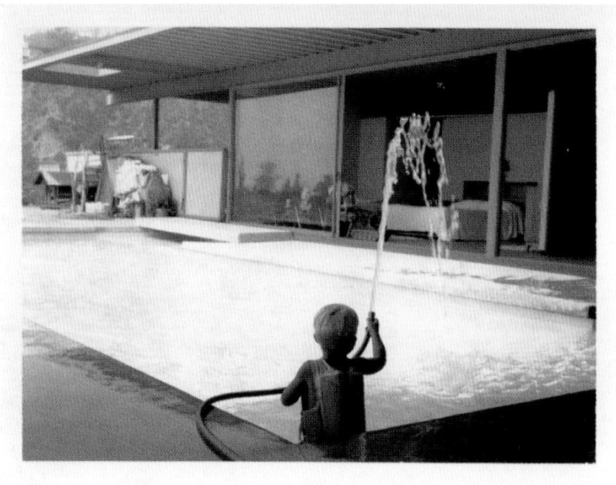

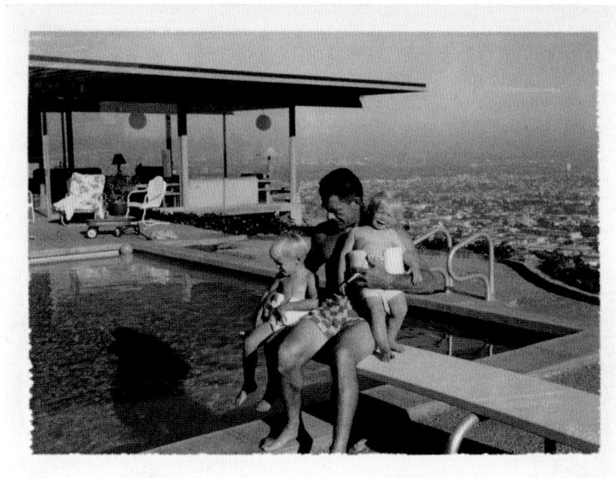

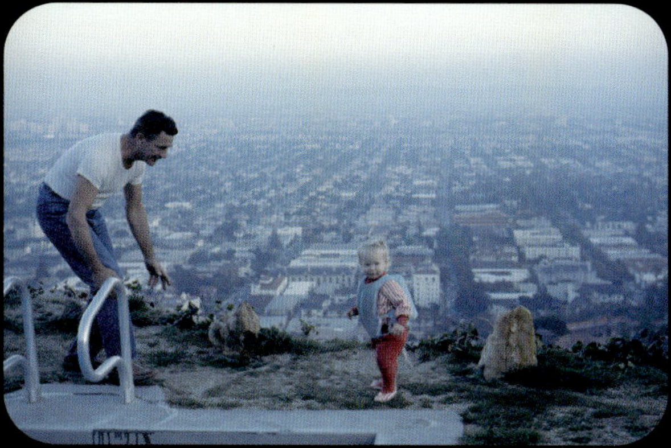
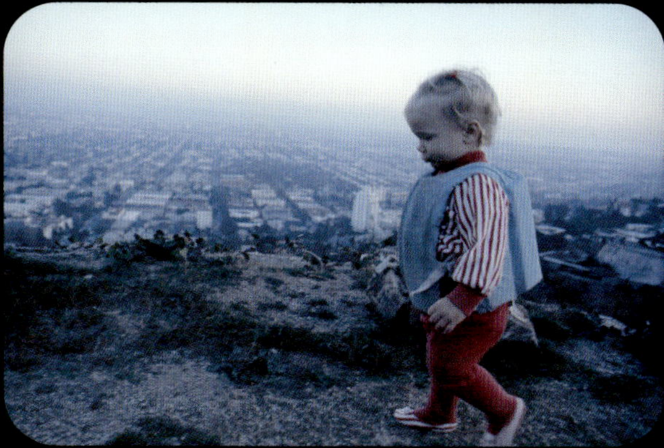
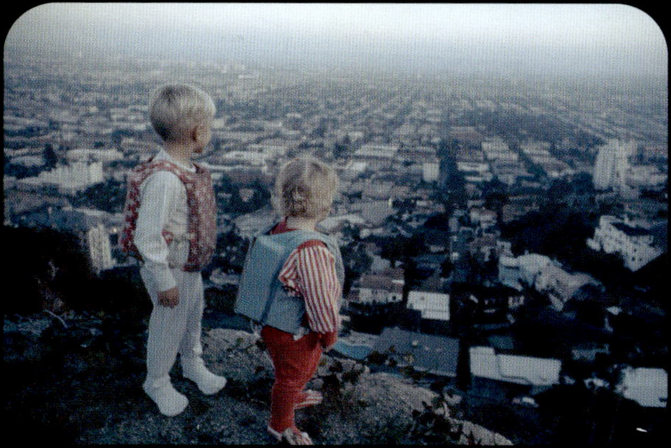
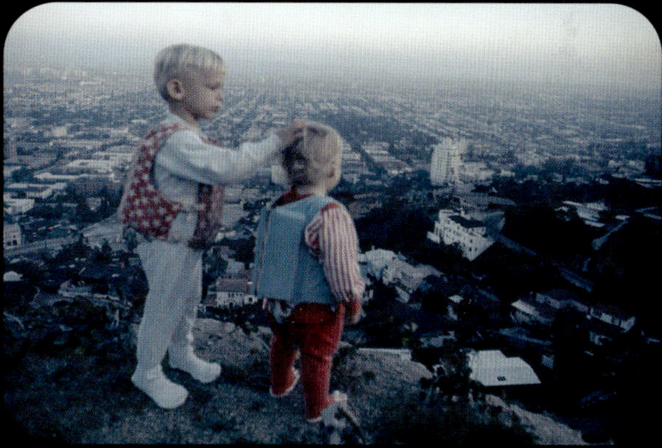
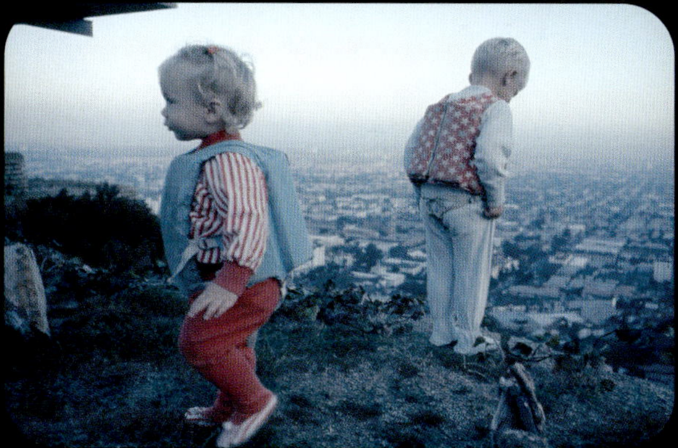
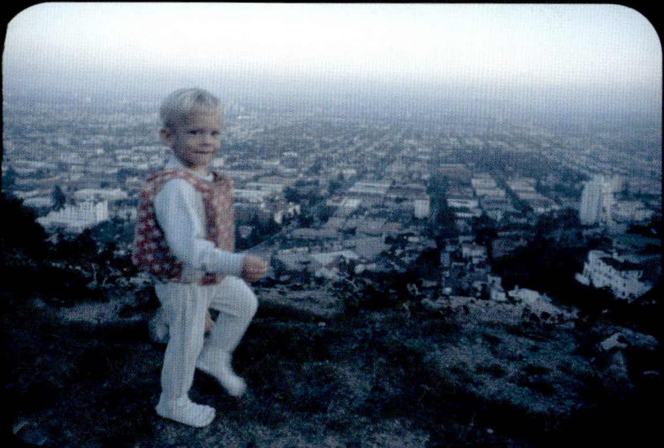

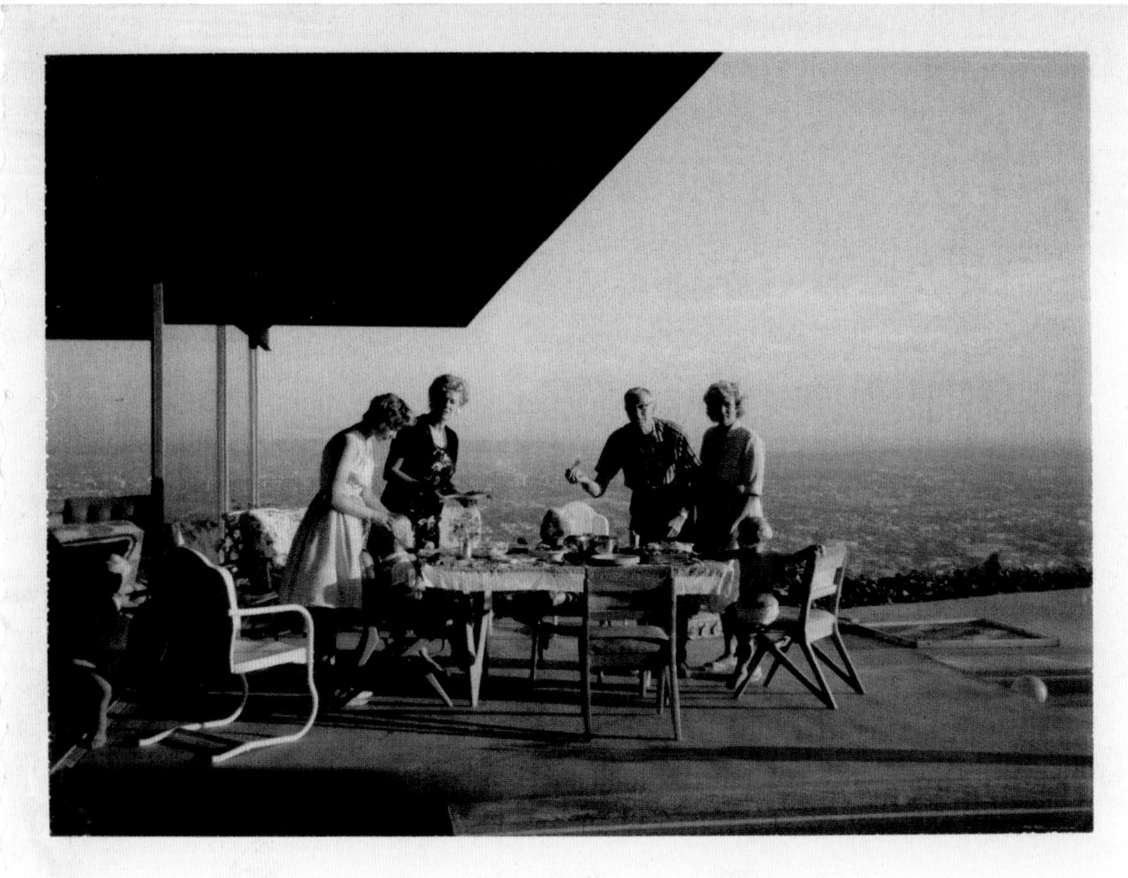

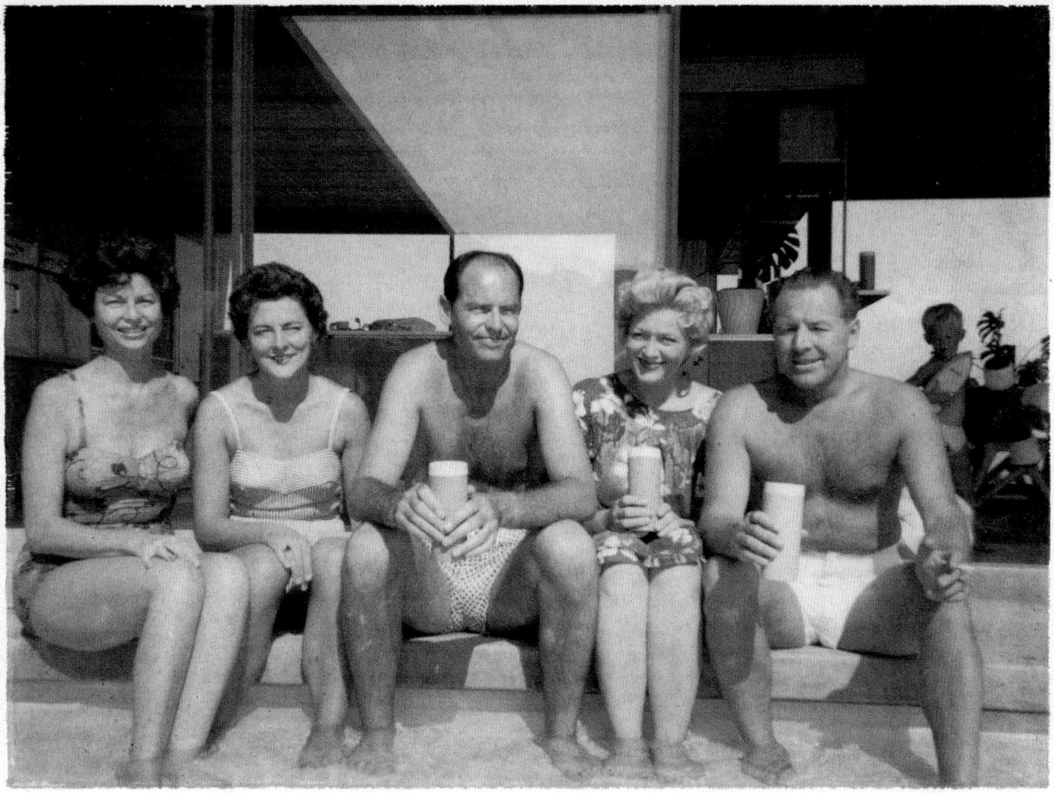

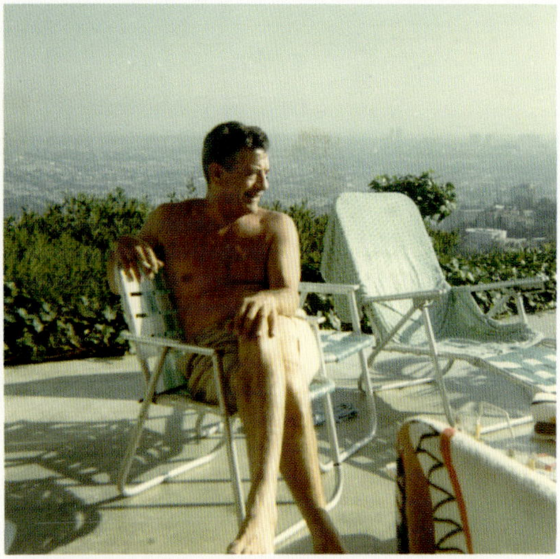

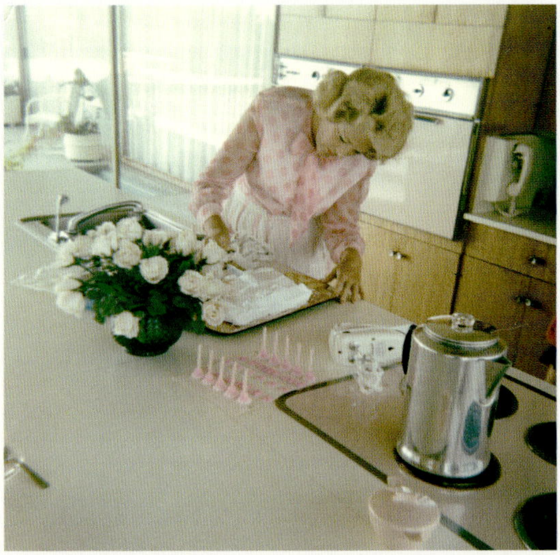

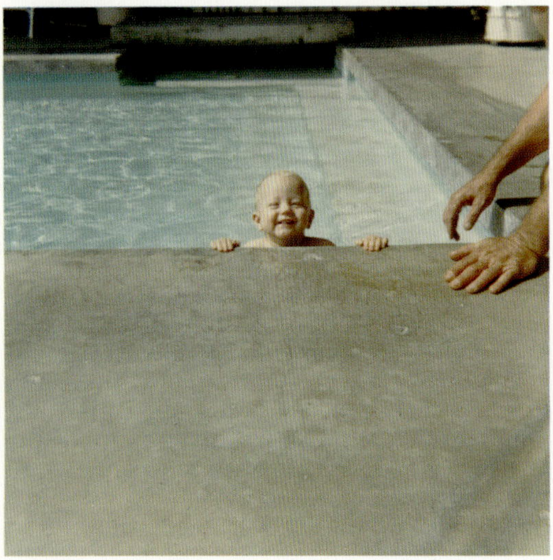

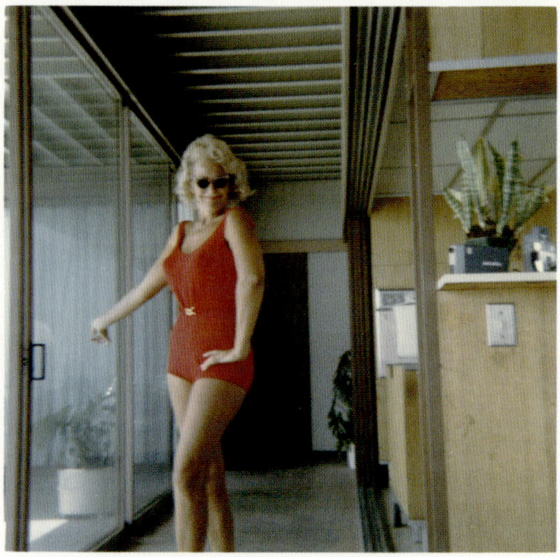

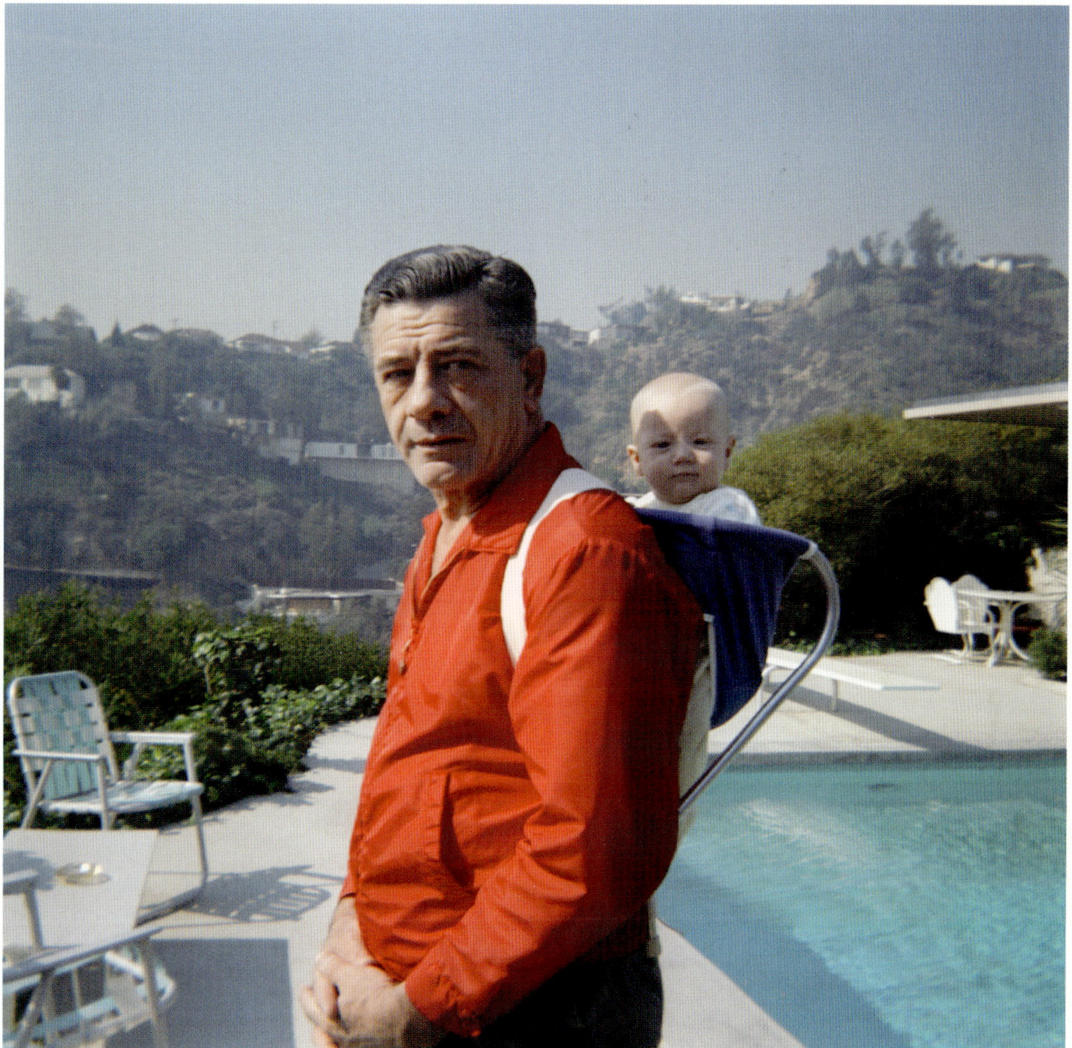

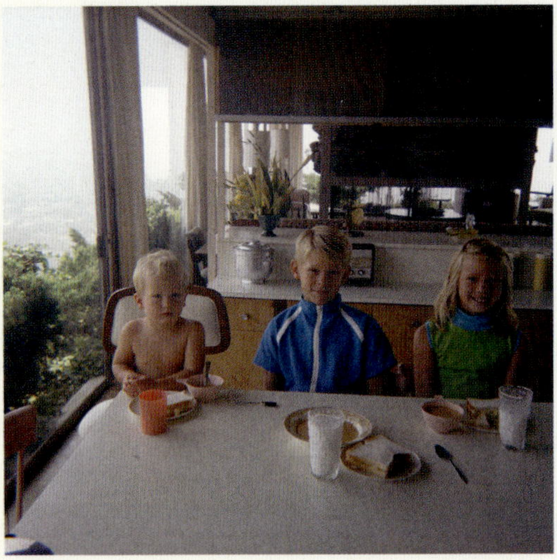

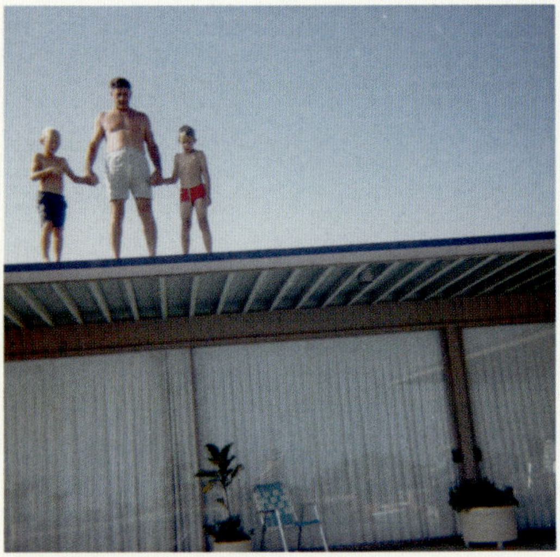

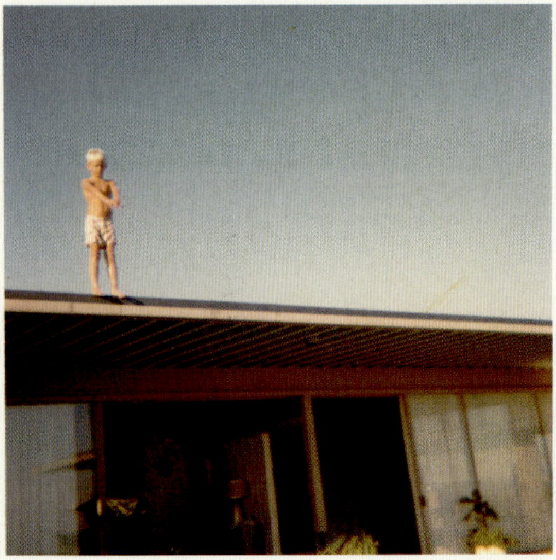

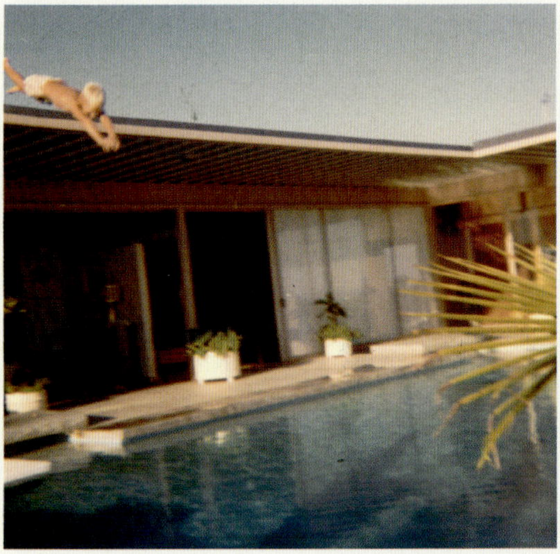

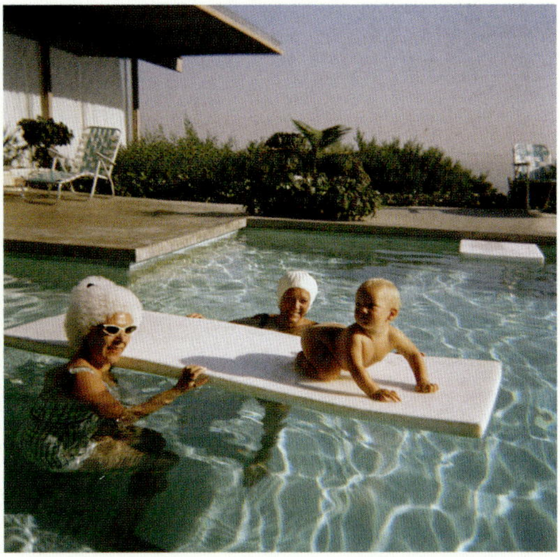

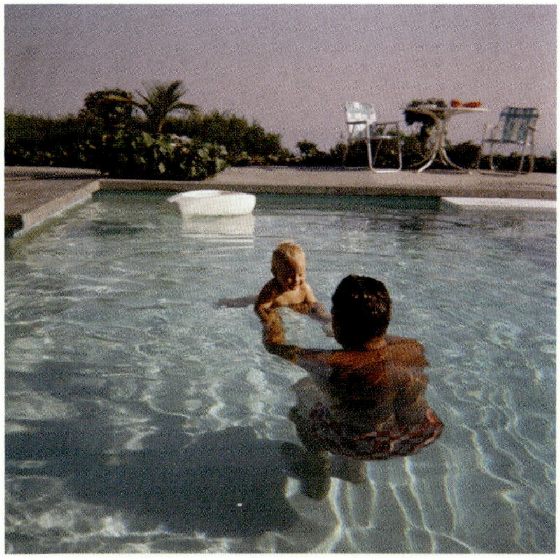

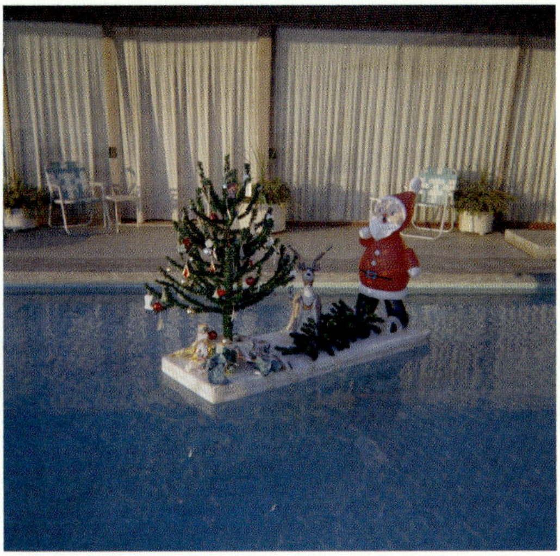

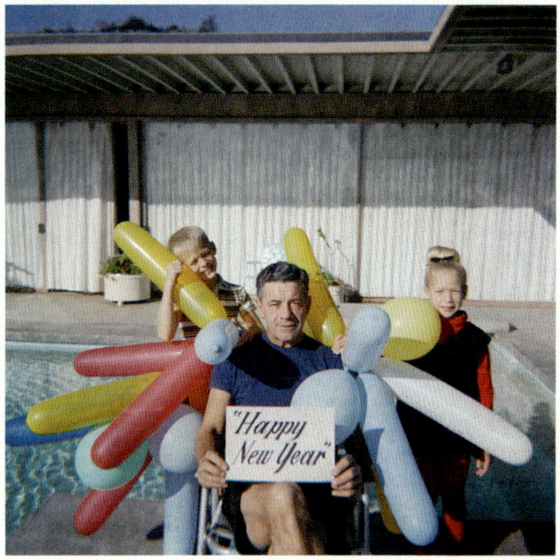
"Happy New Year"

But the house was not really on Hollywood's radar. Six years passed before its next on-screen appearance as the set of "Prescription: Murder," a 1968 pilot for the TV series *Columbo*. Starring Peter Falk as Lieutenant Columbo, a homicide detective in the Los Angeles Police Department, *Columbo* came to be regarded as one of the greatest TV shows of all time. In the pilot, a psychiatrist kills his wife with the help of his mistress (one of his patients), who acts as his alibi. In a dramatic scene, detectives wheel the body out of the Stahl House, steering the gurney beside the pool.

Bruce and Shari remember milling about the crew and cast during the filming of *Columbo*, posing for snapshots with Peter Falk, Gene Barry, and Katherine Justice (who played the mistress). "I just thought she was so pretty," Shari said. "Getting to take a picture with her, I felt very special." It would dawn on her later that this sort of thing didn't happen at her friends' houses.

By then, there was a new member of the family. On September 21, 1966, when Bruce was eight and Shari was six, Carlotta gave birth to Mark Henry Stahl, an unexpected but welcome addition to the family. The baby prompted the next Stahl house riddle: How do you fit a family of five in a two-bedroom, 2,300-square-foot house? Initially, the baby slept in a crib in Carlotta's closet—a spacious closet with drapes instead of doors. In May 1968, Buck divided the kids' room in half with a custom-built wooden partition, with hinged bunk beds that flipped up out of the way. Shari decorated her pink half with dolls and horses. Mark and Bruce shared the other half, wallpapered with cowboys and Indians.

On many holidays, Carlotta's brother, Bud, would come over with his wife and three children, who were the same ages as their cousins. As Buck flipped burgers on the backyard grill, the kids would play Marco Polo, hiding under the concrete bridges where "it was shallow, like a little cave," Shari said. Her grandfather, Carlton, loved to fling handfuls of coins into the pool, mixing collector's items with pocket change. The six kids would dive in at once, a tradition more beloved than Easter egg hunts. One day, when it was just Carlton and Bruce, the old man held out a special prize—a 1902 Morgan silver dollar—and told seven-year-old Bruce that if he dove off the roof, it would be his medal of honor. "I still have that coin," Bruce said half a century later, recalling his grandfather's praise: "Thatta boy!"

The kids never spent the coins they plucked from the deep end, some of which were quite valuable. It was Carlton's way of exposing them to his love of numismatics, and a tradition they would continue with their own children. When it came to money, they had learned from their parents that it was never to be taken for granted, even in times of relative plenty.

With the pool and the personal loan paid off, and occasional extra income from shoots and location fees, money was no longer quite so tight. Buck had found steady work for two decades in the aerospace industry, the nation's second-largest manufacturing employer behind the automobile industry. Around the time Mark was born, he left his job at Garrett Corporation to start his own company, Specialty Seal Co., which sold O-rings and gaskets to aerospace manufacturers. Recognized in a corporate brochure as a leading regional distributor of OmniSeal products, he was asked the secret to his impressive numbers. "Once you've sold an OmniSeal in a given company, permeate it," he said.

Carlotta, staying home with the kids, embodied the ideal of the 1960s housewife. "She was like the mom on *The Brady Bunch*," recalled Michael Hicks, who knew her as the mother of his best friend, Mark. "Everything she did was perfect." Always put together in dresses or neatly pressed slacks, blond curls and red lipstick, she made everything look glamorous, even the ironing of Buck's T-shirts and handkerchiefs. Every morning she would sit at the mirrored vanity in the bathroom, fixing her hair and opening the velvet-lined drawers Buck custom-built for her jewelry. She loved necklaces and bracelets adorned with rare coins given to her by her father, and treasured a charm bracelet, a gift from Buck, with a heart that said, "I love you."

Though the floor plan wasn't particularly expansive, the Stahl house was perfectly suited to Carlotta's passion for food and entertaining. She cooked steak and potato pancakes—Buck's favorite meal—on her pink electric stovetop. She took cake-decorating classes to create magnificent themed desserts. She threw big family parties and poolside barbecues, always experimenting with new recipes and smothering the kitchen island with platter after platter of appetizers. She seemed happiest when her home was overflowing with family, friends, and children, and her laugh filled a room as thoroughly as Buck's booming voice. When she had time to relax, she could often be found floating on a chaise in the pool with a magazine and a glass of cold duck: champagne mixed with sparkling burgundy.

Whenever they had extra money, it went to home improvements. The fireplace was finally covered with the stonework Buck had originally envisioned. After uninvited visitors began sunbathing by the pool and appearing in the carport to steal a glance of the house, Buck turned a 4-foot pony wall into a 7-foot-tall privacy wall separating the courtyard from the carport, so their backyard couldn't be seen from the road. When the Stahls could afford to add carpet, the master bedroom became a family wrestling ring. "Think you can take me?" Buck would growl at the kids, crouched on his hands and rug-burned knees. Three against one always seemed like fair enough odds, but the kids could never take him. No matter how fiercely they clung, he could swat them away like flies. The family still laughs about the day when young Mark, still in footie pajamas, was amusing himself by flicking his father's ear. Buck told him to knock it off.

Flick. Flick. Flick.

"If I catch you," he warned, "I'm going to throw you in the pool!"

Flick.

From the next room, Shari and Bruce saw their brother sail through the open door and land with a terrific splash in the pool. Mark crawled out drenched, crying, and furious. "I'm running away!" he shouted, padding down Woods Drive in sopping pajamas. "And I'm never coming back!" Shari followed the trail of little wet footprints, caught up with her brother, and talked him into coming home.

In August 1967, Buck and Carlotta purchased a second empty lot, adjacent to the house and just downhill, as a real-estate investment as well as insurance against future construction that could potentially block their view. Buck converted "the lot below," as they called it, into a playground for the kids, adding a badminton court, swing set, tetherball pole, and stakes for throwing horseshoes. The kids dug in the dirt and flew kites, which soared on the updrafts created by the cliffs.

In most ways, the Stahl kids lived ordinary childhoods in an extraordinary house. They ate meals on stools at the kitchen island, gobbling pancakes faster than Carlotta could flip them. On weekends, they'd build labyrinthine blanket forts in the living room and wake up to blinding sunshine stabbing through cracks between blankets. "Living in a glass house, you didn't get to sleep in too late," Bruce said. Afternoons found them sprawled on the floor of their parents' room, nibbling saltine crackers and watching *The Beverly Hillbillies* on a console television set in front of the sliding glass door. When friends were allowed to sleep over, they often found it hard to sleep. "The view, the twinkling lights—it was mesmerizing," said childhood friend Michael Hicks. "I had a hard time falling asleep because I didn't want to stop looking at the view."

It was a happy time in the Stahl family life, but the world around them was churning. In 1969, Vietnam casualties were mounting, and 250,000 protesters marched in the nation's capital. There were increasing calls for Civil Rights. It was the year of Woodstock and *Abbey Road*, the last album recorded by the Beatles. Chemical Bank installed the first ATM. Elected in 1968, Richard Nixon was president, and inflation was on the rise. The nation slid into a recession, and the aerospace industry began to contract.

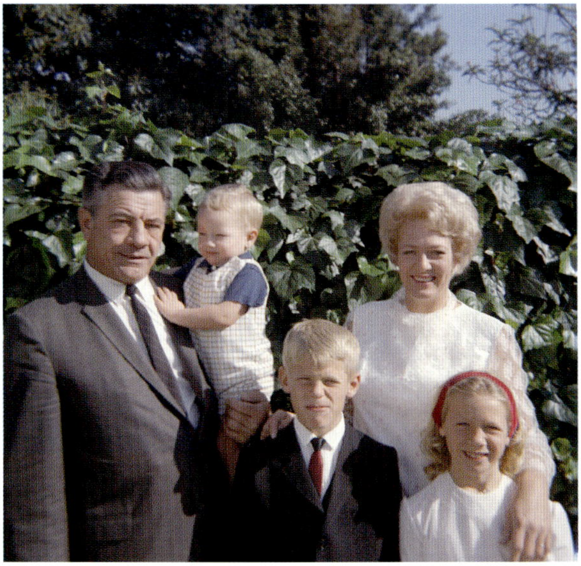

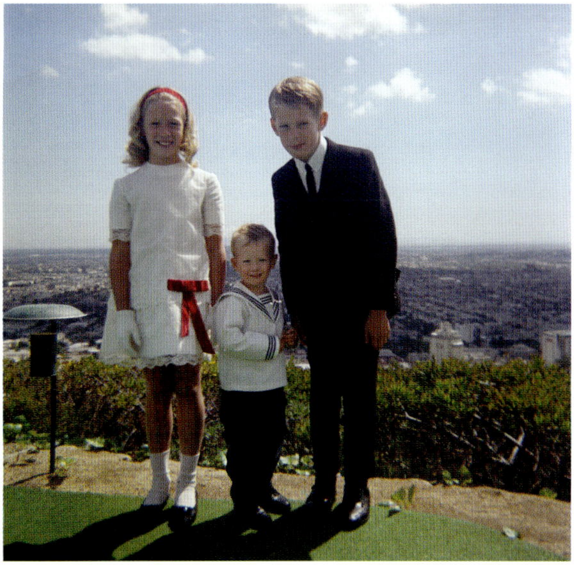

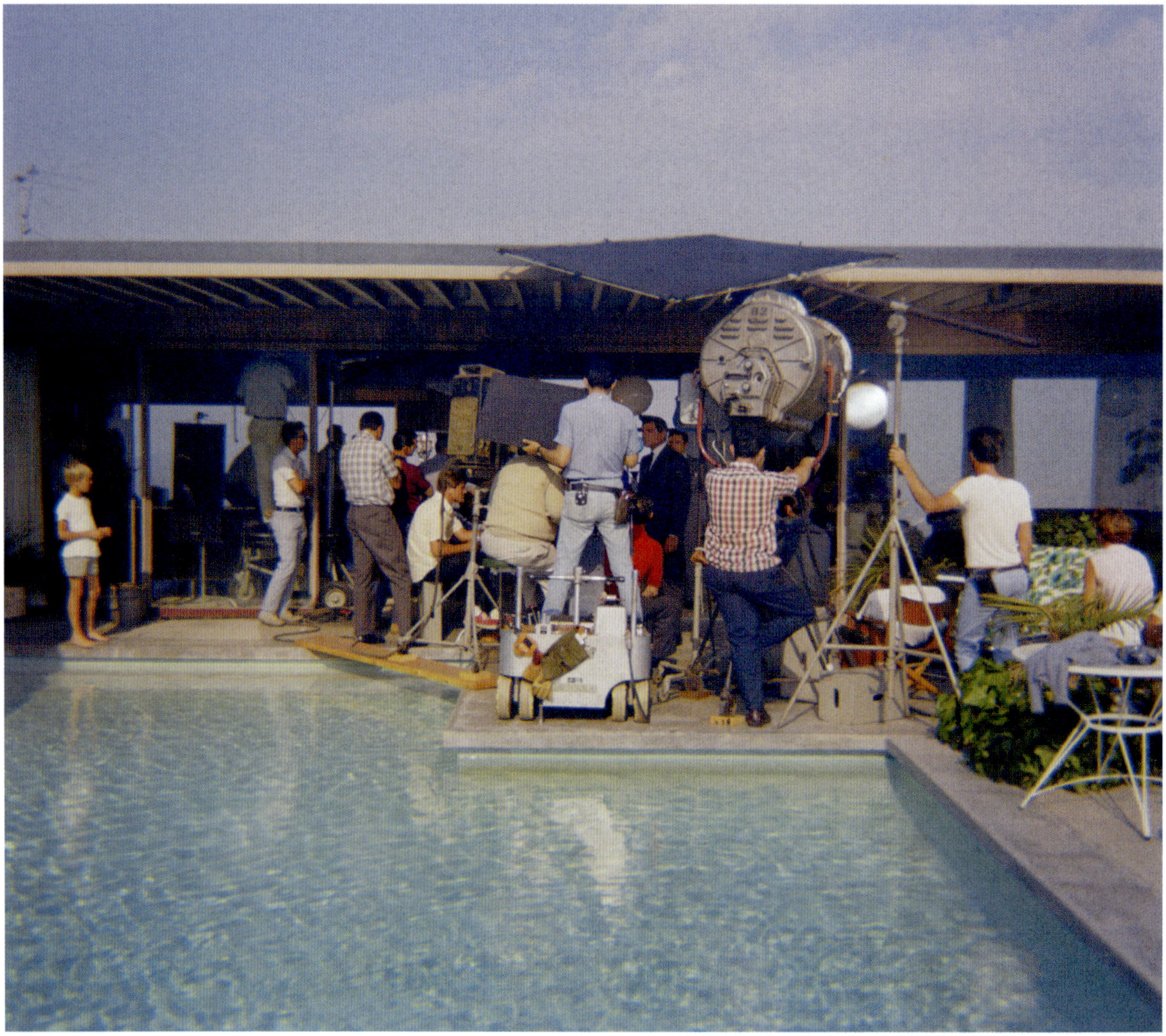

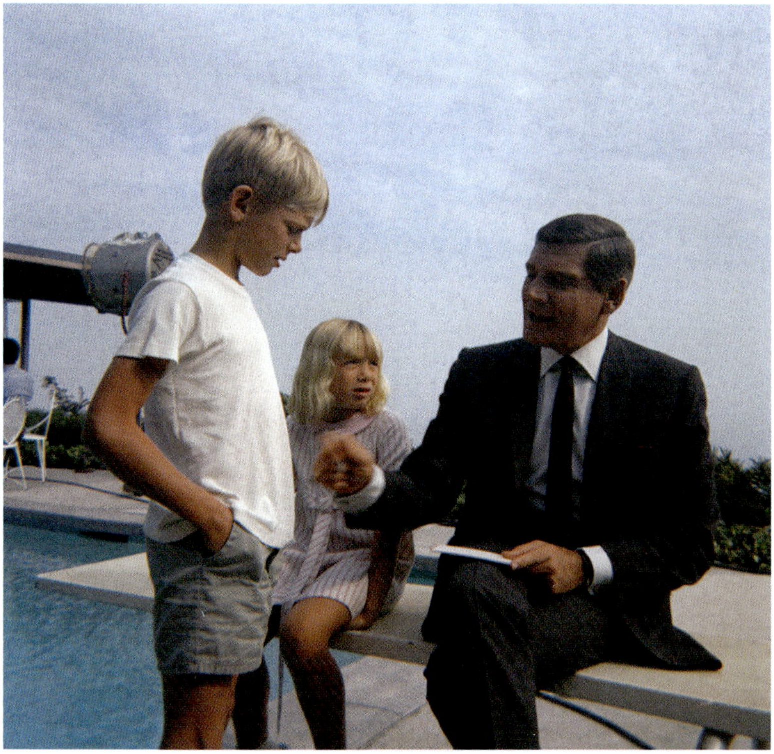

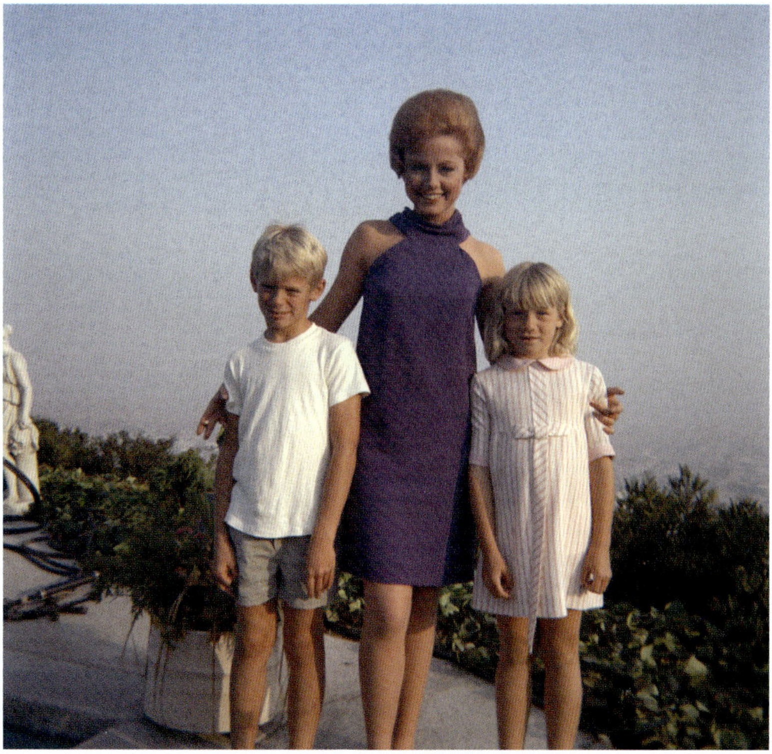

CHAPTER 7
THE MOVE

On July 20, 1969, the Stahl children sprawled on their parents' bedroom floor in front of the wooden-console TV. They watched, transfixed, as a black-and-white image of Neil Armstrong floated across the screen and left a footprint in moon dust. Bruce was eleven, Shari was nine, and Mark was almost three. It was one of their last great memories in the house before they were forced to move out.

That summer, as the aerospace industry faltered in a shrinking economy, Specialty Seal Co. lost customers and Buck's small company went out of business. Like many other Americans, he struggled to find a new job. Almost overnight, the Stahls could not afford to stay in the house they had fought so hard to create. All their savings had been sunk into home improvements and invested in the lot next door, but to Buck and Carlotta, selling the house, or even the

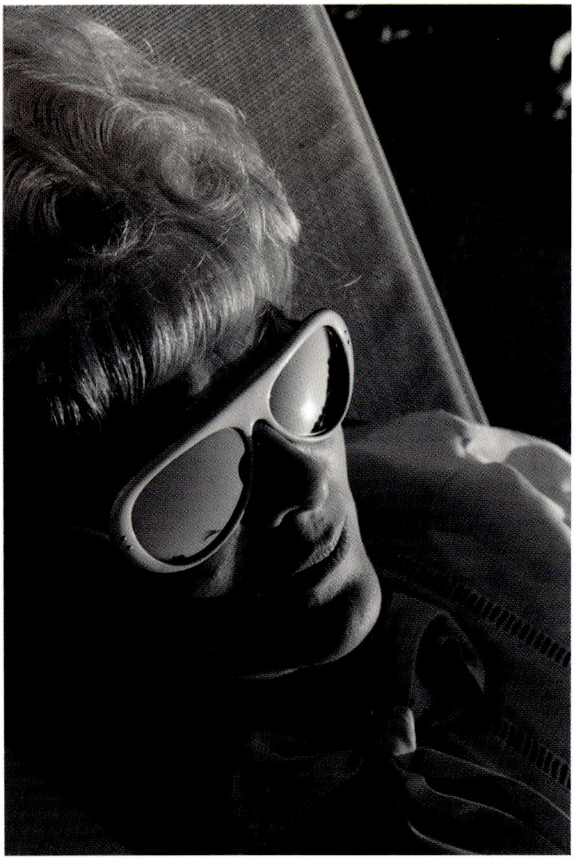

second lot next door, was unthinkable. To keep the house, they would have to move out, at least for a while, and find renters to cover the monthly mortgage—which had increased from $260 to $384 after refinancing to include the second lot. They quickly found a tenant, the manager of War, a funk-rock band formed in Long Beach in 1969 and known for "Low Rider," "Why Can't We Be Friends," and other hit songs of the 1970s. He needed to move in immediately, so the Stahls had only a few days to pack.

The Stahl family moved in with Carlotta's mother, Garnett, who still lived in Carlotta's childhood home on Kenyon Avenue, about a mile from Venice High School. Carlotta's father, Carlton, had recently died, so the move meant her mother wouldn't have to be alone. Buck, Carlotta, and the kids moved into the three-bedroom home, a Spanish casita with stucco walls and a red tile roof. Buck converted the detached garage into a small mother-in-law apartment for Garnett. The kids would run across the backyard to visit their grandma, who always had a pot of pork and beans simmering on the stove.

Having to leave their dream home must have been a crushing disappointment, but the kids never heard their parents complain. Buck found a job with Parsons, a construction company near Salt Lake City, Utah, where he spent two years living and working 700 miles from his family. He rented an apartment in a small town called Tooele. Carlotta and the kids would fly to Utah to visit him whenever they could afford it. "We visited twice," Shari said. "Once with just the kids, and the next time with Mom. I don't remember Dad ever flying home."

Carlotta went back to work, getting a job in data processing for Bank of America. Data was stored on punch cards: stiff cardstock with holes punched in specific patterns that recorded information. Once they were discarded, Carlotta brought them home to make crafts. "She'd fold them, staple them into wreaths, spray paint, and glitter them," Shari recalled.

Bruce and Shari were thrilled about moving so close to their cousins, but they were disappointed when Carlotta's brother moved his family away to Topanga Canyon. Being "the new kids" amplified the trials of adolescence. In seventh grade, Bruce was one of the smaller boys at Marina Del Rey Junior High, and he became a fresh target for bullies. Shari was entering sixth grade at a different school, and she felt vulnerable and lost without her big brother. Mark, still a toddler, stayed home with Garnett.

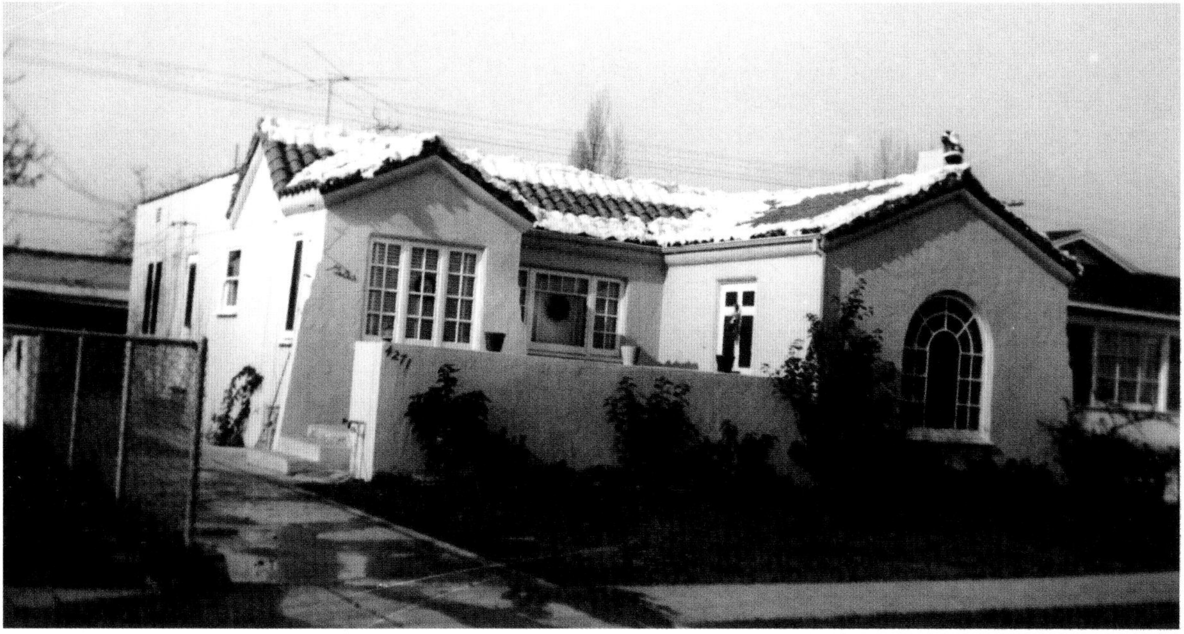

Compared to the only home they had ever known, the kids found "the Kenyon house" dark and claustrophobic, hemmed in on three sides by houses. Shari's bedroom window faced the neighbors' window a few feet away. At night, she felt exposed, worried they could see her through the lace curtains. Bruce and Mark made their room in the den, where the wood-paneled walls were adorned with their late grandfather's collection of arrowheads and coins, and taxidermic deer hooves holding rifles and shotguns. As adults, they would appreciate these family heirlooms, but as kids they found them spooky.

Life "in the flats" was very different from the Hollywood Hills. For the first time, the Stahl kids could roller skate on flat sidewalks and walk to the corner store to buy candy. They could pedal their bikes along Washington Boulevard all the way to the Venice Beach pier. Their new neighborhood was swarming with kids, and soon they had a posse of friends. "It took our lives in a completely different direction," Bruce said.

In junior high they discovered the Culver City ice rink, where Shari learned to figure skate and met her first boyfriend. Bruce ditched his paper route for a job working at the ice rink as a skate guard and Zamboni driver, making $1.75 an hour. The Culver City ice rink was also a practice facility for the NHL's LA Kings. They inspired Bruce to buy his own skates and join a local hockey team, which provided fiercely loyal friends as well as a source of strength and confidence. In tenth grade, after a 4-inch summer growth spurt, Bruce towered over his former bullies and suddenly longed to play football. Buck, whose body still ached from years of busted ankles and broken collarbones, refused to let his son play two contact sports.

One day in tenth grade, Bruce's physical education class had to swim a lap in the Venice High pool while a coach stood by with a stopwatch. Thanks to long days in the pool at "the Hollywood house," Bruce was an instant recruit to the swim team, where he found himself in his element and made lifelong friends. Shari, a lean and athletic 6 foot 1, became a fellow swim-team star. Both would set a Venice High School record in their signature stroke, the fifty-yard freestyle. Bruce's school record—22.15 seconds—would stand for forty-two years.

Mark was only two when they moved, but the course of his life also changed. At the Kenyon house he met his best friend, whose grandparents lived next door. Whenever Michael Hicks was in town, he would dash across the yard to see Mark, a mission he'd later refer to as "running the Happy gauntlet." Happy was the name of Carlotta's parrot, a half-moon conure who flew free during the day. Standing guard on the red tile roof, Happy would dive-bomb the boy as he sprinted across the front porch and lunged for the front door. Michael and Mark would become so inseparable that their families, tired of repeating "Mark and Michael," would refer to them jointly as "Markael." (The moniker survived to adulthood.) They would grow up together and become avid scuba divers—Michael becoming a certified divemaster and Mark a PADI instructor. They would move to Idaho to be college roommates at Boise State University. After graduating college in 1995, they would cofound Markael Productions, a pyrotechnics company. They put on some of the largest pyro-musical fireworks programs in Idaho, including the Boise River Festival, the seventh largest fireworks display in the country. Mark and Michael always joked that their business plan began incubating while they were aiming magnifying glasses at twigs and ants on Kenyon Avenue.

. . . .

When the Stahls moved out of Case Study House #22 in 1969, *Arts & Architecture* was two years out of business. In 1960, John Entenza had taken a job as director of the Graham Foundation for Advanced Studies in the Fine Arts in Chicago. That same year, the debut of the Stahl House marked the beginning of the Case Study House Program's third phase, which broadened the initiative from single-family homes to multiple-family dwellings. Two years into his work at the Graham Foundation, where he continued to champion architecture and art, Entenza found running the magazine remotely too burdensome, and sold it. The new editor, David Travers, continued the Case Study House Program through 1966, when it concluded with a portfolio of thirty-six individual designs, some of which were never built. Though Travers increased the circulation from 8,000 to 12,500 readers during his tenure, advertising did not rise in step. In 1967, after fifty-six years in print, *Arts & Architecture* folded.

. . . .

After two years of working in Utah, Buck found a job in LA. He and Carlotta worked opposite shifts so one of them could be home with the kids. Carlotta's mother was aging, and even if they could have afforded professional childcare, they didn't want to outsource it. On his way to work on the I-10 freeway, Buck would spot Carlotta coming home from the night shift. "Dad would say, 'I waved at your mother on the freeway today!'" Shari said. While the Stahls never stopped missing their house in the hills, the setback forged a stronger family.

"Our parents struggled," Shari said.

Bruce added, "It taught us perseverance."

It took at least six years, but eventually they earned enough money to move back to "the Hollywood house" in 1975. The first renter had moved out, and the second renter longed to be more than a tenant. He had asked, repeatedly, to buy the house, but Buck and Carlotta had no interest in selling.

The new renter left the house in a shocking state—walls painted bright primary colors, large candles in the living room unleashing glaciers of wax onto the carpet. Both sinks in the master bathroom appeared to have been assaulted with a sledgehammer. The swimming pool, neglected, had fermented into a chemical cocktail that ravaged the once smooth layer of plaster, which now grated on a child's tender foot.

Buck and Carlotta ripped out the carpet, fixed what was broken, and slowly made the house back into their home. Bruce, Shari, and Mark moved back into their subdivided room, which seemed to have shrunk in their six-year absence. Bruce and Shari were teenagers now. Mark was nine, but not too young to realize he occupied "half of a half of a room." They were glad to be home, though the notion of "home" had expanded beyond the house. Bruce, a high-school senior, and Shari, a junior, continued to attend Venice High, a half-hour commute down Santa Monica Boulevard and the 405, cruising in Bruce's 1974 Chevy Vega, tangerine with a black racing stripe down the hood. Mark attended schools in the Hollywood area and graduated from Fairfax High School, where he was involved with ROTC. Their world now encompassed the Hollywood Hills—an increasingly exclusive enclave—and the middle-class neighborhoods around Venice Beach. They loved living in the hills but found their people in the flats.

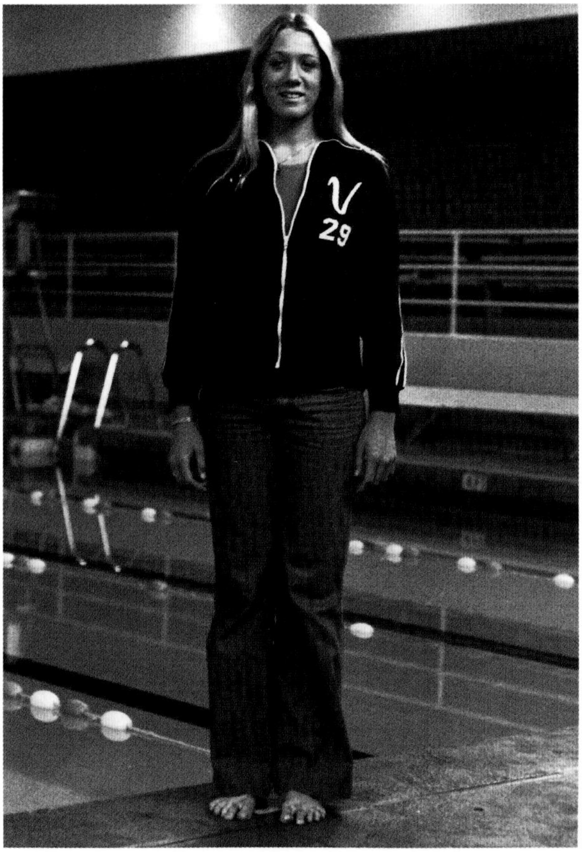

As years passed and the children grew, the house proved capable of accommodating the family's changing needs. Buck and Carlotta chaperoned high-school parties, which always centered around the swimming pool and the kitchen island. When Shari fell in love with photography, she converted the "service porch"—the laundry room between the kitchen and the master bath—into a darkroom. Covering the windows with black felt to block out the light, she exposed black-and-white prints on an enlarger set up on the deep freezer (where Carlotta stored her cakes) and developed them in chemical-processing trays arranged on the washer and dryer.

After graduating high school in 1976, Bruce enrolled in Santa Monica City College, where he studied business and joined the swim team. Shari graduated the following year and moved into an apartment with friends, working as a lifeguard at the Venice High School pool. After Bruce and Shari moved out, the partition dividing their room was removed. Mark enjoyed his own room at last, filling it with books and a giant map marked with pushpins that tracked all the places he had traveled with the Boy Scouts or his parents.

Their erstwhile playground, "the lot below," was put up for sale. After purchasing the lot in 1967 for twenty-five thousand dollars (twice what George Beha offered to sell it for in 1954), Buck held onto it for a decade, even during the five-year move to the flats. Sometime after 1975, he posted an oversized "For Sale" sign on a fence that bordered the cliff. "You could see it from Sunset Boulevard," Shari said. "He had that up for years." Buck refused to sell until he could triple his investment. The lot finally sold in 1977, when Buck retired at sixty-five, for $75,000 to a single gentleman. The man sold it—still empty—in 1988 for $225,000 to a family who built the house that exists there today. The rooftop reaches several feet below the floor of the Stahl House, so the view remains expansive.

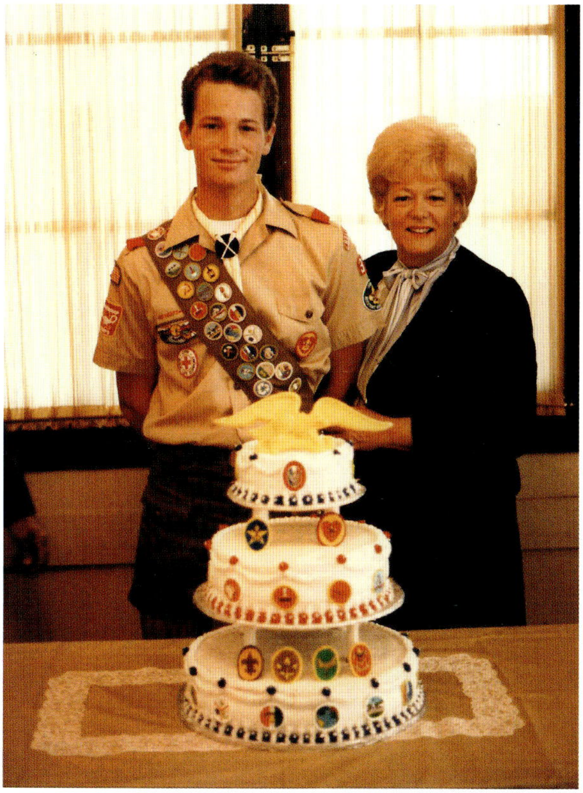

As Buck entered retirement, he had time to take eleven-year-old Mark on hikes and backpacking trips with the Boy Scouts, wearing loafers and Bermuda shorts and carrying a heavy duffel bag thrown over his shoulder, just like he did back in the navy. Mark earned his Eagle Scout rank in 1984, the same year Carlotta retired at fifty-five from Bank of America, where she was ultimately promoted to budget control officer. "She wanted to retire early so she and my dad could travel," Shari said. "They wanted to see all fifty states, so they bought a van with a back seat that converted to a full-size bed. As a joke, she made a license-plate frame that said, 'Buck's Hanky-Panky Van.' He put it on the van right away!" Mark went along, sleeping in a tent by the van when the weather was good. A handful of photo shoots and filming days provided a little extra money for travel.

Case Study House #22 would have a profound and lasting influence on the Stahl kids. Its geometry defined the shape into which their childhood days flowed like water. The persistence they learned from watching their parents fight to realize this dream—and hold onto it through troubled times—would manifest uniquely in each of them.

Shari inherited the tenacity of her father, his refusal to take no for an answer, and his attention to detail. These traits would serve her well in her career in managing finances and payroll, first for large corporations and later for the Stahl House, when tours evolved into a family business. From her mother Shari gained a head for numbers—she would work in budgeting for Bank of America, reporting data to Carlotta, and later would run the payroll department for several large corporations. She also had her mother's deep love for animals. Carlotta, unwilling to hurt so much as a trespassing fly, would scoop bugs and other critters out of the pool and set them free on the hillside. Shari would fill her future home with pets, including a pandemonium of rescued parrots reminiscent of Happy, her mother's half-moon conure, who flew away on Mark's tenth birthday and returned exactly one year later, in the middle of a pool party. Shari would always be drawn to houses festooned with windows and bathed in natural light. One day, she and her husband would buy a hilltop home with a stunning panoramic view—this one of a reservoir in the rugged hills of southeast Idaho.

Mark inherited his father's booming voice, his towering physique, and his take-charge nature. The ultimate Boy Scout, he was always prepared. As a boy, he stuffed his pockets with Hot Wheels, green army men, and essential tools: a Swiss Army knife, matches, a magnifying glass, and a perfectly coiled ball of waxed twine scavenged from his grandfather's shop. As an adult, he equipped his Jeep with everything he might need to assist a troubled motorist. "He would carry extra gas, water, tools, rope, chains, and ice traction plates," Shari said. He became a true Idaho "prepper," his pantry stocked with dried and canned food, military MREs (Meals, Ready to Eat), water purifiers, gas-powered generators, guns and ammo for hunting, and seeds for growing food. In 1996, he would challenge an incumbent for a seat in the Idaho Senate, losing by a narrow margin. Many years later, Mark would dream up the idea to open the Stahl House for official tours.

In the Stahl House pool, Bruce found an element that would shape his entire life. On the swim team at city college, he dominated competitions and shaved a full second off his high-school record—an eternity in a race as furious as the fifty-yard freestyle. His times put him on the radar of nationally ranked colleges and universities. University of California at Santa Barbara head coach Gregg Wilson came to watch Bruce swim at the state championships, where he won his event.

"He got out of the water, 6 foot 4, with these long limbs—he's like an Adonis and a Southern California water rat," Wilson said. "I thought, *holy mackerel!* With his body type, he was the quintessential sprinter protégé." While most nationally ranked swimmers began racing as tadpoles, Bruce only had two years of training and competition. What Wilson saw was raw potential.

As Bruce recalled, "He mentioned the words 'world record.' I looked around like, 'Are you talking to *me?*'"

Bruce turned down several full-ride offers by other universities to be a walk-on at UCSB, a Division I school that offered a modest scholarship, just enough to pay for his textbooks. "I wanted to be the small fish going into the big pond," he said. He played ice hockey and lifeguarded at Venice Beach the summer before moving to Santa Barbara to train at a level he never could have imagined.

"I beat him up pretty good," Wilson said. "But he did everything I asked." In his first year of competition, the swimmer known as "Big B" qualified in three events for the NCAA Division 1 championships. The following year, UCSB offered Bruce a full ride.

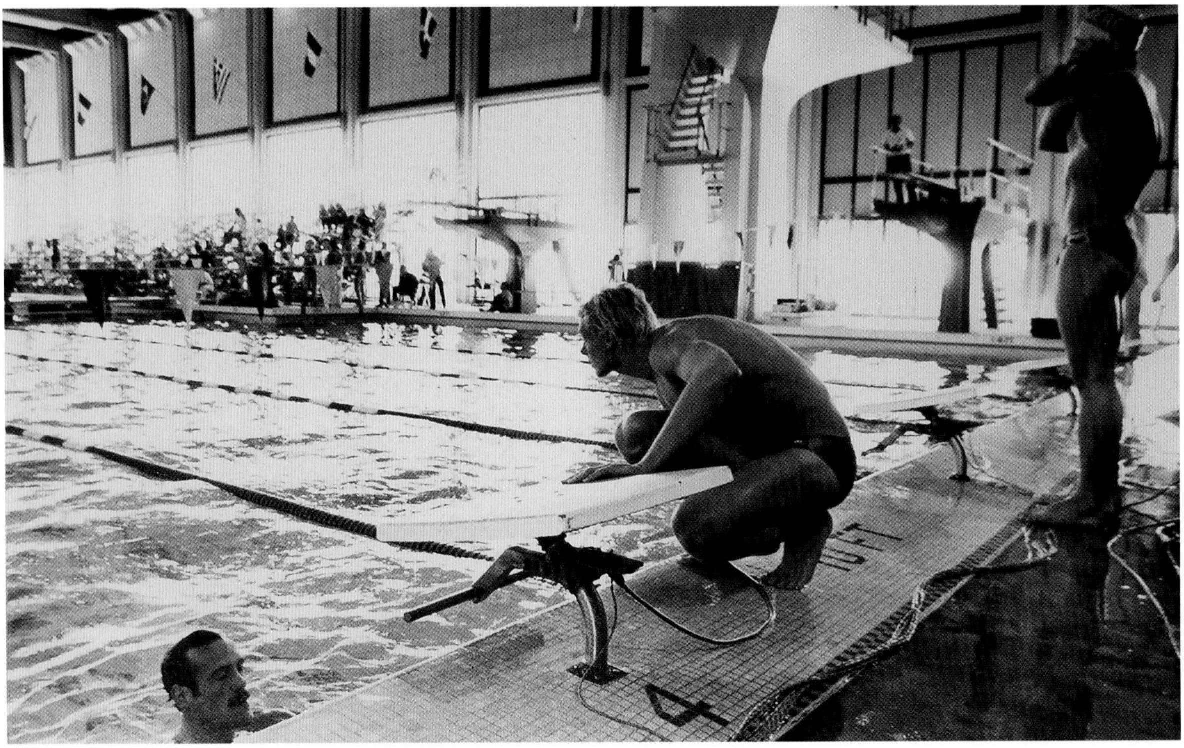

That second year, Bruce helped lead UCSB to its first Pacific Coast Conference championship, launching a twenty-three-year winning streak. The longest in the country, in any sport, any division," said Wilson, who retired after forty years as the Gauchos' head coach. "Bruce was the lynchpin of all this. He was the most valuable on our team—voted by the kids, not me," Wilson said in 2020.

During his senior year in 1980, Bruce trained relentlessly for twin goals: to win the NCAA championships and make the Olympic team. On the ceiling of his dorm room, he taped a photo of the Harvard University pool, where the national collegiate meet would be held.

"When I lay down in bed, it was the last thing I saw," he said. "By the time the race happened, I had already been there."

On the day of the NCAA championships at Harvard, Bruce was ranked No. 2 in the nation. He stepped up on the blocks at center pool, next to his rival, No. 1-ranked Ambrose "Rowdy" Gaines, a five-time NCAA champion from Auburn University. The gun fired and all the swimmers churned toward the finish. Bruce was stunned to discover at the end of the race that he had finished fifth, with Gaines in fourth, something they blamed on a wave created by a collective flip turn that had given a minuscule advantage to the swimmers in the outermost lanes. "This is what makes sprinting so difficult," Coach Wilson said. "The microscopic stuff makes a difference."

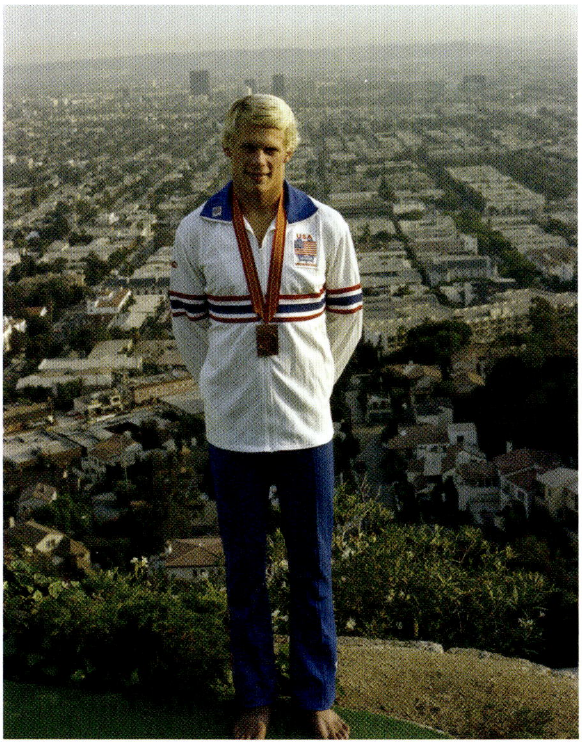

Two weeks later Bruce flew to Austin, Texas, for the national championships.

"All I wanted to do was beat the guy who had beaten me two weeks before," Bruce said. And also his rival, Rowdy Gaines, who then held the world record in the event. Gaines was the first swimmer who had ever clocked a fifty-meter freestyle time under twenty-three seconds flat, and he would go on to become a three-time Olympic gold medalist.

At the gun, Bruce exploded into the water and swam for redemption. When he touched the wall, he squinted up at the clock and saw numbers that had never been recorded in his event: 22.83 seconds. He had beaten the world record by a tenth of a second.

That put Bruce in position for a spot on the US Olympic team to compete in Moscow that summer. Then, in May, President Jimmy Carter confirmed that the United States would be one of sixty-five countries to boycott the Moscow Olympics, a protest against the 1979 Soviet invasion of Afghanistan. "It was bittersweet," Bruce said. "I was training, and then we weren't going." It was an unexpected end to a remarkable swimming career.

Bruce was hired as a lifeguard at Venice Beach and bought a small pool-service business with a route of twenty-eight pools. At first, Carlotta tried to talk him out of what she saw as "a dead-end job."

But Buck told his son, "Whatever you do, son, just give it 110 percent." Bruce built up his business while swimming competitively, qualifying for three US national teams and competing in France, Holland, Mexico, and Brazil. His family couldn't be at every race in person, but he always felt buoyed by their support. He dominated his races in France and the Netherlands. After his victory in Amsterdam, Bruce received a telegram from Buck: "Way to go, boy!"

Looking back, Bruce wonders if he ever would have found this path had it not been for Broadway Federal's pool stipulation, Pierre Koenig's decision to make it the heart of the house, and the unexpected move to the flats, where he found his calling. "My whole life, since I was a little kid, has revolved around pools," he said. "It's still happening today." In his sixties, Bruce continues to run his one-man pool business, servicing dozens of pools in the Hollywood Hills. At least two days a week, he ends the route at his favorite pool, where he'll often sit down and watch the colors of the setting sun mirrored in his calm, childhood waters.

CHAPTER 8

FIRE AND RAIN

September 16, 1979, began as a languorous late-summer Sunday—fair skies after a nine-day siege of smog, hardly any humidity, and a gathering breeze from the south. The beaches were packed. Shari was visiting home with three friends, lying out by the pool in their bathing suits, taking dips to cool off as the temperature rose to 99 degrees. As the wind picked up around 3:00 p.m., Buck smelled something that drew his gaze to the sky. An ominous column of smoke was curling up from a neighboring ridge. Buck never lost his cool, and even now he did not yell. But in the single word he spoke, Shari detected a tone she'd never heard in her father's voice.

"Fire."

The smoke was coming from the southernmost point of the ridge, less than 500 yards across the small canyon, uphill from the flat where Buck and Carlotta had lived as newlyweds. Fanned by 14-mile-per-hour winds, the fire swept up the ridgeline, leaping from house to house along Grand View Drive—a street of magnificent homes with spectacular views. Buck sprang to his feet, shirtless and in Bermuda shorts. Shari and her friends, still in bathing suits, ran out to Woods Drive, where the wail of sirens heralded fire trucks creeping up the hairpin curves. Shari grabbed her camera and photographed neighbors running into the street as black smoke filled the sky.

Hundreds of firemen rushed to the scene, but they still needed help from civilians. Some handed fire hoses to bystanders, including Shari's friend in a black, one-piece swimsuit. Thirteen-year-old Mark manned a garden hose. "They didn't have enough fire crew to help battle the blaze on Woods Drive, so the firefighters asked us to help out," Shari said. "I had always wanted to be a firefighter, so it was thrilling and frightening at the same time." Homeowners climbed on their rooftops to spray down their homes and yards, and one couple scooped water from a drainage ditch. So many garden hoses were flowing at once that the area water pressure dropped dramatically, forcing firefighters to pump water from backyard pools and mobile tanks. Super Scooper airplanes dumped 1,600-gallon blasts of water from the sky.

Buck grabbed a shovel and ran up Woods Drive to help his neighbor, Buck Henry, a co-writer of *The Graduate*, who wrote the screenplay for *Catch-22*, and frequently hosted *Saturday Night Live*. The fire had spread east on the backbone of the mountain and was now roaring south down the rib toward Woods Drive. Henry's house looked out from the highest lot on the ridge. Buck Stahl was digging a fire break around the house as flames began licking at the roof. Sweating under the pressure and the rising heat, he didn't see the six tons of water falling from the sky. It flattened him instantly. He picked himself up, shook it off, and continued to shovel. "It was the only time I've ever seen my father worried or afraid," Shari said.

After four hours, the flames had been extinguished, but the hillside was black and smoldering. The topography had compounded every firefighting challenge: steep hills blanketed with virgin brush, dense neighborhoods of closely packed houses lining the ridgelines, and winding streets with limited access. "The fire crept down the cliff on Woods Drive," Shari said. "It was stopped halfway between Buck Henry's and our house." No human lives were lost, but twenty-three homes were destroyed, including the Goodson House, a wood-and-stone house designed by Richard Neutra. The casualties included Porsches and Cadillacs; grand pianos and sixteenth-century antiques; a 350-page book manuscript, twenty-five years of rock-and-roll diaries, an 1831 Bible, and a pornography collection dating to the 1800s. The owner of Whiskey a Go Go lost two bull terriers, Bo and Annie. An actress mourned a cat named Brains. A freelance photographer who lost fifteen years of negatives and prints was sipping a beer afterward at a neighbor's house, pondering the fleeting nature of material things. He leaned out the window and yelled, "I'm free!"

The next day, four teenage boys were arrested for arson. They had been playing with fireworks near 8611 Hillside Avenue, less than a mile up the road from Buck and Carlotta's first flat. Some 350 firefighters had been called to

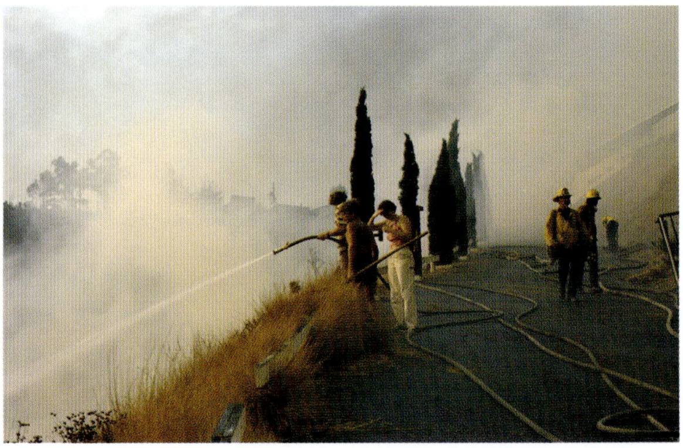

the scene, but residents complained that they took twenty-five minutes to arrive. As the dry brush of the hillsides accelerated the blaze, the narrow, winding, car-lined streets had slowed the fire trucks down. Meanwhile, 20,000 acres simultaneously burned in two other California wildfires.

The *Los Angeles Herald Examiner* reported that most homeowners in the area were badly underinsured and noted that "whatever is done to rebuild the area—with its narrow roads and limited water supply—it will remain one of the city's most visible tinderboxes." Some of the people who lost their homes said they planned to rebuild, but many were uncertain. There would always be another fire, and cliff dwellers were particularly vulnerable.

"The view from up here is spectacular," said a fire captain as he stood in the smoldering remains of a hilltop home. "But I wouldn't live in these hills. Most people want the aesthetic value of wood homes, but at times like this they pay the price; . . . and when a fire heats up, the vegetation can explode like a bomb."

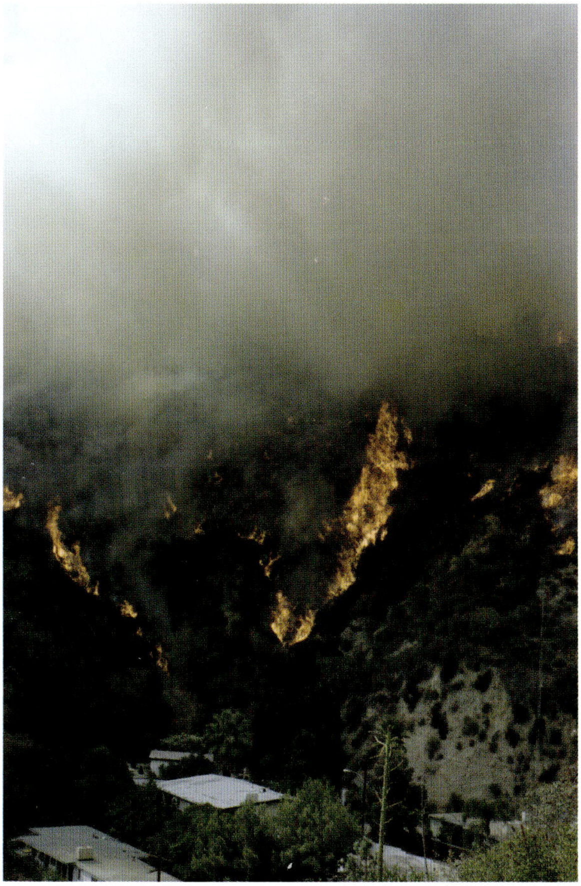

Fire would be an ever-present threat to the Hollywood Hills, where the arid climate, combustible vegetation, and furnace-like Santa Ana winds conspired to turn a spark—from lightning, a cigarette, or a lawnmower striking a rock—into an inferno that could spread through the hills with terrible efficiency. Fires destroyed the vegetation that held together the precipitous slopes, which were already prone to landslides; the cliffs along Woods Drive were constantly sloughing away and leaving small piles of earth in the street. Heavy rains could bring down unstable slopes. One evening in February 1978, Shari drove home through Laurel Canyon just minutes before a flash flood swept an avalanche of mud, debris, and cars down into the intersection of Laurel Canyon and Hollywood Boulevard. Seven people were killed.

Another threat was the inevitability of earthquakes. Of five hundred active faults in the state, the San Andreas and more than one hundred minor faults run through Southern California. This includes the Hollywood fault, which runs along the westernmost base of the Hollywood Hills, less than a quarter mile from the Stahl House.

The 1971 Sylmar quake, a 6.6-magnitude temblor with an epicenter 12 miles from the Stahl House, occurred while the family was living in the flats. The earthquake collapsed schools and hospitals, brought down sections of elevated freeway, and killed sixty-seven people. Bruce and Shari can't recall any significant damage to the Stahl House.

In 1994, the 6.7 Northridge quake injured 8,700 people, killed at least fifty-seven, and caused twenty billion dollars in damage—the costliest earthquake in US history. Freeways collapsed, a three-story apartment building pancaked into two, and so many homes were destroyed or damaged that residents slept in their yards for weeks. Damage occurred as far as 85 miles away, and strong movement was felt in Las Vegas. The Stahl House, just 12 miles from the epicenter in Reseda, survived again, though the tremor shattered two of the plate-glass walls. The steel bones remained intact.

One of the fascinating mysteries of the Stahl House is how, precisely, it is attached to the mountain. In the event of an earthquake or a landslide, what's keeping this house from sliding down the hill? *Life After People*, a TV series on the History Channel, speculated what might happen to the Stahl House in a post-apocalyptic world, when the wildfire-ravaged hillside erodes and then collapses in heavy rains. The dramatic voice-over introduces "California's Stahl House—made entirely of glass and steel," and then cuts to a concrete expert, who imagines "a house like that could potentially sit in a tilted position for some time,

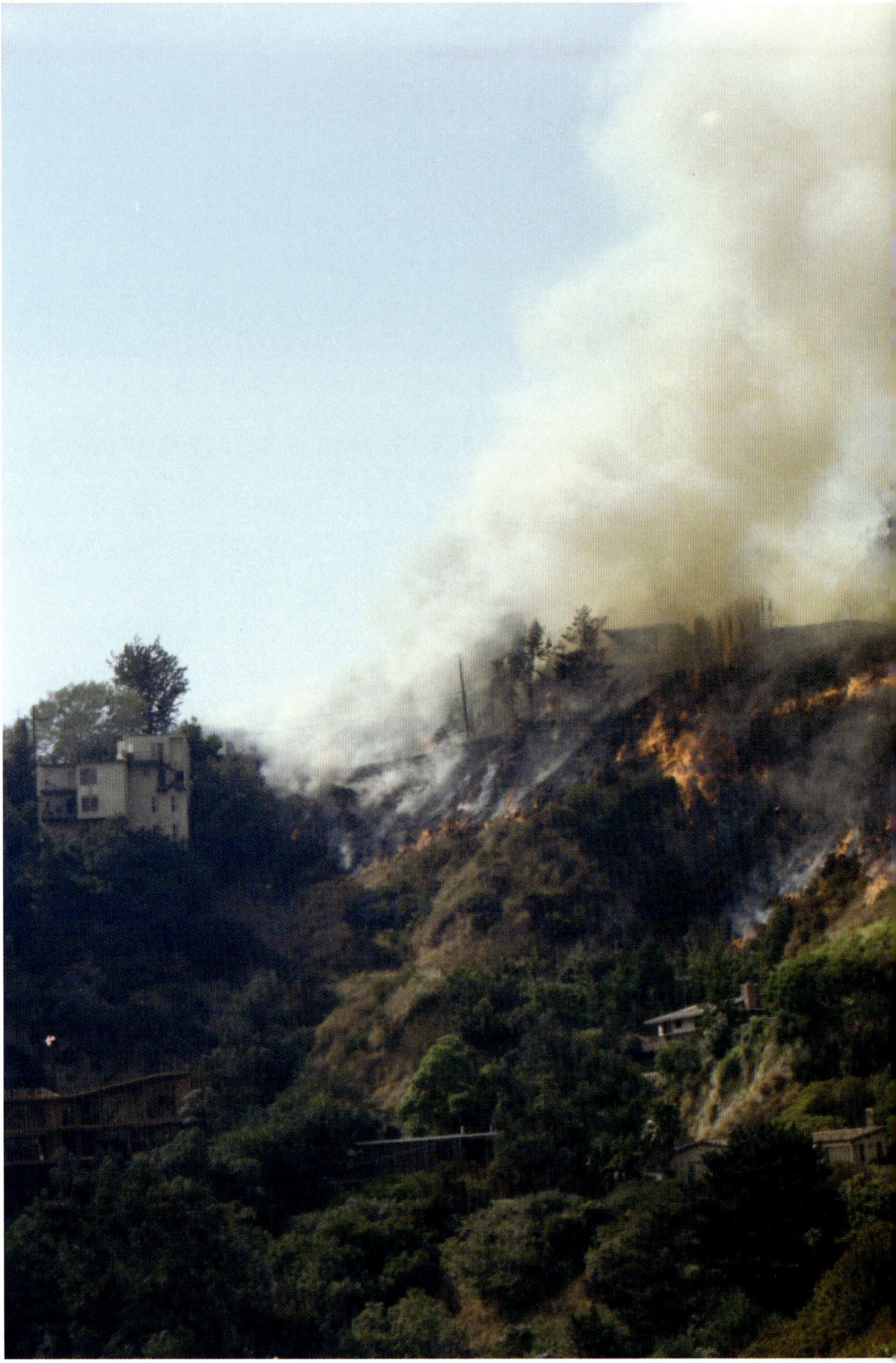

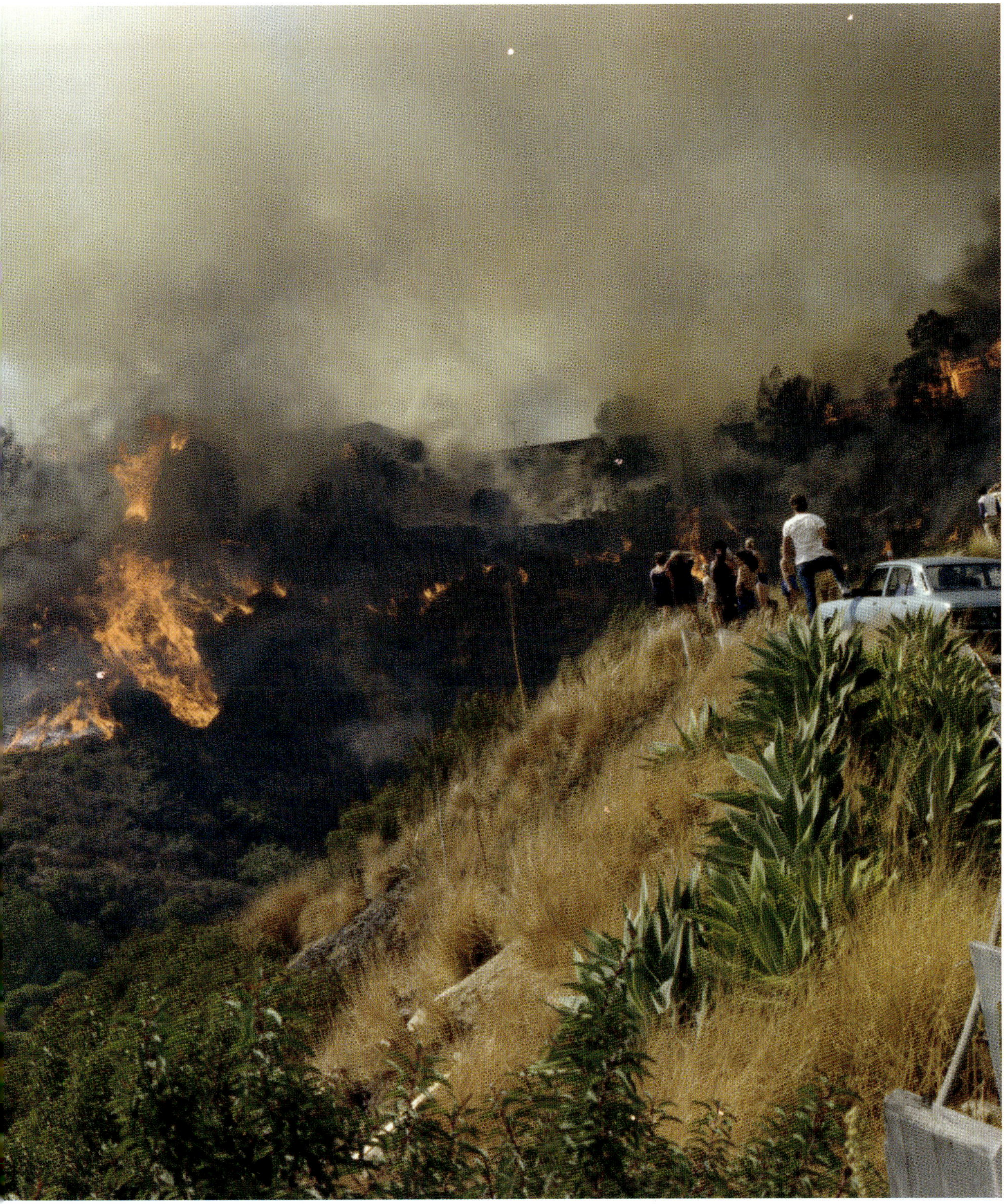

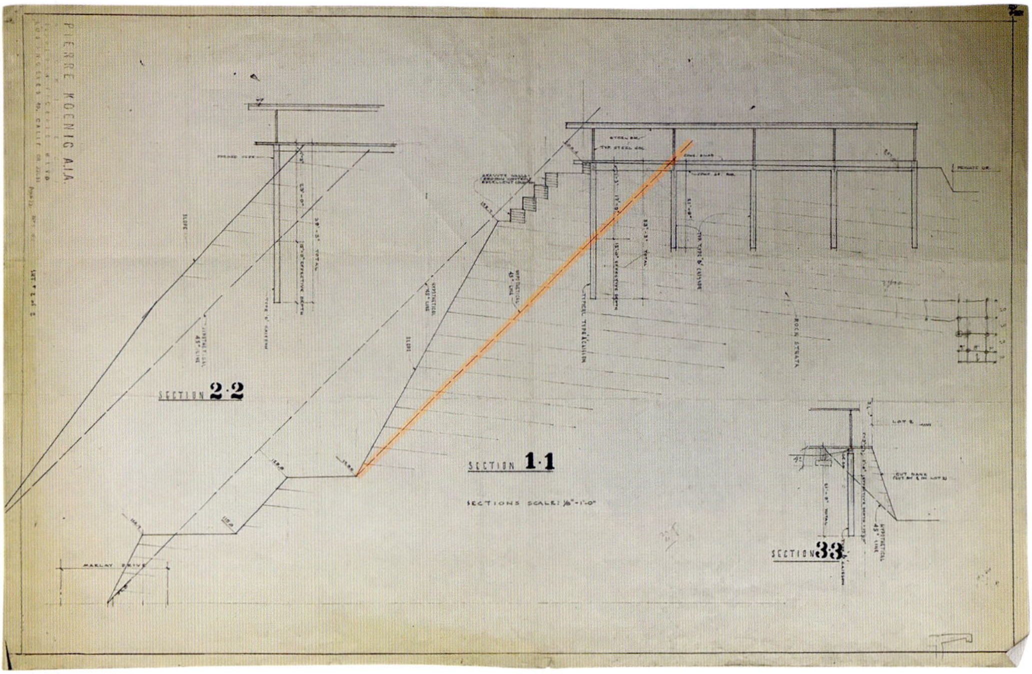

Fig 1: Site section (Sept. 6, 1958) with caissons. The red line indicates the hypothetical 45-degree angle of repose. Should the slope give way, the entire 20-foot bay closest to the cliff would presumably be dangling over empty space.

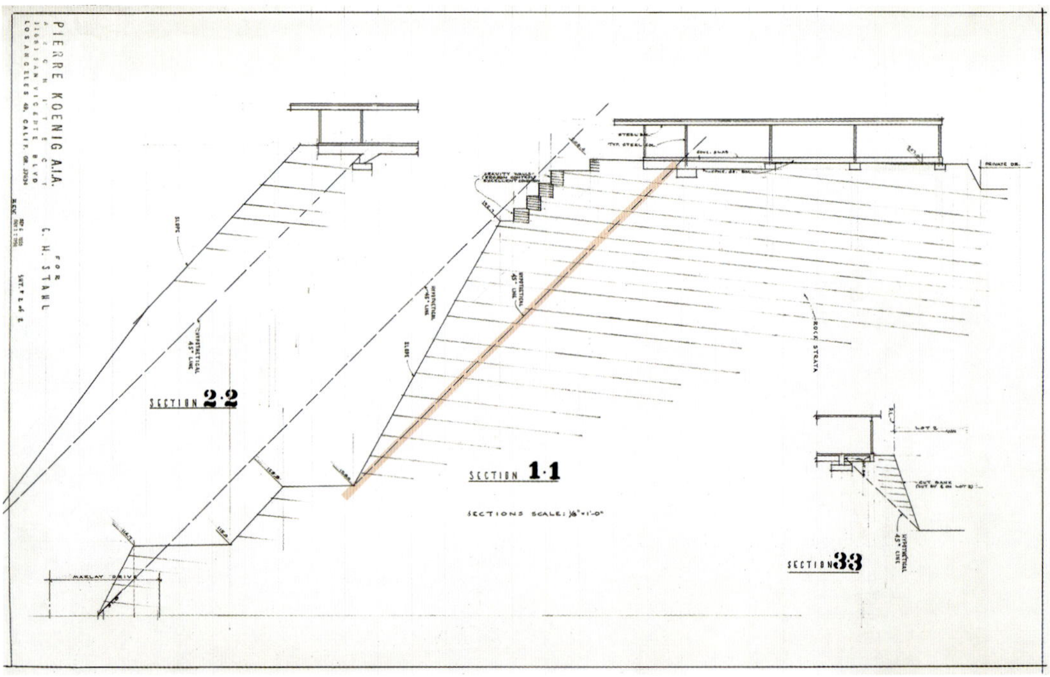

Fig. 2: Revised site section (November 17, 1958) with shortened living room and piers replacing caissons. Note where the angle of repose intersects the house; should the slope give way, the piers s would remain on solid ground, and only 10 feet would presumably be overhanging.

but not a great length of time." A computer-generated animation shows the house (with an impossibly exaggerated overhang) teetering over the cliff as the narrator growls, "and one of the twenty-first century's most iconic homes slides down the hill, crashing the party on the once-fabled Sunset Strip below!"

Many homes in the Hollywood hills are built with caissons, reinforced concrete cylinders plunging deep into the geological strata beneath a house, anchoring the structure to the earth like extra-long tent stakes. Along with massive retaining walls, caissons are commonly used in the construction of new homes in the hills, where gravity and erosion threaten to collapse steep slopes. Caissons are expensive and labor-intensive, requiring drilling anywhere from a few feet to dozens of feet deep, sometimes all the way to bedrock.

Pierre Koenig's site section drawing (Fig. 1), dated September 6, 1958, shows at least five caissons: four measuring 21 feet and 9 inches deep, and one (the closest to the edge of the cliff) plunging 33 feet and 3 inches into the ground.

However, a revised site section drawing (Fig. 2), dated November 17, 1958, depicts no caissons. They appear to have been eliminated and replaced by large concrete blocks placed under the living room, the kitchen bar, and the guest bath. The concrete blocks supported a grid of concrete grade beams (highlighted in blue in Fig. 3) under the kitchen and the living room.

"When we first submitted the plans to the City for approval, we had caissons in mind for supporting this house," Buck said in a 2004 interview with documentary filmmaker Eric Bricker. "And the City said no, no. If that point slid—which it could do very easily—they'd be wiped out like matchsticks." Nine feet below the living room (where he sat as he explained this), "We poured two concrete cubes, 6 foot by 6 foot by 6 foot, reinforced. And then we put the 3-foot-by-1-foot beams resting on those two. So that if this point let go, it would not collapse."

A revised plan (Fig. 3), dated January 6, 1959, seems to support this. The blue highlighted portions indicate piers connected by concrete beams. This plan has chemical erasures that show the shortening of the living room by 10 feet—the key change Koenig made in order to get the City to approve the building permit. This not only reduced the cantilevering portion of the living room from 18 feet to 8 feet (seen in Fig. 2) but also factored in the angle of repose.

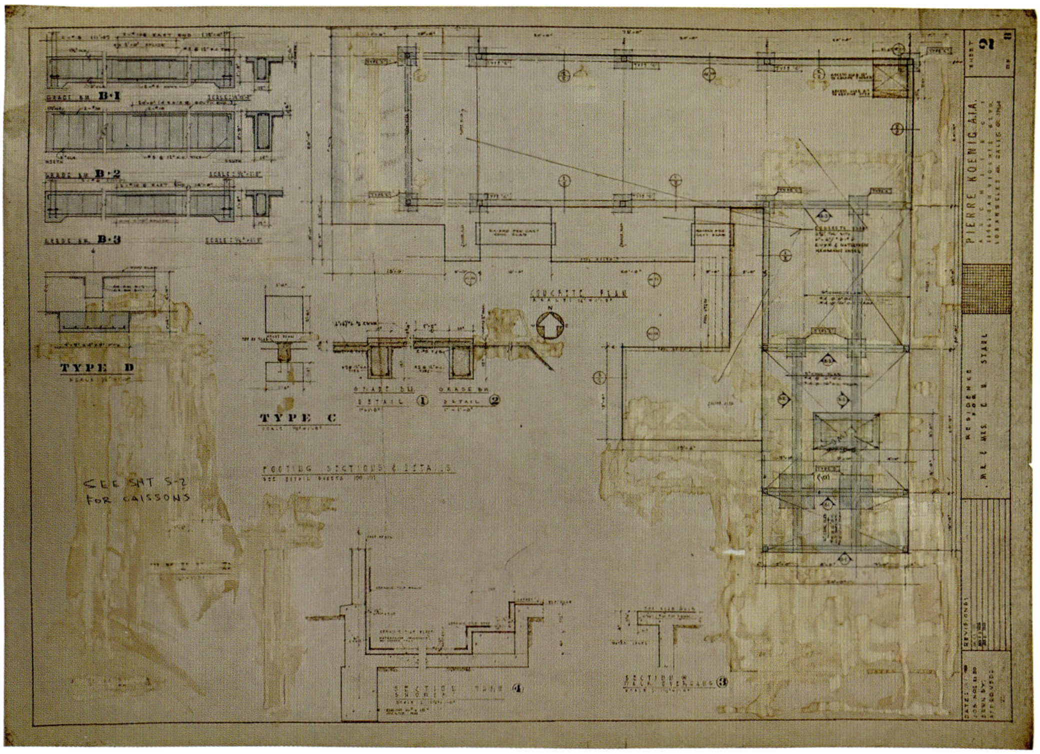

Fig. 3: Revised foundation plan (January 6, 1959). Chemical erasures indicate where the living room bay closest to the cliff was shortened from 20 feet to 10 feet. The blue highlighting indicates the grid of piers and grade beams supporting the house.

The angle of repose is the natural angle that earth, sand, or other granular material will settle into if allowed to seek its own equilibrium. This angle varies, depending on soil composition and moisture, among other things. Cliffs and hillsides steeper than the angle of repose are at risk of shearing off. On the drawings of the Stahl House, a "hypothetical 45-degree angle" was noted and drawn (in Figures 1 and 2, indicated by a red dotted line). If the slope were weakened by an earthquake, landslide, or heavy rains, that portion of the hillside to the left of that line could fall away.

In Fig. 1—the version with caissons—a landslide would leave nearly an entire 20-foot bay of the living room dangling over empty space. In Fig. 2—with the shortened living room bay and the piers—the edge of the house has been pushed back sufficiently from the cliff. Even if the precipitous nose of the ridge sheared off, the 10-foot bay would be suspended in space but remain anchored by the largest concrete blocks.

Colleagues and family members distinctly recall Pierre Koenig referring to caissons when he spoke to architecture students about his house many years later. However, some also remember him mentioning "a large cube of concrete." The Stahl family believes that the caissons were eliminated and replaced by concrete blocks when the living room was shortened. Referring to the concrete blocks, Bruce said, "Dad always talked about counterweights."

At various times over a five-year period, Neil Jackson, professor emeritus of the Liverpool School of Architecture and president of the Society of Architectural Historians of Great Britain, pored over Koenig's drawings and original documents in the Getty Museum Institute's Special Collection for his excellent book, *Pierre Koenig: A View from the Archive* (2019). Jackson studied the drawings above, considered Buck's comments, and offered his interpretation. What Buck referred to as "counterweights" would be the concrete blocks—noted on the plan (Fig. 3) as Type D and Type C foundations. As Jackson explained in an email from Scotland on September 6, 2020, "They acted, in a sense, as a counterweight to the load on the extended cantilever. However, this is not altogether true. In reality, they acted as a pivot upon which the double-cantilevered beam was supported, one end of the cantilever balancing the other end of the cantilever and the space between the two being bridged by the beam."

Eliminating caissons would have dramatically lowered the cost of the foundations, pointed out architect Mohamed Sharif, assistant adjunct professor in the UCLA Department of Architecture and Urban Design. "This is kind of an archive of value engineering," he said of the apparent shift to a simpler, more traditional foundation. The city's push-back—frustrating as it was at the time—might have actually been another stroke of luck in the evolution of the Stahl House. "I think it's a godsend that the City said, 'Move it back.' They could spend more money on the building, rather than just sinking it into the ground—and still have the same floating effect," Sharif said. "It's basically an essay on economy of expression, economy of means and methods."

One of the curious reasons people even wonder about the foundation is that most people presume, based on Julius Shulman's photograph, that the Stahl House hangs out over space considerably more than it actually does. "A lot of people, including architects, come to the house with the preconception that it's a heroic cantilever," Sharif said. "It's not a heroic cantilever. Its heroism comes from elsewhere." In reality, the living room overhang is only about five to ten feet. It is the magic of Shulman's photograph—the contrast of brightly lit glass box against dark void below—that helps create the illusion. The image enhances the spatial ideas (and special effects) of Koenig's design. "Perhaps talk of deep caissons preserves the myth that a structural bay is hanging audaciously off the hillside, when, in fact, only the southwest corner of the hill-facing floor slab does so, but a surprising little," said Sharif, who found these caisson forensics fascinating, but possibly beside the point.

The general consensus appears to be that it is likely there are no caissons. As Neil Jackson wrote, "In the absence of any other drawings, all I can conclude is that there are no caissons beneath the concrete blocks and the foundations are as shown on the cross-sections in your Fig 2." Whatever method was used, it worked. The house has withstood two major earthquakes, and as Bruce said, "It's been sixty years and counting."

The greatest damage to the Stahl House has come from weather, particularly rain. Several of Buck's stone terraces washed away in a heavy rainstorm. "The first two or three left very early, in the '60s," Carlotta said. "This one stayed, the next one down stayed, and a little part of the other one."

Buck was dashed to see his handiwork washed away. "I came home from work one day and saw the things were gone! That was disheartening after building it," Buck said. "I was just thankful there were no cars or people underneath it." The remaining terraces survived, however, and never required reinforcement. They can still be seen today.

When the weather turned, there was nowhere to hide. Thunderstorms rattled the sliding glass doors in their metal tracks in a way that sounded and felt like an earthquake. The most memorable storm occurred in 1982, when strong winds, possibly a microburst, punched through the glass of the famous corner, funneled through the house, and shattered the east glass wall. "The rain was blowing sideways through the house," recalled Shari, who came to check on her parents during the middle of the storm. As the winds raced through the house, glass shelves with vases were blown out of the house, shattering on the lot below.

"I think it originated in Japan and gathered steam across the Pacific," Buck recalled in an interview with *Echoes* magazine. "I was in the kitchen with my son when it blew in one window and blew out another. We were terrified. My son asked, 'What should we do, Dad?' I said, 'Pray!'" Afterwards, the broken walls were replaced with tempered, single-pane safety glass.

Even fair days can be damaging. The direct sun that shines into the living wing during the morning and late afternoon ravages furniture and carpet. The intense light in the cantilevered corner bakes Christmas trees to a crisp. When Carlotta grew tired of sweeping dried pine needles off the presents beneath every desiccated Douglas fir, she bought a silver aluminum tree that lit up and rotated on a motorized base, lighting up the room like a disco ball. For the pool she made a floating pontoon with a small artificial tree, a miniature Santa, and elf-sized presents.

Aside from natural disasters, one of the greatest threats to the Stahl House is time. In any house, things break and corrode over time, but this house poses new riddles. The wires and pipes embedded in the concrete slab make repairs considerably challenging. "The floor has everything in it—the plumbing, the electrical, the radiant heat—virtually everything was put in the slab," Bruce said. "The problem is the water lines were made of galvanized steel pipes. Eventually they rusted out and deteriorated." The pipes embedded in the slab had to be abandoned, and a new plumbing system was run along the ceiling, hidden in closets and the laundry room, between the bedrooms, master bathroom, and the kitchen. (The original radiant heat pipes in the concrete slab still work.)

The Stahls took care to maintain their home, fixing structural issues and making minor changes to keep the house livable and up to date. They extended the stone base on the fireplace. In 1984, the year Carlotta retired, they renovated the kitchen, updating the pink appliances and changing the cabinetry from Philippine mahogany to oak. The kitchen's dropped ceiling, made of plastic egg-crate sheets that concealed the kitchen lights and wiring, was originally held in place by aluminum runners. Buck replaced the aluminum with oak. "I love wood. It adds warmth to a house," he said. "So I redesigned it to have the effect it has [now], of depth and strength." This is one of the changes that Pierre disliked, and Shari and Bruce plan to restore the kitchen as close to

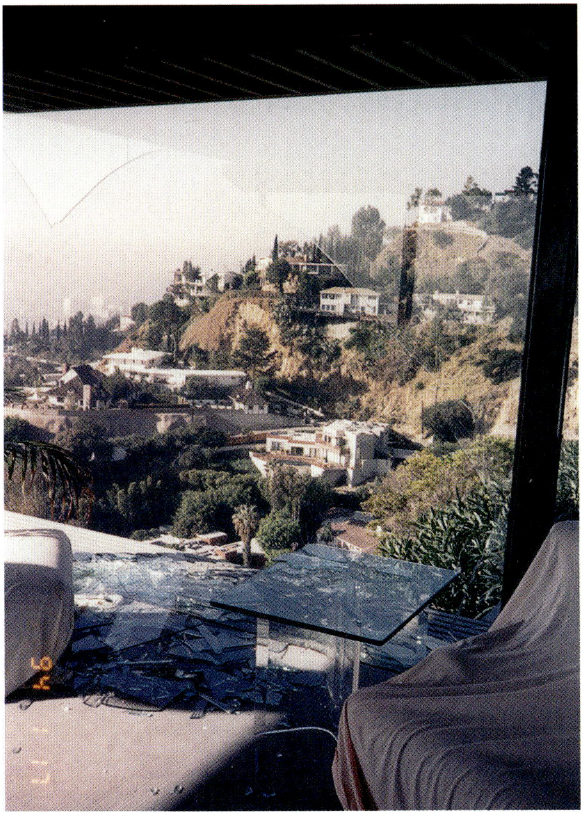

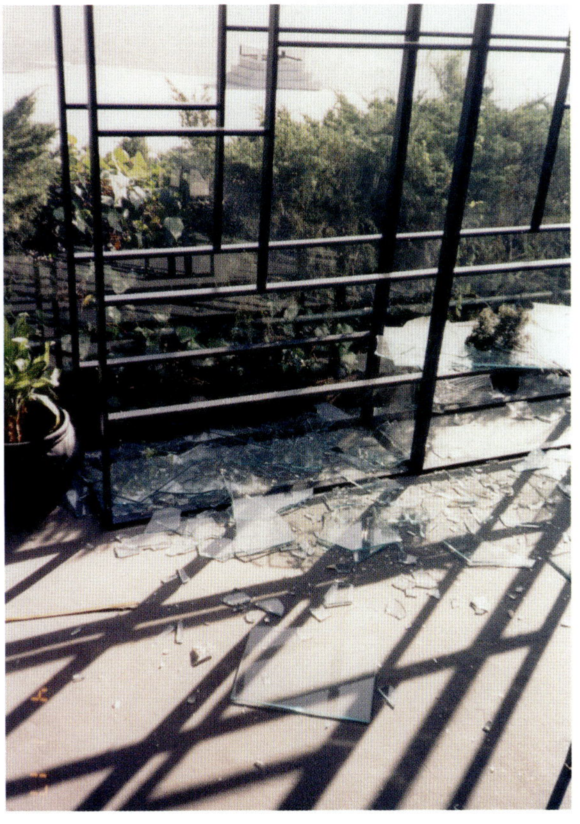

its original state as possible. To the rear wall of the master bedroom, Buck added thin, vertical mirrors, so he could sit with his back to the city and still enjoy the view. (The family wants to leave this as is.)

In 1986, the Stahls added a hot tub on the concrete pool apron where Julius Shulman positioned his tripod all those years before. Visitors always wanted to know where Shulman stood when he took his famous photograph, so Carlotta made a special commemorative plaque with two footprints, his signature, and the inscription: *Julius Shulman Stood Here, May 9, 1960.* (She even borrowed a pair of Shulman's shoes so the footprints would be his exact size.) During tours and on special occasions, she'd place the plaque in the hot tub to mark the spot.

Sometime in the 1980s, Buck surrounded the pool with green Astroturf. But the most egregious change—at least in Shulman's eyes—was the addition of a small catwalk around the exterior of the cantilevered living room, which allowed Buck to wash the windows and hang Christmas lights. Julius Shulman would never let him live this down. "Carlotta, we are going to take down that catwalk, because it hides the view," he insisted. The view, he meant, of the corner he had captured in his photograph. "You can't see the steel suspension, and you realize that the house has been visually destroyed," Shulman said with characteristic bluntness.

Carlotta replied, "We really are, because everybody's against him. All of my children say, 'Let's take it down.'"

Ultimately, the family chose to leave it in place. It's essential for cleaning windows and is often used in photo shoots and filming. "Studios like to be able to put somebody out there," said Shari. "One of my favorite spreads was in *Vogue España*, where the model is standing on the catwalk in a beautiful gown, with the evening city as a backdrop." Sitting on the corner of the catwalk, feet dangling over the city, feels like levitation.

"You're floating," said TerriAnne Drescher, a good family friend who described how the fog rolls off the ocean "like a tidal wave," blanketing the city and erasing the hills until the house appears to be drifting on clouds.

Shari's daughter, Annie, can often be found on the catwalk alone, cross-legged, enjoying the view. "It's her favorite spot in the house," Shari said. "It's been up there so long—to us, it's just part of the house. We have no plans to remove it."

In the eye of the preservationist, these were acceptable "modifications" (as opposed to "alterations" of "character-defining features," which undermine the integrity of a historic house). But Koenig, like many architects, grumbled over any changes made without his blessing.

"They did a lot of things that were not specific to his taste and his way of thinking about a house," said Victor Regnier, his friend and USC colleague. "When the Stahls put green plant materials along the north wall, he felt like it was sacrilege." But for the family who lived there, Case Study House #22 was never a museum piece, an architectural shrine, or an homage to design.

"It's not a museum," Shari said. "It's a home."

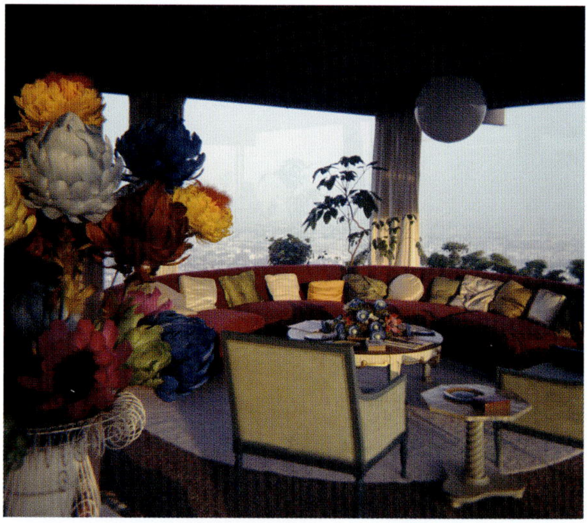

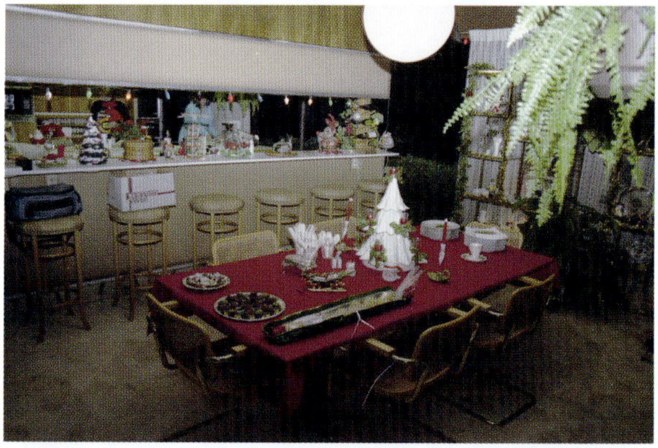

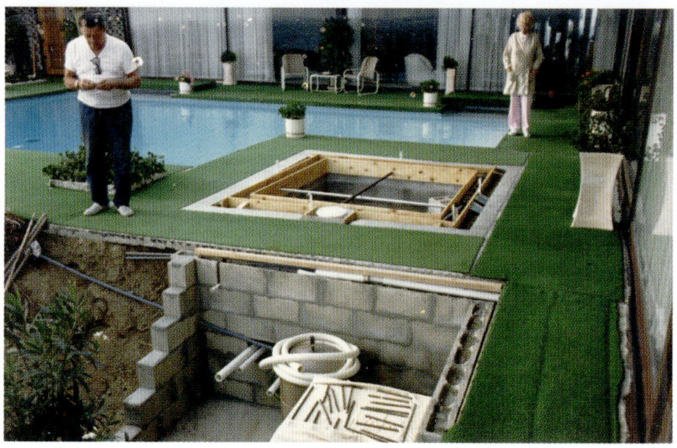

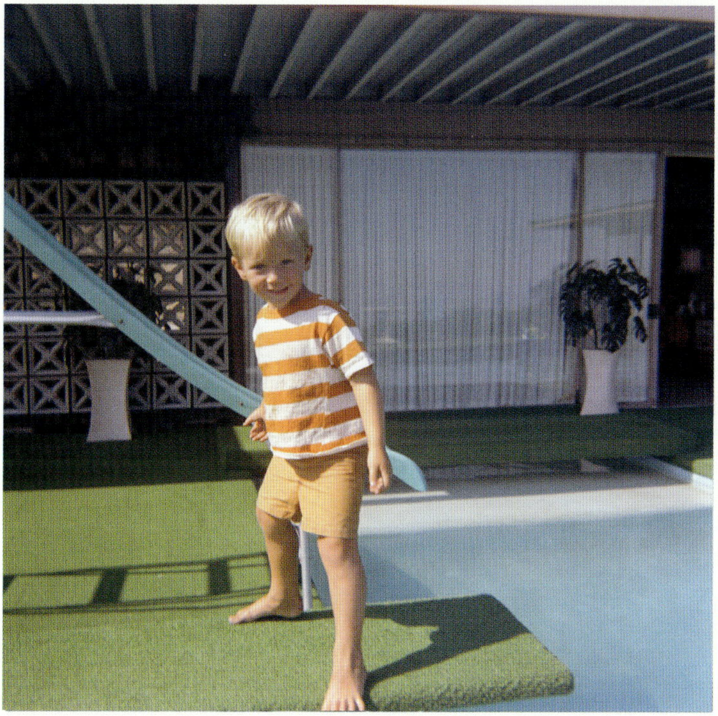

CHAPTER 9
RESURRECTION

One day in October 1989, Buck and Carlotta took their three grown kids to do something that no other family in history can likely claim: They visited an art museum to see their house on exhibit.

"Preview the last thing you'd expect to find in a museum," read the brochure, the cover of which featured Julius Shulman's "Two Girls" photo of their house. It wasn't just photos or a scale model on display. It was a full-size, walk-through replica—a building inside of a building.

The Stahl House mockup was the show-stopping highlight of a landmark exhibition at the Museum of Contemporary Art ("MOCA" to most Angelenos). Blueprints for Modern Living: History and Legacy of the Case Study Houses was one of the most ambitious architectural exhibitions ever produced. It filled the museum's Temporary Contemporary—a 40,000-square-foot former police car warehouse renovated by Frank Gehry in LA's Little Tokyo—with photographs, blueprints, models, design objects, video interviews, ten short films, and full-scale replicas of two houses, plus the façade of a third.

The Stahls had only set foot in one other Case Study House. After touring #21 during its *Arts & Architecture* unveiling, Carlotta had returned a few years later with her kids. "I was too young to understand it," Shari said. "I wanted to go swimming in the water features." Now twenty-nine, Shari was starting to see the Bailey House—as well as her own—with a new sense of appreciation.

As the Stahls entered the exhibition, they stepped into postwar America. As their eyes adjusted to indoor light, they found themselves in a 1945 carport, where a World War II Jeep was parked beneath a corrugated metal ceiling. This was the life-size entrance to Case Study House #4, Ralph Rapson's Greenbelt House, which—until now—had never been built. Published in the September 1945 issue of *Arts & Architecture*, it had never found the right client.

Museum visitors approached the Rapson house as if they were coming home to it, entering through the carport and following a walkway to the eponymous "greenbelt"—a 12-foot-wide interior courtyard flanked by pavilions of glass-walled rooms. On their left they could peer into the bedrooms, and on their right, into a kitchen, living, and dining room that transported them to the 1950s. With a box of Wheaties on the kitchen counter and an electric trainset in the children's room, the house appeared lived in, as if the woman of the house had only just stepped outside to hang the wash (as depicted in Rapson's architectural drawing).

Positioned at the heart of the Greenbelt House, this glass-roofed atrium was the focal point of a house that was, in many ways, antithetical to the Stahl House. Instead of an outward-looking house oriented toward its surroundings, this was an inward-looking arrangement intended for "a more central-urban" location, as Rapson said, where "you didn't have the luxury of a view." It flipped the traditional relationship between home and garden inside out (or rather outside in).

Exiting the Greenbelt House, the Stahls passed a Predicta television, a phonograph, a vacuum cleaner, and other trappings of a postwar lifestyle. A collage of images—*Howdy Doody*, ballpoint pens, newspaper clips of landmark events—formed a visual timeline of the culture and context in which John Entenza's program unfolded. A parade of three-dimensional models, constructed of light, unfinished wood, illustrated the evolutionary progression of Case Study thinking from 1945 to 1966. A partial exterior reconstruction of Case Study House #8 acknowledged the patron saints of modern design: Charles and Ray Eames. In a chapel-like room, Entenza's 1945 manifesto covered a wall. In another, a large screen played a video of architectural writer and historian Esther McCoy—the ultimate witness—being interviewed by Barbara Goldstein, the third and final editor of the magazine Entenza had made famous.

The exhibition was divided by an S-curved wall into "daytime" and "nighttime" areas. Passing through a door in the sinuous wall, the Stahls entered an artificial evening. On a mezzanine beneath the museum ceiling, they found themselves walking through an eerily familiar carport. As they stepped out by the pool, they were struck by the big reveal. Lit from within, their house glowed ethereally, a monument suspended in a starless space as dark as a new-moon night. In the void beyond, where the city should lie, a series of TV sets flickered in the distance. Viewed up close on the lower level, the screens of various sizes played a thirty-minute film of interviews with architects, critics, and homeowners. Seen collectively at a distance, from the Stahl House above, the screens created the illusion of depth and mimicked the glittering lights of the city.

Buck, Carlotta, Bruce, Shari, and Mark wandered through the replica of their home, which had been staged with mid-century furnishings more stylish than any they'd ever owned. It felt like walking through a life-size diorama, or seeing one's little sister dressed up for her first prom. This was the ultimate Hollywood moment—dramatic, compelling, almost real, literally and figuratively transcendental, hovering above history. They were standing in the only Case Study House that would ever be built twice.

Bruce, thirty-one, was so bemused that he couldn't help but turn to the nearest visitor and eagerly blurt, "I grew up in this house!"

"Oh my gosh!" the stranger, a woman, said. "*This* is your *home*?"

It was, and it wasn't. The builders had followed Pierre Koenig's plan, reproducing the house "in faithful detail," as the *New York Times* noted, "down to the furniture in its rooms and the 1950s appliances in its kitchen." Yet there were subtle differences (besides furniture) invisible to anyone but the Stahls. "When you've grown up in a house and you know every inch of it," Bruce said, "you can tell." Shari felt the same way. "Everything was in its place, but not spot on," Shari said. "And it felt dark. Way too dark." Even with the TV screens flickering in the distance, the house was not quite as luminous without the dome of stars above or the shimmer of city lights below. Most visitors were enchanted. To the Stahls, it felt like a strange yet not unpleasant dream. It also impressed upon them that their home, in the eyes of the world, was art.

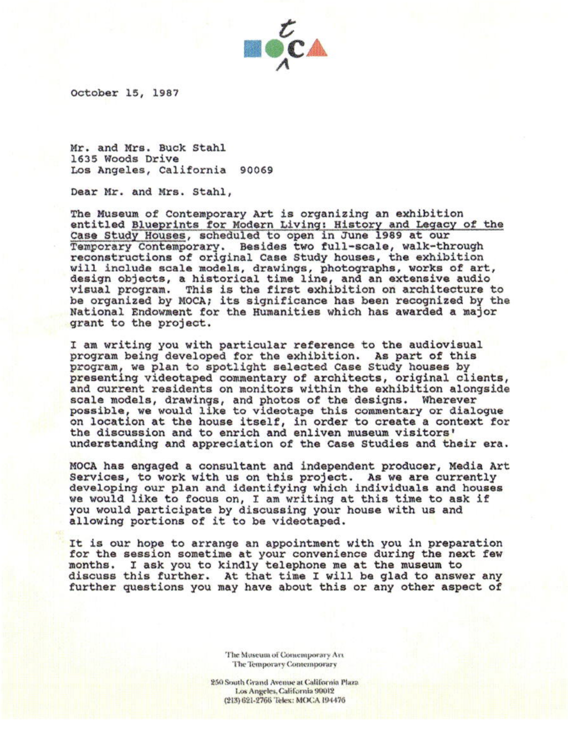

October 15, 1987

Mr. and Mrs. Buck Stahl
1635 Woods Drive
Los Angeles, California 90069

Dear Mr. and Mrs. Stahl,

The Museum of Contemporary Art is organizing an exhibition entitled Blueprints for Modern Living: History and Legacy of the Case Study Houses, scheduled to open in June 1989 at our Temporary Contemporary. Besides two full-scale, walk-through reconstructions of original Case Study houses, the exhibition will include scale models, drawings, photographs, works of art, design objects, a historical time line, and an extensive audio visual program. This is the first exhibition on architecture to be organized by MOCA; its significance has been recognized by the National Endowment for the Humanities which has awarded a major grant to the project.

I am writing you with particular reference to the audiovisual program being developed for the exhibition. As part of this program, we plan to spotlight selected Case Study houses by presenting videotaped commentary of architects, original clients, and current residents on monitors within the exhibition alongside scale models, drawings, and photos of the designs. Wherever possible, we would like to videotape this commentary or dialogue on location at the house itself, in order to create a context for the discussion and to enrich and enliven museum visitors' understanding and appreciation of the Case Studies and their era.

MOCA has engaged a consultant and independent producer, Media Art Services, to work with us on this project. As we are currently developing our plan and identifying which individuals and houses we would like to focus on, I am writing at this time to ask if you would participate by discussing your house with us and allowing portions of it to be videotaped.

It is our hope to arrange an appointment with you in preparation for the session sometime at your convenience during the next few months. I ask you to kindly telephone me at the museum to discuss this further. At that time I will be glad to answer any further questions you may have about this or any other aspect of

The Museum of Contemporary Art
The Temporary Contemporary

250 South Grand Avenue at California Plaza
Los Angeles, California 90012
(213) 621-2766 Telex: MOCA 194476

"Walking through MOCA, it kind of hit me," Shari said. "This must be special. Otherwise, they wouldn't have done this."

The *New York Times* architecture critic Paul Goldberger called the Stahl House and Greenbelt House replicas "the real knock-'em-dead crowd- pleasers" of "a marvelous, voluptuous, sweeping, exhilarating, and at times frustrating exhibition." He acknowledged the TV screens as "either a happy accident or devilishly clever irony." They were, in fact, part of a master plan with an exquisite attention to detail that extended to every inch of the exhibition. Even the metal supports holding up the twenty-two Case Study models were deliberately designed to resemble the abstract lines and dots that appeared on the *Arts & Architecture* cover in January 1945, the issue in which John Entenza announced the Case Study House Program.

The exhibition was supported enthusiastically by Esther McCoy, who chronicled the Case Study House Program more thoroughly and insightfully than any other writer. "I took her to lunch at Michael's," recalled Richard Koshalek, then director of MOCA. "She said, 'Richard, please do an important exhibition on Case Study [Houses].'" Koshalek had first learned of the Case Study program from John Entenza himself, when they met in 1960 at an art event. Entenza's concepts were particularly relevant for a museum founded by artists "to reflect the reality of contemporary art, architecture, and culture," Koshalek said.

In 1984, he tapped Elizabeth Smith, then a twenty-six-year-old assistant curator at MOCA, to oversee a project so ambitious it would take five years to realize. "It was the right time for modernism to be recognized again," Smith said.

"Dawn to dusk" became the unifying narrative of the exhibition, designed by Craig Hodgetts and Ming Fung, architects and partners in a design firm that also created movie sets. "We were thinking about the dawn and dusk of the Case Study House Program," Fung said. "We picked the Rapson House to represent the dawn, on the lighter side of the exhibit. The Koenig house signified the end, so that was in the dusk." To make the experience more empathetic than academic, Hodgetts and Fung positioned the viewer inside the house, rather than outside looking in. "It was really important to do an exhibition on architecture that was accessible to people," Fung said. "We wanted people to envision how the house was lived in."

It was also a nod to Entenza's open-house tours. "One of the touchstones was the fact that when the original case study houses were first built, they were open for the public," Smith said.

Hodgetts and Fung had reached out to Pierre Koenig, who took a sabbatical from USC to help with the exhibition. From the start, they were struck by his unwavering

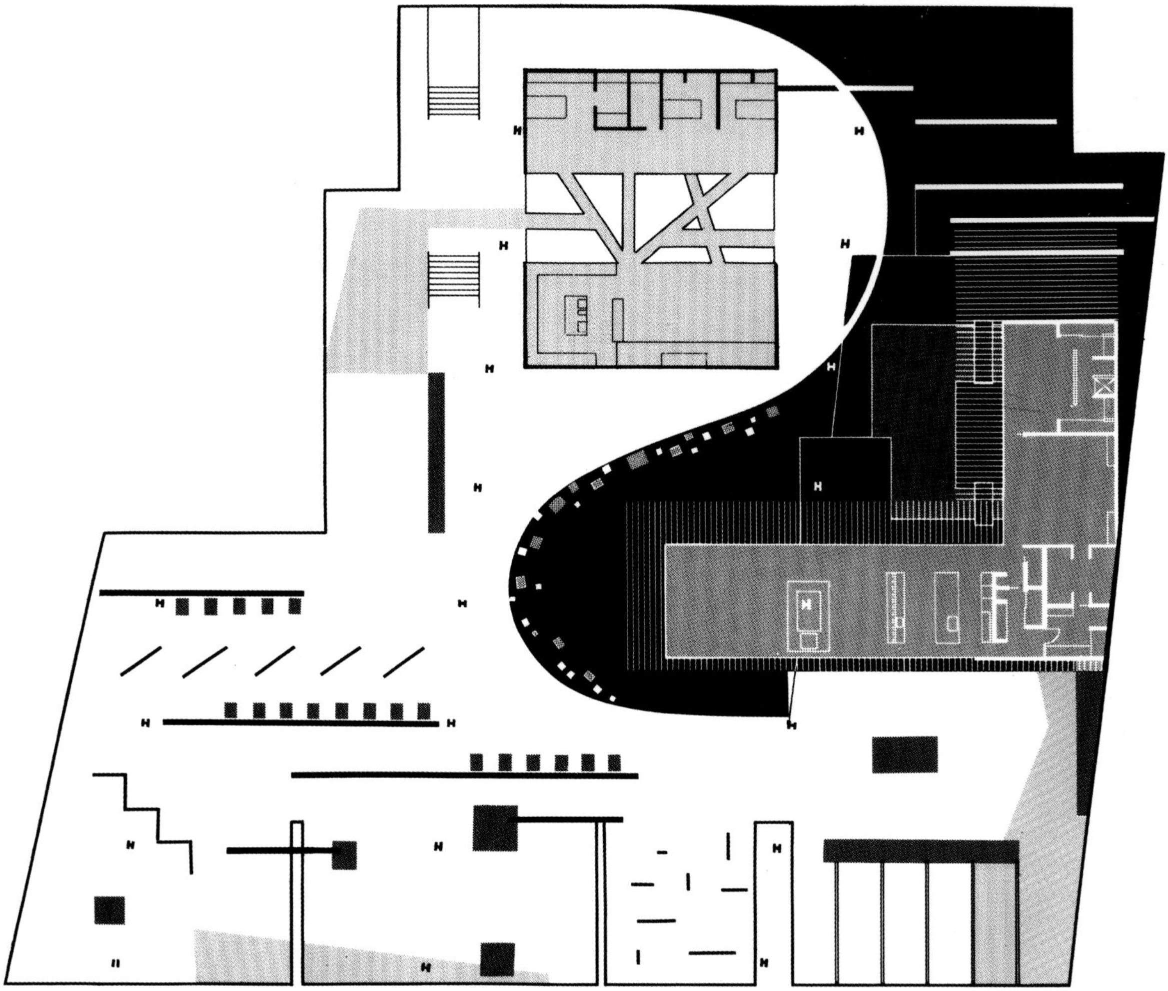

commitment to authenticity and precision. "He insisted it had to be steel," Fung said.

Hodgetts added, "He stressed that if he was going to allow us to make a replica, it had to be a *replica*—full stop." However, the roof would be hung from the museum ceiling, which could not support the weight of steel. A team of movie-set designers instead used wood, sculpted and painted to look like steel. "Pierre came and looked at the roof and said, 'Oh, how great; you made it out of steel,'" Hodgetts recalled.

Added Fung: "We didn't say a word."

The pool presented another challenge. "We were going to have water in the pool," Fung said, "but for all sorts of technical reasons, we couldn't even have an inch." As opening day approached, MOCA's installation expert, John Bowsher, proposed a solution: Because it was a nighttime scene, the pool could be suggested by a swath of black vinyl. Stage lighting would glint off the glossy surface like ambient light off an unlit pool.

While Koenig was advising the designers, Julius Shulman was helping exhibition curator Elizabeth Smith select photos of the Case Study Houses, the majority of which he had photographed. "This is coming back full circle," Shulman observed. "Perhaps people are beginning to realize … that what was done on those days was good, was a contribution." He also saw the opportunity "to invoke the feeling—among students especially, young architects—that, 'Hey, this is good! Let's find out how we can infuse this philosophy into present-day architecture.'"

A month after the Blueprints opening, Esther McCoy celebrated her eighty-fifth birthday with a private party at the Temporary Contemporary. Holding court beside an oxygen tank while smoking cigarettes, she was toasted by friends including architect Frank Gehry and *New York Times* architecture critic Joseph Giovannini, who orchestrated the party with the help of MOCA director Richard Koshalek. "I asked Richard if we could do a black-tie dinner in the space," Giovannini said. "He said, 'Only if I can wait at the table.'" Unable to attend, Robert Venturi—a legendary architect who rejected modernism but adored McCoy—sent a chair from his design collection to enthrone the guest of honor. Michael Sorkin, an architectural critic, was also unable to attend, but roasted McCoy remotely by sending an epic poem that he wrote for her in iambic pentameter.

One of McCoy's last writings was a tribute to John Entenza, who had died of cancer in 1984 at the age of seventy-eight. This essay joined others by Thomas Hines, Reyner Banham, and other great minds of the movement, published in the exhibition's catalogue, a 256-page illustrated book that is still selling thirty years later. In her last weeks, MOCA director Richard Koshalek took McCoy to lunch once more to hear her assessment of the exhibition she had proposed to him years before. "Richard," she said, "I think you did it." Two months after its grand opening, McCoy died of emphysema at home in Santa Monica on December 30, 1989.

The MOCA exhibition—and the subsequent press—acknowledged the great irony of the Case Study program. "Although the Case Study houses did not ultimately achieve John Entenza's vision of revolutionizing public taste and the building industry, the program had a significant international architectural legacy," wrote McCoy. The program failed to establish modernism in a residential setting. The goal of creating prototypes that would bring good design within reach of all people did not come to fruition. The houses were never duplicated (much less mass-produced), and most were not that affordable.

As rational as Entenza's ideas were, there were forces working against them. "It comes down to banks, insurance, the Federal Housing Authority, and the Veterans Administration," said historian Philip Ethington. "They were giving out low-interest loans, but they were prejudiced against modern designs. They wanted things that were solid in the market, with pitched roofs and standard building materials and drywall."

The construction industry was rooted in traditional practices and resistant to change. Building codes discouraged innovation and favored the status quo. Contractors accustomed to building wood houses lacked the expertise, skills, and tools for steelwork. "Esther McCoy told me that the reason the Case Study idea of industrial housing didn't take was because it was predicated on steel construction, and the tolerances for factory work were greater than could be achieved by contractors," said Giovannini. "In Southern California, contractors were working out of the backs of their trucks. They couldn't handle steel. They worked with wood, which is like butter—you can bang it up and cut it. So, tolerances meant that the required expertise was beyond the scope of contractors."

The market for steel houses was limited. Most people could not imagine themselves living in a glass box, as Julius Shulman himself had witnessed. "I would attend some of these houses when they were open to the public," he said. "I listened to people coming through the houses. ... 'I don't want to live in a goldfish bowl!'"

Yet somehow, the ideas—and just as importantly, the optimism—endured. "While there is no doubt that the architects and the editor who set out to build the houses were fired with missionary zeal and hoped to change the world, the program's main impact was esthetic rather than social or economic," wrote Barbara Goldstein, who, with a similar hopefulness, resuscitated the magazine as *Arts + Architecture,* a regional quarterly in print from 1981 to 1985. "It influenced the hierarchy of the postwar house plan; it presented ideas for casual lifestyles, for merging indoor and outdoor space, and for innovations in kitchens and landscapes."

This is, par excellence, an architecture of elegant omission that takes Mies van der Rohe's dictum about *Weniger ist Mehr* (Less is More) even further than the master himself had ever done.

— Reyner Banham, *Los Angeles: The Architecture of Four Ecologies* (1971)

The Blueprints exhibition—one of the most well-attended and critically acclaimed shows ever presented by MOCA—reinvigorated public interest in the Case Study program, both from those who were aware of it and from a whole new generation. Critic Mary Badham noted "the positive response from the largely young audience to both the architectural and the social aims of the Case Study program." Craig Hodgetts and Ming Fung would observe the increasing disappearance of mid-century modern furniture from thrift stores, where their stylists had gathered props for staging the exhibits.

Curator Elizabeth Smith was overwhelmed with positive feedback from practitioners who had taken the exhibits to heart: "I heard from so many younger architects who were inspired by the work that they'd seen in the show and wanted to direct their own work toward a more modern type of vocabulary."

The Blueprints exhibition also revitalized the career and reputation of Pierre Koenig, who had remarked in 1988 that most people thought he was dead. After the Stahl House, he had declined to do another Case Study house. His legacy had faded, and his seminal influence had been largely unsung—even in the USC School of Architecture, where he had been teaching since 1962 but was still an associate professor. "He didn't have much of a following at USC," said Victor Regnier, dean of the architecture school from 1992 to 1996. "When I got to know him, he had only a few close colleagues and had been relegated to our building science program."

After the MOCA show, Koenig began receiving the attention that he (and many others) believed he deserved. "I have been happy for you during this new exposure of the Case Study Houses," wrote architect Jim Tyler in a letter to Koenig. "I believe that it gives you some recognition that is long overdue; I always felt that you were shortchanged on publication of your work and maybe additional clients, because of your quiet demeanor and mannerly approach in dealing with people. Possibly this will bring you new projects and opportunities for the future."

It did. "From 1992 to 1996, he got more attention in those four years than he got in the previous twenty," said Regnier, who pushed for Koenig's promotion to full professor in 1997. The following year, Koenig was named USC Distinguished Professor, a rare honor selectively awarded by the university president "to those whose accomplishments have brought special renown to USC." So far, he is the only member of the School of Architecture to receive this distinction. He went on to receive the USC Distinguished Alumni Award and the Architectural Gold Medal from the American Institute of Architects, Los Angeles.

All his life, Koenig never wavered in his commitment to steel and prefabrication, even when those things fell out of vogue. After years of feeling ignored and undervalued, he finally felt vindicated and validated. "It's pay-off time," Koenig told *Echoes* magazine in 1998. "Now it is all coming back. All those years I have put into it, it is coming back."

The MOCA exhibition had two ancillary programs that illustrated how John Entenza's ideas continued to ripple out into the world. The first came straight from Entenza's playbook: MOCA commissioned several architects to design prototypes to address two of LA's current social needs—affordable multifamily housing and residential units for seniors. The winning multifamily plan, by Adèle Naudè Santos, would be built by the Community Redevelopment Agency of the City of Los Angeles. It stands today on the corner of La Brea and Franklin Avenues in Hollywood.

The second was a series of home tours written and hosted by the Los Angeles Conservancy, a nonprofit group founded in 1978 to protect historic places. On February 4 and February 11, 1990, members of the public were invited into seven houses that represented nearly the entire spectrum of the Case Study House Program. They included a wood-frame house by Richard Neutra (#20), the eternally relevant Eames House (#8), and a steel-and-glass pavilion by Raphael Soriano (1950). Pierre Koenig was the only architect with two houses on the tour.

Koenig had recently overseen the restoration of Case Study House #21, correcting structural issues caused by geological problems beneath the house. (It took longer to restore the house than it took to build it in the first place.) The authors of the tour described "the spartan simplicity" that exemplified his work, praising "the economy of materials and plan that would emphasize the elegance of the structure."

Tour author Mary Alice Wollam recalled meeting with Buck and Carlotta one sparkling night when the rain had washed away the smog. Buck encouraged her to walk on the catwalk suspended over the cliff. "My fingers were like little tentacles," she recalled. "I was holding on to the window as I was walking around the house, over the precipice." When her heart rate finally came down, she began scripting the tour in her mind.

Buck and Carlotta had a warm relationship with the L.A. Conservancy, a group of preservationists who truly appreciated what their house meant, not only to them but to the city. They hosted Conservancy cocktail parties and member-appreciation events where donors and volunteers would mingle in a place that reminded them why they worked so hard to protect buildings they did not own. Once, when a guest fell into the pool, Buck offered his own clothes to the man, who went home in Buck's sweat suit, carrying a plastic bag of sopping clothes.

On the two Saturdays of the house tour, Buck and Carlotta welcomed between six hundred and eight hundred people into their home. Unlike the informal tours Carlotta gave to visitors, these were highly choreographed, as efficient as an assembly line. While guests did not have much time to linger, the experience of being in the place nonetheless left a deep and lasting impression. Some of them would be inspired to protect a building in their own neighborhood. Others would join the Conservancy's Modern Committee (ModCom), which saw an uptick in new, young members. One young man, an architectural preservationist named Peter Moruzzi, would be inspired to do something much bigger.

Moruzzi "made a pilgrimage" from San Francisco to see the MOCA exhibition. "I had seen photos, but I had never been to the house until that tour," Moruzzi said. "It's such a pure expression of postwar modern architecture, and its setting, projected out over a vast expanse of the city—I've never experienced anything quite like that."

Moruzzi subsequently moved to Los Angeles and joined the Conservancy, committed to the notion that advocacy starts with education. People can't be moved to preserve anything they don't understand and appreciate. He would devote years of tireless effort toward getting the Case Study Houses listed on the National Register of Historic Places. Looking back on this moment, thirty years later, Moruzzi would still feel the swell of emotions that washed over him when he first set foot in the Stahl House on that 1990 tour.

"It was life altering."

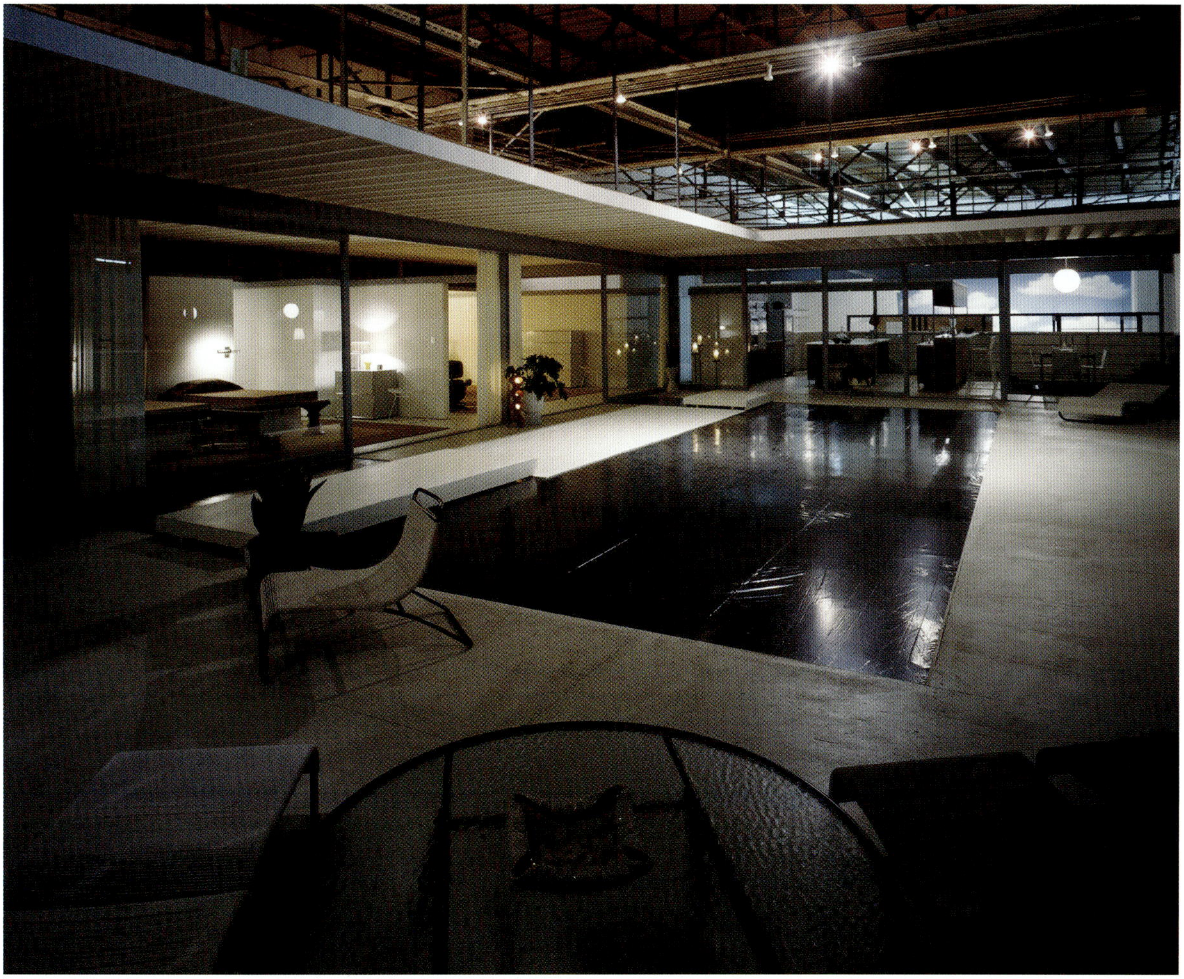

CHAPTER 10
CELEBRITY

Films Featuring the Stahl House

Smog **(1962)**
The First Power **(1990)**
The Marrying Man **(1991)**
Corrina, Corrina **(1994)**
Playing by Heart **(1998)**
Why Do Fools Fall in Love **(1998)**
Galaxy Quest **(1999)**
The Thirteenth Floor **(1999)**
Nurse Betty **(2000)**
Where the Truth Lies **(2005)**
Knight of Cups **(2015)**

In the spring of 1990, the vocal trio Wilson Phillips arrived at the Stahl House to film the video for their second single, "Release Me." In the sultry black-and-white video, directed by Julien Temple, three daughters of 1960s rock royalty harmonized around a grand piano in the cantilevered living room. "It turned out to be the perfect moody setting," Carnie Wilson said, "and it was part of a No. 1 single and video back in the day."

Carnie and Wendy Wilson—daughters of the Beach Boys co-founder Brian Wilson and Marilyn Wilson of the Honeys—had written the song with childhood friend and fellow vocalist Chynna Phillips, the daughter of John Phillips and Michelle Phillips of The Mamas & the Papas.

Four days of back-to-back filming had their stylists and makeup artists napping on the floor of the Stahl House, but the artists were energized and inspired by the "magical vibe" of a location that made them feel "like Hollywood royalty."

"The energy of the house was amazing," Wendy Wilson said. "You just felt like you were right there, in Los Angeles, in the vibe. The house—you stepped in and you felt like you were floating in the air."

The video marked the rise of Wilson Phillips and the beginning of a new chapter for the Stahl House, which quickly became a coveted location for filming and photo shoots. Later that year, Lou Diamond Phillips came to the house to film scenes for a horror movie called *The First Power*. The following year, the house portrayed a bachelor pad in *The Marrying Man*, a romantic comedy starring Alec Baldwin and Kim Basinger.

The pool played a prominent role in several films, including *Why Do Fools Fall in Love*: a 1998 film about Frankie Lymon, a doo-wop singer whose death brings out three widows claiming his estate. Restyled with bloodred shag carpet, the house gets trashed over the course of the movie—windows boarded over with plywood, globe lights busted, furniture moldering in a blackened pool.

"I sure hope they can bring my house back," Carlotta said when she saw it.

In one scene, one of Frankie's wives (Halle Berry) is shoved into the pool by another (Vivica Fox) in a spectacularly vicious catfight. One weekend before filming the scene, Fox and Berry rehearsed the scene at the house. "They went at it tooth and nail," recalled Jane Graves, the key assistant location manager, who was waiting off set and out of sight in the carport. "They were screaming at the top of their lungs and really getting into their performances." In the midst of their raucous rehearsal, an LAPD cruiser pulled up. "Someone had called 911 about a violent domestic dispute," Graves said. "It was two women screaming at the top of the mountain—people were concerned, so they called the police."

In 1999, the house appeared in *Galaxy Quest*, a sci-fi comedy in which Tim Allen plays the star of a defunct science fiction TV show with a cult following. One morning, he wakes up in the living room—facedown, hungover, and pantless—to a crew of friendly Thermians from the Klaatu Nebula, knocking on the glass walls. Carlotta found this delightful. "I just loved those little aliens!" she said.

Curiously, of all the movies that were filmed at the house, none portrayed the house as the home of a family with kids. "In the movies, a glass house and children don't mix," Carlotta said, "and bad guys never have children."

In the nineties, the Stahl House served as a filming location for seven feature films, including *Playing by Heart* (1998) and *The Thirteenth Floor* (1999). It appeared in *Vogue*, and in an LA Gear ad featuring a model on a swing dangling from the roof. The house showed up in Nordstrom's brochures, in a fashion shoot for British *Elle*, a Company Store catalogue filled with down comforters, and in Armani ads that ran in *W* magazine. It was on the cover of at least three music albums.

Requests for filming movies, TV shows, advertising campaigns, and music videos proliferated throughout the 1990s. Buck and Carlotta suddenly found they had a new source of income: location fees, which could range from a couple thousand dollars for a photo shoot to ten thousand dollars—per day—for a movie. The house was now providing for the family.

The Stahl House was added to the "location libraries" of Hollywood location-scouting companies, which catalogued the unique advantages the house offered to moviemakers. The glass walls make it easy to film the interior from the exterior—an arrangement not unlike a set on a soundstage, where rooms can be built with three walls, not four. "You can set up a shot with the pool in the foreground, and through the glass wall you can see right into the house," location manager John Panzarella told the *L.A. Times*. He selected the house for the 2000 film *Nurse Betty*, starring Greg Kinnear, Renée Zellweger, and Morgan Freeman. "You can shoot a McMansion any time you want, and no one will remember it. It just satisfies my creative juices to get great architecture into movies."

Now that Buck and Carlotta were both retired, with the shoots being managed by location companies and trusted site reps, the couple finally had the time to travel, making epic road trips in "Buck's Hanky-Panky Van," and bringing Mark along. As the children grew older, they would take over as site reps, along with Bruce's wife, Melisa.

Hosting a film crew is a spectacle in which dozens of people descend on a house in what appears to be mass chaos. First come the people who cover the floors, Bubble Wrap doors, and pad surfaces that might get dinged or damaged. Then they bring in wardrobe, which must be steamed and organized. The models arrive for hair and makeup, which usually takes a couple of hours. Stylists and photographers stage the set, taking Polaroids and adjusting the light. When the shoot begins, it's orchestrated madness, like a hive of bees working in concert.

This is when homeowners are generally expected to make themselves scarce. Buck and Carlotta sometimes escaped to the kids' bedroom—which they had converted into a guest bedroom and office—and drew the curtains. Some crews were so big they spilled out of the house and into the neighbors' driveways, which they rented out for space to unload, turn trucks around, park vehicles, or cater meals for the crew. On such shoots, Buck and Carlotta often had to move out of the house for a few days. But they didn't mind, particularly when filming agreements included a room at the famed Chateau Marmont, the 1929 boutique hotel on Sunset Boulevard, downhill from the Stahl House. Carlotta always requested a view of the hills, not the city, so she could look up at her house.

When shoots were small, Carlotta welcomed the crew into her home as if they were guests. "She was everybody's mum," said Catherine Meyler, a location agent who has represented the Stahl House for decades. "She treated the people on the shoot like her kids. That's another reason people liked going up there so much. Usually you have to take your shoes off and be very careful. Sometimes something gets damaged because people are so tense. Carlotta made everyone feel so relaxed. Very rarely was there ever any damage. People took care, out of respect."

Carlotta was protective of her home's integrity, and she flat-out rejected offers from adult photographers and filmmakers hoping to shoot at the house. A strict no-nudity policy was written into all contracts. On one fashion shoot, Carlotta was sitting in the house when she noticed a topless

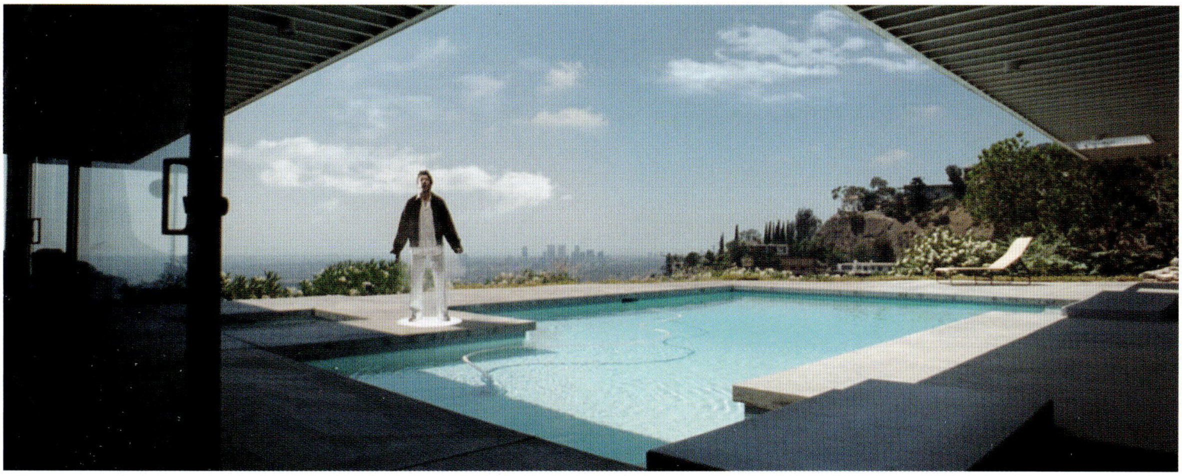

Tim Allen in Galaxy Quest.

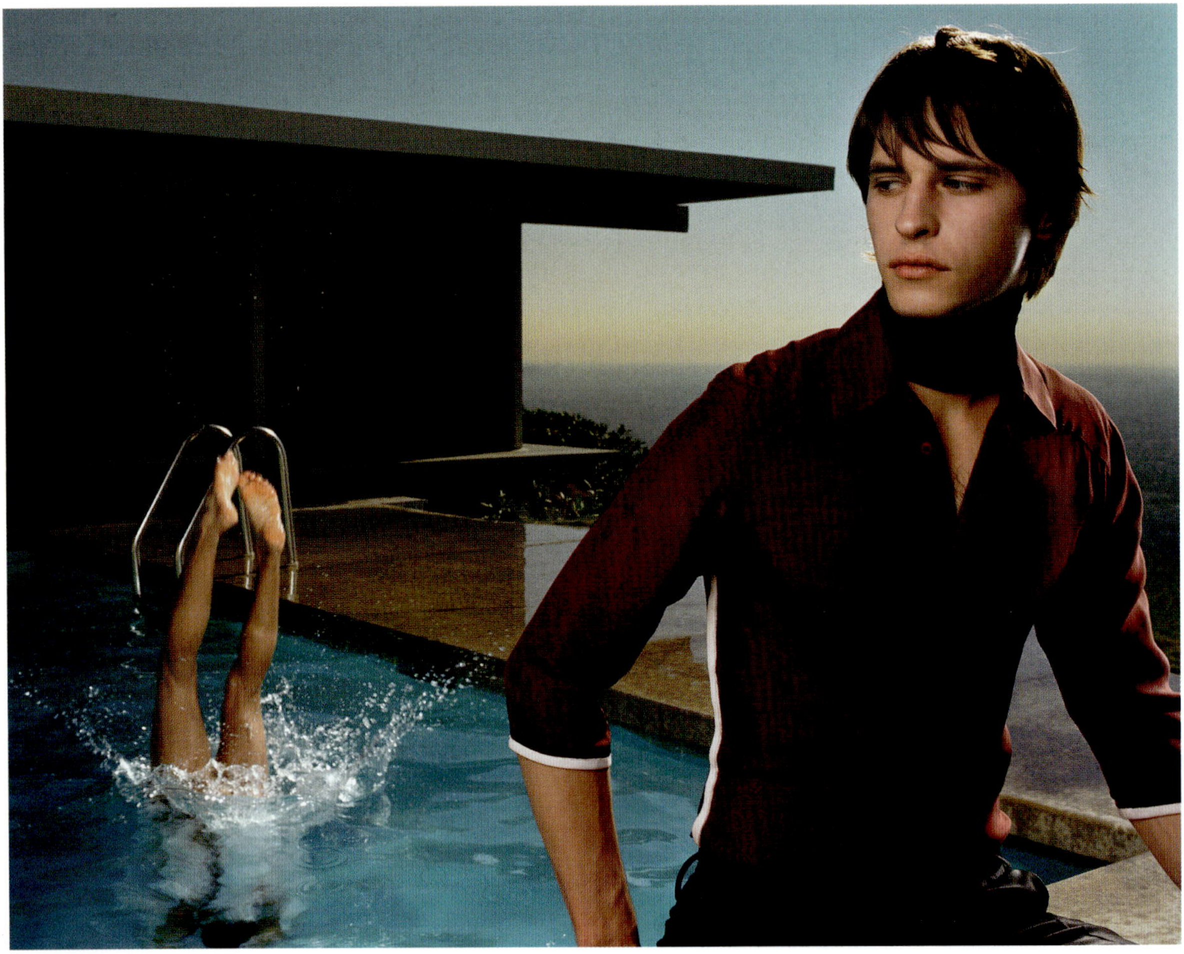

Miu Miu ad campaign.

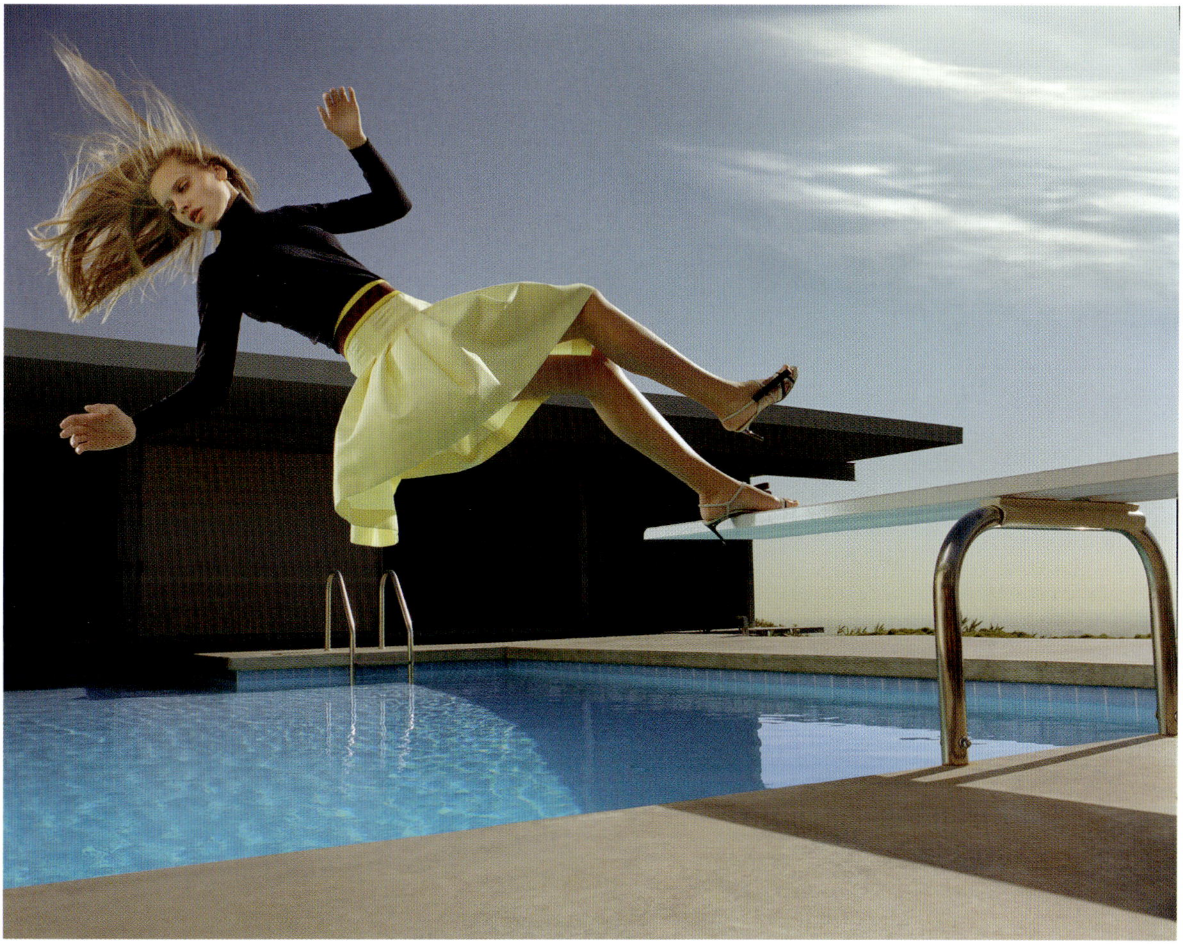

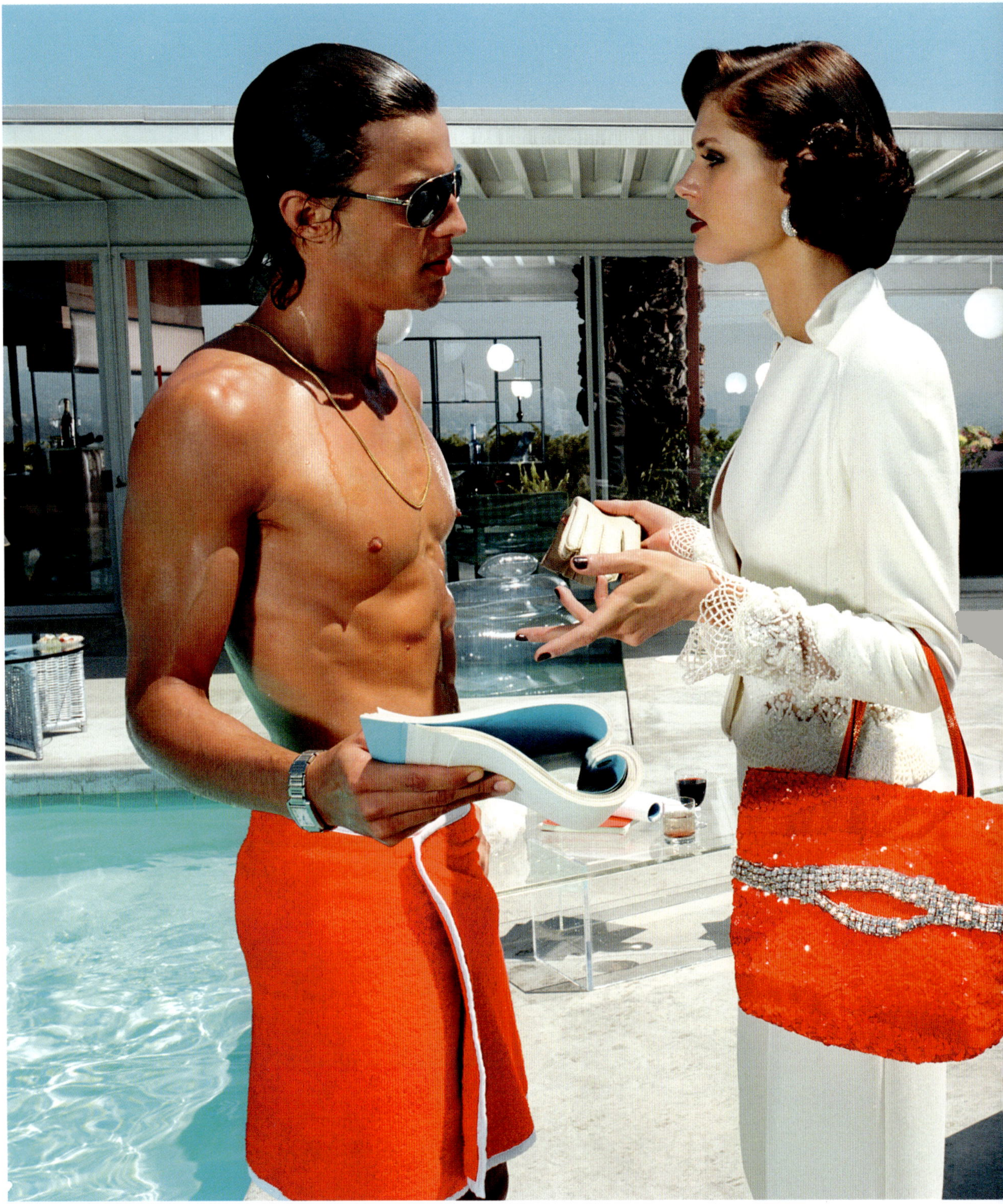

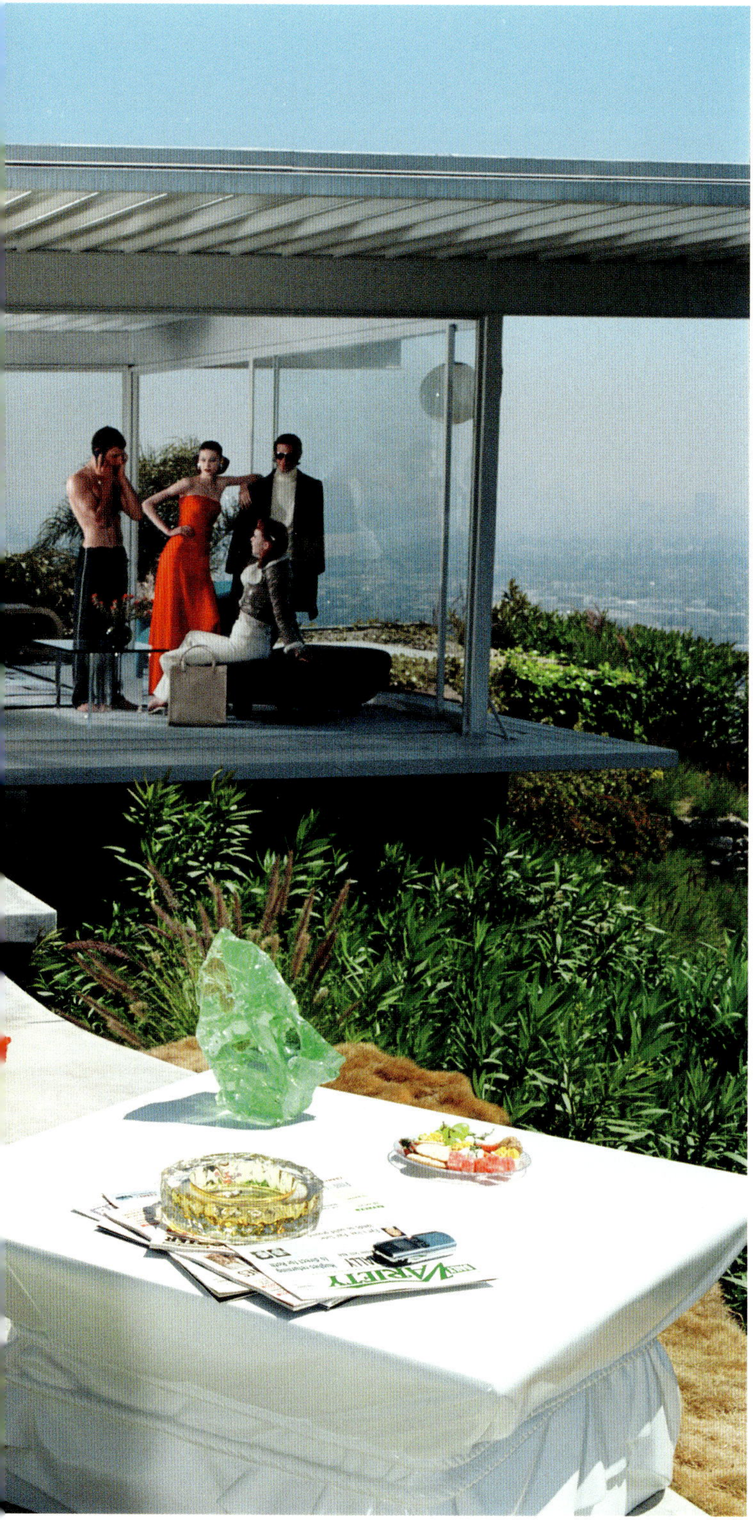

Valentino ad campaign.

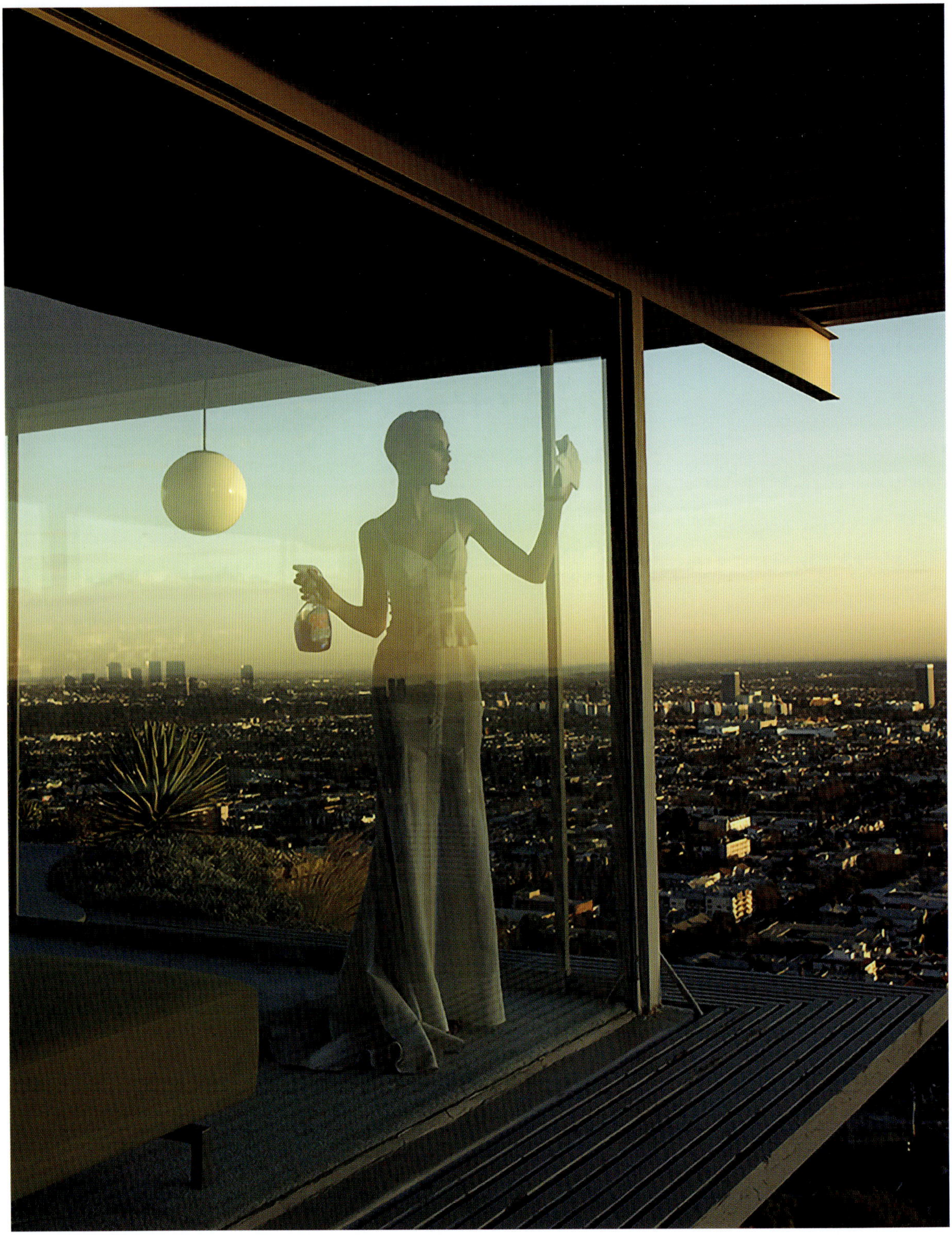

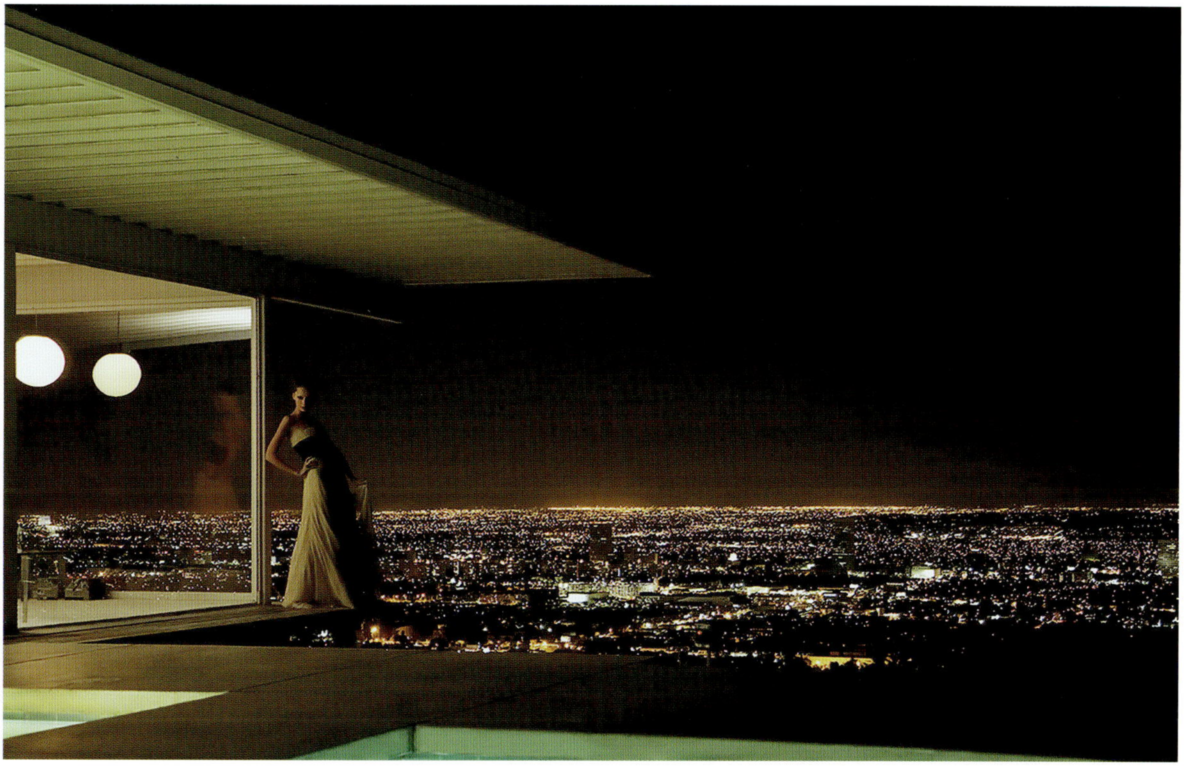

Vogue España

model facing her. The woman had her naked back to the camera, but her naked front to the house. Carlotta was very upset. Phone calls were made. It was explained that the shot would show bare shoulder, the model's face in profile, and the purse—nothing more. But an assistant was promptly dispatched to buy pasties or something (anything!) to cover the model's nipples. Future contracts were amended to prohibit both nudity and "implied nudity." (The policy remains in place today.)

Bruce, Shari, and Mark grew up immune to being starstruck. So many A-list celebrities passed through their house they can hardly recall all the names. "Charlize Theron did a L'Oréal commercial or something up here," Bruce said. "We've had Heidi Klum and Seal when they were still married. In between shots he was singing."

Bruce's wife, Melisa, recalled, "It felt like we were getting a private concert, Seal singing in the house."

Jennifer Garner filmed a Neutrogena commercial at the house. Christie Brinkley narrated a video for an airline. Cameron Diaz posed in a swimsuit for the cover of *GQ*. Gisele Bündchen modeled Victoria's Secret lingerie. Rascal Flatts shot an album cover. Paris Hilton straddled a motor scooter. Lindsay Lohan did a fashion shoot. The list goes on and on: Jennifer Aniston. The Olsen twins. Natalie Portman. Cindy Crawford. Kevin Bacon. The cast of *Entourage*. "I try not to talk to the actors," Shari said of her work as a site rep, tasked with handling the house, cast, and crew with professional detachment. She's there to answer questions about the house, make decisions on how it is used, and help direct traffic on the narrow neighborhood street. Mostly, she tries to stay out of the way. "I have my job to do. They have theirs."

Photographers love shooting at the house. "It's one of my favorite places in the world," said photographer/director Dewey Nicks. "It screams of title sequences and that golden age of Los Angeles architecture." Perhaps because the house is not very big, he said that no matter which lens he chooses, "it fits into the frame of a camera very well." Wide-angle captures the pool and expansive view. A normal lens crops the pool and roofline into geometric compositions. A telephoto emphasizes the way the light bounces off the glass or the hint of blue that suggests a pool. And a shoot there carries cache. "There is something about procuring a shoot at the Stahl House as a photographer in LA that lets other photographers know you're working on a great project. It's a name-drop. You would name-drop that in one of those 'brag-plain' conversations: *Oh my gosh, we were up at the top of the hill all day . . . couldn't come down . . . shooting the Stahl House. . . .* War stories with a very sexy punchline."

The house shoots well not only because of its natural light and glamour but also because of its ability to disappear or play a supporting role. "The house provides a sort of frame for still photography," said Meyler, the location agent who has been called the Eileen Ford of modernist homes. "Your eye goes to the model. The house becomes a frame, a subtle there-but-not-quite-there element."

One of her favorite shoots was a Valentino campaign photographed by Stephen Meisel, a fashion photographer considered one of the industry's best. Based in New York, Meisel came to Los Angeles to shoot high fashion and high architecture together, producing imagery with a near-mythical glamour. "If you imagine all those models standing around in a studio, the effect would be totally different," Meyler said. "The fact that it's so high up and overlooks the whole city also brings in this hierarchy where you're above it all. This is all happening at a higher level than the rest of the city."

For many of these still shoots, Carlotta and Buck were present, sitting in the kitchen and bemusedly observing the spectacle unfolding in their backyard. Carlotta welcomed celebrities and supermodels into her home with the same unaffected hospitality she extended to architecture students. "I think the girls warmed to Carlotta because she was so genuinely kind to *them*; she didn't know if anyone was famous, or their level of fame," Meyler said. "They were just visitors, and she was gracious and warm to everyone. I think she felt maternal toward the girls, and they could really relax and enjoy themselves. That was reflected in the photos."

There are many working houses in Los Angeles and around the world. They have stunning bones, or ethereal light, or a commanding view, or some combination of elements that can be put to infinite creative use by photographers and filmmakers. What is it about the Stahl House that makes it the apotheosis of such houses?

"There's a confluence at that one particular house," said Philip Ethington, USC professor of history, political science, and spatial sciences. "There are other Case Study Houses, but none of them achieved that kind of fame." The first time Ethington saw the house was in the Shulman photograph in a college textbook about twentieth-century America. "I can still think back to being fascinated by that picture in college. I just remember staring at it." That photograph encapsulated the soul of a house and the spirit of a singular moment in history. What struck Ethington when he finally set foot in the house, many decades later, was its expansiveness in spite of its small footprint and simple design. "When you get there, it's just a shoebox! Two glass shoeboxes jammed together in an L design. And yet it's so expansive! You can see through it. Everybody shoots it with wide-angle lenses and makes you think it's this huge thing. But when you're in it, you realize how small it is."

Some believe that what sets the Stahl House apart has everything to do with the lives that unfolded within it.

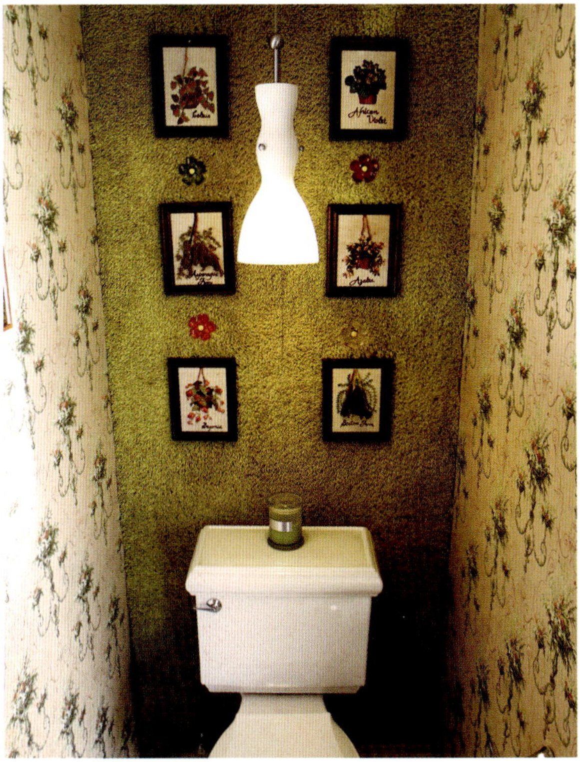

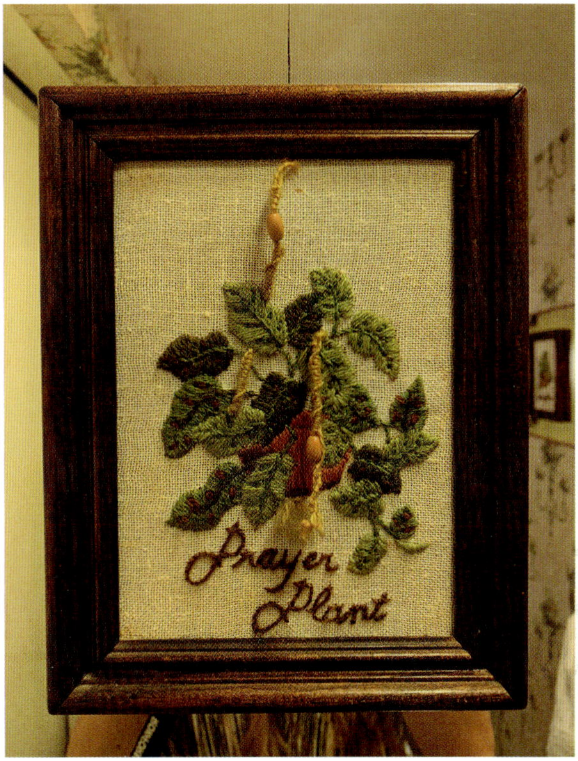

Catherine Meyler believes "soul" comes through in photos. "When it's lived in properly by a family like the Stahl family, it tends not to look like a set. It has photographs of family members. It has tchotchkes that might not be period-appropriate but might be very dear to the family. It makes the house a home. And that creates an atmosphere, a feeling that is very tangible. It's difficult to recreate," said Meyler. "The reason people loved going to the Stahl House was that it was a home."

"Your environment really plays a big part in how you express yourself," said vocalist Wendy Wilson. "Every house has its own energy. This house just felt very welcoming. You just felt like there was a lot of presence. For a moment, that was our house."

Even those parts of a house that don't appear on-screen or in photographs can inspire the creative atmosphere and influence the results. For example: the powder room, just off the kitchen, virtually never appears in photographs, films, or publications. The floral wallpaper is dated, faded by time, and dotted with water spots. The wall behind the toilet is covered in green shag carpet. Cross-stitched pictures of flowers and plants, embroidered by Carlotta, are framed on the walls. Between them are plastic daisies that Shari, as a child, presented as a gift to her parents. "I found them in a neighbor's trash," she said, laughing. If original fabrics and textiles are the preservationist's barometer of integrity, the powder room—never updated or changed—is the most authentic and endearingly personal room in the house. Visitors love it or hate it.

"I love the guest bathroom, which is kind of its own world in and of itself," said Josh Agle, the artist better known as Shag, whose mod oil paintings have an international following. "You can see where Mrs. Stahl was going to head with the rest of the decor. I'm glad she did the one room. And I'm glad she stopped there."

While this bathroom is rarely photographed, it is an example of the X factor that influences the final product of creative work performed at a charismatic location. "Very often you'll hear people say, 'Oh, it's just a close-up of her head; they could have shot that anywhere,'" Meyler said. "Which isn't true. Photographers and directors like to be inspired by their surroundings. Obviously, the architecture and the light are the main draw—the quality of light at the Stahl House is amazing because it's so pure and natural—but as the photographer or director is walking around, they start soaking up the atmosphere and what's around them. By the time they're ready to take a picture (particularly when Carlotta was there), they're relaxed and happy and inspired by *everything* around them, smitten with charm, and the shots reflect that."

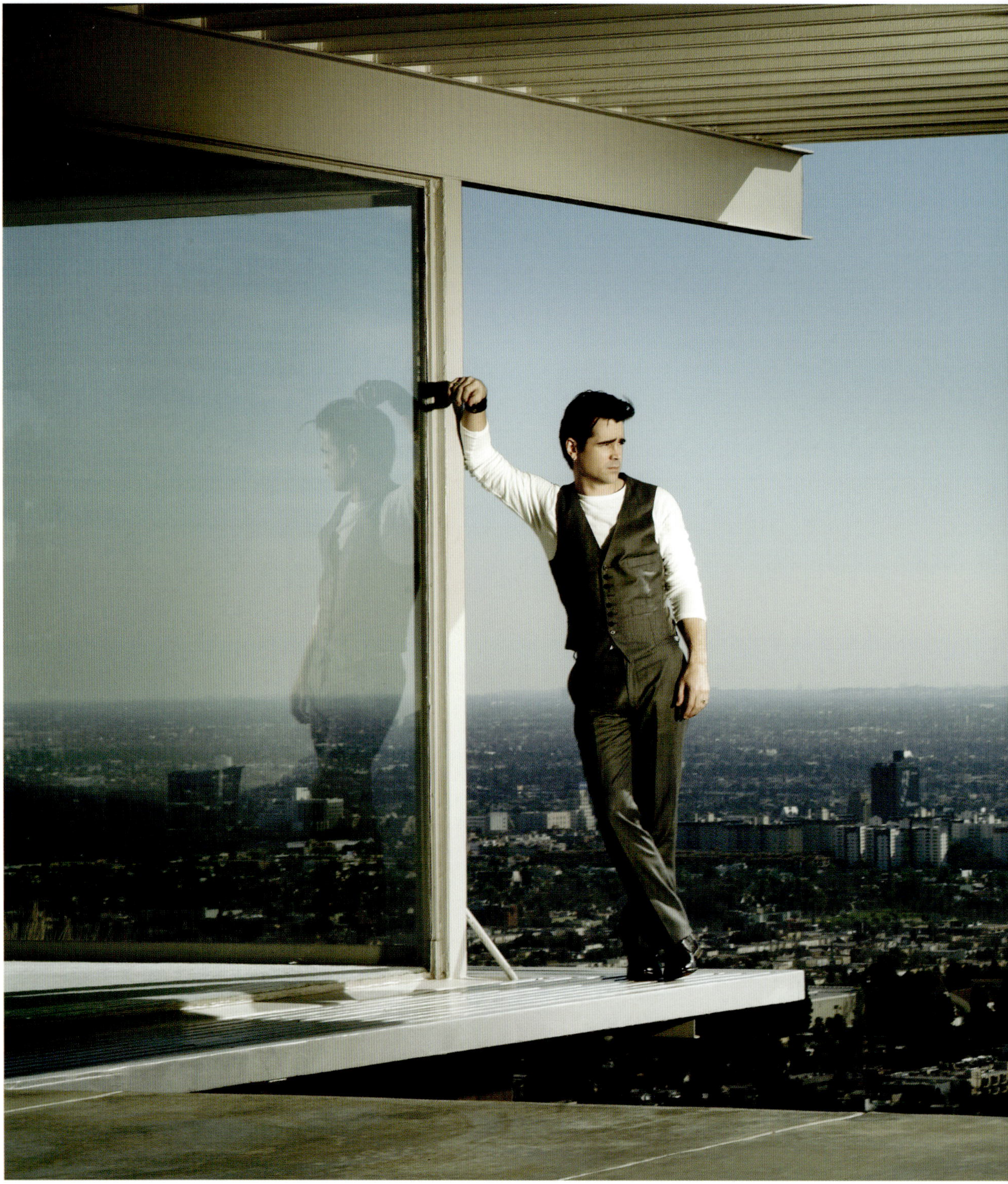

Colin Farrell

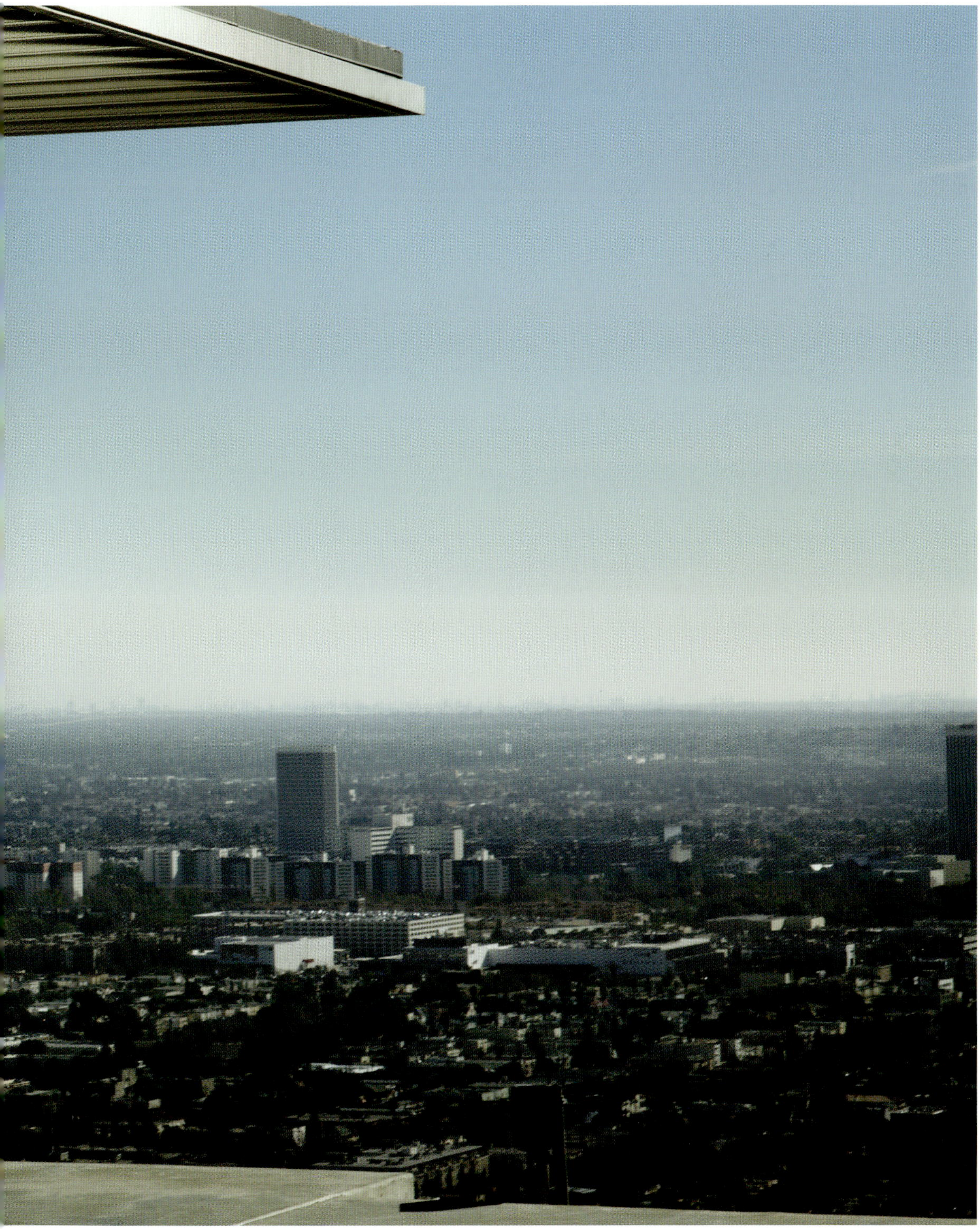

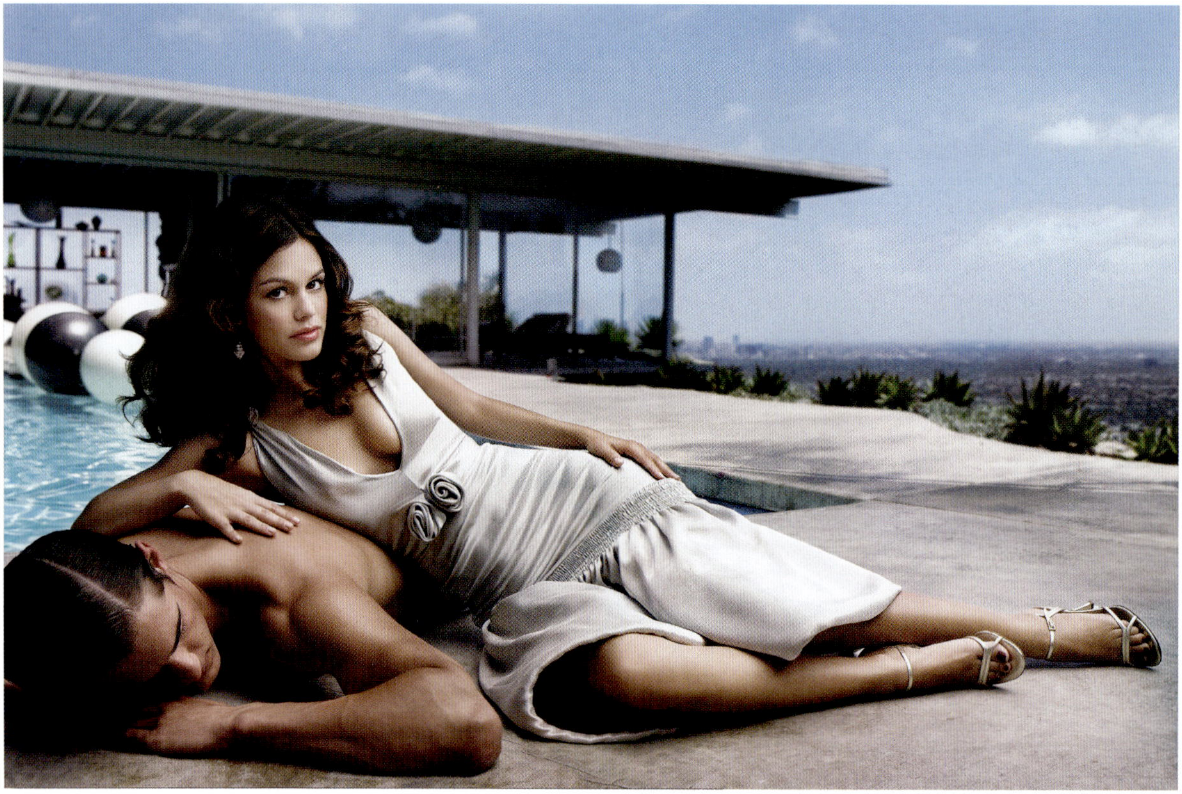

Rachel Bilson

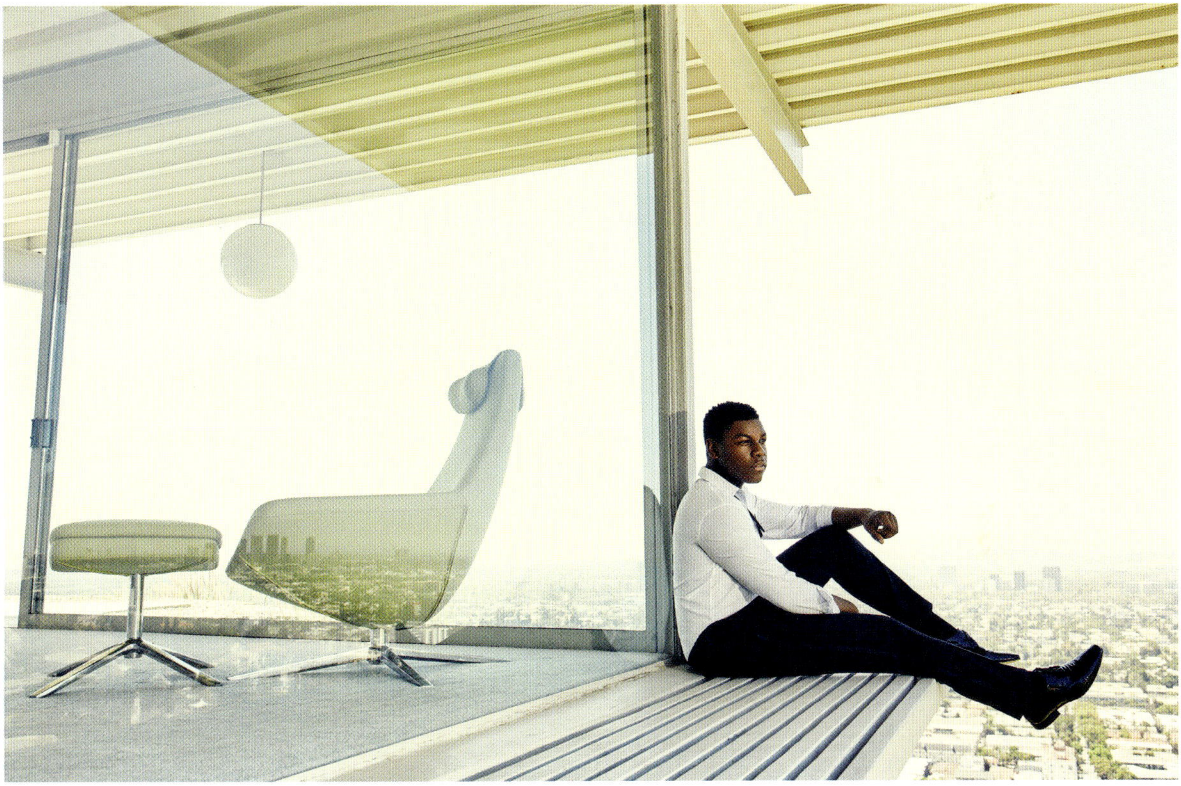

John Boyega

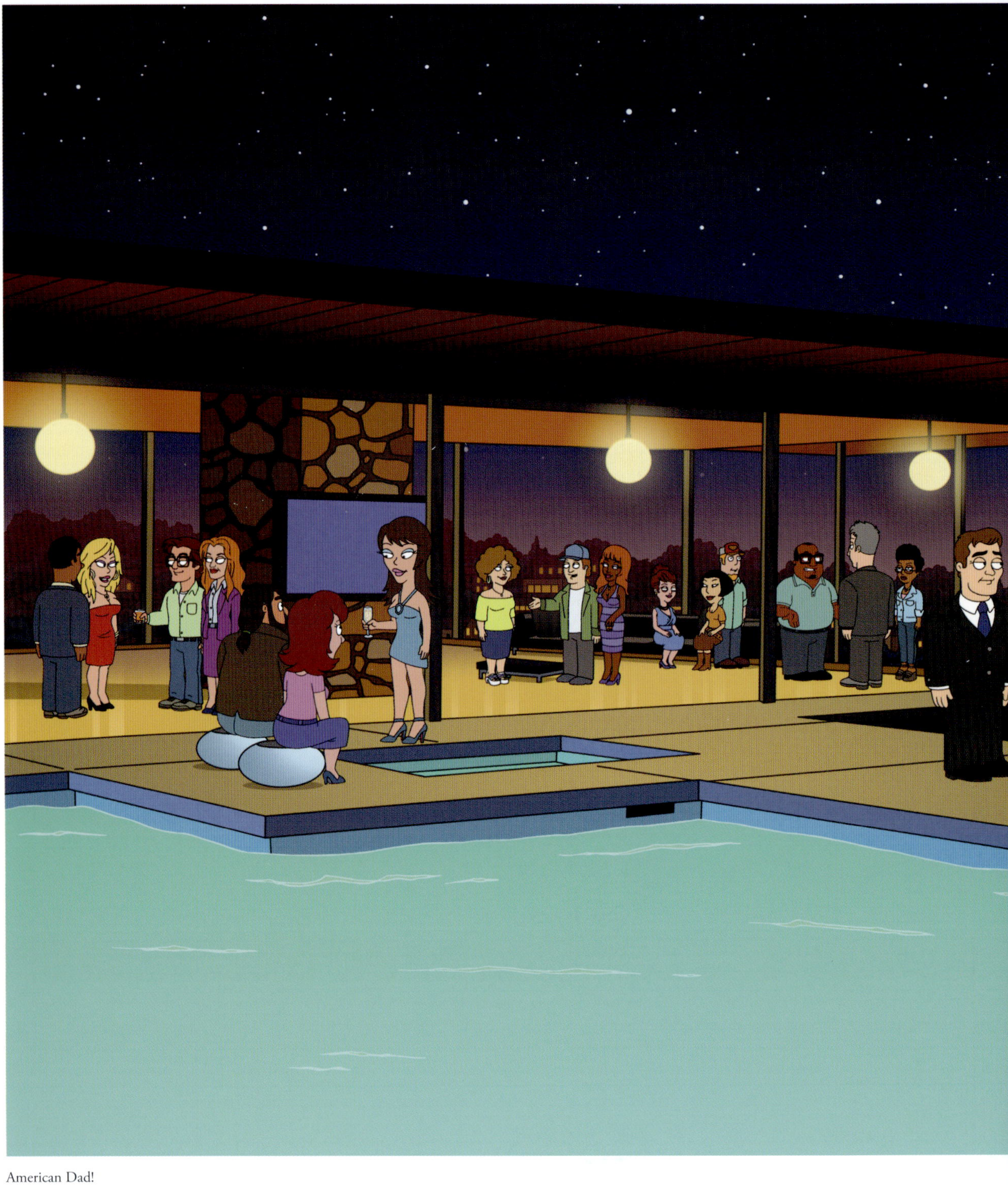

American Dad!

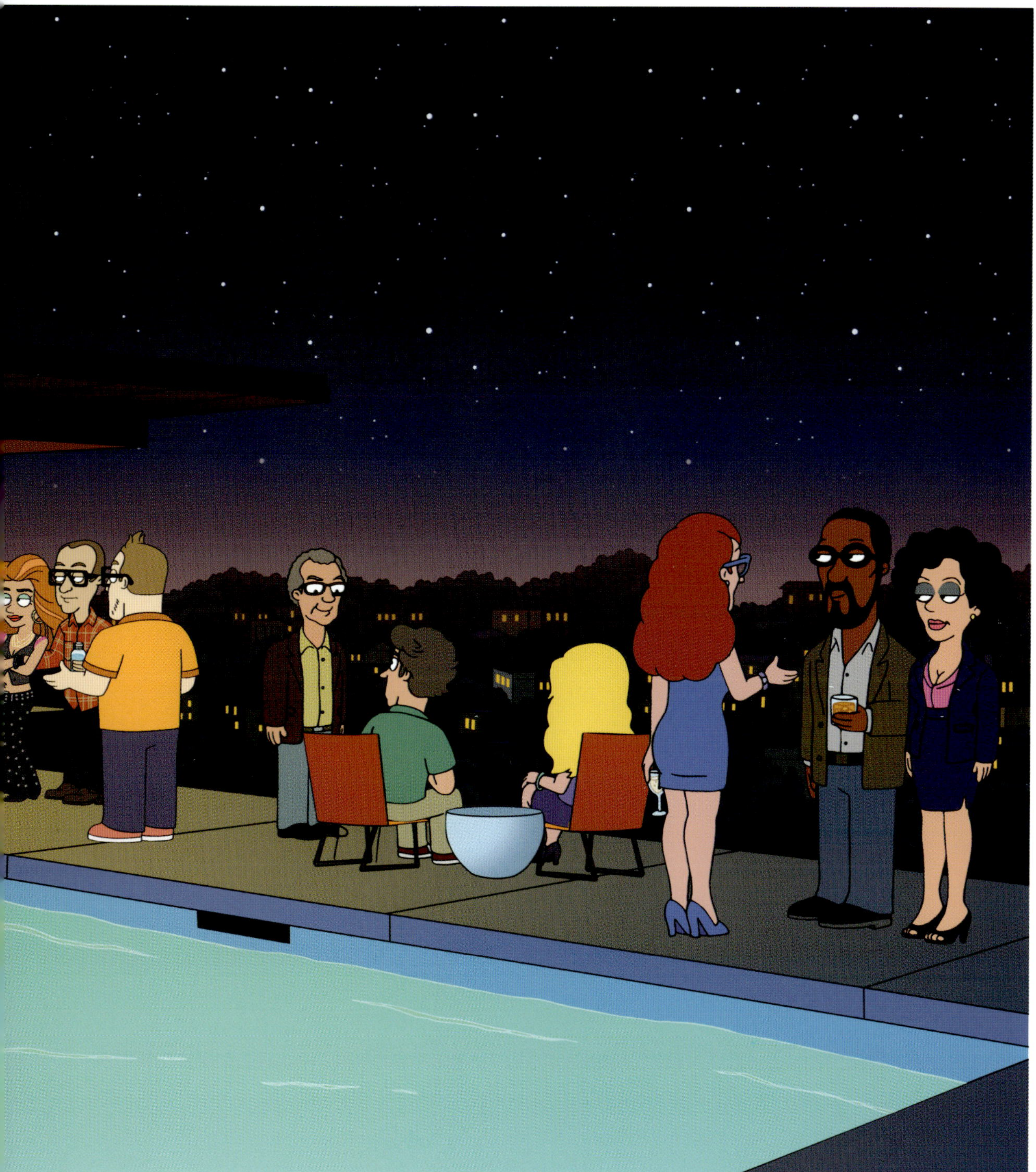

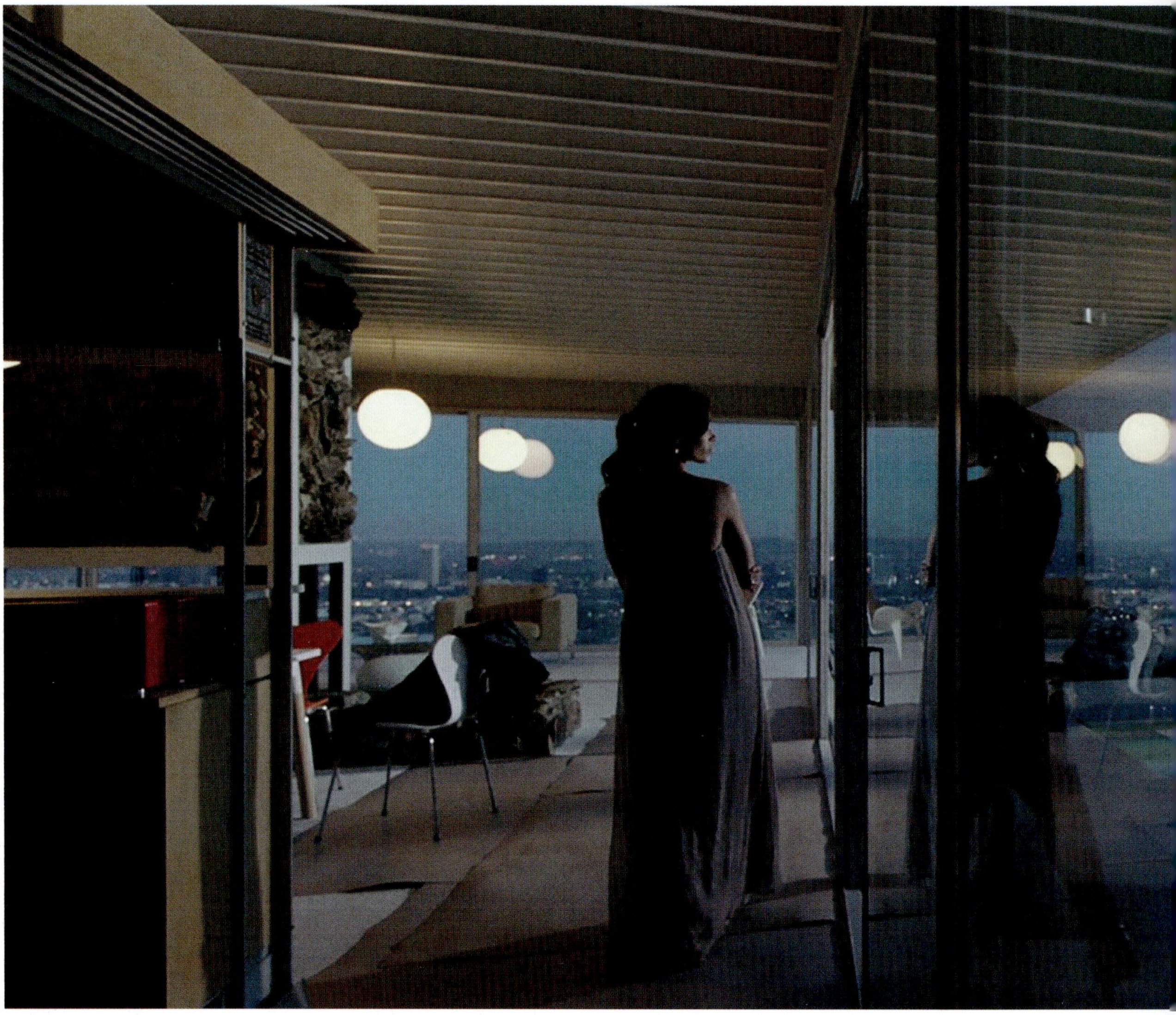

Knight of Cups

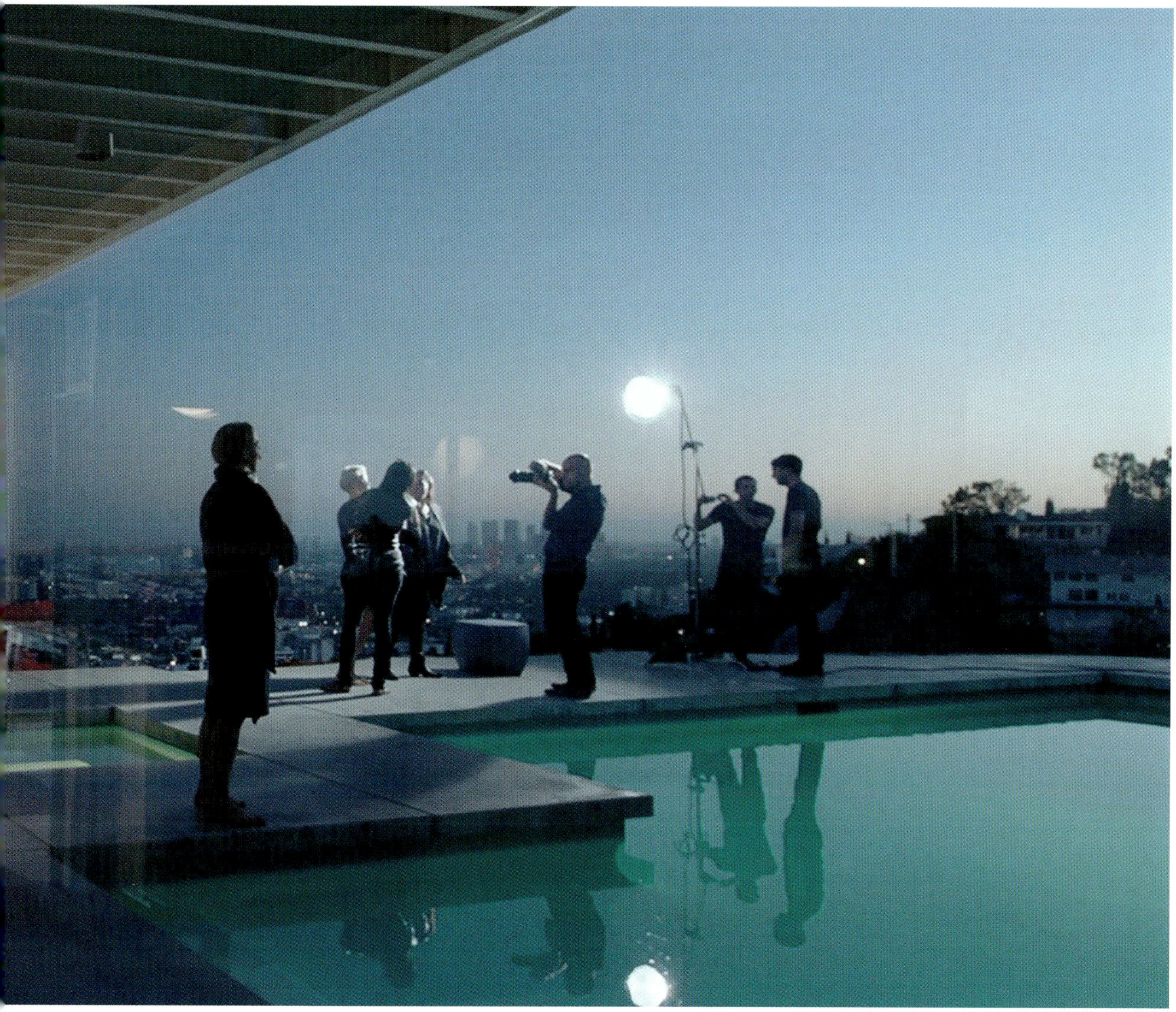

"It's not to say that cleaner, starker houses don't shoot well," Meyler said. "Houses like the Stahl House just shoot better. They have intrinsic charm."

If a house can have a résumé (which many locations do), the Stahl House should have a special section dedicated to its influence on fine art and pop culture. Aside from the thousands of photographs published in newspapers, books, and magazines—the house is widely believed to be the most photographed home in the world—Case Study House #22 has inspired many derivative works. It has appeared in episodes of *The Simpsons* and *American Dad!*, portraying the ultimate Hollywood Hills party. It has been recreated with LEGO and gingerbread and reimagined as a safe house in one of the best-selling video games of all time, *Grand Theft Auto: San Andreas* (2004). It is beautifully portrayed in modernist house paintings by British artist Andy Burgess, who has been called "the next David Hockney."

To celebrate the twentieth anniversary of the Modern Committee in 2004, the Los Angeles Conservancy commissioned a mod painting by the artist Shag. Chris Nichols, then head of ModCom, asked Shag if he could incorporate three recently protected landmarks—Capitol Records, the Cinerama Dome theater, and Pann's, a Googie coffee shop—into the painting. Shag combined them in an imagined cityscape that served as the backdrop for a fantasy party at the Stahl House. Julius Shulman appears in the painting, as does Chris Nichols, who is holding an oversized bottle of champagne. Why did Shag choose the Stahl House? "To me, the California dream has always been a house with a city-lights view over a swimming pool," the artist said. "That's the Hollywood 'You've made it' dream."

Another painter, Carrie Graber, saw her whole oeuvre transformed by her first visit to the Stahl House. "There's nothing in the world that could stop somebody from having their breath taken away," she said. "You've seen pictures, but it doesn't capture the whole 360. You step out there and you're on top of the world." That night, after dark, someone took a couple of snapshots of Graber lying by the luminous pool, looking out at the city lights through the transparent house. Graber had been a figurative artist for fifteen years, but she felt compelled to translate this moment into an oil painting. During a show in Palm Springs during Modernism Week, the painting attracted a whole new group of fans. Today, modern architecture defines her work. Some of her most popular works are a series of *Case Study Paintings*, as she calls them, that sell for six thousand to nine thousand dollars apiece.

Art imitated art in a fashion shoot by Vincent Peters for Miu Miu, an Italian high-fashion brand associated with

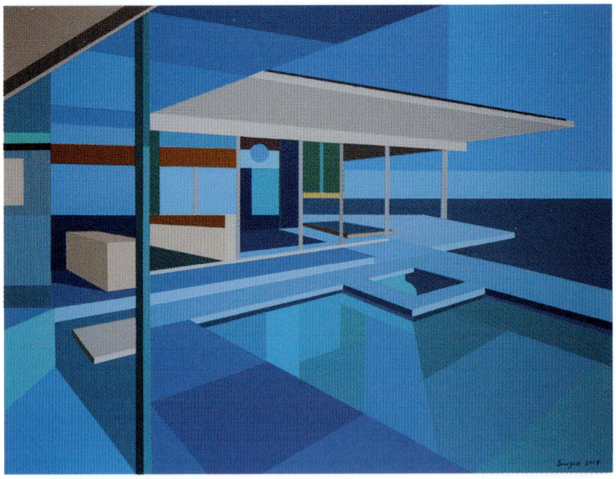

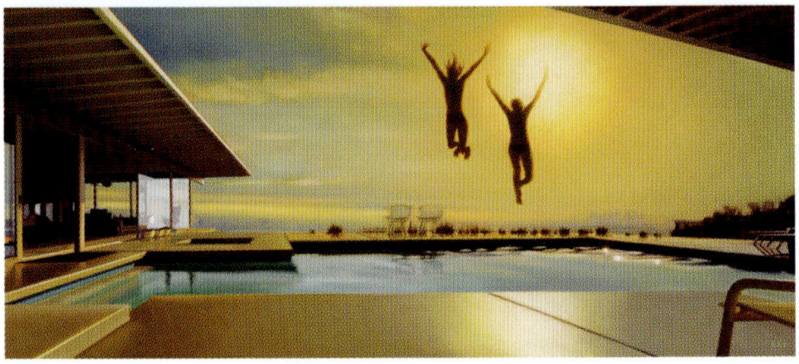

Prada. Stylists transformed the Stahl House to resemble a 1967 pop-art painting by British artist David Hockney. In a meeting with billionaire fashion designer Miuccia Prada, Peters had been pressed to come up with a concept on the spot. "*A Bigger Splash* was a painting that was generally on my mind, as I was always fascinated by the mood and lighting of the artwork," Peters said. "I loved the idea of just falling and the movement in space." One of Hockney's most famous paintings, *A Bigger Splash* depicts a modern house with a swimming pool in the moment a diver has vanished into a splash. To simulate the flat-roofed house in the painting, stylists blacked out the windows of the Stahl House. Models dressed in Italian clothes appeared to be falling into the pool, captured on film a split-second before the big splash. (Wearing harnesses under their clothing, they were suspended by a crane parked in the street.) In 2000, the ads ran in *Vogue, Elle, Harper's Bazaar, Marie Claire, W* magazine, and other prominent glossies.

Interestingly, Pierre Koenig's Case Study Houses inspired David Hockney himself in the 1960s. "I came to Los Angeles for two reasons," he told editor Dian Hanson at a 2009 dinner party. "The first was a photo by Julius Shulman of Case Study House #21. ..."

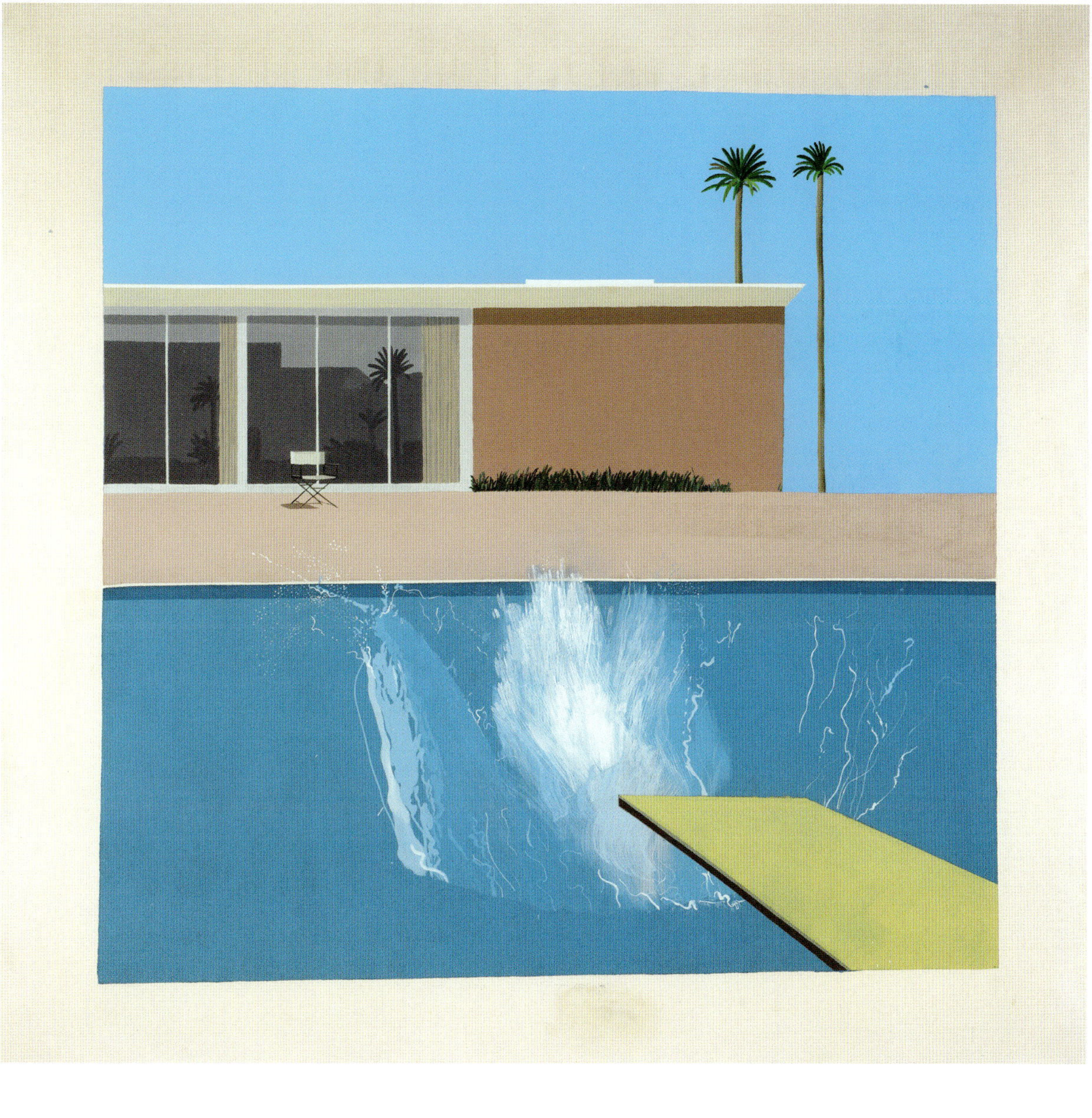

David Hockney, "A Bigger Splash," 1967

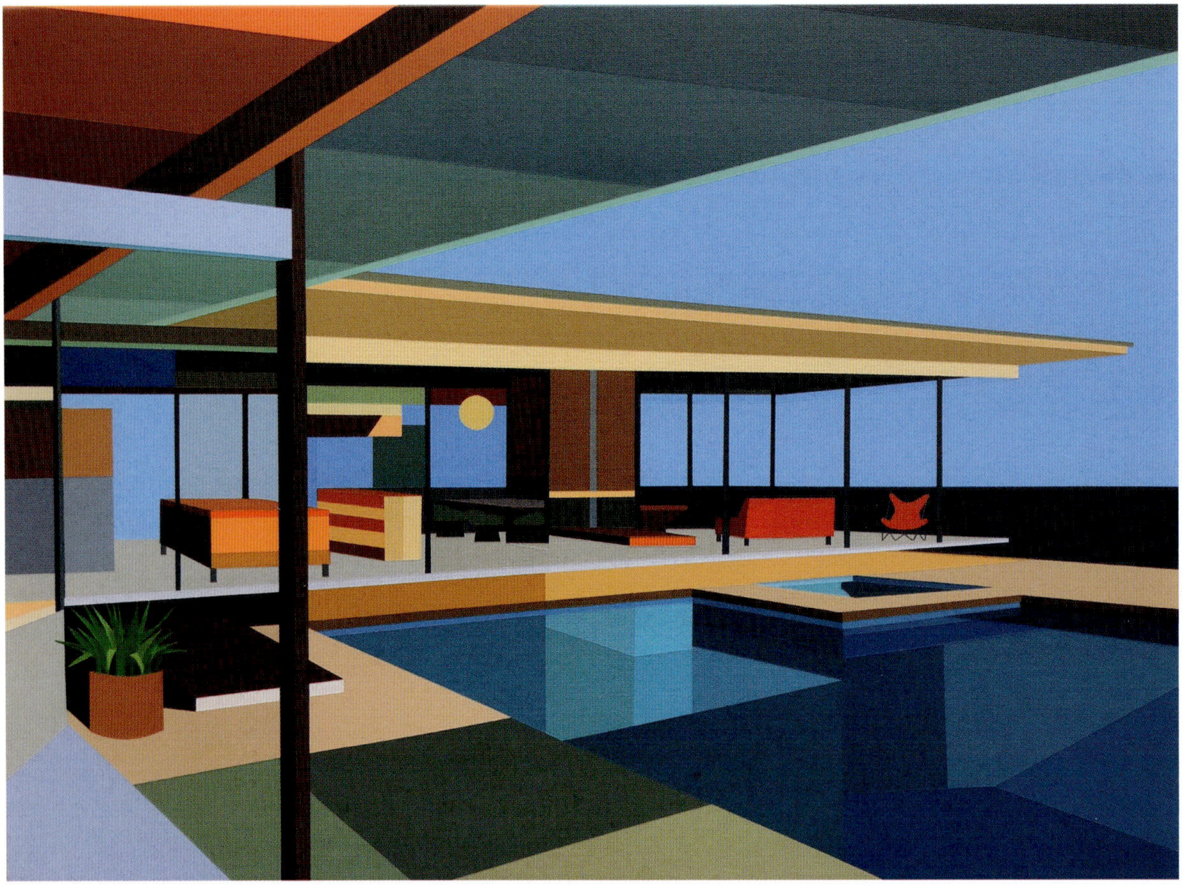

Artwork by Andy Burgess

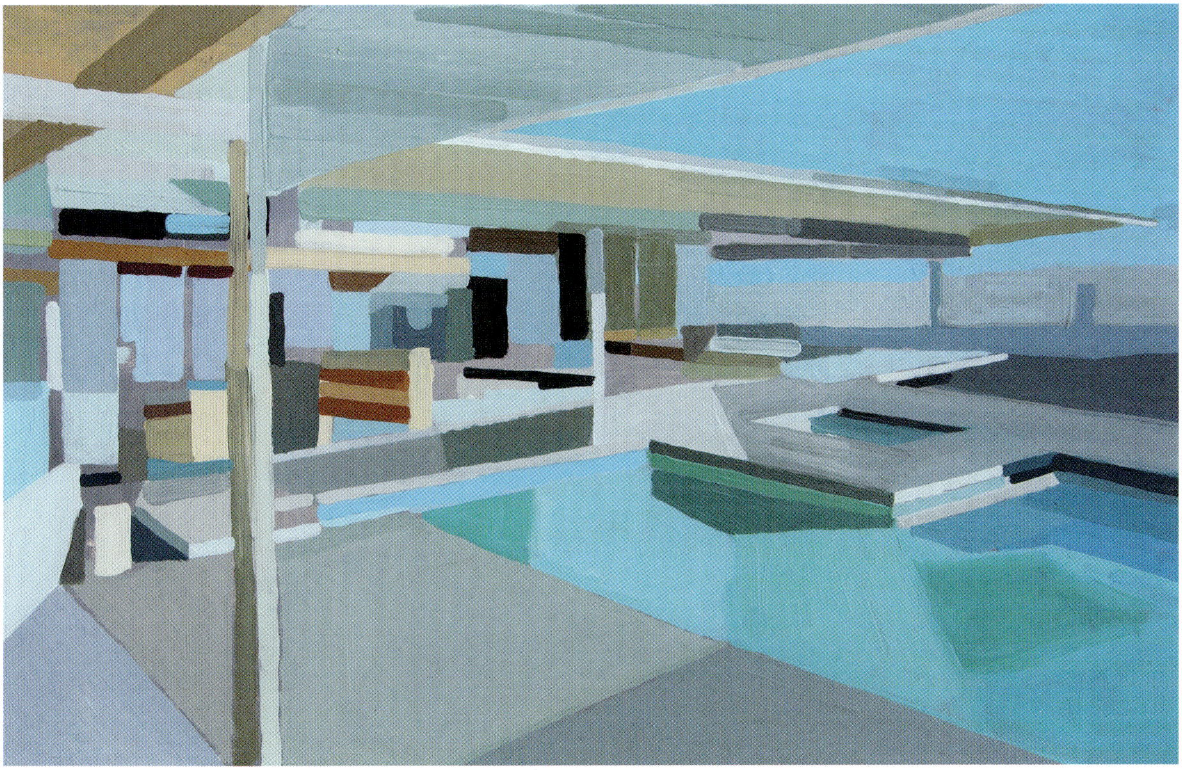

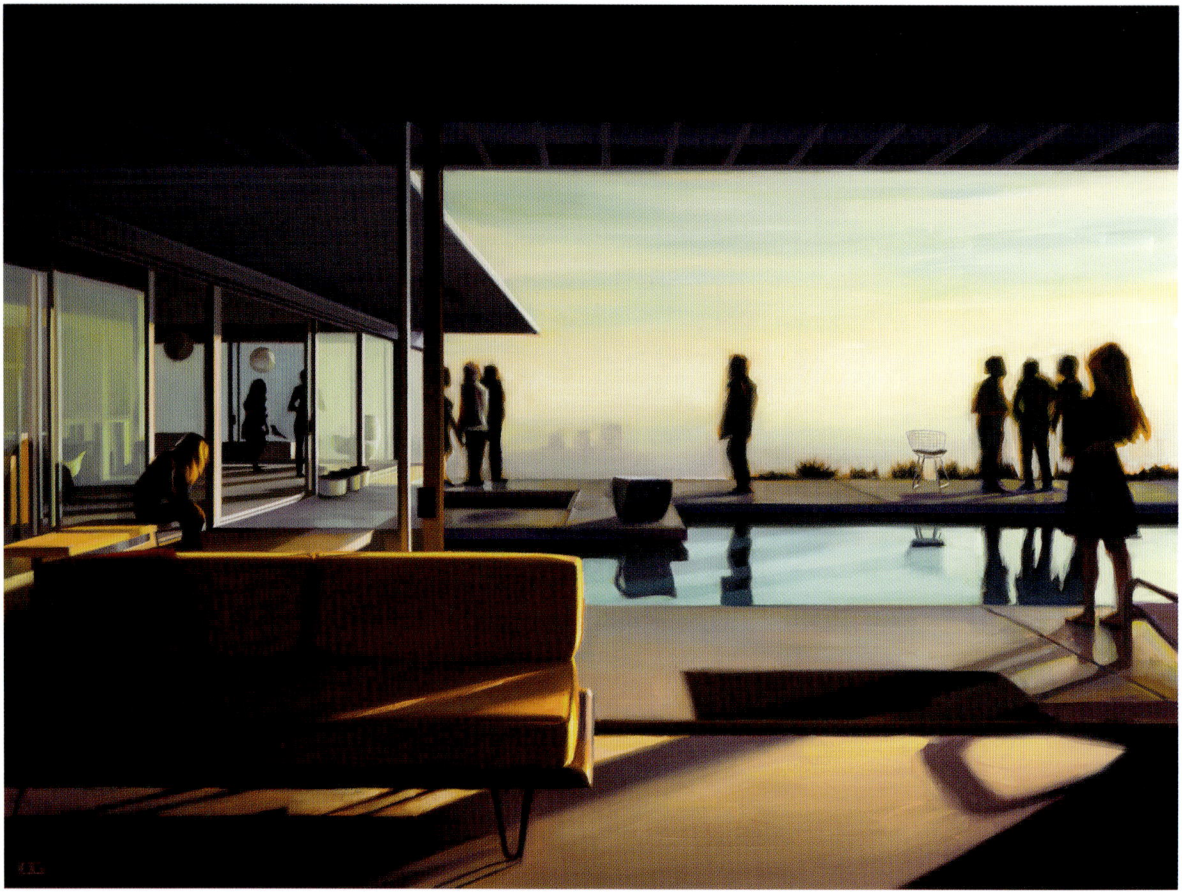

Artwork by Carrie Graber

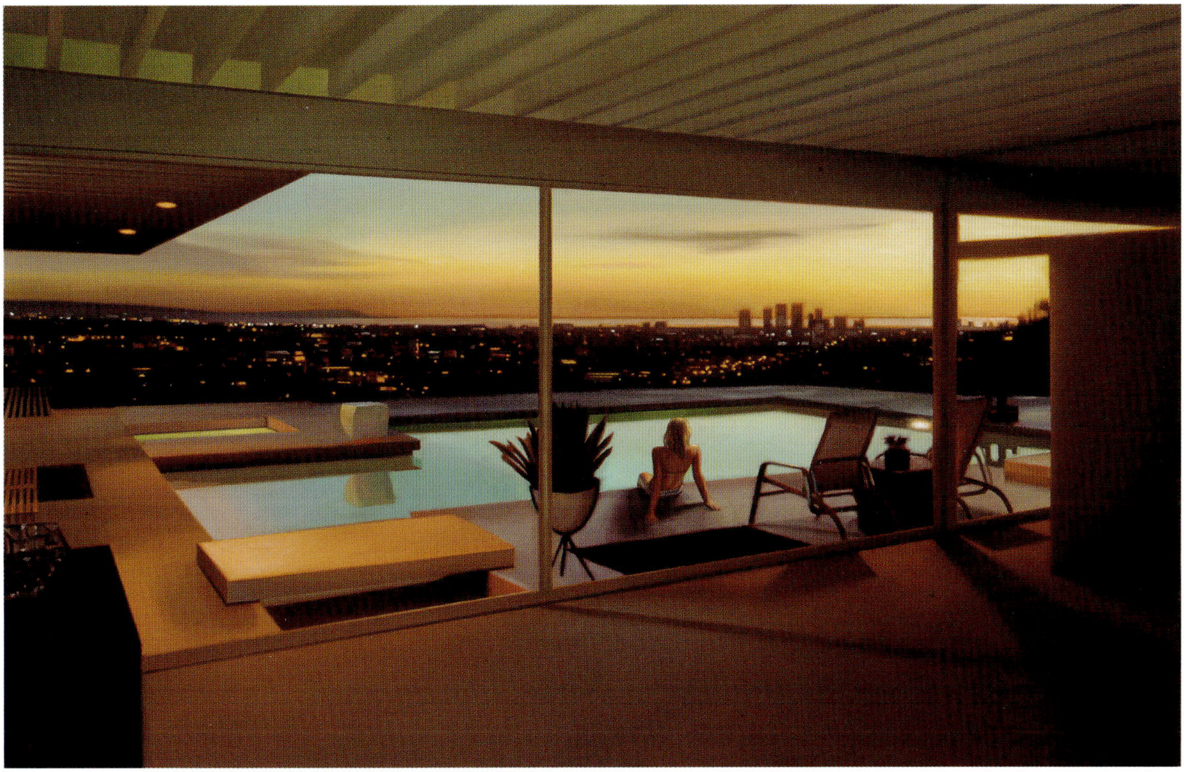

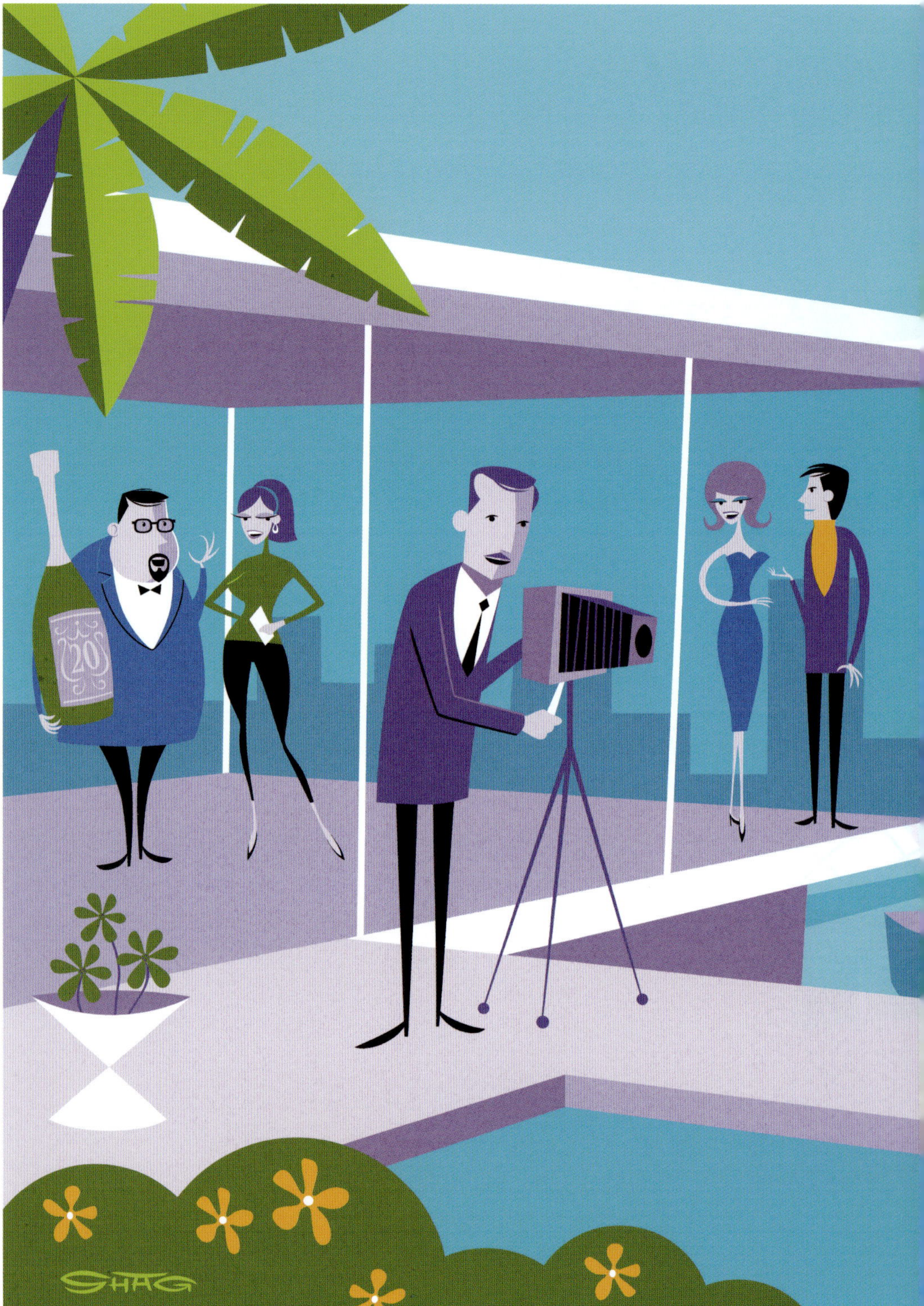

Artwork by Shag

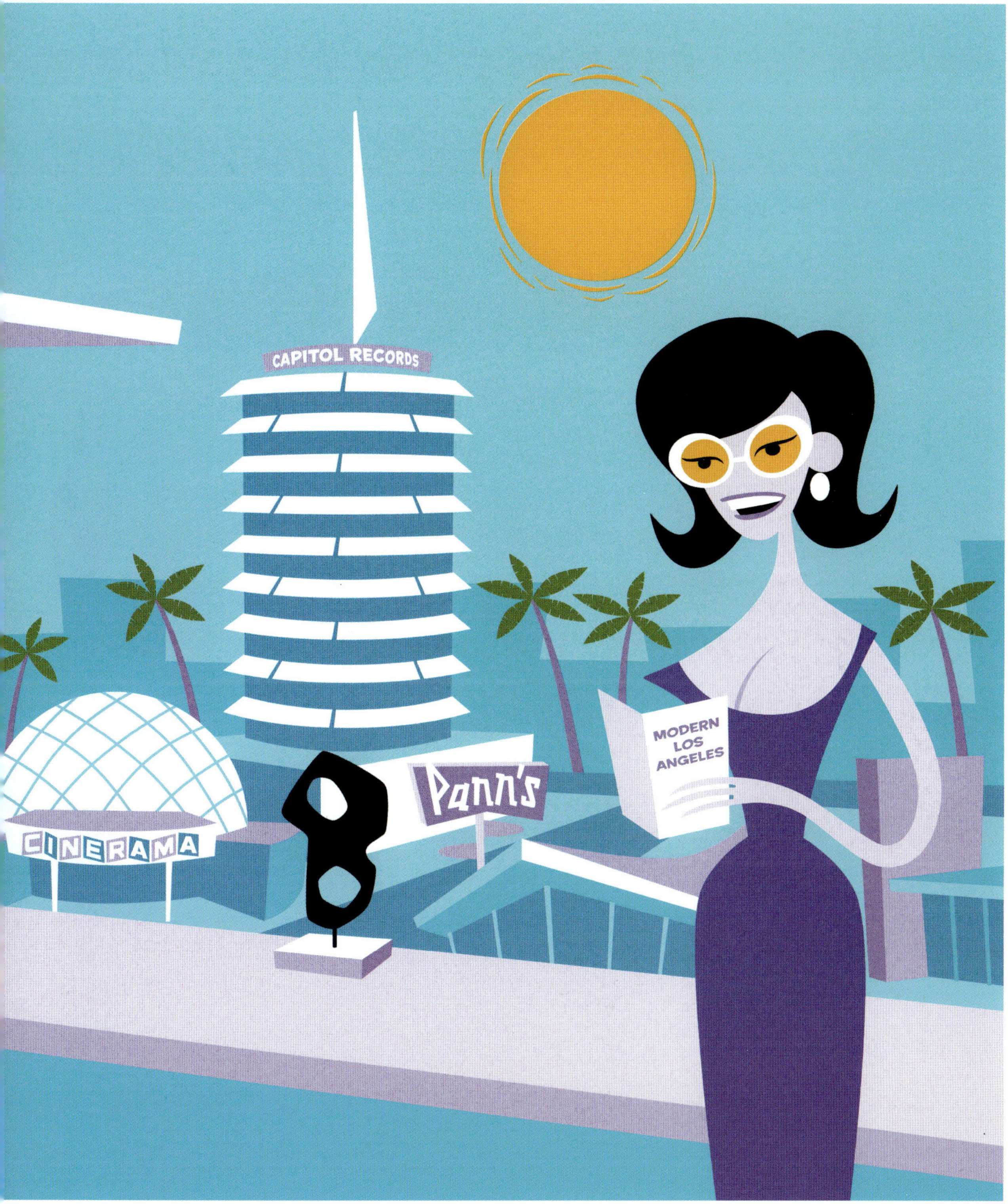
CAPITOL RECORDS
CINERAMA
Pann's
MODERN
LOS
ANGELES

CHAPTER 11
OPEN HOUSE

Carlotta always opened her door to strangers. They arrived in pairs, in classes or groups, sometimes alone, usually uninvited. They were students or tourists or movie buffs, design lovers or preservationists, writers, photographers, historians, or artists. The one thing they shared was the compelling need for this pilgrimage. They just wanted a glimpse of her home.

Even before the 1989 MOCA exhibition, Carlotta and Buck would come home to find uninvited guests swimming in the pool, reclining on a chaise lounge, or just standing there, awestruck, drunk on the view. Sometimes the trespassers came and went unobserved but left traces: toys on the bottom of the pool, furniture moved from its normal location, wet footprints that dried in the dust on the pool deck. Even after Buck raised the carport wall and installed a locked door, some still managed to find a way in. "They go around, they sneak through the sides, and then they poke around the edge, and eventually one will knock," Carlotta said, laughing. "By the time I get out there, they're standing in the middle of the road. It's almost comical. It really is. And I always assure them that I will always have time for them to come in."

After the MOCA exhibition, the Stahl House pilgrims seemed to multiply. In the era of film and photo shoots, the house became a celebrity—a world-famous personality with its own fans and paparazzi. Buck preferred to shoo them off (and certainly he tried). But Carlotta would always open her door, wave them in, and ask, "Want a Coke?"

In 1994, USC School of Architecture Dean Victor Regnier started teaching a class called The Great Houses of Los Angeles. The course highlighted famous architects and one significant house designed by each. After lectures and readings, the class visited each one for a three-hour tour, during which they could wander around and connect theory with reality. Pierre Koenig always guest lectured to the students during their visit to the Stahl House, which was a highlight—both for students and for Professor Koenig.

"He just adored it," Regnier said. "I would introduce him and tell the story of how he almost failed first-year design." (Many students could relate.) "It was the highlight of the course to go to that house," Regnier said. Even if students had never heard of the Stahl House, they recognized it from films and commercials. "It was a déjà vu experience for them."

Coming back to the Stahl House provided an opportunity to reunite Buck and Pierre, whose relationship had been strained for years. It began in 1960 with one corner of the roof—the one immortalized by Julius Shulman—which wasn't draining properly. "The rainwater was supposed to run through the gutters and drain towards the street, but instead the rain drained off of the famous corner, down the cliff," Shari said. "Erosion was a concern." Buck had brought this up before the house was completed, and Koenig had promised to address it, but the issue was never satisfactorily resolved. Buck refused to make his final four-hundred-dollar payment to Koenig until it was fixed. (Neither happened.) The two men—whose common streak of stubbornness had once drawn them together—stopped speaking and simmered in resentment for years.

Years later, Buck's assertions that he had "given Pierre the idea for the house" upset Koenig. As Bruce recalled, "Dad always said, 'He can have the credit. I've got the house.'

"It was almost as if both decided to take more credit for it than was due," said Regnier. "I don't think Pierre wanted to give Buck credit for the kind of ideas he had or the work he carried out on the site. Buck, I'm not sure he would have even hired Pierre if he realized how complicated this house would be."

At some point, Carlotta engraved the glass carport door with the initials CHS. Most visitors assume it's a nod to the Case Study House program. Some people would ask if it was a typo. "I know exactly what I did," Carlotta would say. "It's my husband's initials." She would never in her life say one unkind word about Koenig, whom she adored. But this was her quiet, subtle way of honoring Clarence Henry Stahl. "I felt that my husband deserved a little credit."

Regnier credits Carlotta and Gloria Koenig, Pierre's second wife, for helping him nudge the two stubborn men in the direction of reconciliation. "I think there was a little pillow talk from the two spouses, saying, 'C'mon, start acting like a human being!'" Regnier said. "I don't think they became best friends; I think they were just able to see one another's perspective a little more clearly."

No one has ever opened a house to the public like the Stahls have. They have brought architecture to the public. —Julius Shulman

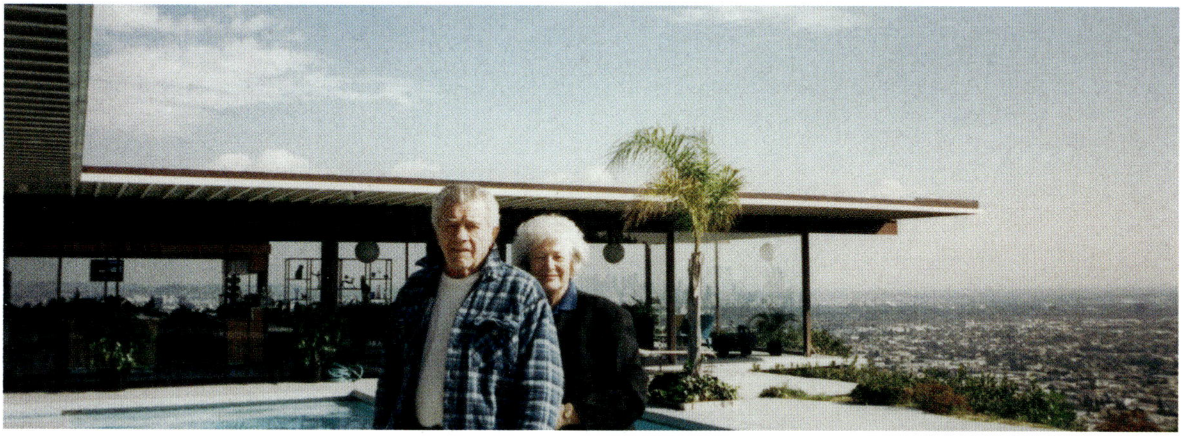

There had also been longstanding tension between Koenig and Julius Shulman, whose acclaim for his photograph of the Stahl House had eclipsed Koenig's fame for designing the house. "Who made whom?" said Randy Koenig, Pierre's son. "My dad said the picture of the two ladies is what made Julius Shulman."

For his part, Julius Shulman certainly didn't help matters by frequently and openly saying, "The picture of Pierre Koenig's house is now a classic, and suddenly Pierre Koenig becomes a hero, based on one picture. 'Oh, you're the guy who did that building.'"

Even after MOCA elevated Koenig's reputation as a master of mid-century modern, his resentment lingered. He was known to say, "Architects need to build the buildings before photographers can show them off."

....

In 2000, Buck and Carlotta were giving a tour to a group of architecture fans from Japan when Buck, then eighty-eight, slipped on the walkway over the pool. He lost his balance, fell against the glass, and landed with a sickening crunch on the concrete bridge outside the kitchen. At the hospital, doctors confirmed what Buck already knew: he had broken his hip. He came home in a wheelchair with Carlotta, seventy-one, as his caretaker.

The doctors said Buck would walk again. But he never stopped using his wheelchair. "Once he broke his hip, he was frightened to get up and walk," Bruce said. His mind stayed sharp—he had always loved to read, and when his eyesight started failing, the kids bought a device that magnified books on a screen. He enjoyed books about architecture, particularly if they featured his house, which more and more seemed to do. Carlotta struggled to care for him. He was heavy to help in and out of the wheelchair. And then she started forgetting to pay the bills and had trouble balancing the checkbook.

The children recognized the signs of early dementia. To take care of her aging parents, Shari quit her job at Countrywide Home Loans, where she had risen to vice president. Still living in Riverside with her husband and daughter, she drove to her parents' house every day, a three-hour round-trip commute, even though she left at 6:00 a.m. to avoid rush hour. She helped her mother pay bills and lifted her father into the shower. She did all the little things that a house demands, things her parents could no longer do: pulling weeds, painting walls, helping Bruce with the pool, reorganizing closets, cooking, cleaning, and washing windows. "It was the hardest job I ever had, but the most gratifying," Shari said. "I got to spend time with my parents."

One day in 2005, Buck collapsed in the shower. Shari was unable to lift him. She called Bruce, who lived across town in Lake Balboa, to come help. Once they got him dressed and back in his wheelchair, Buck seemed to be okay. But the next morning, when he wheeled himself into the kitchen for his piping-hot cup of coffee, Shari noticed something didn't seem right.

"How are you, Dad?" Shari asked.

"I don't feel good," he said.

He had never said that before.

Buck hated going to the doctor. So Shari was surprised—and very alarmed—when he agreed to a trip to the emergency room. It was pneumonia. Soon it spread to both lungs, and Buck was put on a ventilator. In the ICU, he begged to come home. But the doctors said he'd get better, and his family felt it would be wise to bring him home after he regained some strength.

"He just wanted to go home," Shari said to Bruce, remembering.

"I think he wanted to die in his home," Bruce said. "At this point we thought there was still hope."

Buck died in the hospital on April 26, 2005, at the age of ninety-three. It was two days after his birthday and one year after Pierre Koenig's passing. Carlotta, Bruce, Shari, Mark, and TerriAnne Drescher, a family friend, surrounded his bedside. Mark read Psalm 23:4 aloud in his soft, deep voice, as Buck entered the valley of the shadow of death.

"We really thought he'd be coming back home," said Shari, thinking about that moment.

Bruce sighed.

"And he never did."

By this time, the steady stream of pilgrims had increased to a level that explains why Hollywood stars have agents and handlers. "Nothing less than one thousand in a given month," Carlotta estimated in 2004. "And I'm not counting the still shoots, the commercials and everything—they come in big groups." When unexpected visitors showed up, she would still dash around the house, sweeping everyday clutter into drawers and the oven, where it wouldn't spoil the minimalist lines or detract from the maximum view.

She had a particular soft spot for students, who came from all over the world. Fifty-five Japanese architecture students squeezed into the house on one visit. "I don't stop the kids," she said. "I always tell them, 'You kids are the future—no telling what you're going to invent! So, let's just go for it.' They come in and walk around, ask some questions. It's usually a half hour, forty-five minutes, and then they're off to try to get in another house."

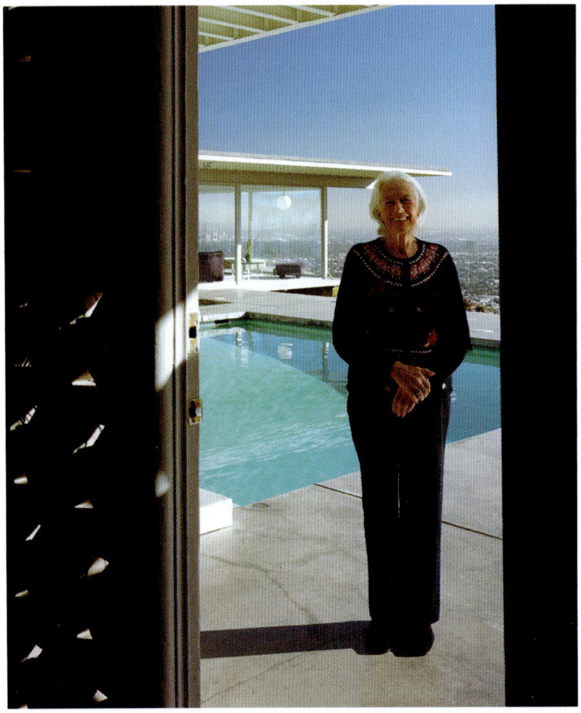

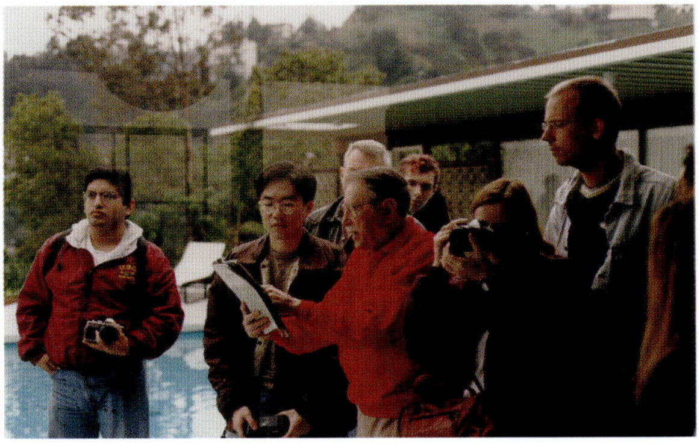

At the same time, Carlotta was showing symptoms of progressing Alzheimer's. Halfway to the grocery store, she'd wonder where she was going. Shari realized her mother was going for night drives when a security guard for a shoot noticed the car pulling away at night. Mark was living in Idaho. Bruce was running a business and raising three young kids. Shari and her husband, Berndt, had adopted a daughter in 2003. Instead of dividing her time between their home in Riverside and her mother's house in Hollywood, Shari moved her entire family—husband, daughter, two dogs, and two parrots—under the same steel roof. Buck's closet became a cozy bedroom for four-year-old Annie, who grew closer to her grandmother even as Carlotta's mind slipped away.

In 2007 the American Institute of Architects listed the Stahl House as number 140 on the America's Favorite Architecture list, which included monuments, hotels, museums, libraries, skyscrapers, and the White House. It was one of eleven structures in Southern California and the only privately owned home on the list.

That same year, Shari and her family moved to Idaho, where Mark had settled down after college. "We were just tired of the traffic and congestion and wanted to spend more time home than on the freeways," Shari said. In the mountains outside Boise, they found land, space, privacy, and almost zero traffic. Carlotta's Alzheimer's had progressed to the point where it was no longer safe for her to live alone, so she joined them in Idaho.

For the first time in forty-seven years, no one lived full-time in the Stahl House.

In 2008, the *Los Angeles Times* named the Stahl House one of "the best houses of all time in Southern California." In order to manage the growing demand for shoots, tours, and filming, the family had founded a business and started restoring the house as close as possible to its original state. It was a full-time job (actually, two). Mark oversaw ongoing maintenance and restoration work, commuting from Boise to Hollywood, where there was always something to fix or to oversee at the house, where he served as a site rep. Shari ran the business from Idaho, where she cared full-time for Carlotta. The house had evolved into an enterprise with two employees.

Then came the recession of 2008. Almost overnight, film budgets dried up and bookings stopped. Maintaining the house was expensive and a never-ending responsibility. But selling it wasn't an option. Buyers inquired, but Carlotta needed her home, even though she could no longer stay there full-time. Alzheimer's had stolen her ability to live on her own, but it would not take her house.

It was Mark who conceived the idea for the next chapter of the Stahl House: tours. Paid public tours would continue Carlotta's legacy of opening her home to others, rather than closing it off like some modernist shrine. The income from tours would also fund ongoing maintenance and the mounting costs of restoration.

In 2009, Stahl House Inc. began booking tours. "At first, I thought there would be just a few people who would come," Shari said. "Boy, was I wrong."

At first, Mark led the tours himself. Some days, no one showed up. Then stories began to appear in the press, word spread, and he received help from a family friend, Andrew Edelstein, who was a docent at the Eames House. "It started out one day a week," Edelstein said. "Five tours on a Saturday. Mark would do one, then I would do one, so we'd have a break." When *Dwell,* an architectural magazine that celebrated modern design, held a convention in town, they gave tours every forty-five minutes from 10:00 a.m. until 6:00 or 7:00 p.m. for three days straight. Soon after, tours began to sell out, sometimes months in advance. The staff of docents grew, and many became family friends.

The three Stahl siblings had always been close. But now that they were working toward a common goal, they grew into a team, finding their own roles and rhythms. Shari oversaw finances and studio requests, Mark was in charge of tours and marketing, and Bruce took care of the pool and helped with restoration projects. The house held them together.

By this time, Julius Shulman was two years shy of becoming a centenarian and still enjoying a golden life with an unnatural arc that seemed all apex and no denouement. The photos he once sold for thirty-five or fifty dollars were now selling on the fine-art market for two thousand to twenty thousand dollars. His images had been exhibited everywhere from the Getty to the Guggenheim. He was the subject of a documentary biopic called *Visual Acoustics: The Modernism of Julius Shulman*, and he had received just about every award a photographer could win. He still called himself "the great Shulman."

He had no agent, zero assistants, and nine phones. "He favors portables, because they enable him to place the receiver on his walker and wheel it around like a slumbering baby so he can attend to it the moment it stirs," wrote Mary Melton. He lived alone in his Raphael Soriano home, his base camp for almost five decades, where his phones continued to ring. Sometimes it was the mayor of Berlin—other times Brad Pitt, who shared his love of modern architecture.

Carlotta saw him for the last time in 2005, at his ninety-fifth birthday party at the Getty, which had recently acquired Shulman's archives. The party coincided with the opening of an exhibit called Julius Shulman, Modernity and the Metropolis. Sitting before an audience under a wall-sized projection of the Stahl House, he reflected on his career with Wim de Wit, head of the Getty's special collections. Shulman was still Shulman. "I sell more architecture than the architects," he declared. "Often people were more impressed with my photographs than with the houses themselves."

At the reception, where Shulman cut into a cake shaped like a Nikon camera, Gloria Koenig came over to greet Carlotta. They were widows now. After a sudden onset of leukemia, Pierre Koenig had died five years earlier, on April 4, 2004, at the age of seventy-eight. He continued teaching at USC until the very end, and he was in the middle of building a two-story glass-and-steel home on the beach in Malibu—a house that he described as having "views that rival the Stahl House."

In his obituary, Elizabeth Smith acknowledged that throughout his career, he never strayed from his ideals. "Until the end of his life he remained an ardent believer in industrial materials and prefabricated systems—the idea that life could be improved through architecture."

Koenig never lost faith in the power of minimalism. "Simplicity is the essence of beauty," he told his friend Steve Diskin, who asked him in 1995 to describe his creative process on camera. "Solving the problem with the minimum means" was his answer. "When I start to work, it's very complex, and I keep working until I work out all the complexity."

Koenig didn't enjoy looking back at the postwar years, a time that seemed to hold great promise for architecture but one that, despite his best efforts, he now saw as unwilling to embrace the possibilities the era presented. He saw the past as dark and ignorant. "I thought that I could somehow influence what the future could be," he said. "We thought we could change the world. We were so strong and so powerful and so in control that we could make a whole new utopian world." While he believed that his life's work had "made some impression," it was "not really as overwhelming as I thought or hoped it would be." And yet he had discovered a peace in the process, in giving himself to his work.

"You forget yourself. You project everything into your work, sacrifice yourself for your work. But it's worth it.

What's a life for? A life is supposed to be something you give. And I happened to give myself to my work. And I think that's the way it should be."

Almost a year after Pierre Koenig's death, Julius Shulman packed up 260,000 prints, color transparencies, and negatives in his office. "When the archive was driven away, that was the most emotional I've ever seen him," his daughter, Judy, told *Los Angeles* magazine editor Mary Melton. When Melton asked Julius about that day, he showed her a letter from Richard Neutra. "Julius Shulman and surely his work will survive me," Neutra wrote. "Films are stronger, and good glossy prints are easier shipped than brute concrete and stainless steel—or even ideas."

In November 2007, Julius Shulman was asked to sit for a portrait by photographer Tim Mantoani, who was documenting famous photographers holding their most iconic image. For his book, *Behind Photographs: Archiving Photographic Legends*, Mantoani wanted to photograph Shulman holding his "Two Girls" image of the Stahl House. "I think for all of us, as you grow up, there are just certain images that linger," Mantoani told the *San Diego Union-Tribune*. "Images that recorded history and also helped define it." Shulman consented, but he didn't want a big to-do. He didn't have time to go to Mantoani's studio in San Diego, but he agreed to be photographed at home.

Setting up his equipment in Shulman's home office, Mantoani rigged a tripod with a 55-pound antique camera with a long accordion-like bellows. A large-format Wisner 20 x 24, it would capture an image on poster-size Polaroid film. This setup was particularly sensitive to light leaks, so Mantoani worked carefully. "I was concerned about fogging the film with too much ambient light around the film back," he said.

But he felt rushed by his notoriously impatient subject, who barked at him for moving a table to compose the shot. "Don't move anything without asking!" Shulman snapped.

Shulman, dressed in a powder-blue shirt and vest, sat on a stool and held a poster of his famous shot. He didn't smile, but the catchlights in his eyes captured their intensity. Mantoani ducked under a big black cloth, adjusted the lens, and captured the first exposure. Then he examined the results. "When I peeled the Polaroid, there was a huge blue streak from a light leak," he said. But when he showed the blemish to "One-shot Shulman," the master paid him the ultimate compliment: announcing the shoot was over—no need for a second shot.

He saw the light leak as a fine metaphor (and perhaps an excuse to be done). "It's all about me—letting in the light," Shulman said. "I love it! We're done, kid."

In January 2009, *Los Angeles* magazine published Mary Melton's "Lens Master," a ten-thousand-word profile of Shulman that would win a PEN Center award. Arranged in "36 exposures"—the number of shots on a roll of 35-millimeter film—the story presented a kaleidoscope of scenes from different parts of the photographer's long life. Even in his final years, Shulman was still answering a constantly ringing phone, still bursting with the confidence that rankled some and charmed many. "Why, I'm more famous than ever!" he had exclaimed in an unveiling of *Julius Shulman. Modernism Rediscovered*, a three-hundred-dollar, three-volume collection of Shulman's photos.

Six months after the *Los Angeles* magazine profile summed up a life that spanned nearly a century, Julius Shulman died in his Soriano steel-and-glass home on July 15, 2009. He was ninety-eight years old.

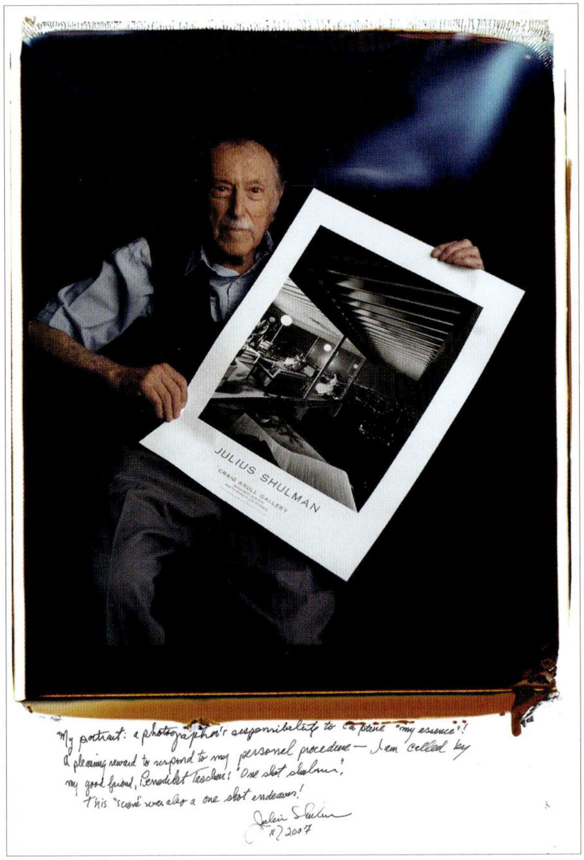

Every morning, just as she had for half a century, Carlotta awoke to a view of water and sky, only now her perch was in the foothills outside Boise, Idaho, and her view was of Lucky Peak Lake. She now lived with Shari, Berndt, and their daughter, Annie, in a hilltop home designed by Arthur

Dennis Stevens, who studied under Frank Lloyd Wright. Mark bought a house on a neighboring hill. From her bedroom window, Shari could see his lights wink on in the gathering dusk and know he was home safe.

As Carlotta's Alzheimer's progressed, she began to confuse Mark with Buck. But while most memories faded or bled together, those of her house were indelible. "I want to go home," she would say. The house was the anchor to her past, her life. And that memory never faded.

"With Alzheimer's, it was the one thing she remembered vividly," Shari said. "I wasn't her daughter anymore. I was the lady who took care of her. But she never forgot her house."

For as long as she was able, Mark would fly with Carlotta back to LA to spend two weeks at her house, so she could be in the place that made sense to her and calmed her. Eventually, as Alzheimer's took hold, these trips became less frequent. Near the end, as her condition deteriorated and she required near-constant care, Carlotta briefly resided in the memory-care unit of a retirement home in Idaho.

On the day Carlotta turned eighty-two, Shari, Mark, Berndt, and Annie brought her a cake and sang "Happy Birthday." Brimming with love and bracing for the inevitable, they found her smile as beautiful then as it ever was.

In Carlotta's last days, her three kids and her brother never left her side. They took turns sleeping in a chair in her room so she wouldn't have to be alone. Eleven days after her birthday, on July 25, 2011, they whispered, "I love you," and watched her fade away.

....

One day shy of two years after Carlotta's death, on July 24, 2013, the Stahl House was listed on the National Register of Historic Places. It was the culmination of a fifteen-year effort by Peter Moruzzi, the preservationist Carlotta had welcomed in 1990 on a MOCA exhibition tour. That tour had been the "life-altering" moment that was part of the twenty-three-year path leading to this major milestone.

"This is perhaps the most iconic house constructed in the Case Study House Program," Moruzzi wrote in the application, describing the house as "a superlative architectural statement in steel and glass" and "the work of a master architect." He also found it essential to acknowledge the people who lived there, and why that mattered. "The house has been continuously owned and maintained by the Stahl family," he wrote. "It retains a high level of integrity." Combined with its listing as a Los Angeles Historic-Cultural Monument, and protection at the state level, Moruzzi said in 2020: "It's about as protected as something can be."

Randy Koenig, Pierre's son, is an architectural lawyer who frequently speaks to architectural groups, including the American Institute of Architects. "Every single time, [someone from] the Frank Lloyd Wright Foundation [will] come up to me and shake my hand and say, 'Congratulations, your dad's house is more photographed than Fallingwater.' They're very gracious about it. 'Your dad's house is the most famous house in the world.'"

Today, more than seven thousand visitors tour the Stahl House each year, nearly one-third of them from some other country. The number one question docents hear is: "What about the family who lived here?"

The answer to that question is mostly missing from all those newspapers, books, and magazines. "The house is the celebrity," Shari said. "Not us."

This house is so much of a celebrity, in fact, that it needs a manager and an agent. That is now Shari's full-time job. As vice president of Stahl House Inc., the family-owned company that manages the house, she works seven days a week and wears too many hats: accountant, tour and studio booker, webcam checker, restoration coordinator, payroll chief, tax-return wrangler, parking officer, ombudsman, and phone dispatcher for lost tour guests trying to navigate the spaghetti-like roads of the Hollywood Hills. Most days she works remotely from her home office in Idaho: a sunny, window-lined room that's also home to eight rescued parrots. Like young children, her birds vie for her attention whenever she picks up the phone, and their fury erupts like an orchestra of belligerent pterodactyls. Their chorus explains why a flock of parrots is officially termed "a pandemonium." She goes by Shari Gronwald now, and when people call with requests she can't accommodate, they demand to speak to her manager.

Every few months, Shari boards a plane in Boise and flies into Burbank to spend a few days working at "the Hollywood house." She drives the company car—Buck and Carlotta's 1998 Oldsmobile Silhouette minivan—on freeways that spike her blood pressure, threading through a city so different from the one she knew as a child. As she climbs the serpentine surface streets, she sees mansions where she once played in empty lots. But when she unlocks the carport door that wears her father's initials and steps into the courtyard, the pressure of the city gives way to something she only feels here. Walking across the pool, on the concrete bridges under which she once played as a child, sliding open the glass door to the kitchen, she feels a sense of peace as enveloping as swimming under still water—where the noise and the rush of the world disappears, the moment suspended in time and place.

"It's that feeling of calm—*I'm home*," Shari said. "I open the door, and I can hear my parents talking. I walk in every room, just to take it all in. That presence—it reminds me of my childhood and being safe."

Shari sleeps in "the kids' room," where the closet door slides open to reveal a computer and her tiny office. She hides her suitcase in the Jack-and-Jill bathroom, the only spot in the house closed off to tours. A faint noise in the ceiling vent—a tinny *tink-tink-tink*—is familiar and comforting, like the house is whispering, "Welcome home." Every inch of the place triggers a memory. In the kitchen, she can see her mother pulling a cake from the oven, her father sipping coffee with his Danish and listening to the news on a portable TV on the end of the kitchen island—his favorite spot in the house.

It would be nice to live here full-time, but fame has made that all but impossible, unless you like waking up to strangers peering in through your bedroom window. Privacy and private property seem like notions of a bygone era, as anachronistically quaint as vacuum tube radios and Bakelite rotary phones. Those have been replaced by camera phones and the invasion of trespassing drones, which she waves away with the agitation of someone swatting at hornets. The first time she heard one buzz over the cliff, its camera lens aimed through her window, Shari was so incensed she called the police.

"Can I shoot at it with my BB gun?" she asked.

"No, ma'am," a voice said flatly.

"Well, then I'll just throw rocks at it."

"Ma'am," the voice said. "You can't do that."

Although no one lives there full-time, the Stahl House is still very much a home. Bruce and Melisa, who live in west Van Nuys, sometimes spend time there with their three nearly grown children, Shane, Sara, and Skyler. As often as possible, Shari and Berndt fly from Idaho with Annie, the only grandchild to have lived there briefly. Annie loves sitting on the edge of the catwalk, talking on her cell phone, bare toes dangling over the city.

Mark, Buck and Carlotta's youngest child, died tragically and unexpectedly just a few months after the house was listed on the National Register. Shari and Bruce dedicated themselves to fulfilling Mark's plan, as painful as it is to carry on without him. The tours he started have now eclipsed filming and shoots as top priority of the Stahl House. They feel it opens the door to sharing their parents' legacy with others.

"The Stahl children are keeping the house open so people can go experience it," said Linda Dishman, director of the Los Angeles Conservancy. "When you touch a building, it imprints in your brain differently. It's one thing to see beautiful photographs, but it's nothing like being there. There are certain houses that are like that, that need public access."

The Stahl tours have no velvet ropes. Visitors are welcome to sit on the couch, and excuse themselves to the powder room, where the original wallpaper, the green shag carpet on the wall behind the commode, and Carlotta's framed embroidery have remained unchanged since the 1970s. Their furniture did not survive the ravages of time and unrelenting light—the living room turns black couches purple in a matter of months—so the house is currently staged about every two years by Design Within Reach. As with the 1960 *Arts & Architecture* photo shoot and the 1989 MOCA exhibition, the house is styled with furniture that Buck and Carlotta could never have afforded.

Docents tell the story of how the Stahl House came to be, and then give the guests unscripted time to wander and imagine. "I was impressed with the tour, but also that they gave you time at the house, to just hang out, sit outside by the pool, be in the living room," Dishman said. "I think there was a real respect there for the experience of people. It's not just about the tour. It's about letting people experience the architecture."

The tour attracts visitors of all stripes—architects and scholars, historians and preservationists, Case Study experts and mid-century modern fans. Most who know something about the house expect to know the story. "This is by far [one of the]—if not *the*—most iconic house in LA," said Jordan Nedeff, a Los Angeles real estate broker on a tour in 2018. "It's burnt in everybody's imagination."

"Don't you think it's really kind of defined Los Angeles?" said Cary Berglund, a reporter for NBC News, who came on the same tour. "This is the kind of architecture that put LA on the map."

It is rare to meet a first-time visitor who isn't visibly moved. "I'm still in awe right now," Nedeff said on his first Stahl House tour. Despite an intimate working knowledge of high-end LA homes, he found himself choking up. "I don't want to cry … it's a masterpiece."

Even people who know the trivia, who have seen the house on the silver screen and in the pages of glossy magazines, who have Shulman photos framed on their walls or saved as their iPhone home screens, are stunned when they see it person. Sometimes they find themselves starstruck, as if meeting a celebrity. "When you walk through those doors for the first time, it takes your breath away in a way you could never have imagined," said Berglund. "Nobody could capture what the reality is."

Those who come expecting a typical tour often encounter something more profound. "Architecture is a transformative experience, and I believe buildings and places can be portals to parts of our soul," said Eric Evavold, an architectural tour guide based in Los Angeles. "The Stahl House is a portal."

It transports many people through an intimate story to which they can relate. "These people had a vision, and they made it happen," said Jeannie Vasquez, a young artist who found herself empathizing with Buck and Carlotta's story. "He only had one income. They had kids. It's like all the real-life struggles that a lot of couples face. But they created this. It's pretty inspirational."

Bruce frequently drops by, unannounced, lingering discreetly in the background of a tour, because the enthusiasm of visitors always recharges him. When people learn his identity, he is invariably peppered with questions. He doesn't mind. Like Carlotta, Bruce gets a huge kick out of seeing people's reactions. "I call it 'the wow moment' when they come through the door," Bruce said. "I love seeing the look on their faces."

Docents say the Stahl House tour is different from others. "If you've ever been to Fallingwater, or even the Eames House, it doesn't feel like the Stahl House," said docent Andrew Edelstein. "It has the feeling of a family home."

Visitors say the same thing. "How do I even articulate this? How do I even explain what I've just seen?" mused Eleanor Schrader, distinguished instructor at UCLA Extension. "My first impression is: This is someone's *home*. It came through very clearly, even though it's probably the most famous house in the world. There's just such a joy of coming here. There's such a warmth here."

Photos of Buck and Carlotta greet visitors throughout the house and their presence is palpable. "I wish I could have been here when they lived here," said Berglund, the NBC reporter. "That's the only thing missing … time travel."

Perhaps that's what sets Case Study House #22 apart: the difference between a house and a home. Pierre Koenig once said, "In architecture, if you can get both the intellectual stimulation and the emotional stimulation at the same time, then I think it's a work of art."

Case Study House #22 is, to many, a work of art, the capstone of Koenig's great legacy. As long as it remains in the family—the only Case Study House in the care of original owners—the Stahl House also will be, above all, a home.

One August day in 2019, Bruce's oldest child, Shane Stahl, did a cannonball off the flat steel roof, landing with an epic splash in a pool overflowing with cousins, uncles, aunts, and a floating, inflatable palm tree. The hot tub bubbled with mountains of suds—a tradition Carlotta started with her grandkids. "She'd always put a big ol' glob of dish soap in the jacuzzi," recalled Shane, Carlotta's first grandchild, now 6 foot 3 and built like his tall, lean father. "That would happen nearly every time we came during the summer. We'd be in the jacuzzi—bubble monsters—and grandma would bust out all the kitchenware." Tupperware transformed into buckets, pots and spoons became drums, and the mountains of suds were fashioned into quivering hats and beards. "The bubble tradition was definitely passed on."

It was the first big family reunion since the extended family had gathered at the house for the memorials of Buck, Carlotta, and Mark. Except for their absence, it was just like old times. Mark's best friend since childhood, Michael Hicks, was there taking pictures. Bruce, sixty-one, and Shari, fifty-nine, were jumping off the roof, silhouetted by a cloudless sky. "That's the rite of passage when you go to the Stahl House," said Shane, who has perfected the cannonball. Now twenty-four, Shane was not too old to dive for handfuls of coins, tossed into the pool now by Shari. He could still recall the aroma that always welcomed them home—his grandmother's caramel, chocolate-chip cookies.

Until recently, this house was simply "Grandma and Grandpa's house." The house where his sisters and cousins would open presents on Christmas Eve, hunt for Easter eggs, and celebrate birthdays, usually with a special cake from Carlotta. They took photos with their prom dates here, the city an ultimate backdrop. To celebrate his college graduation, Shane threw a party with friends and a beer-pong table by the pool. "The older I get, the more I appreciate how legendary the house is," Shane said, "and my grandpa having this idea of what he wanted and finding an architect to bring it to fruition."

Every Monday and Thursday, Bruce ends his pool route at the house that still welcomes him home. After skimming bugs off the surface, emptying the filter, and testing the water's chemistry to ensure it stays perfectly blue, he cracks open a beer and sits down on an outdoor bench. Surrounded by memories, swimming in sky, he gazes at the panorama that's constantly changing, that never gets old. The sunset always looks different up here, and it's never the same two days in a row. The thrum of Los Angeles is ever present, but here it is faint and removed, almost soothing, like the white noise of waves breaking on some distant shore.

When it's time to leave, he arms the alarm and slides the glass walls closed. He walks over the concrete bridges, looks back at the pristine pool, and opens the carport door. Before he crosses the threshold to the world outside, he says softly, "Goodnight, Mom. Goodnight, Dad. Goodnight, Mark."

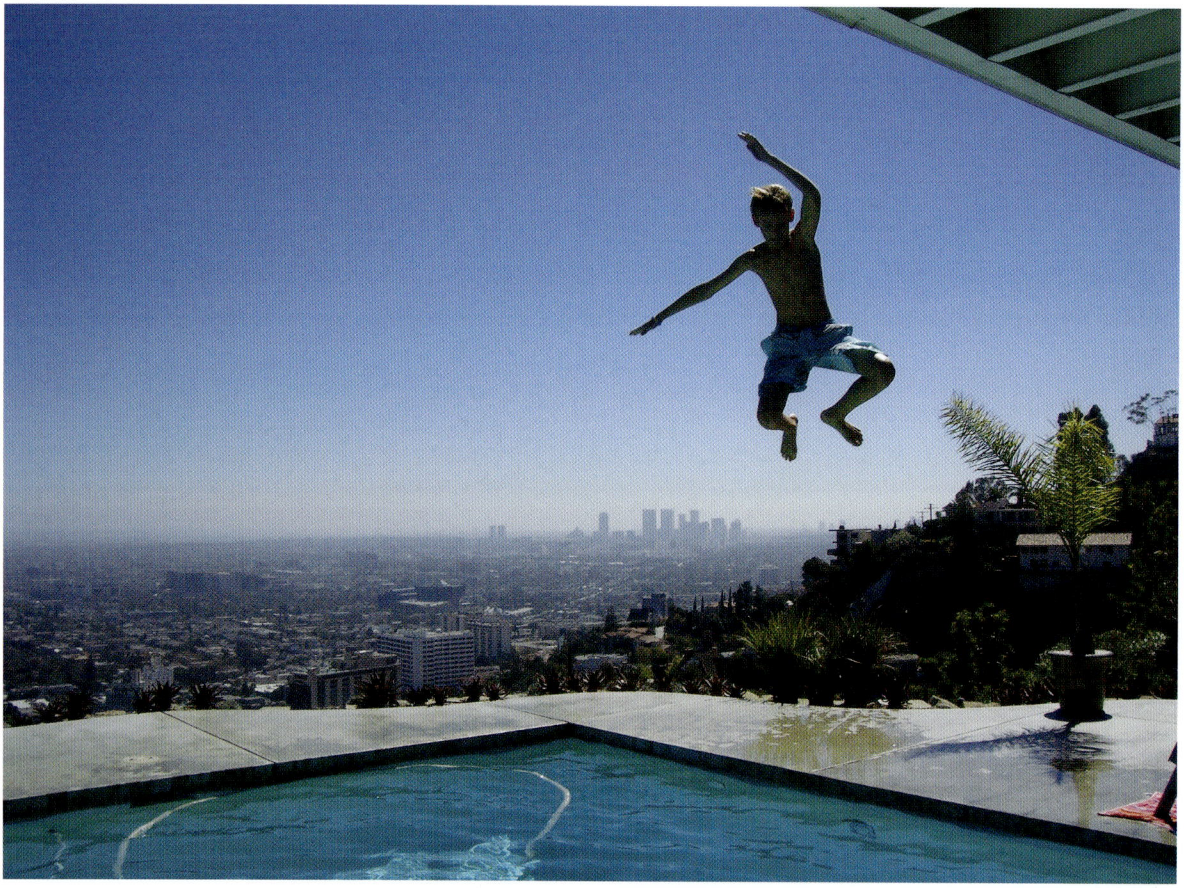

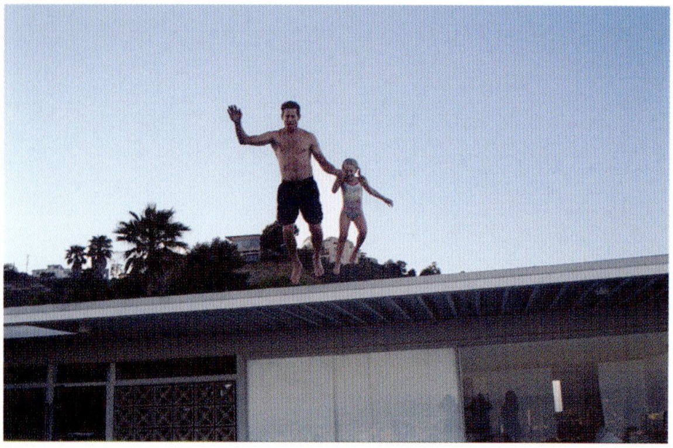

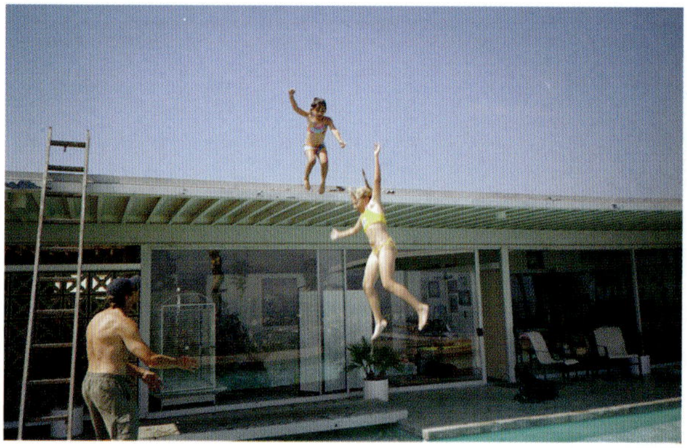

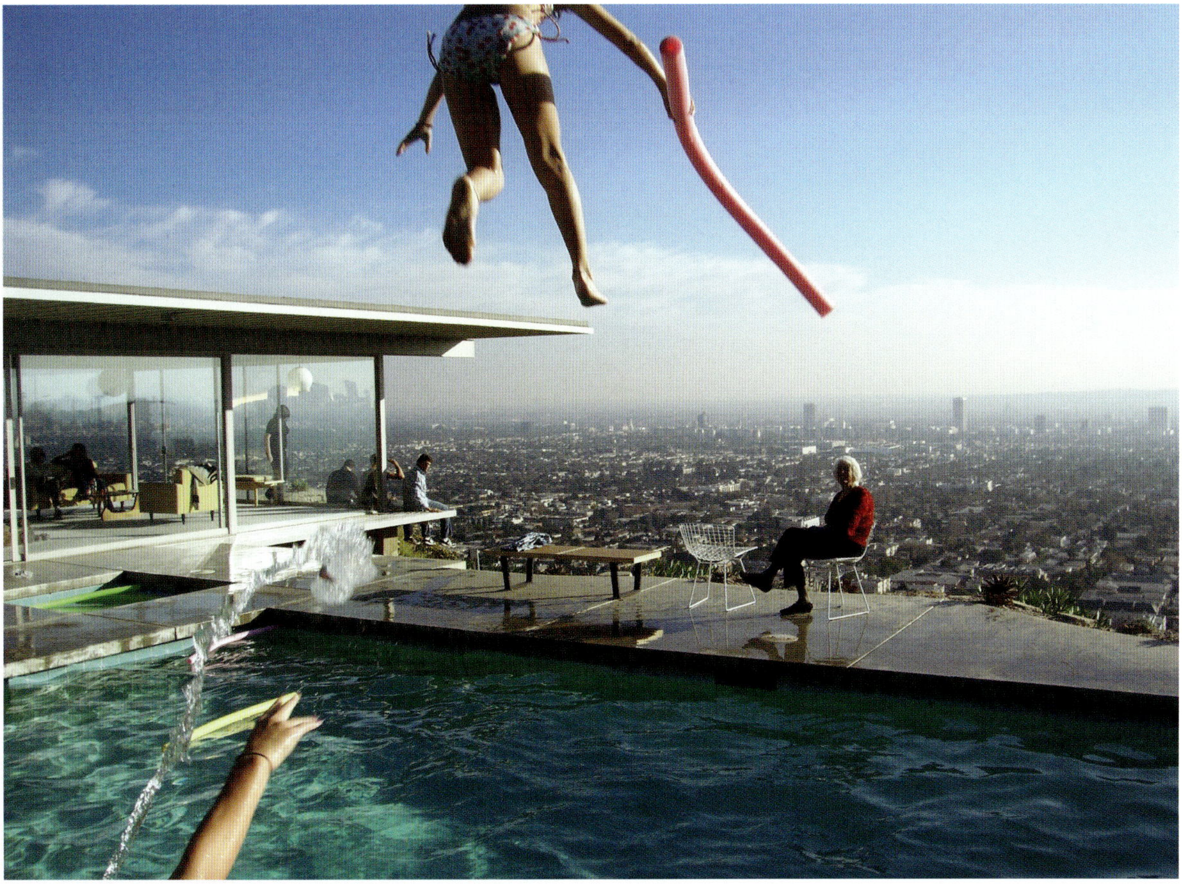

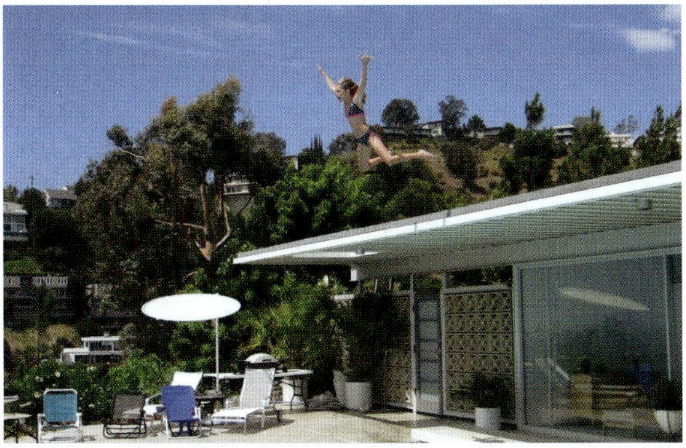

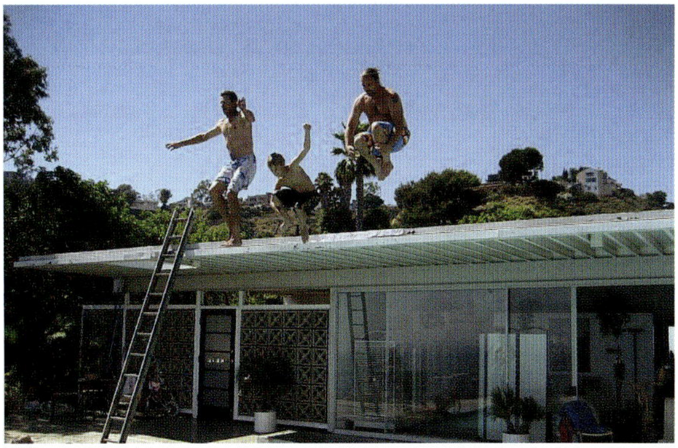

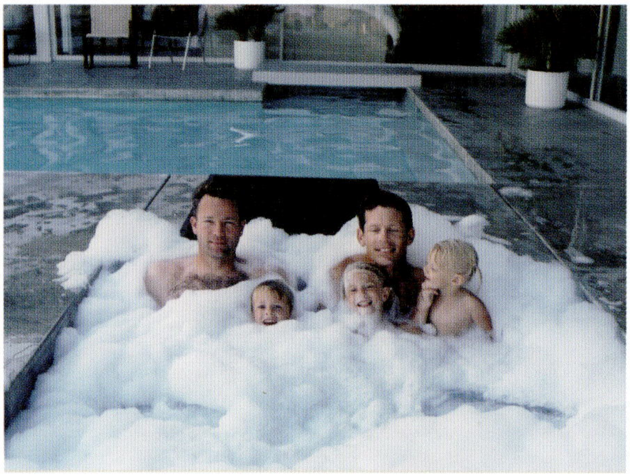

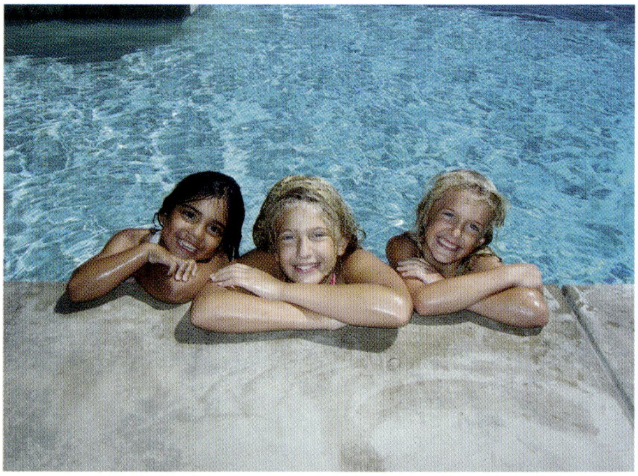

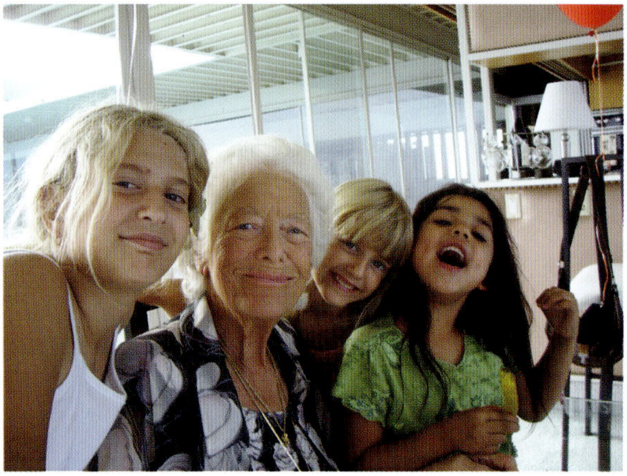

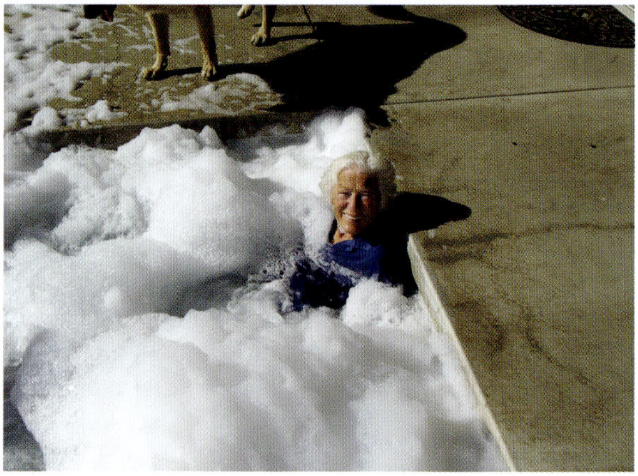

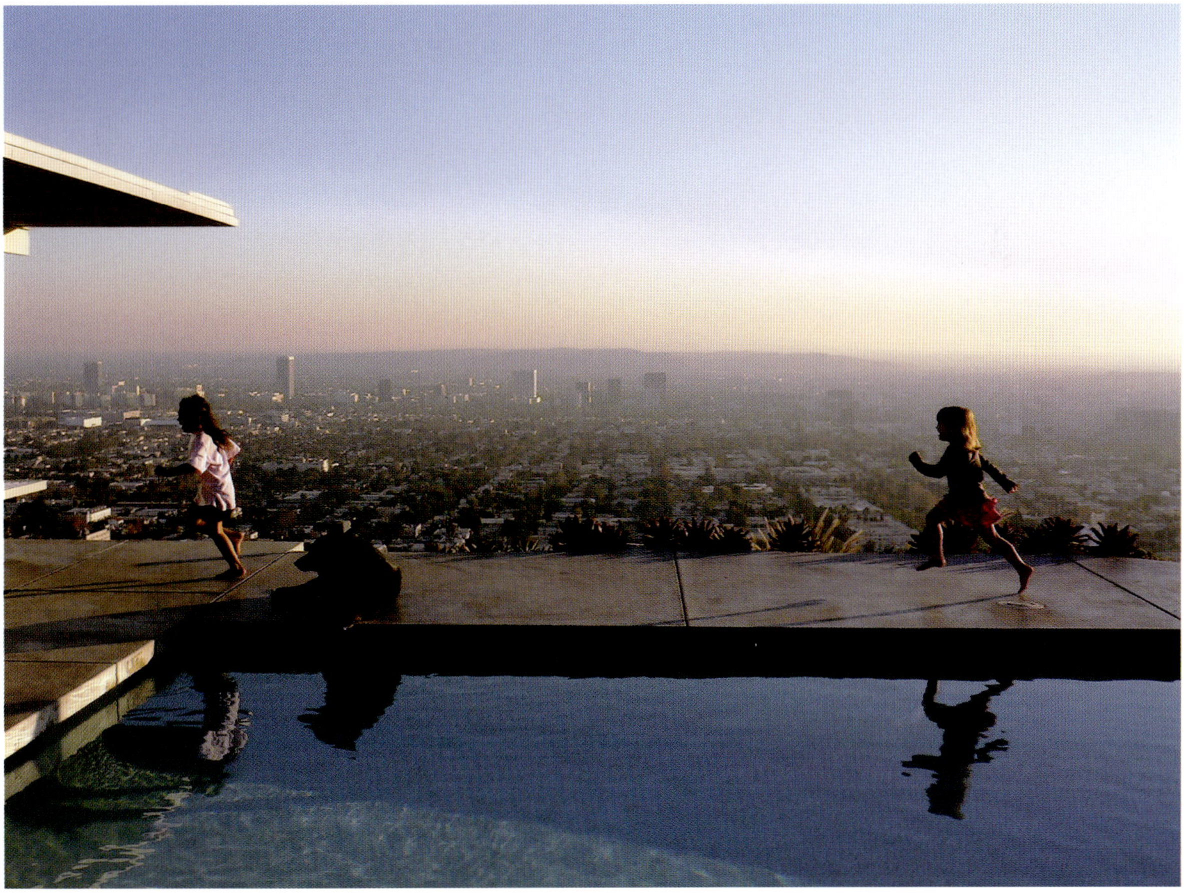

EPILOGUE:
THE REUNION

When Julius Shulman snapped what is perhaps the most famous picture ever taken of Los Angeles, could he have imagined, could any of his subjects have imagined, that a single image would encapsulate the promises, hopes, and dreams of L.A.'s future—and conjure our fantasies of its past?

—Mary Melton, *Los Angeles* magazine

Some of the world's best ideas, discoveries, inventions, and stories begin with a simple question.

In the fall of 2000, Mary Melton began a new job as an editor at *Los Angeles* magazine. Prepping ideas for her first story-pitch meeting, she thought about Julius Shulman's most famous photograph, an image she had long admired. Melton, thirty-one, had always wondered: *Who were the "Two Girls" sitting in that dreamy living room?* That question led to an idea, which she proposed in the meeting: "Let's track them down and—if they're game—restage the photo."

"That photo has always fascinated me," Melton said. "It was selling such a fantasy of what it means to live here, and in that moment in time. It's possibly the most iconic photograph taken of Los Angeles. I had long wanted to know who they were, these two girls in the photograph. I started to dig around."

After months of digging, phone calling, and schedule-wrangling, Melton drove to LAX to pick up one of the women. "I'm going to see this woman who has been in my mind for decades," Melton said, recalling the moment twenty years later. "I'm getting goosebumps talking about it." She was driving her 1987 Toyota pickup truck, a red long-bed, thinking: *Condé Nast would have sent a car.*

In Shulman's photograph, Ann Lightbody is poised on the left, one elbow raised, with her back to the city lights flickering through the open glass door. She was twenty-one years old—hardly a "girl"—a student majoring in history and political science at UCLA. She was engaged to Jim Jennings, the USC student working part-time as a draftsman for Pierre Koenig in 1960.

Four decades after the shutter opened and closed on that moment, Lightbody stepped off the Southwest flight to meet Melton, who had found her and, through the magazine, flew her down from Seattle. Now sixty-two, Lightbody was the assistant dean at the University of Washington's School of Business Administration. Her hair was short, her smile radiant, and she still carried herself with the poise of the era she had unwittingly come to embody. "She was absolutely lovely and sweet and funny, and had a great personality," said Melton, who put Lightbody up at the Roosevelt, the Hollywood hotel where David Hockney had painted a multi-million-dollar mural on the bottom of its famous Tropicana Pool.

The next day, on April 4, 2001, Ann Lightbody stepped into the Stahl House for the first time in forty-one years. One by one, she watched them all come through the door—the complete cast of characters whose lives had intersected in such a singular way to make the Stahl House famous.

Here came Cynthia Murfee (now Tindle), her dear friend from Pasadena High, with whom she had sat still in the dark for seven long minutes during the first part of Julius Shulman's tricky double exposure. A grandmother now, retired from the school district, Tindle was living in Hermosa Beach. She was carrying her four-month-old granddaughter, whom she was babysitting. Wearing skirt suits now, instead of white dresses, the two women embraced and smiled through the tears. "Ann and Cynthia hadn't seen each other in forty years," Melton said. "It was just like two girlfriends from college."

There was Pierre Koenig, dressed in all black, gray curls wild and windblown from a drive in his green Fiat Spider convertible. Koenig, seventy-five, was working as an architect and a professor at the USC School of Architecture. He had brought his wife, Gloria, an architectural historian and author. Julius Shulman, ninety years old and leaning on a cane, was making his way around the living room, effervescing with energy and ideas. He had "retired" in 1985, but he was working on a few pet projects, including photographing the Getty. The architect and the photographer were still getting calls nearly every day about the house in which they were standing. Nearby was Shulman's former photo assistant, Leland Lee, who had helped rig the lighting all those years ago, replacing lightbulbs with flashbulbs that popped in the second phase of the double-exposure.

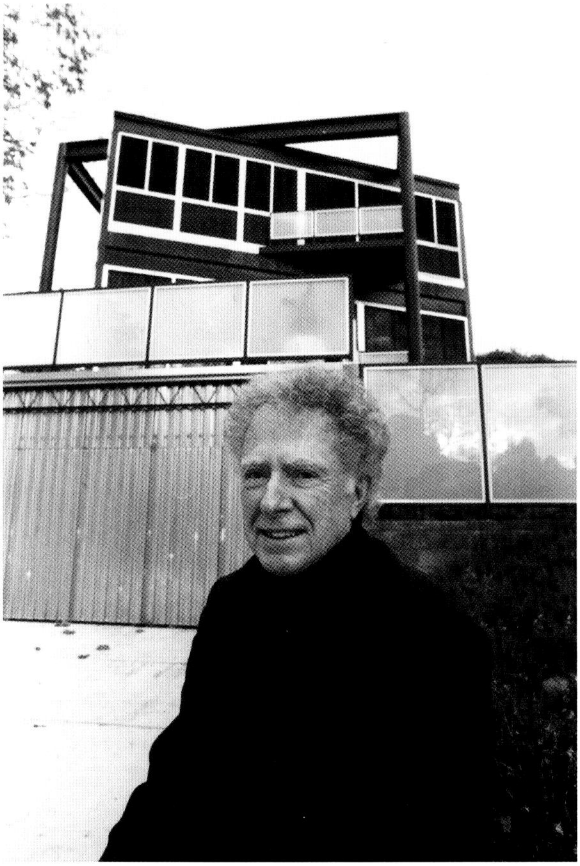

Across the room were the beaus who had invited Lightbody and Tindle to the 1960 shoot. Jim Jennings and Don Murphy were architecture students back then, Kappa Alpha frat brothers, and roommates at USC. Jennings and Lightbody were engaged at the time, and Tindle and Murphy were courting. Lightbody and Jennings later married, had a son, and divorced. Murphy and Tindle dated for a few years but broke up and married other people. Murphy was working as an architect in Sierra Madre. Jennings had worked as an architect and remarried. Accompanying him now was his new wife.

And there were Buck and Carlotta, welcoming yet another round of guests, watching yet another story unfold in their storied home. Carlotta, seventy-one, was as put-together as always, dressed in white slacks and a crisp, white blouse, with a blazer the color of ballet shoes. Her honey-blonde hair had gone white, but she still wore her favorite red lipstick. Buck, three weeks from his eighty-ninth birthday, was using a wheelchair, as he had been ever since he broke his hip. He was smaller now, a bit hard of hearing, and age had softened his booming voice. But his mind was still sharp, and he could recall every detail about planning and building his house.

Though the reunion was recreating the most iconic moment in Stahl House history, this gathering was historic in its own right: Never before had *all* the players been together in one place at one time. When the group had convened forty-one years before, Buck and Carlotta were absent. Yet they would forever be intimately tied to that moment. As Carlotta recalled, "When anybody comes in the house for the first time, they say, 'Are you one of those girls?'"

"The Stahls had never met 'the girls,'" Melton noted. "The girls hadn't seen each other in forty years. But when they took their seats in that familiar glass-walled perch, it was as if they'd never left."

On the catwalk outside the living room, USC history professor Philip Ethington was cleaning the windows with Windex and a big rubber squeegee. "Julius invited me to go along on this thing," said Ethington, a historian whom Shulman had come to consider both a friend and a personal chronicler. "He kind of treated me as his core historian. He wanted me to witness these historic moments." A professor of history, political science, and spatial sciences, Ethington would later write the script for *Visual Acoustics*, a documentary about Julius Shulman produced by Eric Bricker. He had first encountered the famous photograph as a college student reading a textbook about twentieth-century America. Now, as he watched the two women reunite on the other side of the glass, he thought: *Ann Lightbody—what a perfect name for someone in a photographic masterpiece!*

As the professor washed the windows, another unsung player snapped his photo. It was Chris Nichols, a member of the Los Angeles Conservancy's ModCom, which was working to get the Stahl House listed on the National Register of Historic Places. As a writer for *Los Angeles* magazine, Nichols had helped Mary Melton track down Cynthia Tindle, a keystone to orchestrating this reunion. "I loved the idea of deconstructing this moment in time," Nichols said. "I loved having the opportunity to work professionally with my heroes, my idols."

The photographer chosen to capture this next moment in Stahl House history was David Glomb, a self-taught architectural photographer with a delightfully eclectic resume. As an architecture major, he'd gotten a college job at Disneyland—"I was Winnie the Pooh!"—then worked as a Hollywood sound engineer on films including *Grease* and *Rocky Horror Picture Show*. Like Shulman, Glomb had a serendipitous start in photography. As a favor for a friend, he took a few photos of an Angelo Donghia interior; a designer then saw those images and hired him. "I just got job after job," Glomb said. "I was very lucky, being in the right place at the right time." Decades later, Shulman noticed Glomb's work and reached out. "He had been getting calls for work," Glomb said. "Since he was retired at that point, he called to see if I would help him." They had partnered on various assignments, including photographing the Cathedral of Our Lady of the Angels for the cover of *Architectural Record* and reshooting Richard Neutra's famous Kaufmann Desert House. Though they collaborated as equals, Glomb was often misidentified as Shulman's assistant.

Unlike many photo shoots at the Stahl House, this one was small and intimate, with just a handful of people, most of whom would be in front of the camera. "I knew it was historic," Glomb said, "because all the players were still alive." He couldn't stand exactly where Shulman had stood, because that would now be in the hot tub. So, he backed up and stood on the concrete footbridge, composing the image in his mind.

While Glomb set up his equipment, everyone else reminisced about that day in May of 1960. They remembered the unfinished kitchen, the plaster dust, the pool, and the view. Mary Melton took notes and turned on a tape recorder as they mused about how it all came together.

"They said, 'Wear a dress—you might be in a picture,'" Tindle recalled. "We all went together, like we were on a date. Don had a '55 Chevy with turquoise sides. They were the greatest cars going. Nobody was living in the house. The kitchen was empty. It was pretty wonderful—you step out of your bedroom and you're in a pool. It was just a casual evening of fun. I happened to like Don, so I wouldn't have cared if I just stood there."

Leland Lee, Shulman's assistant, remembered the speed with which Shulman worked, but also his patience for shifting light and his attention to every detail. "You had to wait for the right light, especially with night pictures," Lee said. "We had to maneuver and place lights, mostly to avoid reflections in the glass. Sometimes it would help to open a sliding glass door."

Shulman remembered what he was thinking when he positioned Lightbody and Tindle in the living room. "I wanted to breathe some air into the house, not to pose them with their faces in the camera necessarily, but to get a feeling of natural activity, as well as using them for scale," he said. "After all, architecture is for people."

Mary Melton asked Lightbody and Tindle to think back to that seven-minute interlude in the dark. What were they saying when the flashbulbs popped?

"What were we talking about? Probably Don and Jim," Tindle said. "I didn't think, 'Oh gee, I'm going to be in something famous.' I'm not a person who likes to have people looking at her. If I had known, I might have been a little nervous about how I looked or gone out and bought something new for the occasion. Yes, I was in a dress, but in 1960, you didn't go out without wearing a dress. You would never have gone out wearing jeans or pants."

"We were just chatting," Lightbody said. "We only had dreams at that time."

Tindle said, "With Ann and [me], you can put into our conversation whatever you think we were talking about. We were young and about to start the adventure of life. There were a lot of places you thought you were going, and all the places you didn't."

When David Glomb was ready, each person took their place in the shot.

Carlotta wheeled Buck out to the pool patio and stood by his side. Pierre, holding a blueprint tube, stood behind them, next to his masterpiece. Lightbody and Tindle took their seats in the famous corner. Shulman, front and center, stood next to a camera on a tripod and held a print of the photograph whose fame and mystique had brought them all together.

Standing behind the photographer, Melton saw the constellation of people she had wondered about for years. In the distance, just over Pierre's shoulder, she could see her office, housed in a thirty-story building on Wilshire Boulevard. For years to come, she would look out of that office window, remembering this very moment at the house up on the hill.

Click.

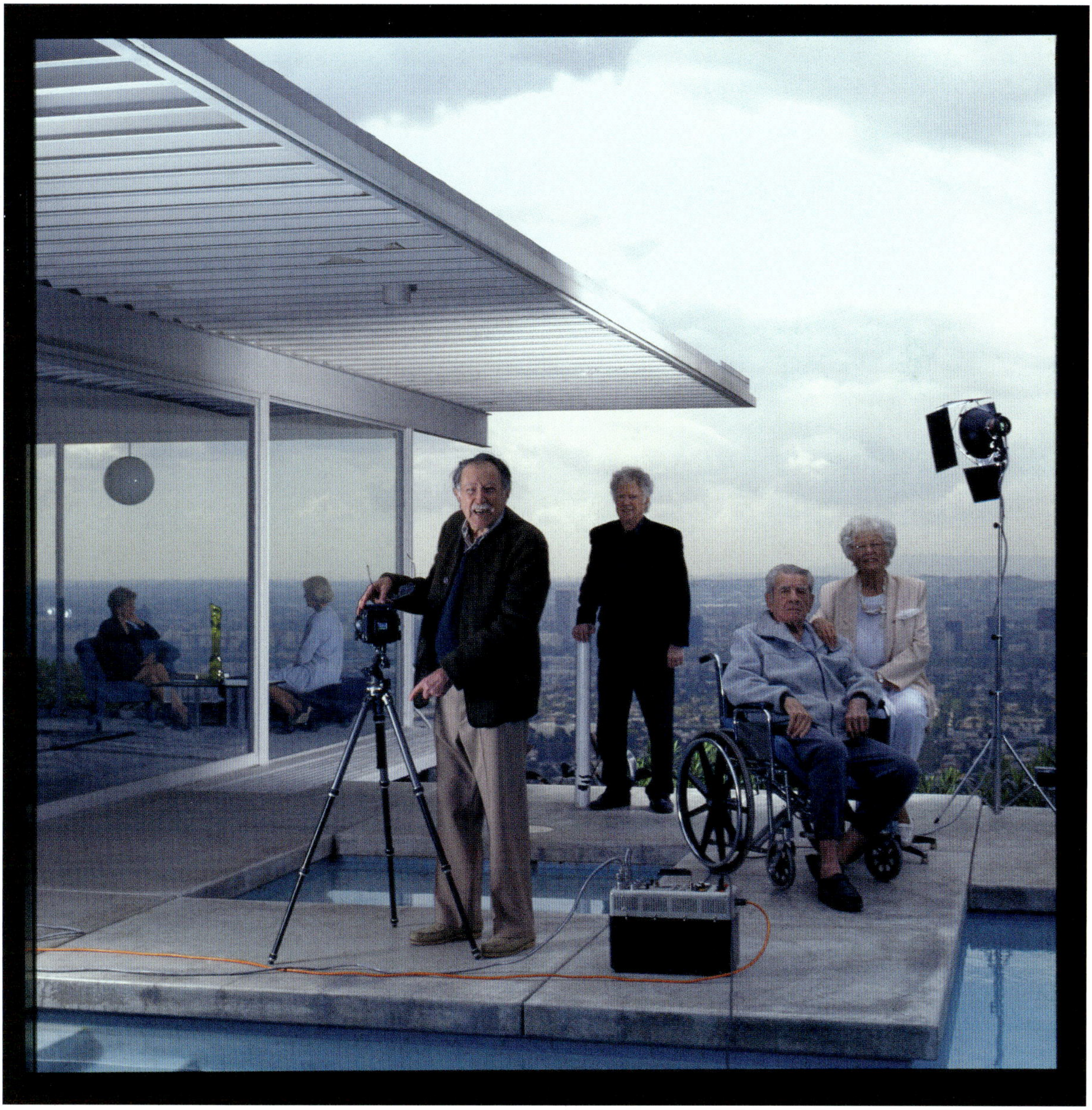

Left to right: Ann Lightbody, Cynthia Tindle, Julius Shulman, Pierre Koenig, Buck Stahl, and Carlotta Stahl.

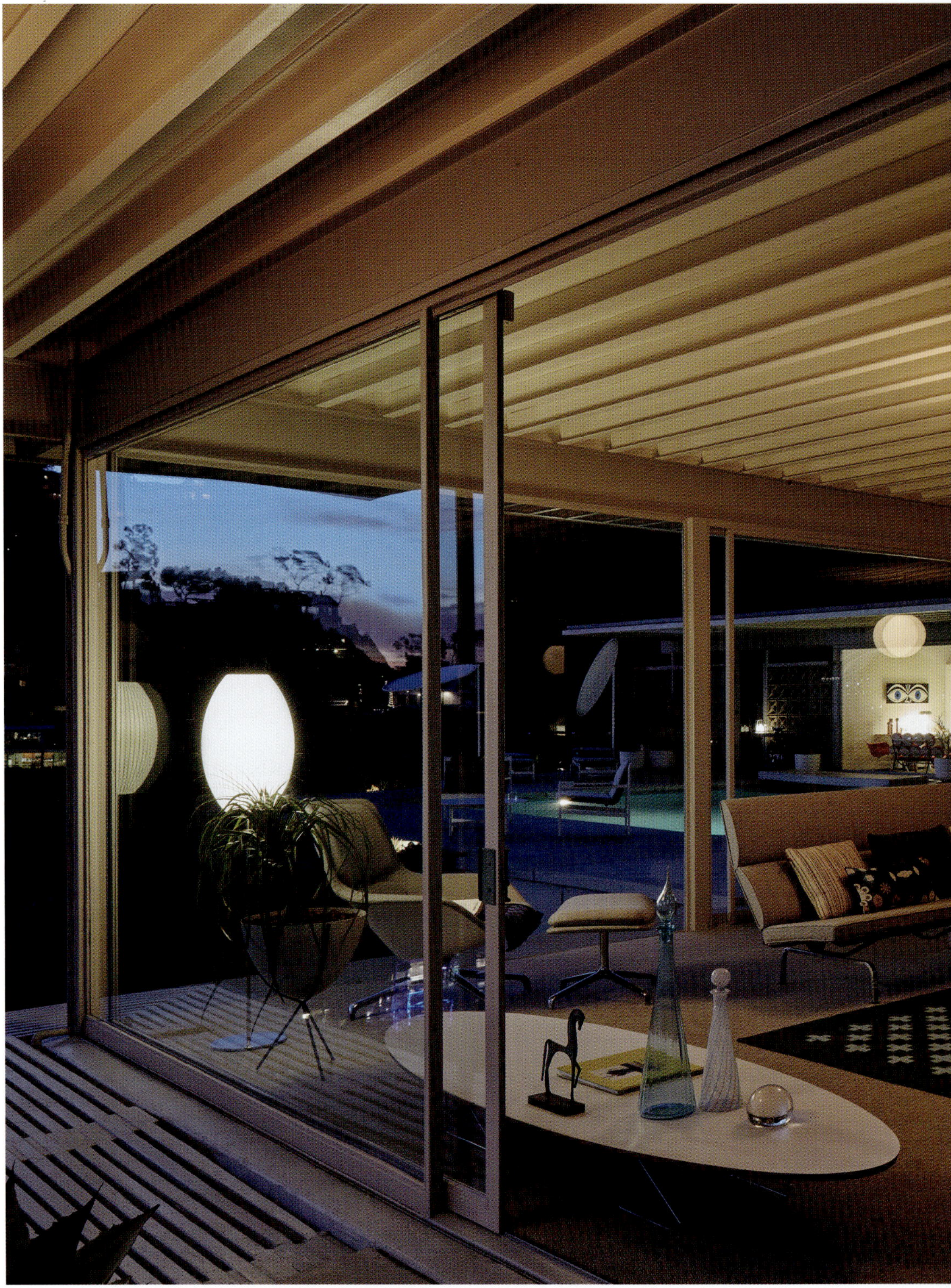

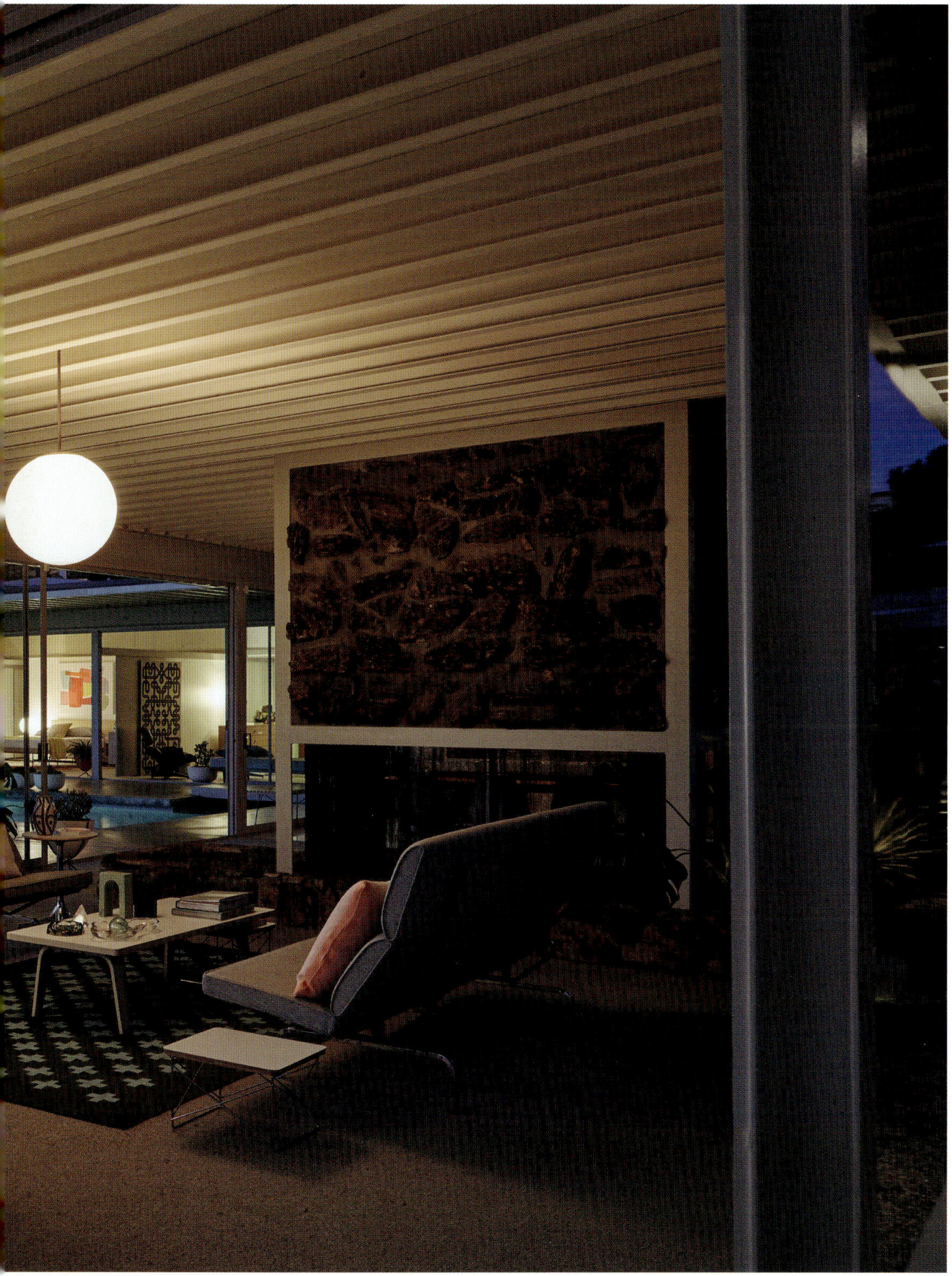

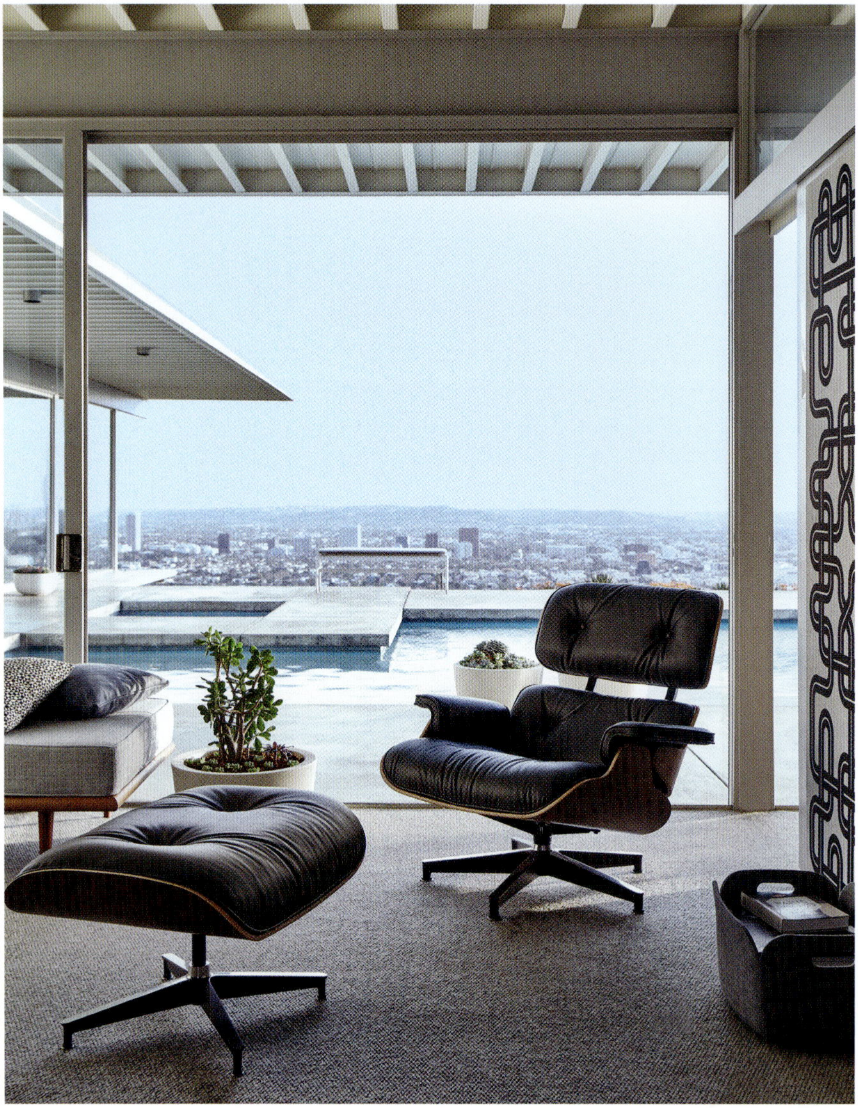

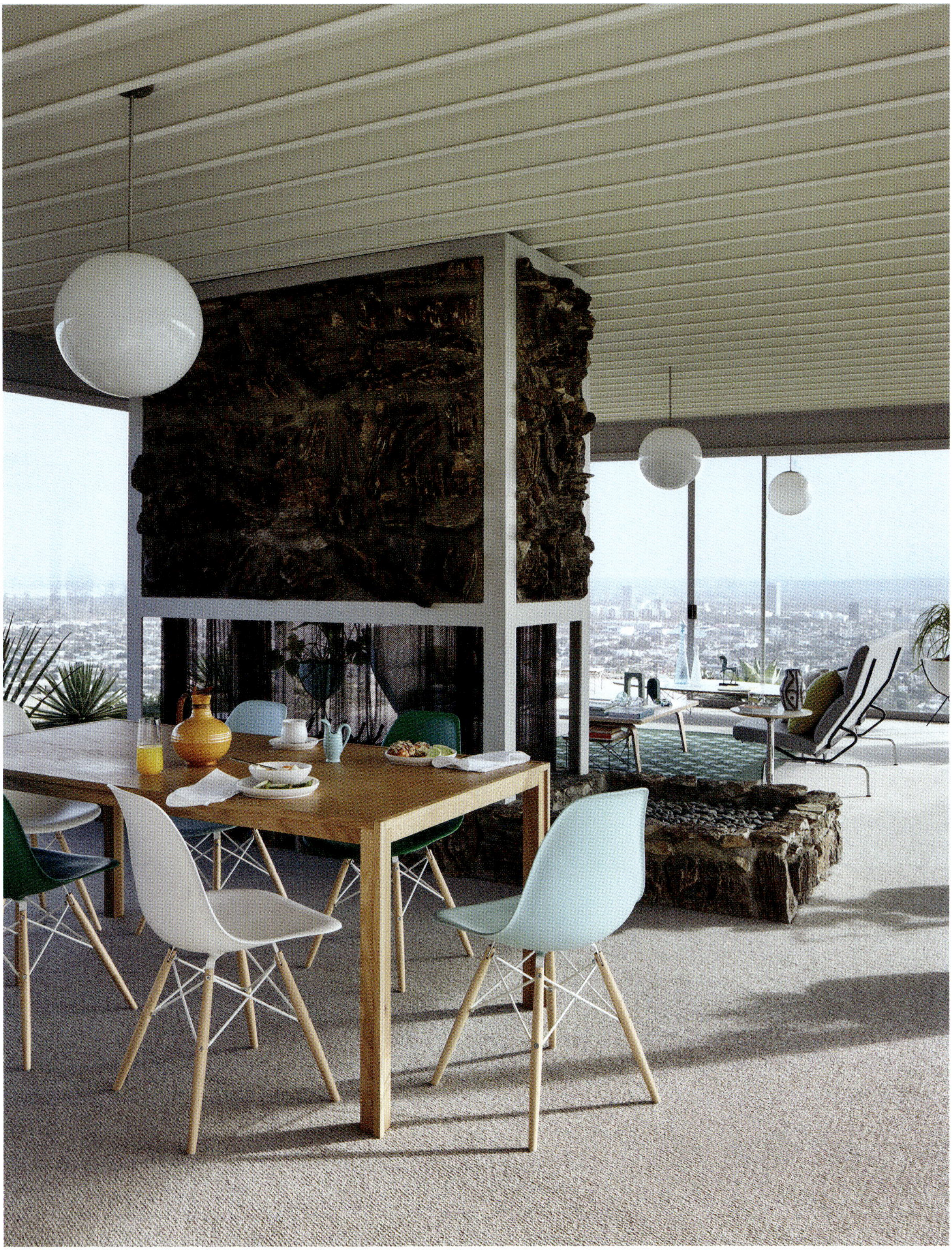

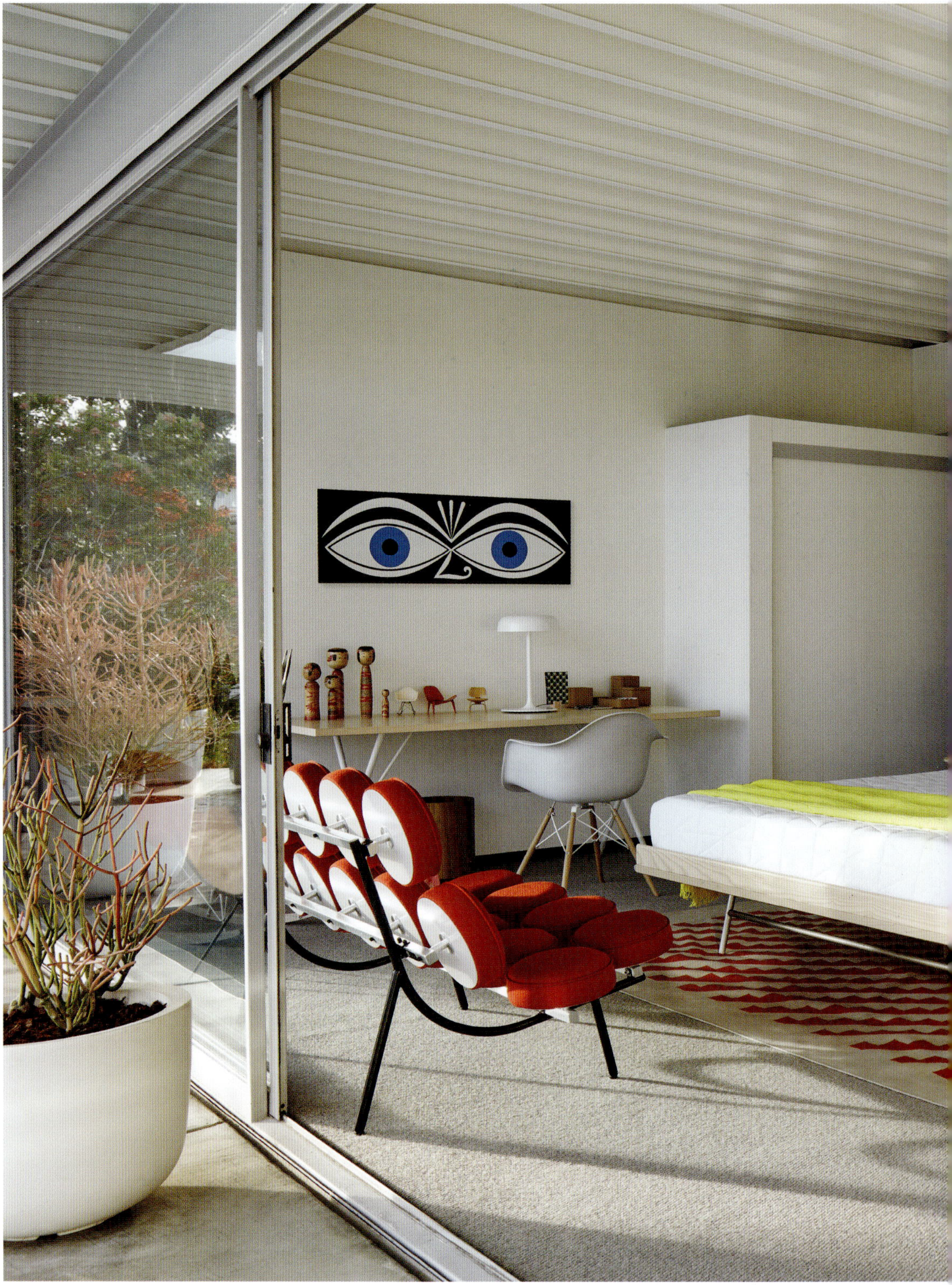

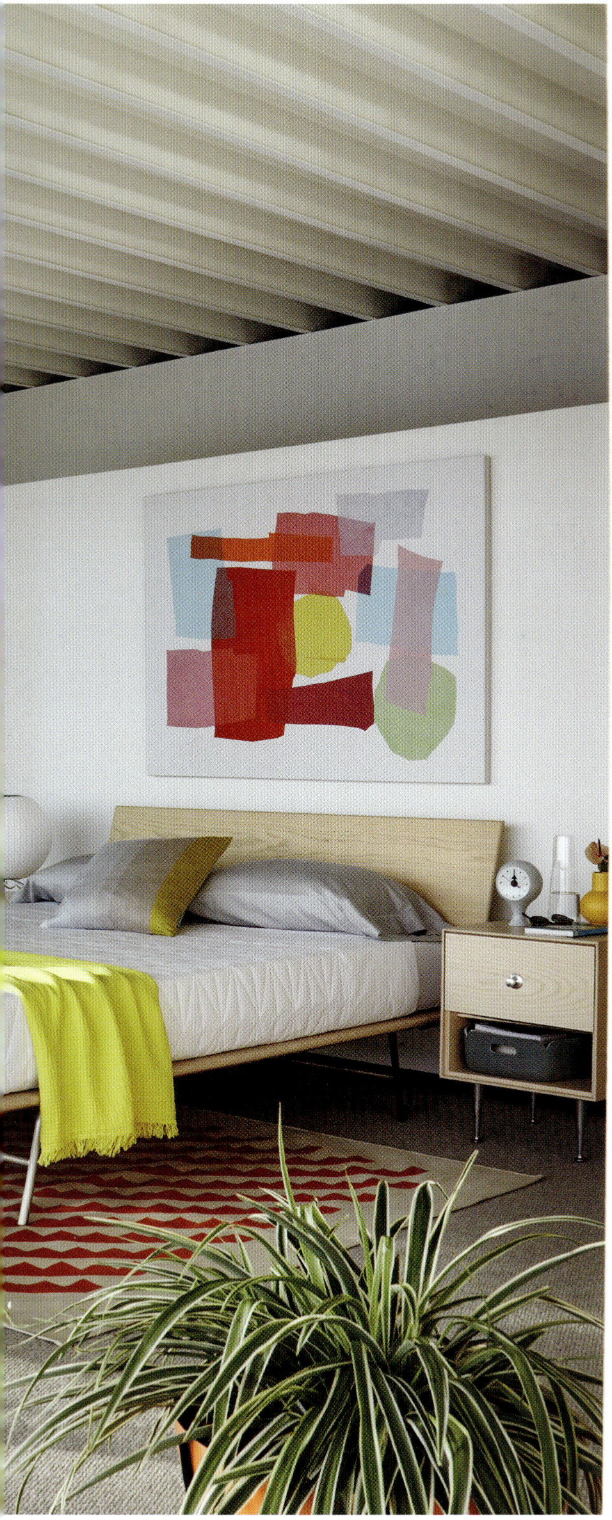

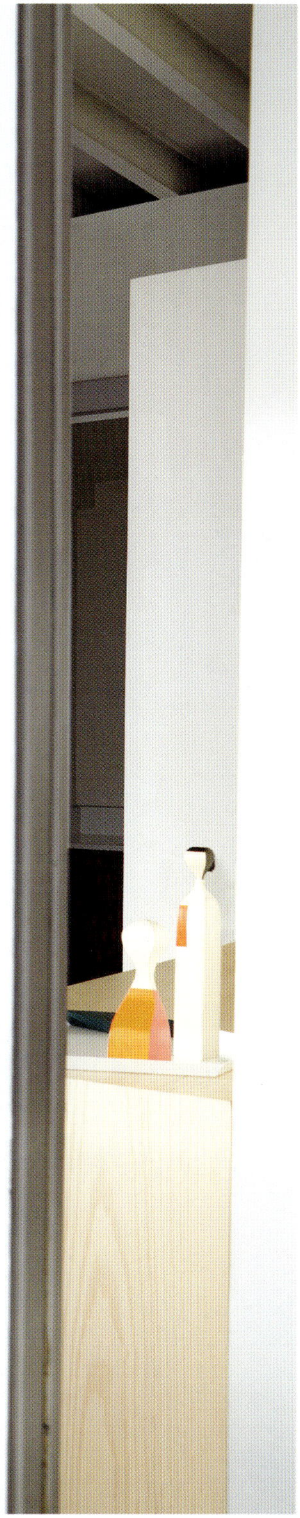

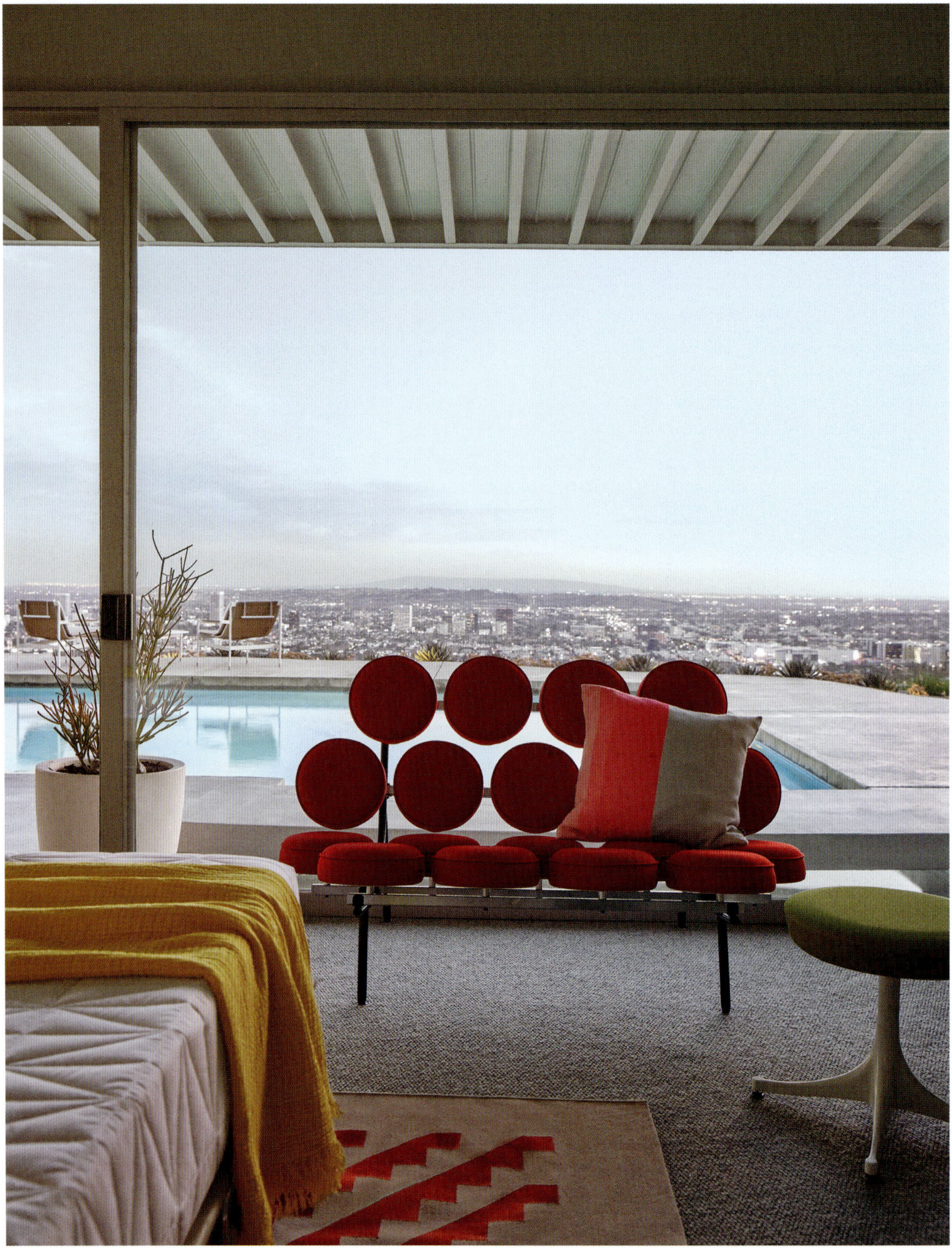

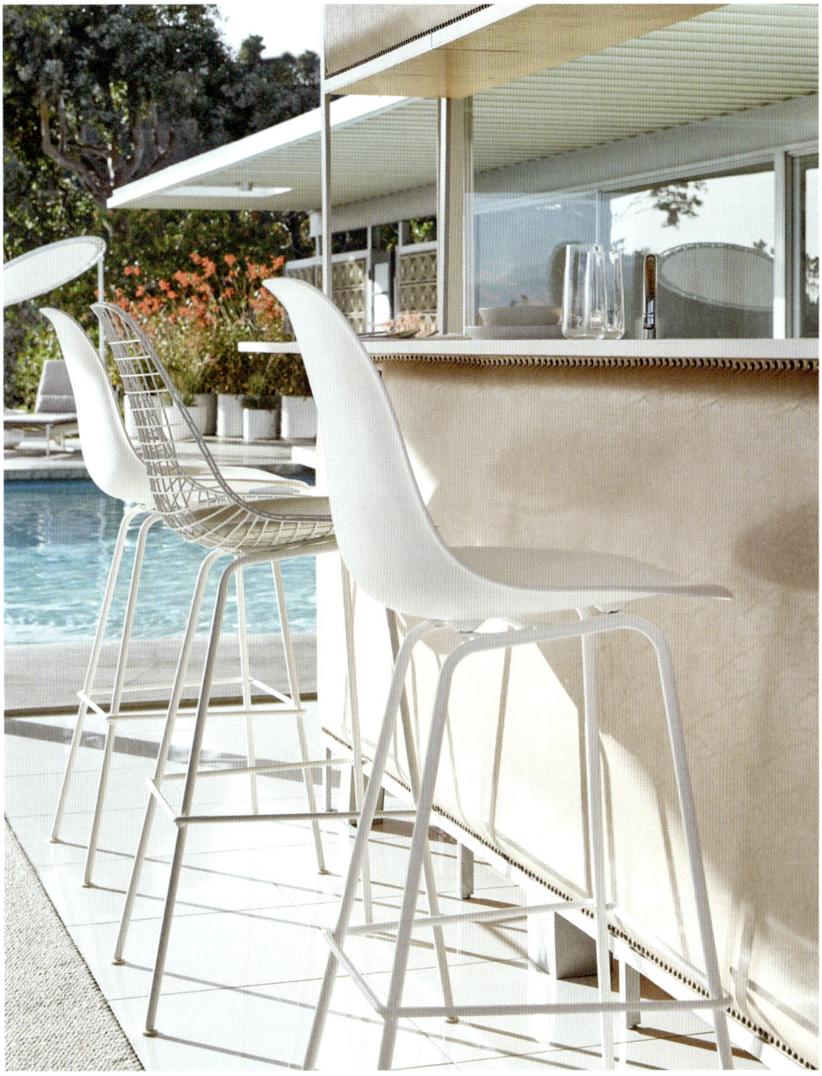

NARRATIVE ENDNOTES

Instead of formal endnotes, as one would find in an academic book, we decided to take a narrative approach. We sought a format that would be useful to scholars and historians on the hunt for primary sources, but also something the non-academic reader might actually read—with interest! This section includes details, technicalities, stories we couldn't quite verify, and points of debate. These asides would have stalled the narrative momentum in the chapters, yet seemed important enough to publish in a biography of the Stahl House.

This book required two years of deep research, employing the skills of both the journalist and the historian. Great efforts were made to fact-check what we hope will serve as the definitive history of this storied house. Some of the fact-checking led us down rabbit trails to fantastic stories.

First, a quick word about the research and reporting. This portrait of Buck and Carlotta's life emerged largely through interviews with their children, Shari and Bruce, and surviving members of their family. These interviews were conducted between January 2019 and January 2021. (Mark had passed before this phase of the project began.) Whenever possible, memories of facts and dates were corroborated with photographs and historical documents from the Stahl family archives, which Mark and Shari meticulously organized and scanned. These private archives are not available to the public, and they included a number of photographs, documents, and records that can't be found in public archives. We'll mention a number of those items as examples, but it's not an exhaustive list.

Kim, Shari, and Bruce spent a couple of days at the Getty Research Institute Special Collections, located at the J. Paul Getty Museum in Los Angeles. The Getty archive (as we'll call the GRI from here on) is home to the Pierre Koenig Archive and the Julius Shulman Architectural Photography Archive. Aimee Lind, a heroic archivist, pulled out everything in either collection that was related to the Stahl House. Wearing white gloves, we studied architectural drawings, memos, photographs, newspaper clips, magazine tear sheets, personal letters, and other historical papers. We photographed every architectural drawing brought out for review, because many of them were hieroglyphic to us without interpretive help. We later reviewed the photographs with architects, historians, and experts who helped translate.

Characters who could not be interviewed were given voice through dialogue documented in a variety of sources. Whenever possible, we tried to source direct quotes from recordings (audio and video) and interview transcriptions. However, many quotes came from secondary sources, published in newspapers, magazines, and books. For direct quotes not obtained in an interview by the author, the interviewer or source is attributed upon first reference in the text. For subsequent quotes, repeated attribution was limited for the sake of narrative flow.

To aid the future historian, scholar, or journalist, some comments on sources are provided.

CHAPTER 1: THE DREAM

Many of the numerous stories Buck told his children were corroborated through fact-checking. There were a few we were unable to verify, but neither could we disprove. As part of the family lore, we found them interesting enough to mention here.

Regarding Buck's job painting airplanes: Shari and Bruce, as well as family and close friends, recall Buck saying one of the planes he lettered was the Spirit of St. Louis. The plane, built in San Diego, stopped briefly in St. Louis on May 11–12, 1927, on its way to New York, where Charles Lindberg would begin his historic solo, nonstop flight across the Atlantic. Buck would have been fifteen years old during that layover, supporting this family legend. However, historical photographs taken prior to leaving San Diego show the name was already painted on the plane.

According to Dr. F. Robert van der Linden, curator of air transportation and special purpose aircraft at the Smithsonian Institution's National Air and Space Museum (which exhibits the Spirit of St. Louis), the lettering on the nose and tail of the plane was painted in April 1927 by Albert B. Crygier, an employee of Ryan Airlines, the San Diego manufacturer of the plane.

"While some touch-up of the aircraft was possible when the Spirit visited St. Louis," van der Linden wrote in an email to the author, "Mr. Crygier was the primary painter." We thought Buck's story was worth noting in the context of family lore.

Buck's football career has been reported and published in numerous articles and mentioned by people who knew him (including Pierre Koenig) in recorded interviews. Attempts to verify this fact with historians and official football records were inconclusive. Profootballarchives.com shows no player named Buck Stahl or Clarence Stahl on any team rosters of the era. Historians note that football record-keeping at that time was spotty, and many athletes played under pseudonyms. Athletes who played in exhibition games or training camps may not have been recorded on team rosters.

Much of the dialogue between Buck and Carlotta Stahl in this chapter (and elsewhere in the book) was captured in recorded interviews generously shared by interviewers.

Director Eric Bricker filmed his interviews with Buck and Carlotta in their home on August 25, 2004. Portions of this interview appear in *Visual Acoustics: The Modernism of Julius Shulman* (2008), his documentary about the life and career of Julius Shulman. Bricker provided the uncut footage for use in this book, and it yielded a number of quotes that did not appear in the film.

Other rich dialogue came from an oral history interview with Buck and Carlotta by historian Philip Ethington. His interview, recorded in audio form, took place in the Stahl House on May 9, 2001. It can be found in the Getty archive. Also helpful were an interview with Carlotta by Fumie Yamanaka in July 2004 (transcription found in the Stahl family archives) and Ginger Moro's article, "Case Study House #22 in 2000," *Echoes* magazine, Fall 1999, vol. 8, no. 2.

Key sources from the Stahl family archives included the agreement with contractor Robert J. Brady, and a letter from John Entenza to Buck and Carlotta approving the Pierre Koenig house to be part of the Case Study House program, designating the house as Case Study House #22.

CHAPTER 2: THE CONFLUENCE

Neil Jackson's meticulously researched and footnoted book, *Pierre Koenig: A View from the Archive* (Los Angeles: Getty Research Institute, 2019), is one of the most comprehensive sources we found on the architect's life and work. In addition to rich biographical details, the book contains a number of photographs, drawings, and architectural plates that are of great use to the scholar and historian.

Jackson, professor emeritus at Liverpool School of Architecture and president of the Society of Architectural Historians in Great Britain, corresponded by email from Great Britain. He took a great deal of time to review primary sources and thoughtfully answer many questions about Koenig's work that few others could answer with such authority.

An extremely valuable insight into Koenig's personal history was a series of recorded interviews conducted by Mohamed Sharif, Los Angeles, January through November 2003, DVD4, Copyright © 2016 by in-D media. These unpublished interviews exist in Sharif's private archive, and he kindly shared them with us. Per his request, we direct-quoted very sparingly from them in this book. Sharif also kindly corresponded a great deal with us via Zoom chats, phone calls, and by emails, translating some of Koenig's architectural drawings and answering technical questions about architecture and construction processes, historically and today.

Other helpful books on Koenig included: *Pierre Koenig* (London: Phaidon Press, 1998), by James Steele and David Jenkins; *Pierre Koenig 1925–2004: Living with Steel* (Los Angeles: Taschen, 2007), by Neil Jackson; and *Case Study Houses* (Los Angeles: Taschen, 2016), by Elizabeth A. T. Smith.

Many of Julius Shulman's biographical anecdotes and quotes in this chapter were documented in an oral history interview with Shulman by Taina Rikala De Noriega, January 12–February 3, 1990, for the Archives of American Art Oral History Program. The full transcript is available at the Archives of American Art. Other quotes came from videos, including: "Voice of the Photographer," The Annenberg Space for Photography, accessed online at *youtube.com/watch?v=Eto9mHoXLYg*; Julius Shulman, narrating a photo documentary about his life and images for the series *SHELTER*, accessed online at *youtube.com/watch?t=129&v=u6i-YguE1zaU&feature=youtu.be*.

Useful books on Shulman include *Julius Shulman Los Angeles: The Birth of a Modern Metropolis* (New York: Rizzoli Classics, 2016) by Sam Lubell and Douglas Woods; *A Constructed View: The Architectural Photography of Julius Shulman* (New York: Rizzoli, 1999) by Joseph Rosa and Esther McCoy; *Julius Shulman: Architecture and its Photography* (Cologne: Taschen, 1999) by Peter Gossel, et al.; *Julius Shulman: Modernism Rediscovered* (Cologne: Bibliotheca Universalis, 2018) by Pierluigi Serraino and Julius Shulman; and *Julius Shulman's Los Angeles* (Los Angeles: J. Paul Getty Museum, 2011) by Christopher James Alexander.

Many useful facts and quotes appear in the following articles: "Home of the Steel Ideal," by Jonathan Glancey, *The Guardian*, November 7, 1998; "Julius Shulman: Capturing the Essence of California Architecture," by Steve Proffitt, *Los Angeles Times*, October 9, 1994; "Lens Master," by Mary Melton, *Los Angeles* magazine, January 2009; "A Shot In The Dark: The Unknown Story Behind L.A.'s Most Celebrated Photograph," by Mary Melton, *Los Angeles* magazine, June 2001; and "Julius Shulman, Photographer of Modernist California Architecture, Dies at 98," Andy Grundberg, *The New York Times*, July 17, 2009.

Particularly useful primary sources, archived at the Getty Research Institute (unless otherwise noted), included: Pierre Koenig, "Areas in Relation to Structure," in idem, "Housing, Wood, and the Community."Pierre Koenig papers and drawings, 1925–2007, 2006. M30, box 147, folder 12. Pierre Koenig, "What is the Best Dwelling Type?," in idem, "Housing, Wood, and the Community." Pierre Koenig, Untitled (lecture, San Francisco Museum of Modern Art, San Francisco, CA, June 20, 1990). Pierre Koenig papers and drawings, box 147, folder 12. Pierre Koenig, "Acceptance Speech Gold Medal Award Ceremony, Oct. 28, 1999," Pierre Koenig papers and drawings, box 51, folder 6. Esther McCoy, *The Second Generation* (Salt Lake City: Peregrine Smith, 1984), 28. "Pierre Koenig, Candidate for Promotion to the Rank of Full Professor, School of Architecture, University of Southern California," 1996, collection of Neil Jackson.

CHAPTER 3: THE CATALYST

Some of the most valuable sources of information about John Entenza are the writings of Esther McCoy, an architectural historian who is considered the greatest chronicler of the Case Study House Program, and who was also a close personal friend of Entenza. A wealth of primary sources can be found in the Esther McCoy papers, circa 1876–1990, bulk 1938–1989, Archives of American Art, Smithsonian Institution. A finding aid for her papers can be downloaded in PDF form at aaa.si.edu/collections/esther-mccoy-papers-5502. A particularly useful essay about John Entenza and *Arts & Architecture* is filed in box 20, folder 50.

The three phases of the Case Study House Program are described in Esther McCoy's book, *Case Study Houses: 1945–1962* (Second edition, Los Angeles: Hennessey & Ingalls, 1977 was the copy we used; the first edition was published in 1962 under the title *Modern California Houses*).

The archives of *Arts & Architecture* are owned by the David Travers Family Trust. Select issues, from January 1945 to July–August 1967, are available for free download in PDF form at artsandarchitecture.com. The family of David Travers, John Entenza's successor (1926–2017), generously granted us permission to reprint certain articles and illustrations from the Case Study House years.

Arts & Architecture, under Travers, ceased publication in 1967. From 1981 to 1985, the magazine was published by editor Barbara Goldstein, who subtly renamed it *Arts + Architecture*, replacing the ampersand with a "+". In 1998, Barbara Goldstein edited a book, *Arts & Architecture: The Entenza Years* (Los Angeles: Hennessey & Ingalls), that included a curated selection of pages published in the magazine between 1943 and 1959. The introduction, epilogue, and an essay by Esther McCoy provide rich details about John Entenza's life and persona.

The brief description of the evolution of modernism was written with guidance from historian Philip Ethington, chair of the history department at the University of Southern California. Ethington wrote a similarly helpful condensed history of modernism for *Visual Acoustics: The Modernism of Julius Shulman*, a 2009 documentary directed by Eric Bricker.

The anecdote about Entenza telling Koenig to have Shulman shoot his house has been published in numerous sources; the direct quotes used here came from Mary Melton's article, "A Shot In The Dark: The Unknown Story Behind L.A.'s most Celebrated Photograph," *Los Angeles* magazine, June 2001.

Pierre Koenig's description of his conversation with John Entenza about Case Study House #21 was published in Neil Jackson's book, *Pierre Koenig: A View from the Archive* (Los Angeles: Getty Research Institute, 2019), citing Jackson's interview with Koenig in Los Angeles on July 13, 1988.

Other quotes and facts were sourced from "Homes of the Fabulous '50s," by Sam Hall Kaplan, *Los Angeles Magazine*, May 1987; and "Real Homes for Real People," *L.A. Style Magazine*, September 2009; and Taina Rikala De Noriega's previously noted interview with Julius Shulman.

CHAPTER 4: THE PLAN

This chapter's narrative draws heavily on published sources and aforementioned interviews by Eric Bricker, Philip Ethington, and Mohamed Sharif. Ginger Moro reported great dialogue in "Case 22 in 2000," *Echoes* magazine, Fall 1999, vol. 8, no. 2, 82. Neil Jackson's *Pierre Koenig: A View from the Archive* provided details and insights. Reyner Banham's seminal book, *Los Angeles: The Architecture of Four Ecologies* (London: Penguin Press, 1971) provided historical and cultural context. The February 1956 and May 1958 issues of *Arts & Architecture* were also useful.

The Stahl family's private archive yielded a wealth of historical documents unavailable elsewhere, including: Photographs of Buck's model, dated 1956, taken at 5405 Slauson Ave., Culver City, CA 90230; the formal agreement between Koenig and the Stahls, dated November 20, 1957, and signed by Buck on Dec. 4; a log of payments made to Pierre Koenig; Pierre Koenig's fifty-five-page document providing scope of work, materials, and finishes, workmanship by sections to build the house; a document showing itemized costs by type; Buck's two letters to steel companies requesting work on the house; the Broadway Federal Savings and Loan original application; letters from Broadway Federal Savings and Loan to Buck approving the loan, noting requirements for a pool and a two-car carport; the Broadway Federal loan-payment book; the Catalina Pool Co. original Estimate Sheet and Agreement; and the original California Federal Savings and Loan application and letters of acceptance for the pool.

The Stahl family had many discussions about how to share the story of their father's model in a way that would honor his vision without in any way diminishing Pierre Koenig's mastery and legacy. Koenig's unique mind and abilities are unquestionably responsible for this masterpiece. "Without Pierre, this house would never have happened," Bruce Stahl said many times. "My father had a vision, but Pierre made it a reality."

However, for this to be an honest and definitive account of the Stahl House, it's important to acknowledge the tension caused by Buck's model, both in the architectural community and between the Stahl and Koenig families personally.

"There has been some dispute about whether or not Stahl provided Koenig with the idea for the building," wrote historian Neil Jackson in *Pierre Koenig: A View from the Archives*.

Buck spoke about his model openly to visitors, but photos of the model were not made public until a few years after Buck and Koenig died. In a June 27, 2009, feature story in the *Los Angeles Times*, Barbara Thornburg wrote that "the original inspiration for the design may not have come from architect Pierre Koenig but rather his client, Buck Stahl."

The three-page newspaper feature in the Home section included a previously unpublished 1956 black-and-white family photograph of Buck posing next to his model. The caption noted that the photo was "taken more than a year before Koenig was hired" (a fact supported by the agreement in Stahl family archives, signed by Buck on December 10, 1957). In the story, Thornburg observed that the model "bears more than a passing resemblance to the iconic design attributed to Koenig."

Shari, Bruce, and Mark had long wanted to share their father's story but held off on doing so publicly until after both men had passed, hoping to avoid stirring up bad blood. They believe their father deserves some credit for the original concept of the L-shaped glass house. They also acknowledge that only Koenig could have elevated and refined Buck's ideas to create a masterpiece. Like Carlotta, they saw the house as a wondrous meeting of minds, a confluence of ideas. "It was a collaboration," Mark Stahl told Thornburg. "Pierre bought into my dad's vision but made alternations to make it buildable."

Gloria Koenig, Pierre's widow, told Thornburg: "Pierre used to say that every client thinks they designed their house."

Asked about Gloria's comment in a 2020 phone interview, Randy Koenig, Pierre's son, said, "Those are my words. She actually consulted with me."

Both Randy and Gloria were upset by the appearance of the model and the assertion of co-authorship. "Everyone wants to design a house. I've built a couple of houses, and I always become the architect," said Randy, an architectural lawyer, with a good-natured laugh. "But I'm not the licensed architect. I think it's good that everybody thinks that they design their own house. I think it's a compliment."

Randy said his father did not see Buck's model. "My dad never saw that model, never knew about the model," Randy said. "That model never showed up, or was mentioned, or shown to my dad for … at least eleven or twelve years. And I remember, it was very significant. My dad was very upset that Buck was taking some credit. It simply isn't true." We are grateful to Randy for graciously having this conversation and sharing his statement for the record.

Others in the architectural community have expressed a spectrum of views about the model. Our intention in sharing them here is not to discredit anyone, but rather to give voice to the diversity of perspectives for readers to consider. It is a complicated and fascinating part of the history of the Stahl House. To avoid it would seem disingenuous.

Historian Neil Jackson, who studied Koenig's work as closely as anyone, acknowledged the *LA Times* story and photo of the model in *Pierre Koenig: A View from the Archive*, offering this perspective: "The similarities between Buck Stahl's proposal and Koenig's solution should not be unexpected, for Stahl's requirements, when applied to the site, offered few other options."

Joseph Giovannini, an architect and renowned architectural critic, recalled Buck telling him he had "given Pierre the idea for the house."

In the 2009 story, Giovannini said, "I dismissed it as typical owner hubris at the time." Then he saw Buck's model and changed his mind. "The gesture of the house cantilevering over the side of the hill into the distant view is clearly there in the model," he told Thornburg. "But it is Pierre's skill that elevated the idea into a masterpiece. This is one of the rare cases it seems that there is shared authorship."

Elizabeth A. T. Smith, who curated the MOCA exhibition, provided further interpretation. "The design indeed shares certain similarities with what was later built, but Pierre Koenig would never have introduced curving forms into his work, and I'm struck by the pronounced arc of the house's wings in Buck's model," she said. "From this I can infer that Koenig adhered to the basic attributes of Stahl's concept but refined the design into something more rigorous, geometric, and 'pure' in its form and materials —in essence adapting it to his own vocabulary."

When Philip Ethington conducted an oral history interview with Buck and Carlotta in their home on May 9, 2001, Carlotta showed him a photograph of Buck's model but asked him not to publicize it. "She was very ginger about it, out of respect for Pierre," Ethington said in a phone conversation on January 21, 2021. "I didn't know what to do with it. I felt like I was privy to some secret."

In the deep research conducted for this book, we found no recorded interview in which Pierre Koenig mentioned the model. In many interviews, he referenced Buck's ideas and what he did to adapt them. Buck built the model explicitly to show architects exactly what he and Carlotta wanted. However, we found no conclusive evidence that Koenig saw the model in person. All we know for certain is that, at some point, Koenig saw at least a photograph of the model and acknowledged its existence.

Architect Mohamed Sharif, who was interviewing Pierre Koenig for a documentary, took a private tour of the Stahl House with Koenig in 2003. Sharif described this moment vividly in an email on January 22, 2021: "Carlotta brought out photos of the model, recalling Buck's hands-on involvement in fashioning the home before he met Pierre. A silent Pierre smiled as Carlotta spoke. It seemed like a non-arrogant, unspoken acknowledgment that—while Buck had conceived the house with the enthusiasm of a design aficionado—it was he, the expert architect, who had painstakingly advanced and disciplined it into the renowned lyrical composition and framework for a new lifestyle."

CHAPTER 5: GROUND BREAKING

Randy Koenig, Pierre's son, shared a wonderful story we've never seen published in the many accounts of Julius Shulman's Stahl House shoot. In an interview on October 23, 2020, Randy recalled: "My dad raised me as a single parent. I had to go around to all his job sites with him. My strongest memory was: I was there when they had the famous shoot with the models. I was there. I had to sit in the car, outside. All I remember was raw concrete. My dad made me sit in the car the whole time. I had been up there many times, and I was mortified that I was not allowed in."

Many of the construction details came from records in the Stahl family archives, including original job contracts for the septic system and installation, a Rusher Heat original work order for the radiant heat system, and change orders from contractor Robert Brady. Buck's agreement to reduce the contractor's fee by $450 by doing cleaning and other manual labor at the job site was detailed in Change Order #4. A few biographical details about Robert Brady were included in a Dun & Bradstreet report dated June 1, 1959. A Bethlehem Steel ad mentioned Raymond Equipment and Welding Company. The original letter from John Entenza to Buck and Carlotta, dated April 1, 1959, is a highlight of these private archives.

Direct quotes came from Eric Bricker's interviews, from "A Milestone in Steel," Pictorial Living, *Los Angeles Examiner*, July 17, 1960; "Case 22 in 2000," *Echoes* magazine, Fall 1999, vol. 8, no. 2; and "Lens Master," *Los Angeles* magazine, January 2009. Paul Goldberger's quote was cited by Claudia Luther in "Julius Shulman Dies at 98; celebrated photographer of modernist architecture," by *Los Angeles Times*, July 17, 2009.

Pierre Koenig's April 19, 1960, letter to general contractor Robert Brady can be found in Pierre Koenig papers and drawings, box 1A, folder 1, Getty Research Institute, along with Pierre Koenig, "Areas in Relation to Structure," in idem, "Housing, Wood, and the Community."

CHAPTER 6: THE GEOMETRY OF HOME

Most of this chapter came from interviews with Bruce and Shari, Michael Hicks, Bud and Ann Gates, and other family members. Some quotes came from Michael Bricker's interview. An OmniSeal brochure in the Stahl family archive added a bit of color to Buck's job in sales. The film *Smog* can be viewed on YouTube.

One of the best childhood gems was cut from this chapter. One day, as young Shari and Bruce ate lunch by the pool, a monkey appeared. Bruce and Shari tell it best:

Bruce: *We were sitting there in our swimsuits, eating. All of a sudden, this monkey came up the hillside, grabbed one of our grapes, and was hanging there eating it. It had one of those really long tails.*

Shari: *Probably a spider monkey.*

Bruce: *We were going, "Mom! Mom! There's a monkey here!" Didn't it end up biting you?*

Shari: *It did.*

Bruce: *Yeah, because you tried to touch it or something.*

Shari: *Well, Dad was able to get it inside the house because it was obviously a pet. It was lost.*

Bruce: *It was a pet that got loose.*

Shari: *Dad was like, "Don't pull his tail!" We were over there pulling his tail, right? Finally, the monkey had enough. He just turned around and just bit me, right here. [Points to upper arm.]*

Kim: *How old were you?*

Bruce: *We were pretty young. Under ten.*

Shari: *They ended up calling animal control or something. It was someone's pet that got out; it was probably somebody who lived right down there, down below.*

Bruce: *It was one of the strangest things.*

CHAPTER 7: THE MOVE

Most of this from interviews with Shari and Bruce. A phone interview with former UCSB swimming coach Gregg Wilson brought Bruce's swimming scenes into sharper focus. Certain details came from *Arts & Architecture: The Entenza Years*, by Barbara Goldstein.

CHAPTER 8: FIRE AND RAIN

The question of whether the Stahl House was built with caissons turned out to be one of the most confounding riddles of this book. The bottom line: The Stahl family and a number of experts believe it is very likely there are no caissons. In the absence of a complete set of drawings, short of tearing down the house, there is no way to be 100 percent sure. In the building of any house in any era, changes may occur on the job site without being fully documented.

A number of photos in the Stahl family archives document the house in various stages of construction, including the pouring of the slab. We weren't able to find any photos that showed the type of drilling rig that would have been necessary to drill deep holes for caissons.

Architectural drawings from the Getty Museum Institute Special Collections and the Stahl family archives were studied in sequence, according to their revision dates. Several architects were consulted, including Mohamed Sharif, who toured the Stahl House with Pierre Koenig and Neil Jackson, an architectural historian who probably spent more time than anyone studying Koenig's drawings and papers at the Getty.

The consensus seems to be that the drawings suggest the caissons depicted in the original plan were removed and replaced by concrete blocks. This change appears to have been made around the time the living room was shortened by 10 feet, pulling the edge of the building away from the precipitous nose of the ridgeline—the slope of which exceeded the 45-degree angle of repose that determined the farthest point at which the building should protrude.

In *Pierre Koenig: A View from the Archive*, Jackson noted another change that seems to support the notion that caissons were edited out. "Because the building codes would have required the steel fireplace to be supported by caisson foundations, thus increasing the cost of the substructure considerably, Koenig welded it to the roof deck so that it was suspended above the concrete slab," Jackson wrote on page 46. "Only when the floor screed was poured was the fireplace secured in position. The roof of the kitchen is similarly attached to the roof deck, but now by steel tension wires, for stability during earthquakes."

Jackson found in the Getty archive a written statement in which Koenig explains how his design addressed the risk of erosion and earthquakes: "The piers [concrete blocks] are not under the columns [vertical steel beams supporting the roof] in this case but are set back from five to seven feet. In this way any possibility of damaging erosive action is eliminated. The columns are bearing at the ends of the concrete beams and are encased with twelve inches of concrete for resistance to seismic forces. With glass on all exterior walls except the street side, all horizontal forces can be resisted in this manner." The original document is in the Getty archive. See: "Case Study House 22 Pierre Koenig," 1, n.d., Pierre Koenig papers and drawings, box 1A, folder 1.

Regarding the plan in Fig. 3, Neil Jackson shared some interesting history about the nature of the document and the marks we refer to as chemical erasures, for lack of a better term. In an email on January 21, 2021, he wrote:

This drawing is what we used to call a copy neg in the days before computers. It is a sheet of tracing paper with a chemical film on the reverse side. To create a copy neg, this treated tracing paper is put through the printer with the original drawing, also on tracing paper, placed on top. An ultraviolet (I think) light is shone through the two drawings and then the copy neg is passed through ammonia vapour. The end result is that the image of the original drawing appears on the reverse side of the copy neg (hence the name). This allows the draughtsman, using a razor blade or a craft knife, to scratch away the unwanted lines from the reverse of the sheet and to draw new lines on the front of the sheet, which has not been damaged. This copy neg. now becomes the updated, master document and paper prints can be made from it by passing it through a printer. Your fig. 3 looks like it has been wiped down with a liquid, probably white spirit (denatured alcohol?), such as one would use to clean paint brushes. I think it unlikely that this was done to remove the original lines, since it would be too difficult, with a liquid, to maintain that degree of accuracy.

The September 1979 fire was mistakenly called the "Mt. Olympus Fire" in the morning edition of the September 17, 1979, *Los Angeles Times* and renamed the "Laurel Canyon Fire" in the Late Final edition. In stories published on September 17, 1979, the *Los Angeles Times* reported that twenty-four homes were lost. A September 25, 1979, story in the *LA Herald Examiner* said some of the houses initially counted did not actually exist.

For detailed coverage of the fire, see:
Laurie Becklund, "Four Boys Arrested in Laurel Canyon Fire," *Los Angeles Times,* September 17, 1979, Late Final edition. Janet Clayton, "Firemen, Lifeguards Battle the Elements," *Los Angeles Times,* September 17, 1979. Jill Stewart, "Major LA Wildfires—and What Areas Could Burn Next," *LA Weekly,* January 16, 2014.
Ted Thackrey Jr., "Mt. Olympus Fire Razes 18 Homes," *Los Angeles Times,* September 17, 1979.
Roderick Thorp, "From the Ashes of Laurel Canyon, Some Burning Questions," *LA Herald Examiner,* September 25, 1979.

Earthquake details came from: University of California, Berkeley Seismology Lab *https://seismo.berkeley.edu/blog/2017/02/09/today-in-earthquake-history-san-fernando-1971.html,* and "1994 Northridge earthquake" on History.com, *www.history.com/topics/natural-disasters-and-environment/1994-northridge-earthquake.*

CHAPTER 9: RESURRECTION

Interviews with Craig Hodgetts, Ming Fung, Richard Koshalek, Elizabeth A. T. Smith, Peter Kirby, Mary Alice Wollam, and Peter Moruzzi yielded a wealth of new insights and anecdotes about the Blueprints for Modern Living exhibition and its home tours. Interviews with Bruce and Shari recreated the scenes of the Stahl family's visit to the museum. An oral history interview of Julius Shulman, conducted January 12 through February 3, 1990, by Taina Rikala De Noriega for the Archives of American Art, was particularly useful. The full transcription and an audio excerpt can be accessed online at *www.aaa.si.edu/collections/interviews/oral-history-interview-julius-shulman-11964.*

Peter Kirby filmed interviews with architects and other experts for short films that played in a continuous loop on TV screens in the nighttime part of the exhibition. They can be viewed online at *https://vimeo.com/433240005/4b27b0b5cf.*

Sources from the Stahl family archives included: A letter from MOCA assistant curator Elizabeth A. T. Smith to Buck Stahl, January 11, 1988; a MOCA mailing announcing the exhibition; an invitation to a preview of the exhibition on October 14, 1989; a flyer advertising the symposium on October 21, 1989; and the symposium program.

Published sources for this chapter included: Mary Banham, "Blueprints for Modern Living: History and Legacy of the Case Study Houses:

Museum of Contemporary Art, Los Angeles, 17 October 1989–18 February 1990," *AA Files,* no. 20 (Autumn 1990). Paul Goldberger, "When Modernism Kissed The Land of Golden Dreams," *New York Times,* December 10, 1989. Barbara Goldstein, "The History and Legacy of the Case Study Houses," *Architecture: The AIA Journal,* December 1989. Neil Jackson, *Pierre Koenig: A View from the Archive* (Los Angeles: Getty Research Institute, 2019). Sam Hall Kaplan, "Low-Cost Homes: The Case Study Legacy," *Los Angeles Times,* November 26, 1989. Allan Temko, "Blueprints for Beauty," *San Francisco Examiner,* December 10, 1989. Elizabeth A. T. Smith, *Blueprints for Modern Living: History and Legacy of the Case Study Houses* (Cambridge, MA, and London: MIT Press, 1999). Leon Whiteson, "Case study redefined residential architecture," *Austin American-Statesman,* October 15, 1989.

CHAPTER 10: CELEBRITY

This last line of this chapter, a quote by artist David Hockney, caused considerable consternation and gnashing of teeth, so difficult was it to fact-check. "I came to Los Angeles for two reasons," Hockney reportedly said in 2009. "The first was a photo by Julius Shulman of Case Study House No. 21. …" The second reason was AMG's *Physique Pictorial,* a magazine of homoerotic nude photography featuring the work of photographer Bob Mizer. (The quote was truncated in the chapter because it would have required a lengthy explanation unrelated to the subject of this book.)

The quote was cited in "The pull of Hockney's pool paintings," an essay by Matthew Sperling for *Apollo,* an international art magazine. The essay begins with Hockney's quote and examines the motif of the swimming pool: "the setting for many of his major paintings of the 1960s and 1970s," many of which "became defining images in the cultural identity of Southern California."

To those familiar with Case Study House #21, which has no swimming pool, Hockney's quote in this context begs the question: *Did he really mean Case Study House #22?*

If he did, it would bring full circle the narrative in the chapter, which includes a scene of Case Study House #22 being styled for a fashion photo shoot in homage to Hockney's famous painting, "A Bigger Splash." In other words: art imitates art imitates architecture. (The story about that shoot, by the way, was shared by photographer Vincent Peters in an email.)

Many attempts were made to reach out to Hockney with the simple question: *Did you really mean #22?* It's a fairly common and rather understandable error to confuse #21 and #22, given their common architect and photographer. Email requests to fact-check this seemingly simple matter were dispatched to gallery owners, friends of the artist, and handlers at David Hockney Inc. The response: "The artist is currently deeply engaged in his painting and responding to few requests."

Finally, we reached out to Dian Hanson, cited in the Apollo essay as the "interviewer" who elicited the quote in 2009. We asked if we could see the interview transcription, realizing it might be of limited use if Hockney simply misspoke. Perhaps the context in which it was said would yield a bit more insight.

"It was used in my book *Bob's World,* a monograph of [*Physique Pictorial*] photographer Bob Mizer," she said in an email conversation in late 2020. (Hockney was apparently a big fan of Mizer.) "There is no transcript, as he told it to me at a dinner party. He was drinking and telling jokes and may very well have misspoken, as #22 is the most famous Case Study photo by Shulman. Julius was not there to weigh in, and more important at the moment was the Bob Mizer part."

Hanson felt it was important to include the second half of David Hockney's quote, because it was the part more pertinent to the dinner-party conversation in which it was said.

The rest of this chapter, and particularly its photos, ripped us out of the comfortable world of archives and schooled us in the machinations of Hollywood's cult of celebrity. We learned some stuff. For example: In order to publish a photo of a celebrity that ran in some magazine, one must get permission from the photographer (who often requested a four-figure fee), the magazine, and the celebrity. Many emails to celebrity agents and managers disappear into a black hole. Those who do respond often want to know, "Who else is going to be in the book?" before making any decision. Such was the case for a still shot from the film *Why Do Fools Fall in Love,* featuring the famous catfight between Halle Berry and Vivica Fox, who claw each other into the Stahl House pool. We regret that this image did not make it in the book. Neither did the frame from *The Simpsons,* in which Homer Simpson "goes Hollywood" and appears at a Stahl House party of the sort that never really occurred at the Stahl House. Fox declined to let us include *The Simpsons* but agreed to *American Dad!.* (If you Google "Homer Simpson at the Stahl House," this unobtainable image will appear for your viewing pleasure free of charge.)

Many requests for celebrity interviews were, not shockingly, dismissed by publicists. Other requests yielded pleasant interactions with people whom fame has not managed to spoil.

One of those people was Wendy Knutson, of the vocal trio Wilson Phillips. Wendy described in a phone call the ethereal experience of filming the music video for "Release Me" at the Stahl House. She also helped us fact-check a couple of matters, such as Buck's story about the Mamas and The Papas living in the house across the street. That turned out to be true, though we learned it was only two members of the band who lived there, and not the whole band, as we had presumed.

Another generous supporter was Catherine Meyler, a location agent who represents many properties (including the Stahl House) for use in photo shoots, TV shows, movies, and commercials. Called "the Eileen Ford of modernist homes" by writer Laurie Pike, Catherine was our guide to navigating the celebrity network. She was able to articulate as well as anyone what makes the Stahl House a favorite location of photographers and filmmakers.

The actress Kelly Lynch, a great advocate and spokesperson for modernism, was also a wonderful interviewee and enthusiastic supporter of our book. In 1995, Robert Bergman photographed her at the Stahl House for *W* magazine (see image on facing page). The shoot, Lynch recalled, was a recreation of a scene in the movie *American Gigolo,* and the Stahl House was "a character on its own," with a mood that changed with the light. In a 2020 phone interview, Lynch recalled a visit to the Stahl House with Pierre Koenig, who told her, "This is the crown of my work." Mark Stahl was still living there at the time. "One of the bedrooms was kind of messy," Lynch said. "[Pierre] looked at me and said, 'People live here.' It's a good thing. That's what you want. You can imagine sleeping well there."

Lynch and her husband, Mitch Glazer, consider themselves "custodians" of John Lautner's Leo Harvey House 1950, where they live and occasionally open their home for architectural tours. "To really experience mid-century houses, you have to be in them and see the world through them. Looking at them is one thing, but being in them is another."

CHAPTER 11: OPEN HOUSE

This chapter was based largely on interviews. Interviewees included Victor Regnier, Randy Koenig, Lynn Mantoani, Mary Melton, Peter Moruzzi, Linda Dishman, Michael Hicks, Melisa Stahl, Shane Stahl, and, of course, Bruce and Shari. Some quotes came from previously cited interviews by Eric Bricker, Taina Rikala De Noriega, and Ginger Moro. Quotes from various people who attended the Stahl House tour were filmed by Michael Hicks on a tour in 2018.

Peter Moruzzi's application for the National Register of Historic Places contains some vivid and insightful writing. Some of Pierre Koenig's poignant reflections were captured in a short indie film produced by Steve Diskin, a close friend of Koenig's. The film, *Four Friends: How Designers Think They Work* (copyright Steve Diskin, 1995), can be viewed online at *https://vimeo.com/50390665.*

EPILOGUE: THE REUNION

This scene was reconstructed through interviews with Mary Melton, Chris Nichols, Philip Ethington, as well as the dialogue included by Mary Melton in her excellent story, "A Shot In The Dark," for *Los Angeles* magazine, June 2001. We tried to find Ann Lightbody and Cynthia Tindle to interview them, but sadly we were unable to make contact.

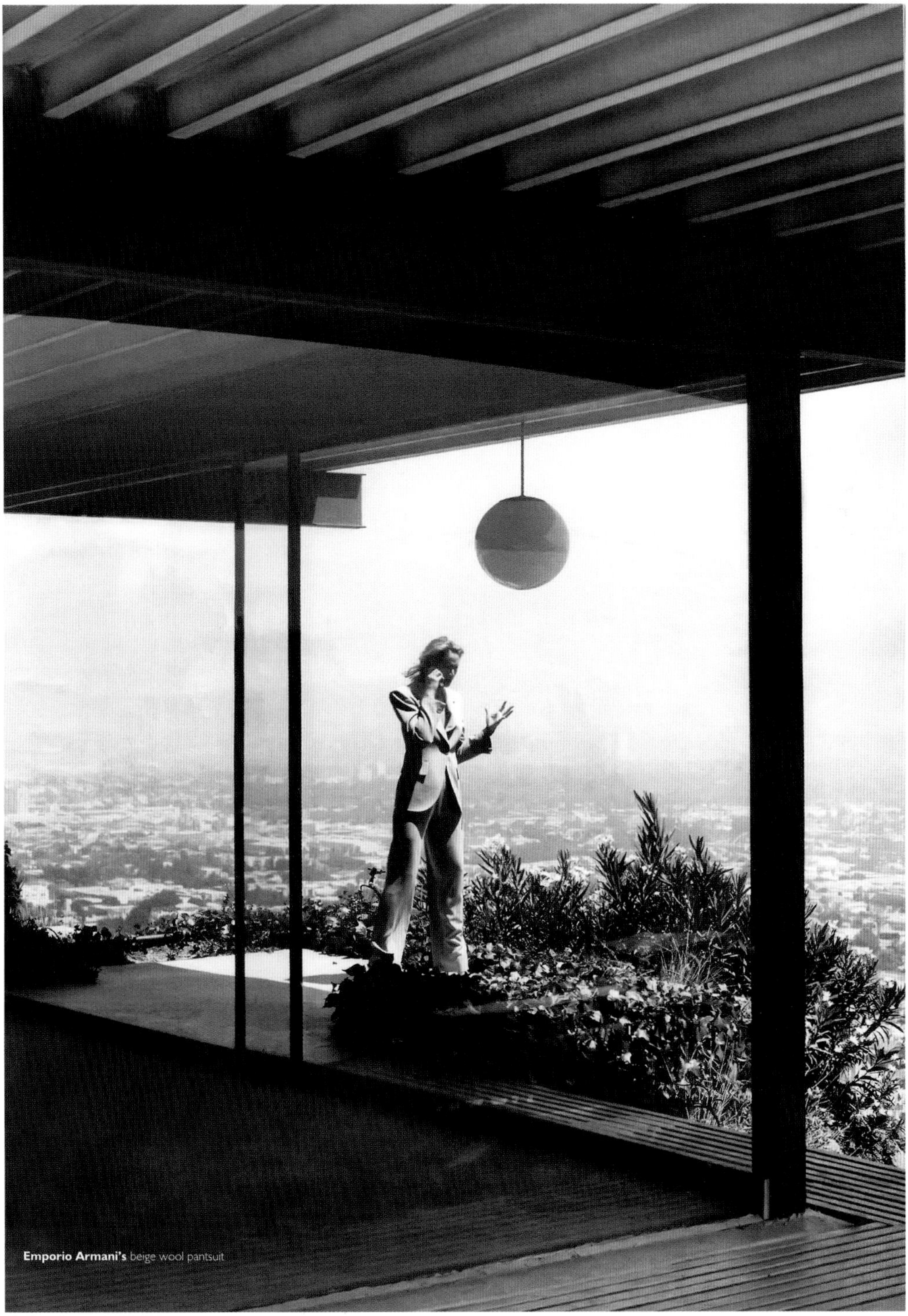

Kelly Lynch in Emporio Armani for W *magazine.*

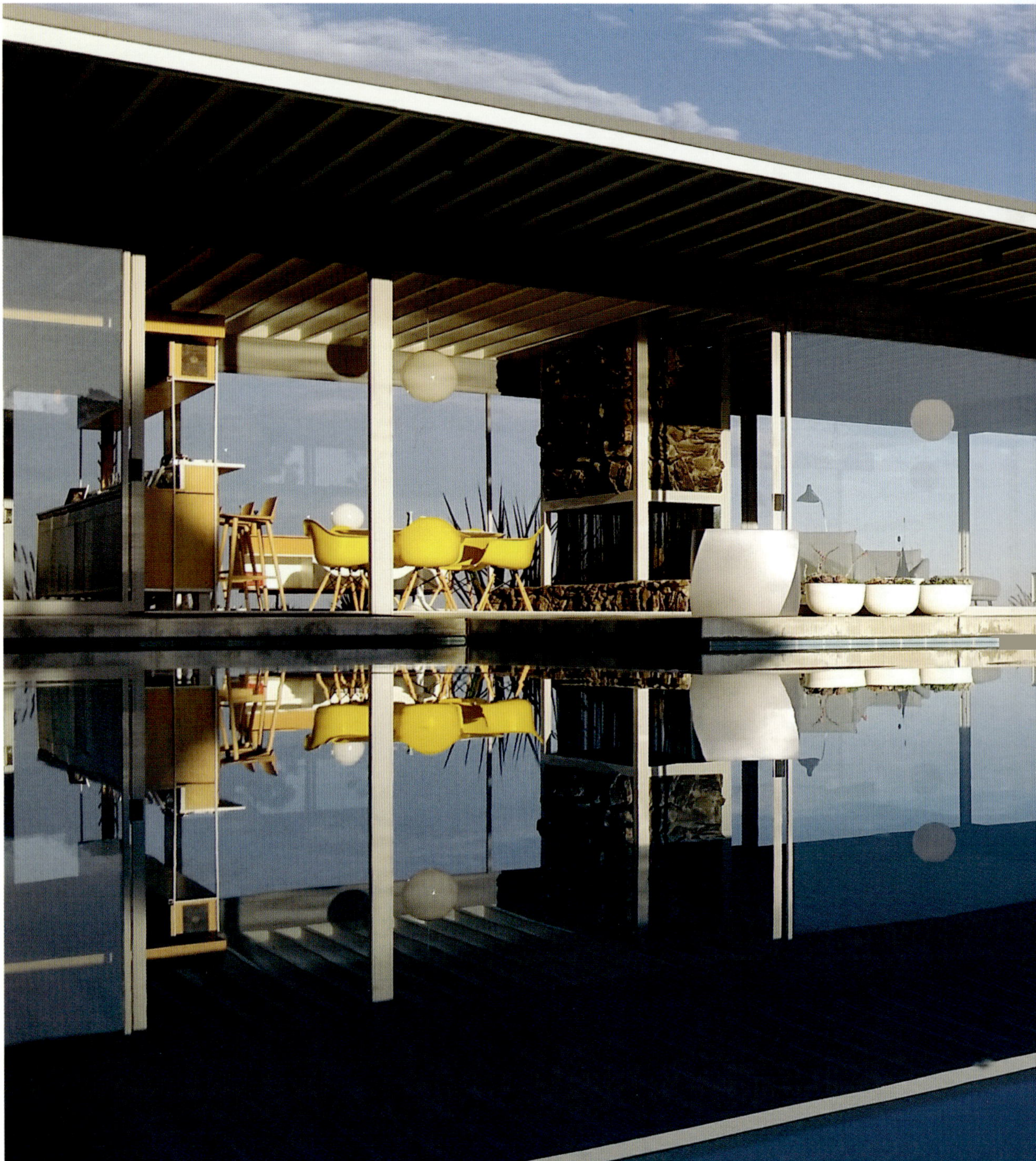

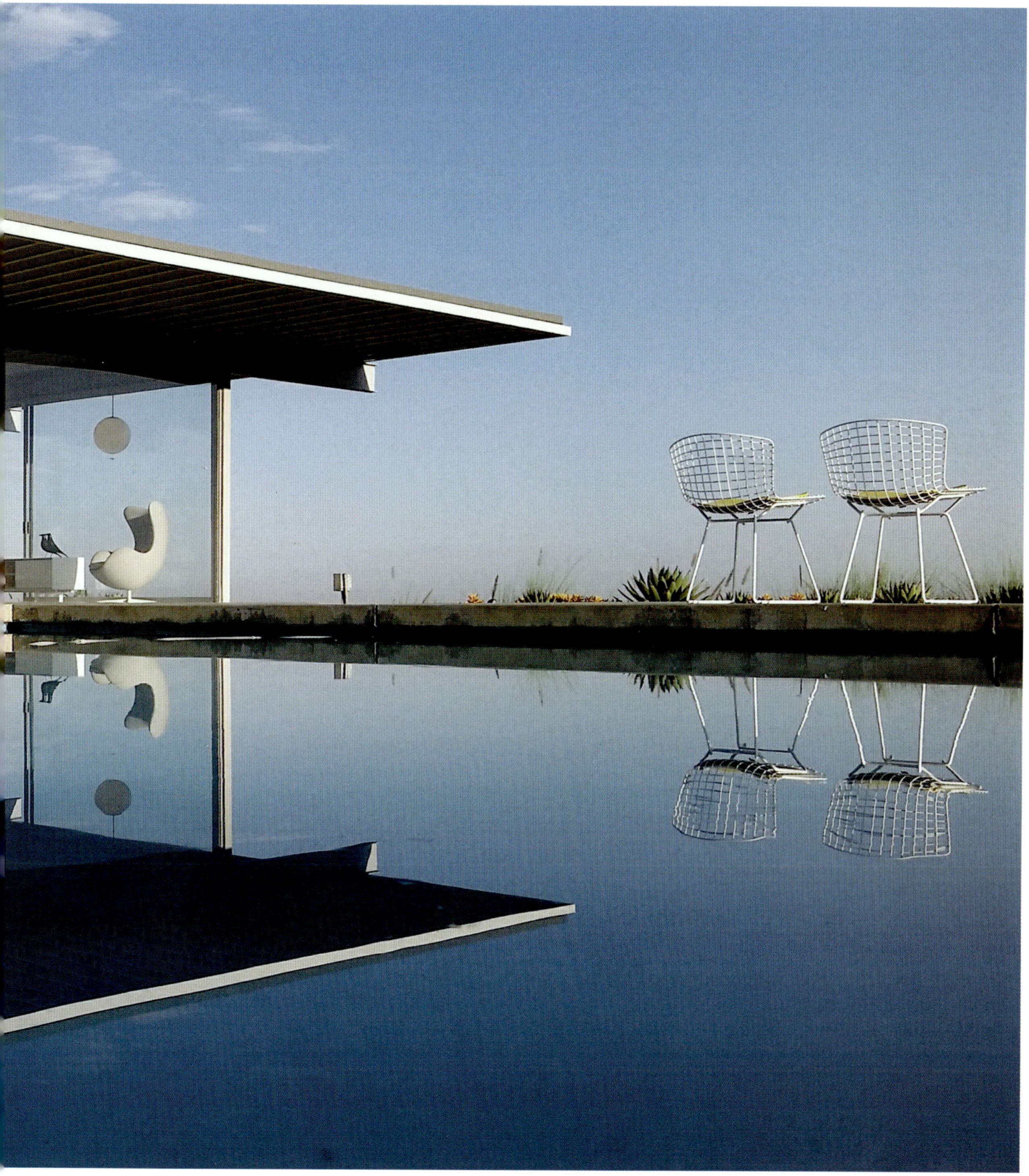

IMAGE CREDITS

Cover	Julius Shulman, © J. Paul Getty Trust. Getty Research Institute, Los Angeles (2004.R.10)
2	Bruce Stahl, Stahl family archives
24	Pierre Koenig (contact sheet), ca. 1960, Getty Research Institute, Los Angeles (2006.M.30), Bethlehem Steel
29	Pierre Koenig (contact sheet), ca. 1960, Getty Research Institute, Los Angeles (2006.M.30), Bethlehem Steel
30	© J. Paul Getty Trust. Getty Research Institute, Los Angeles (2004.R.10), Pierre Koenig
31	© J. Paul Getty Trust. Getty Research Institute, Los Angeles (2004.R.10), Pierre Koenig
32	© Gerard Smulevich, Julius Shulman
33	© Slav Zatoka, Slav Zatoka Images, Julius Shulman
36	© Eames Office LLC (eamesoffice.com), Charles and Ray Eames, John Entenza
38	*Arts & Architecture*, January 1945; © Travers Family Trust. Used with permission
39	*Arts & Architecture*, January 1945; © Travers Family Trust. Used with permission
40	*Arts & Architecture*, May 1959; © Travers Family Trust. Used with permission
	Arts & Architecture, October 1959; © Travers Family Trust. Used with permission
	Arts & Architecture, February 1960; © Travers Family Trust. Used with permission
	Arts & Architecture, June 1960; © Travers Family Trust. Used with permission
41	*Arts & Architecture*, October 1959; © Travers Family Trust. Used with permission
47	Julius Shulman, © J. Paul Getty Trust. Getty Research Institute, Los Angeles (2004.R.10), Paul R. Williams, 1952
50–51	© J. Paul Getty Trust. Getty Research Institute, Los Angeles (2006.M.30), Pierre Koenig papers and drawings, Stahl House, Case Study House #22 (plan), ca. 1960
52–53	© J. Paul Getty Trust. Getty Research Institute, Los Angeles (2006.M.30), Pierre Koenig papers and drawings, Stahl House, Case Study House #22 (plan), ca. 1958
54–55	© J. Paul Getty Trust. Getty Research Institute, Los Angeles (2006.M.30), Pierre Koenig papers and drawings, Stahl House, Case Study House #22 (plan), ca. 1960
62–65	Pierre Koenig Papers and Drawings, Construction Site, Stahl Residence, Case Study House #22 (Los Angeles, CA), ca. 1960, Getty Research Institute, Los Angeles (2006.M.30), Bethlehem Steel
68	Pierre Koenig Papers and Drawings, © J. Paul Getty Trust. Getty Research Institute, Los Angeles (2006.M.30)
69–93	© J. Paul Getty Trust. Getty Research Institute, Los Angeles (2004-R.10), Julius Shulman Photographs
95–103	© J. Paul Getty Trust. Getty Research Institute, Los Angeles (2004-R.10), Julius Shulman Photographs
120	Shari Stahl Gronwald, Stahl Family archives
130	© J. Paul Getty Trust. Getty Research Institute, Los Angeles (2006.M.30), Pierre Koenig papers and drawings, Stahl House, Case Study House #22 (cross sections), ca. 1960
131	© J. Paul Getty Trust. Getty Research Institute, Los Angeles (2006.M.30), Pierre Koenig papers and drawings, Stahl Residence
141	© Marvin Rand Archive, MOCA exhibit "Blueprints for Modern Living, History and Legacy of the Case Study Houses"
143	© Paramount Pictures Corp. All Rights Reserved. *Galaxy Quest*, directed by Dean Parisot, 1999, film still courtesy of Paramount Pictures Corp., Tim Allen, used with permission
144	© Vincent Peters, Miu Miu campaign
145	© Vincent Peters, Miu Miu campaign
146–147	© Steven Meisel, Valentino campaign, art+commerce
148–149	© Patric Shaw, *Vogue España*, Trunk Archive
152–153	© Brian Bowen Smith/August, Colin Farrell, used with permission
154	© Mark Seliger/AUGUST, Rachel Bilson, used with permission
155	© Miller Mobley/AUGUST, John Boyega, used with permission
156–157	*American Dad!* © 2019 Twentieth Century Fox Television. All rights reserved, episode: Twinanigans
158–159	© Emmanuel "Chivo" Lubezki / Dogwood Pictures, *Knight of Cups*, directed by Terrence Mallick, 2015, Nicolas Gonda, Christian Bale, Freida Pinto, used with permission
160	© Andy Burgess, © Carrie Graber, used with permission
161	© David Hockney Collection Tate, U.K., David Hockney, "A Bigger Splash," 1967, Acrylic on Canvas, 96 x 96 inches, used with permission
162–163	© Andy Burgess, used with permission
164–165	© Carrie Graber, used with permission
166–167	© Shag, LA Modern, Josh Agle, used with permission
172	© Tim Mantoani, Behind Photographs Archiving Photographic Legends, used with permission
179	© Scott Radnidge, used with permission
181	© Courtesy of University of Southern California, on behalf of the USC Libraries Special Collections, Irene Fertik-Photographer, used with permission
183	© David Glomb, used with permission. Reunion photograph of Julius Shulman, Pierre Koenig, Buck and Carlotta Stahl, Ann Lightbody, Cynthia Tindle.
184–191	© Images courtesy of Design Within Reach and Mark Seelen
197	© Robert Erdmann/August, Actor Kelly Lynch as seen in *W* magazine, used with permission
198–199	Bruce Stahl, Stahl family archives
201	© Brian Bowen Smith/August, used with permission
202–203	Stahl family archives, master bedroom
207	© Kim Cross, used with permission
208	© Kim Cross, used with permission

All other photographs courtesy of the Stahl Family Archives.

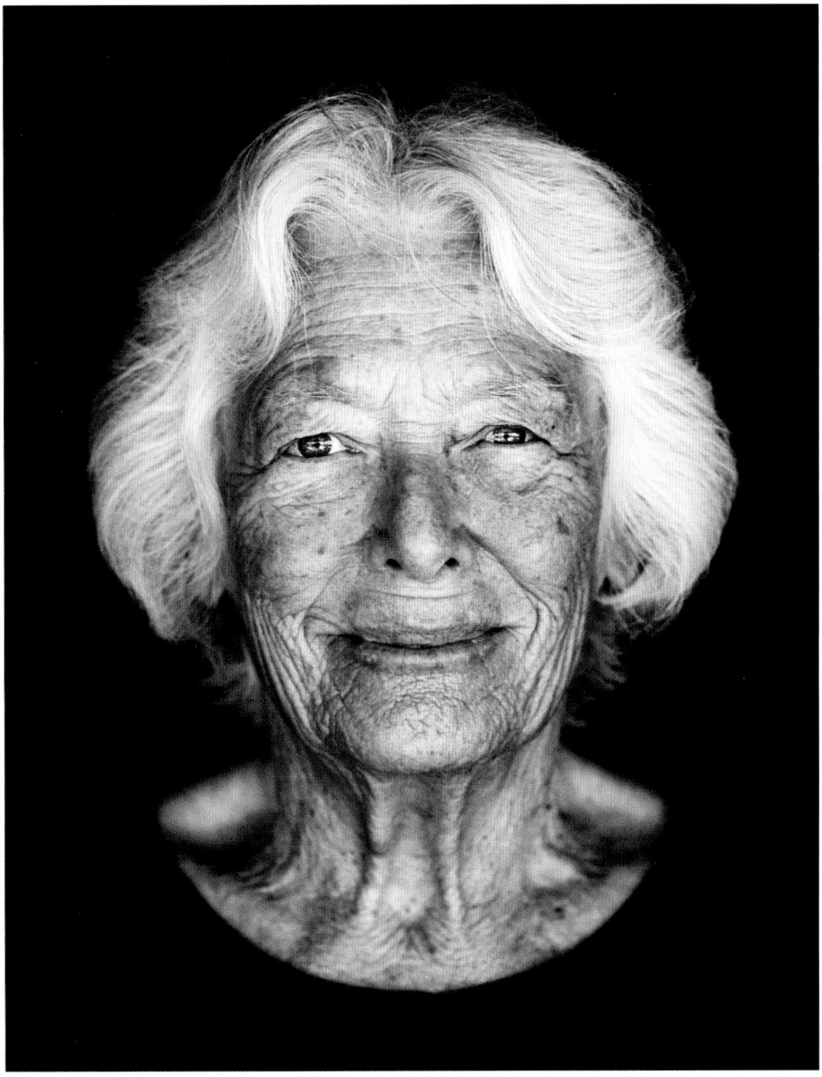

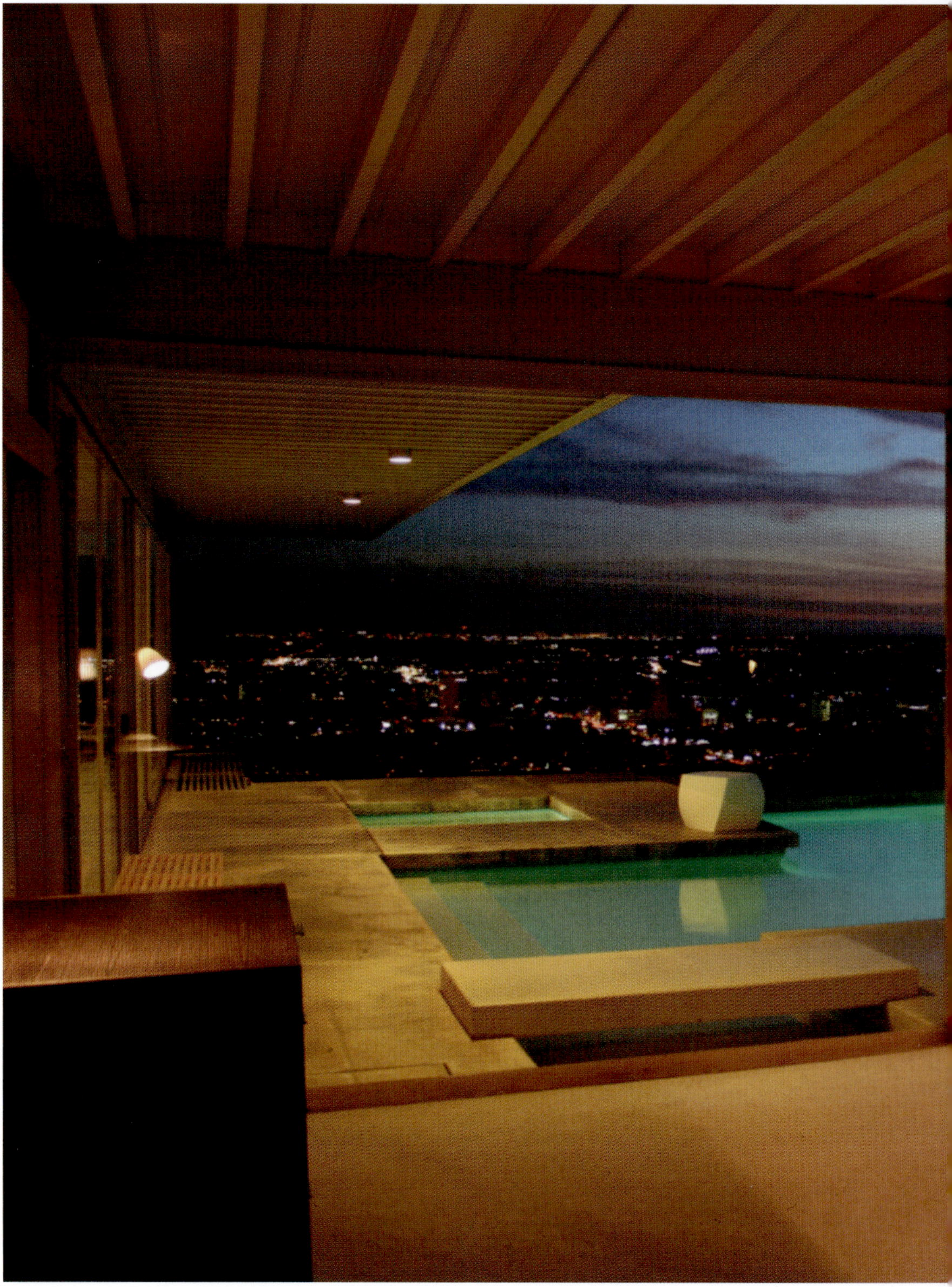

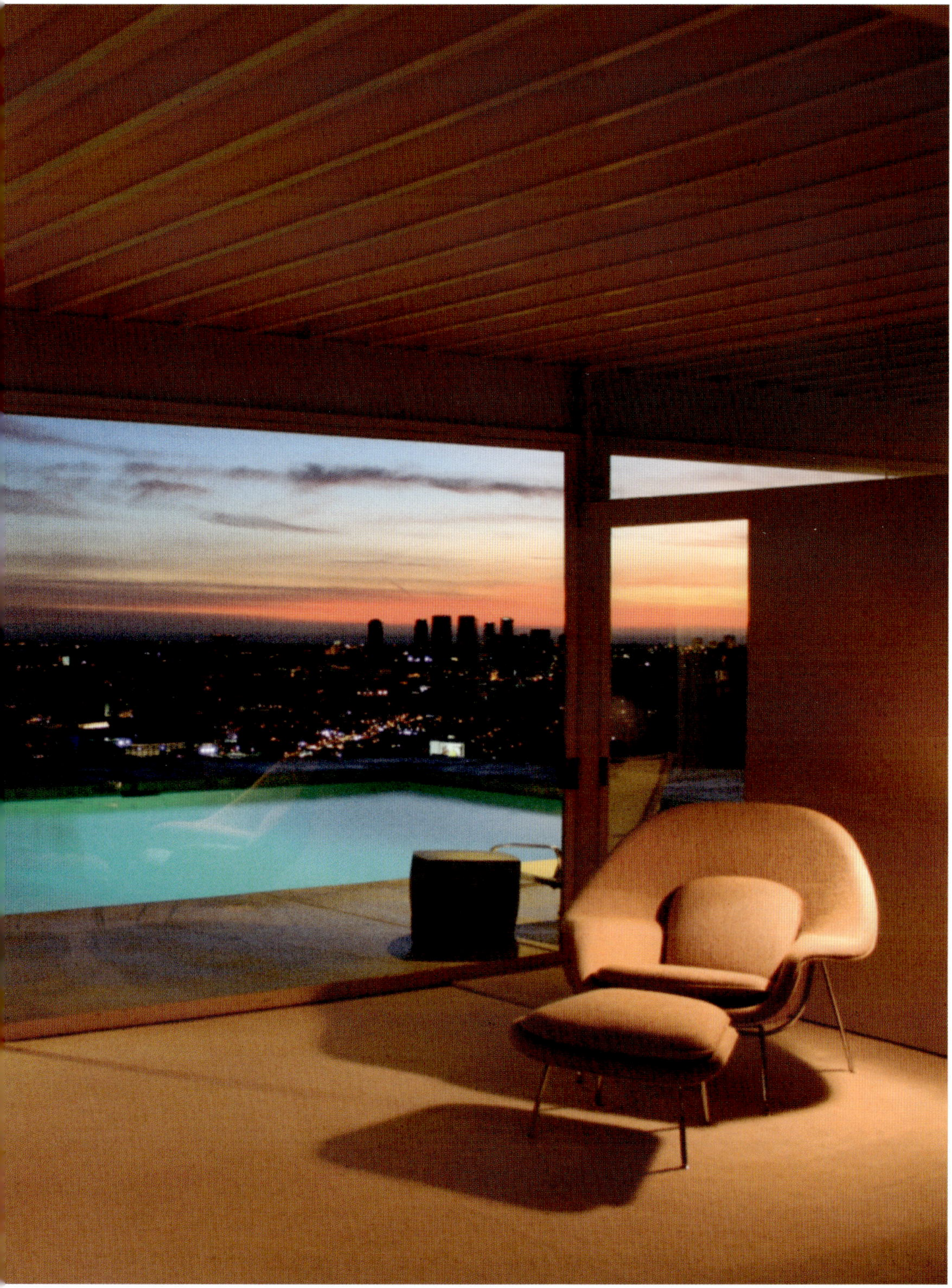

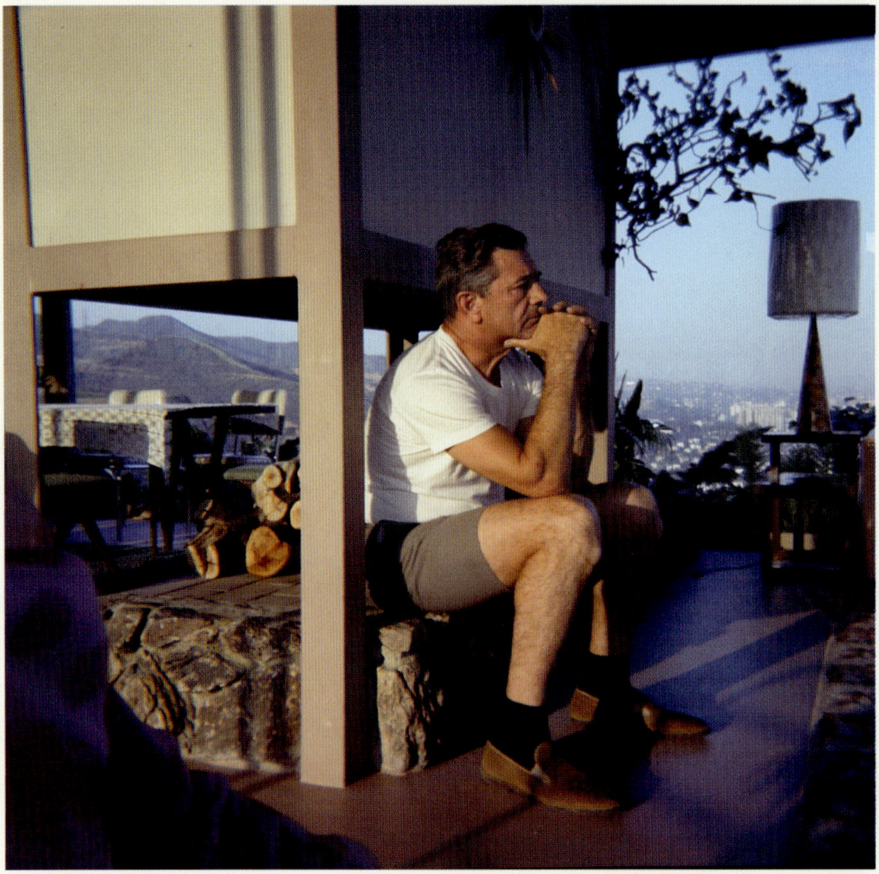

ACKNOWLEDGMENTS

This book is a monument to the perseverance of Shari Stahl Gronwald and Bruce Stahl, who've been on a ten-year journey to publish a definitive account of the Stahl House.

"Nothing about building this house was easy," Bruce said, "and neither was this book."

Shari, a meticulous planner and project manager, curated the Stahl family archives, combing through mountains of primary sources for details and facts that would have been lost to memory. She energized every interview with her wickedly funny sense of humor and kind heart. This book was in many ways a leap of faith and an act of trust on both sides.

Bruce, a natural storyteller, was a fountain of memories. As someone with a hands-on role in the physical upkeep and restoration of the Stahl House, he was key in describing some of its structural peculiarities. His contributions include many spontaneous phone-call pep talks, as well as his insistence that immersion reporting requires jumping off the Stahl House roof into the pool.

Kim trusted us and embraced this journey of telling our story. Her research skills are peerless and obsessive, and when she adopts a subject, she pours everything she has into the story, follows up relentlessly, and runs to ground any scent of clue or discovery. She is a truly brilliant writer. It has been such a fun and educational endeavor and we are proud we found not only a writer but a friend.

Michael Hicks, the lifelong best friend of Mark Stahl and an emerging documentary filmmaker, served as storytelling wingman. Thanks, Michael, for strategy sessions on narrative structure, vetting ideas, reading drafts, and sharing my obsession for research and fact-checking.

Aimee Lind at the Getty Museum Archives identified many of the drawings and documents related to the Stahl House in the vast archives of Pierre Koenig and Julius Shulman. We are also grateful to the David Travers Family Trust, the Marvin Rand Archives, and Dr. F. Robert van der Linden, curator of air transportation and special purpose aircraft at the Smithsonian National Air and Space Museum.

We are deeply grateful to the historians, writers, and scholars who shared interview recordings, transcripts, notes, photographs, and videos with the author. These primary sources gave authentic voice to characters no longer around to be interviewed. Documentary filmmaker Eric Bricker shared uncut video footage of interviews with Carlotta and Buck. Mary Melton shared personal notes from her 2000 interview with the Stahls and helped recreate the scene of the reunion. Other recorded interviews were shared by Peter Kirby, Fumi Yamanaka, and Steve Diskin. Craig Hodgetts and Ming Fung provided documents, photographs, and interviews about their pivotal Blueprints for Modern Living exhibition at MOCA.

Philip Ethington, who was adopted by Julius Shulman as his "sort of personal historian," went above and beyond to help us accurately convey the historical and cultural context of this story. Phil shared valuable primary sources, including interviews he conducted. He was also an eyewitness to some pivotal moments in Stahl House history. Through this project he became a wonderful mentor, teacher, and guide to modernism.

Mohamed Sharif was also extremely generous with his time and expertise. He shared firsthand memories of his time with Pierre Koenig, as well as his recorded 2003 interviews, which are part of his personal archive. As an architect, he helped decode drawings and address technical questions about the construction of the Stahl House.

Neil Jackson provided support and detailed insights from England, spending hours poring over dated drawings and other historical documents to help accurately interpret and address several technical matters, particularly the evolution of the Stahl House foundations. His knowledge of Koenig's life, buildings, philosophy, and legacy are truly impressive. Buy his books. All of them.

A number of architects, historians, curators, preservationists, critics, writers, and other experts enriched this story with context, anecdotes, details, and insights. Heartfelt thanks goes to Randy Koenig, Victor Regnier, Richard Koshalek, Craig Hodgetts, Ming Fung, Elizabeth A. T. Smith, Chris Nichols, Peter Moruzzi, Linda Dishman, Mary Alice Wollum, Barbara Goldstein, Allison Arieff, Sam Lubbell, Jickie Torres, Carrie Graber, Catherine Meyler, Jane Graves, Josh Agle (Shag), Vincent Peters, David Glomb, Lynn Mantoani, Dian Hanson, Wendy Knutson, Carnie Wilson, Kelly Lynch, Dewey Nicks, and Carol LeFluffy.

Many friends and family members shared photos, sat for interviews, and corroborated memories. We're grateful to Bud and Ann Gates, Jim and Barbara Gates, Bobby Duemler, TerriAnn Drescher, Gregg Wilson, Andrew Edelstein, Melisa Stahl, and Shane Stahl for enduring recorded interviews. Thank you to Berndt, Annie, Sara, and Skyler for their love and support.

For permission to include images in this book, we'd like to thank: David Glomb, Slav Zatoka, Gerard Smulevich, Andy Burgess, the Hockney Studio and the Tate museum, Design Within Reach and Herman Miller, Mark Seelen, the Eames Foundation, Marvin Rand Archives, Vicki Rand, Vincent Peters, Nicolas Gonda, *Knight of Cups*, Emmanuel "Chivo" Lubezki, Dogwood Pictures, Paramount Pictures, Tim Allen, Fox/Disney, Steven Meisel, Miller Mobley, John Boyega, Brian Bowen Smith, Colin Farrell, Patric Shaw, *Vogue España*, Rocco Ceselin, Third & Army, Hunter & Gatti, Massimo Dutti, David Gandy, Robert Erdmann, Kelly Lynch, Mark Seliger, Rachel Bilson, Irene Fertik, and USC.

We are indebted to the friends who donated the space and time for monastic writing retreats, without which this book would have greatly suffered in the chaos of a pandemic. The proposal evolved on a remote Idaho ranch overseen by Jerry and Terry. The manuscript was born in Rick and Shauna's cabin. Many chapters came to be in a tiny cabin on Jamie and David's sheep ranch. And the final revision was completed and filed from David and Ruth's snowed-in ranch house.

It takes many minds and eyes to bring a book into the world. Leslie Meredith, our nurturing agent, refined the illustrated proposal and matched it with the perfect art publisher. Steve Crist and Gloria Fowler of Chronicle Books took a good story and shaped it into an object of beauty. From idea to endnotes, editor Glenn Stout elevated the narrative with an ear for prose, an eye for logical holes, and a gift for historical research. Bronwen Dickey contributed surgical line-editing skills as well as writing-music playlists and moral support dispatched with a wicked sense of humor. Michael Heacock, Emily Hagopian, Lindsay Bierman, Alysia Burton Steele, and Art Meripol served as lifelines for many questions about architecture and photography. In moments of kismet that dovetailed two previously beleaguered paths, novelist Anthony Doerr introduced Kim to writer Alan Heathcock, and Alan connected Kim with the Stahls.

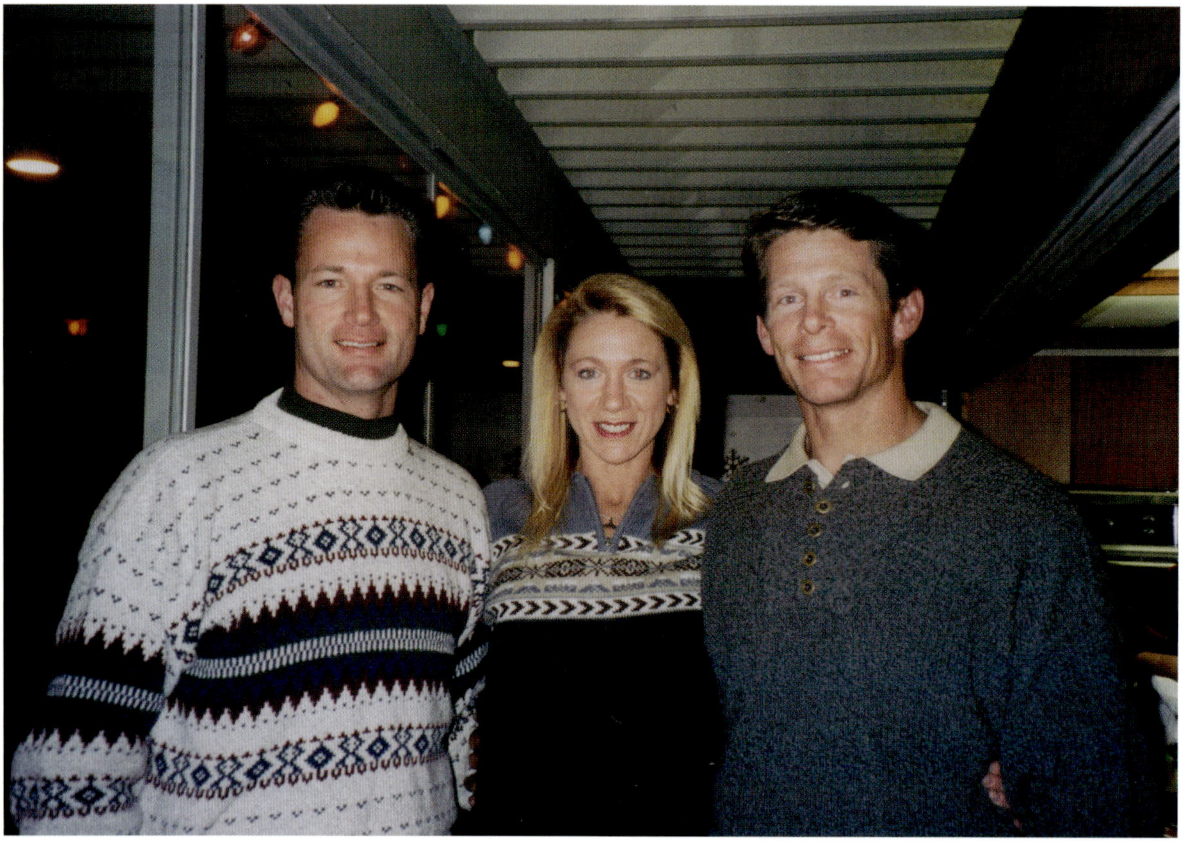

To my husband, Berndt, thank you for all of your love, for putting up with my endless work schedule, for giving me the extra time needed to work on this book, and for encouraging us to complete what we set out to do so many years ago. To my daughter, Annie, thanks for the love that you give me even when "all I do is work," for making me lunches when I'm too busy to eat, for showing Austin the Stahl way of doing cannonballs off the Stahl House roof, and for being with me during this journey. I'm eternally grateful to Mom and Dad for their endless love and support, and to Mark for being such a great brother, best friend, and making me laugh all the time. I miss you all dearly.

—Shari Stahl Gronwald

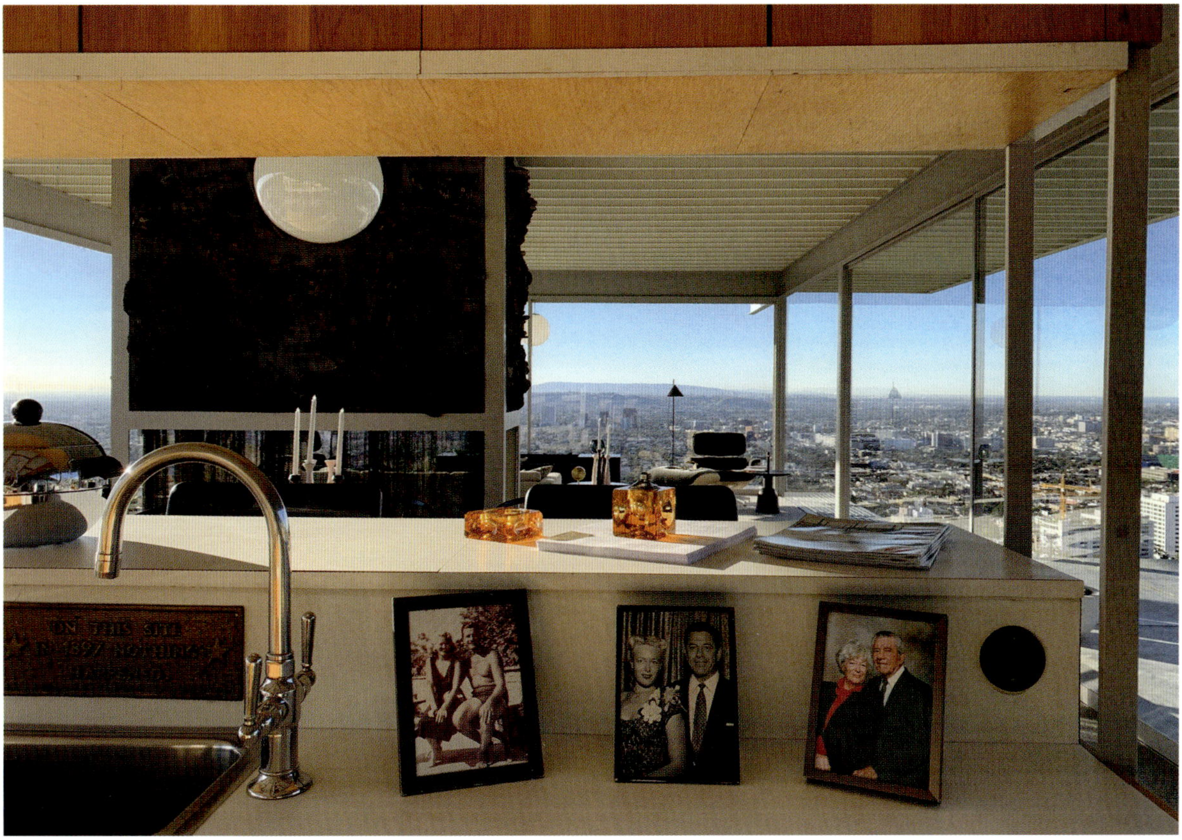

To my wife, Melisa, and my kids, Shane, Sara, Skyler, I would like to thank you for your love and support, for helping us tell this story of your grandparents and of this wonderful house that they built. To Mom, Dad, and Mark, I miss you dearly. Mom and Dad, thank you for always believing in us and standing by our decisions. For picking us up and dusting us off and telling us that we can do it—I will never forget that. Mark, I miss you, I miss our talks, I miss our friendship, I think of you every day. I love you guys very much.

—Bruce Stahl

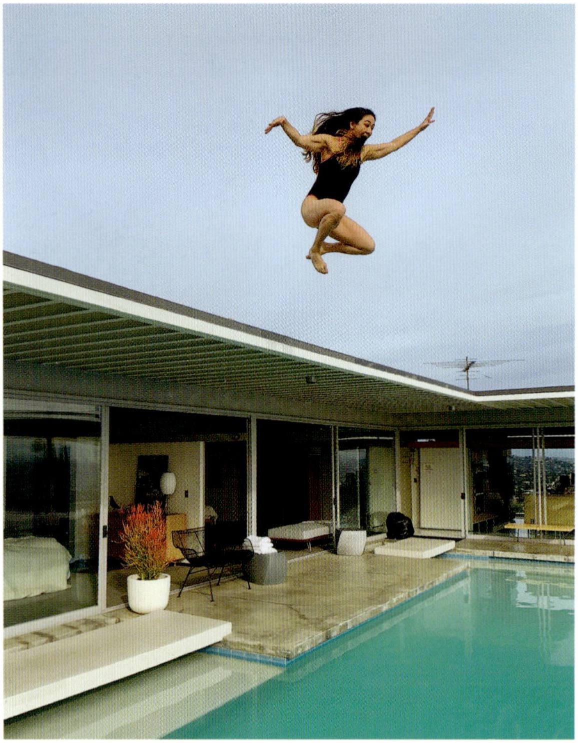

Without a loving and supportive family, I couldn't write a sentence, much less a book. To my husband, Eddie Freyer, thank you for understanding that stories are my love language, for living with my creative mess, and for giving me the time, space, and freedom that writing demands. To my mom, Joyce Cross, thank you for all the deadline meals, for teaching me never to act my age, and for never once trying to talk me into a sensible career. And to my son, Austin, thanks for sharing a love of wheelies, backflips, dirt jumps, and architecture. I can't wait to do cannonballs off the Stahl House roof with you.

—Kim Cross

THE STAHL HOUSE
CASE STUDY HOUSE #22

The Making of a Modernist Icon

By Shari Stahl Gronwald, Bruce Stahl,
and Kim Cross

Art Director and Editor: Gloria Fowler

Design: Carrie Worthen and Ben Pope, Thirdthing

Production: Kayleigh Jankowski

Copy Editor: Sara DeGonia

Rights Clearance: Shari Stahl Gronwald

About the Authors

Bruce Stahl and Shari Stahl Gronwald are siblings who grew up in Case Study House #22 and who own and care for it to this day. They generously open their home up to architectural tours and as a film location. Both are committed to honoring their parents' legacy by sharing the full story of how this miraculous home came about.

Kim Cross is a *New York Times* best-selling writer specializing in meticulously reported narrative nonfiction. Her stories have been recognized by the *New York Times*, Harvard University's Nieman Storyboard, the Columbia Journalism Review, and Best American Sports Writing. Her first book, *What Stands in a Storm*, was one of Amazon's Best Books of 2015.

ISBN: 978-1-7972-0943-2
Library of Congress Cataloging-in-Publication Data available.
Manufactured in China.

CHRONICLE CHROMA

Chronicle Chroma is an imprint of Chronicle Books
Los Angeles, California

chroniclebooks.com/chroma

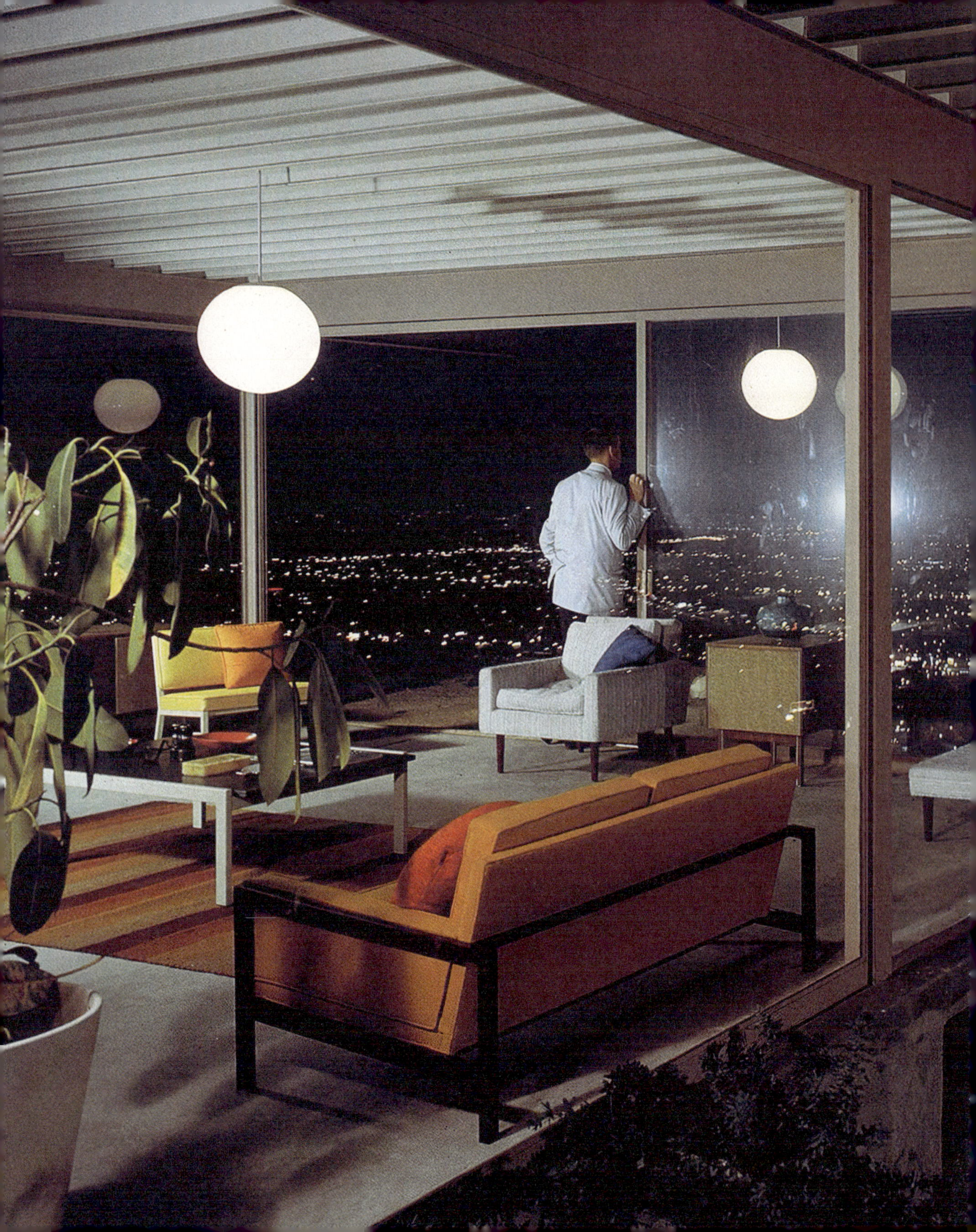